P9-DVB-663

 ORACLE®

Oracle Press™

Rapid Modernization of Java™ Applications

Practical Business and Technical Solutions for Upgrading Your Enterprise Portfolio

G. Venkat

Mc
Graw
Hill
Education

New York   Chicago   San Francisco
Athens   London   Madrid   Mexico City
Milan   New Delhi   Singapore   Sydney   Toronto

Cataloging-in-Publication Data is on file with the Library of Congress

McGraw-Hill Education books are available at special quantity discounts to use as premiums and sales promotions, or for use in corporate training programs. To contact a representative, please visit the Contact Us pages at www.mhprofessional.com.

Rapid Modernization of Java™ Applications: Practical Business and Technical Solutions for Upgrading Your Enterprise Portfolio

Copyright © 2018 by McGraw-Hill Education (Publisher). All rights reserved. Printed in the United States of America. Except as permitted under the Copyright Act of 1976, no part of this publication may be reproduced or distributed in any form or by any means, or stored in a database or retrieval system, without the prior written permission of Publisher, with the exception that the program listings may be entered, stored, and executed in a computer system, but they may not be reproduced for publication.

Oracle and Java are registered trademarks of Oracle Corporation and/or its affiliates. All other trademarks are the property of their respective owners, and McGraw-Hill Education makes no claim of ownership by the mention of products that contain these marks.

Screen displays of copyrighted Oracle software programs have been reproduced herein with the permission of Oracle Corporation and/or its affiliates.

1 2 3 4 5 6 7 8 9   LCR   21 20 19 18 17

ISBN   978-0-07-184203-7
MHID   0-07-184203-9

Sponsoring Editor Lisa McClain	**Technical Editor** Tomas Nilsson	**Production Supervisor** Lynn M. Messina
Editorial Supervisor Jody McKenzie	**Copy Editor** Lisa Theobald	**Composition** Cenveo Publisher Services
Project Manager Anubhav Siddhu, Cenveo® Publisher Services	**Proofreader** Rick Camp	**Illustration** Cenveo Publisher Services
Acquisitions Coordinator Claire Yee	**Indexer** James Minkin	**Art Director, Cover** Jeff Weeks

Information has been obtained by Publisher from sources believed to be reliable. However, because of the possibility of human or mechanical error by our sources, Publisher, or others, Publisher does not guarantee to the accuracy, adequacy, or completeness of any information included in this work and is not responsible for any errors or omissions or the results obtained from the use of such information.

Oracle Corporation does not make any representations or warranties as to the accuracy, adequacy, or completeness of any information contained in this Work, and is not responsible for any errors or omissions.

I dedicate this book to my family. Without their support, this project would not have been possible.

To my wonderful wife, Priya, who endured the long hours I spent researching, writing, and editing this book. She made it possible for me to juggle my passion for this endeavor, my work commitments, and my family life. Without her patience, sacrifice, and encouragement, I would have given up on this project a long time ago. She is the bedrock of our family and makes it possible for all of my ideas and fancies to take flight. This dedication cannot fully express my gratefulness for all that you do. I love you very much!

To my loving daughters, Brinda and Leela, whose laughter and entertaining antics kept me focused and relaxed, especially during tight deadlines! They are the sweetest children I could ever hope for. Thank you, girls, for giving up so many bike rides with me so that I could finish this book.

I would also like to thank my parents for instilling in me a love of learning, letting me dream big as a child, and supporting me in all my pursuits.

About the Author

G. Venkat is currently the CEO of bitWise Academy, a next-generation AI-driven eLearning platform that introduces adaptive and personalized computer science education to students in Grades K–12. The bitWise Integrated Curriculum blends traditional computer science tools and programming languages with STEM, art, music, and games into an interactive learning environment.

Venkat is a serial entrepreneur, venture partner, conference speaker, book author, but most of all, a true technology enthusiast. For the past two decades, he has been a global technology management veteran with hands-on engineering and executive management experience in R&D, innovation and strategy, development of tools and platforms, and delivering disruptive go-to-market solutions for multiple industry verticals.

As the former global head of the Technology Modernization and IT Strategy Practice at Infosys, he led several large-scale, mission-critical consulting engagements at Fortune 500 companies including Apple, Volkswagen, US Cellular, Northwestern Mutual, Allstate, CVS Caremark, Nationwide, Aon, Caterpillar, Sears, United Airlines, Motorola, and Chase Manhattan. Venkat is a business and technology strategic advisor specializing in Business Transformation, Technology Modernization, Portfolio Management, Business and Technology Strategy, Business Case Creation, Product Evaluations, and Application Portfolio Rationalization initiatives.

Passionate about working with open-source technologies spanning the entire application stack, his research interests include artificial intelligence, machine learning, chatbots and conversational UI, big data, IoT, distributed computing, cloud computing, large-scale high-performance computing, and other emerging technologies. Venkat advises multiple startups in the areas of AI, ML, deep learning, image processing, IoT, and real-time communications platforms. He holds a B.Tech. degree from the Indian Institute of Technology, Madras, and an MS and PhD (ABD) in Interdisciplinary Studies (Aerospace and Computer Science) from the University of Alabama, Tuscaloosa.

About the Technical Editor

Tomas Nilsson was a product manager for Java SE at Oracle for more than nine years, covering both the technical as well as commercial aspects of the Java SE ecosystem. Perennially curious, his areas of interest range from bit manipulations in the JRE to effective marketing strategies and how to create the best Agile development team. He is currently the product manager for the Data Intelligence Service at Snow Software.

Contents

Foreword

Amidst the ever-changing and ever-expanding technology universe, one thing remains clear: technology continues to advance at a rapid pace. These advances are apparent in every aspect of our lives, from smart homes and smartphones to our businesses running in the cloud. Though we experience technology's impact across our personal and professional lives, the enterprise undoubtedly has faced the greatest challenges in keeping pace with the rapid advancements over the past few decades.

Since ARPANET first appeared in the 1969, technology has moved in only one direction—forward—and it's moving fast. In the 1980s, after the Internet became ubiquitous in universities and large businesses, we saw the invention of the World Wide Web and hypertext, vehicles that brought networking and Internet access into the modern home.

For the developer, computer programming's mixture of mechanics, mathematics, assembly language, and frustration quickly evolved into programming applications using revolutionary languages of the time such as FORTRAN and C, leading to businesses adopting computers en masse and giving rise to the formation of the developer community. New companies emerged to create software and tools that enabled developers to execute rapid builds and deployments of business applications, an initiative pioneered by Oracle with its relational database and first released as a commercial offering in 1979. Sun Microsystems, Hewlett-Packard, IBM, and Microsoft all followed closely behind with their own innovations. Intel and Sun Microsystems led the charge on microchips, where Moore's Law postulated exponential growth in the chip's power. Today, we hold quad-core processors in the palm of our hands as we browse the Internet, check our e-mail, or execute a business application all from a smartphone.

It is safe to say that we have not advanced this far and this fast by operating on FORTRAN and Smalltalk alone. Java, unveiled by Sun Microsystems in 1995, arose from a need for a developer-friendly language that could take on the Internet. Java's arrival changed the game. It introduced write once, run anywhere; it championed open-source libraries and components. Just as Linux disrupted operating systems, Java similarly transformed applications. Hundreds of thousands of business applications were now being written in Java and deployed to Linux servers. Technology was moving forward, and fast.

Although the advances were great and the excitement palpable, enterprises saddled with fixed IT budgets were not in a position to move forward at this rapid pace. While new applications were being written in current versions of Java, older applications languished. Over time, this problem exacerbated to where many organizations routinely and simultaneously supported several Java versions, oftentimes where support for those major and minor Java versions had already been discontinued, resulting in gaping security holes and unknown business risks.

When Oracle acquired Sun Microsystems in 2008, it embarked upon streamlining Java releases, nomenclature, updates, and support, as well as further enabling the developer community. Oracle recognized the challenges faced by the modern enterprise. Despite Oracle's commitment to propel businesses forward with Java, several companies still confronted challenges associated with inadequate budgets, limited resources, and a lack of tools necessary to keep applications modernized and current with the latest Java platform. The enterprise has struggled to keep pace, while technology continues to advance. This has long created a gap in the industry, and this book addresses these challenges head-on.

The June 2012 launch of Oracle Cloud delivered the industry's broadest and most integrated public cloud with services across IaaS, PaaS, SaaS, and DaaS. The cloud applications of today already provide industry-specific solutions integrated with mobile, social, and analytics technologies across many channels of engagement. Intelligent applications that leverage machine learning and AI algorithms are being fueled by the explosion of available data and digital information from a multitude of sources.

Almost every enterprise, large or small, has begun its cloud journey. Business transformation and the unavoidable IT modernization are not one-time activities; they are continuous processes that must fluidly and flexibly adapt to ever-changing business needs. The author's experience as a developer, an enterprise consultant, and a business leader lend a unique perspective to this book. There is something to be gained by almost every enterprise contributor—application owners, business users, financial controllers, operations, technical architects, developers, CIOs, and executives can all benefit from the best practices and proven techniques for addressing the challenges of modernizing Java applications. The insights and practical approaches in this book will serve as a guide to navigate current modernization challenges and look ahead to the vast technological opportunities of tomorrow.

Thomas Kurian
President, Product Development
Oracle Corporation

Preface

How to Use the Book

The flow of the book is designed to be customizable based on the role of the reader. It is expected that the readership will broadly fall into four categories:

- **Architect** Enterprise architect, technical architect, domain architect, or solutions architect
- **Business** Business roles such as an IT manager, application owner, functional analyst, or business analyst
- **Developer** Application developer, software engineer, or other technical roles
- **Executive** Senior management roles such as director, CTO, or CIO

Based on their roles or areas of interest, not everyone will be interested in reading all the chapters in the order they are presented. Four suggested custom trails can be followed based on a reader's role and interest:

- **Architect** Chapters 1–14
- **Business** Chapters 1–5, 9, 10, 12–14
- **Developer** Chapters 1, 2, 5–11, 14
- **Executive** Chapters 1, 3, 12–14

Acknowledgments

I would like to acknowledge and express my gratitude to the many people who supported me during the course of writing this book. This book is a compilation of my experiences and consulting engagements with both large and small enterprises over the past two decades. I first presented this concept at the Oracle OpenWorld / JavaOne 2014. The session was well received and led to Brandi Shailer, former acquisitions editor at McGraw-Hill, reaching out to me to discuss a book proposal in October 2014. This book has been a labor of love since then and I have enjoyed every minute of it, especially the countless all-nighters and gallons of coffee that got me to the finish line!

Shortly after I started writing this book, Brandi accepted a content manager position with LinkedIn. Two amazing individuals, McGraw-Hill senior editor Lisa McClain and editorial coordinator Claire Yee, joined the project and wholeheartedly evangelized this endeavor. Their unrelenting support and belief in my vision throughout the various phases of research, development, and content generation was instrumental in the successful completion of this book. Thank you Lisa and Claire! I would also like to thank Lisa Goldstein and the wonderful folks at Oracle Press for collaborating with McGraw-Hill to guide this project to completion. I want to thank Tomas Nilsson, Senior Principal Product Manager for the Java Platform at Oracle and the technical editor for the book. His timely comments and technical review of the chapters allowed me to elevate the technical quality of this book. Thanks to McGraw-Hill editorial supervisor Jody McKenzie and senior production supervisor Lynn Messina, as well as Anubhav Siddhu and his team at Cenveo for their tireless efforts during the copy editing, proofreading, and publishing phases of this book. Their diligence transformed my manuscripts into a print-worthy publication—all within incredibly tight deadlines!

My sincerest appreciation to Thomas Kurian, the esteemed president of Oracle, Product Development and Platforms, who wrote the insightful foreword to this book. He is an industry visionary who was able to predict the importance of the cloud on business transformation and the way IaaS, PaaS, SaaS, and DaaS could accelerate business and technology adoption, making IT modernization and application portfolio management the core essence of enterprise strategy. Mr. Kurian anticipated the need for an all-encompassing reference book discussing application modernization in general, and the Java platform in particular, in a way that resonates with enterprise business and technology units. Thank you to Kothanda Umamageswaran, vice president of development at Oracle, for his support and faith in my ability to deliver a compelling book.

There were several individuals with decades of industry experience who graciously accepted to serve as external reviewers for specific chapters or portions of the book. Their expertise ranged across engineering, architecture, IT management, business, product management, finance, and operations. My humble gratitude and appreciation to Kaushal Kurapati, VP Product at Mastercard; Priya Venkat, general counsel at Edgewater Networks; Murali Gomatam, president at 3K Technologies; Ganapathy Dharmasankar, independent consultant and former senior architect of technology modernization at Infosys; Neeraj Kulkarni, director, Business Applications Development, Wisconsin Department of Revenue; and Marek Novotny, senior software engineer at RedHat. I also received considerable encouragement from industry leaders such as Sri Shivananda, SVP and CTO at Paypal; Dilip Venkatachari, VP at McKinsey and Company; Sohrab Kakalia, CEO of Thrive Solar Energy and former VP of Innovation and Technology at Infosys; and Rick Offenbecher, CIO at Wisconsin Department of Revenue. Thank you very much for your support.

Last, but not the least, there are innumerable people who have worked with me, influenced me, and helped me acquire the knowledge and expertise to write this interdisciplinary book. I am grateful for our interactions over the years and many of those experiences are reflected in this book.

To all of you who made this book possible, especially if I missed naming you individually, a very sincere THANK YOU!

Introduction

The release of Java in 1995 completely changed the way enterprises approach application development. We can endlessly debate whether Java made Internet applications popular or whether the Internet made Java popular. No other technology has enjoyed the rapid ascension that Java has encountered. It has become the most widely adopted programming language in the world. We can also thank Java for the explosive advances in open source, making Linux extremely popular for server-side deployments. This serves as an apt introduction to this book by capturing the rise of Java since its launch and by sharing key events about its history.

History of Java

Java made its debut on May 23, 1995, at the SunWorld conference. John Gage made the announcement along with Marc Andreesen that Java would be incorporated into the Netscape Navigator browser. At that time, the number of people working with Java was less than 50.

Fast forward to the present where Java is the most popular language, with more than nine million developers using Java worldwide. It is the number one development platform with more than one billion downloads each year. Java currently runs on more than three billion devices today, and with the explosion of handheld devices and IoT platforms, that number could very soon expand to tens of billions.

The official Java 1.0 programming environment was made available for public download at Sun Microsystems' 1996 inaugural JavaOne event. The event showcased about 100 exhibitors, including established companies and brand-new startups; more than 6000 attendees; and announcements for several exciting product launches, including more than 100 new books.

With more than 10 million computers connected to the Internet at that time, and all the major operating systems vendors—including IBM, Microsoft, and Apple—licensing Java from Sun Microsystems, the JavaOne conference was a sheer state of euphoria with endless possibilities for the modern developer.

By 1997, the number of developers working in Java had exploded to 400,000, and soon it became the number two programming language in the world, even as the attendance for JavaOne swelled to 10,000. The following year, Java really started to come into its own, with more than two million downloads of the JDK. JavaOne 1998 attracted more than 15,000 attendees. The release of JDK 1.2 was a significant milestone with several new libraries added to the Java platform along with modifications to existing libraries. The Swing API and the EJB 1.0 were two fundamentally new additions to the Java platform. The Java division grew to employ more than 800 people during that time.

By 1998, although more than 150 companies had licensed Java technology, the adoption of Java for large-scale applications in the enterprise was still quite slow. JDK 1.2 became instrumental in changing the perception of a rapidly evolving Java into a stable JDK, and the introduction of EJB led to a perception that the Java platform was finally ready to build enterprise-class applications. In 1999, Sun split the Java platform into three areas: J2SE, J2EE, and J2ME. The Java Platform was rebranded as the Java 2 Platform Standard Edition (J2SE), Java 2 Platform Enterprise Edition (J2EE), and the Java 2 Platform Micro Edition (J2ME). J2EE 1.2 was released along with Java Server Pages (JSP 1.0). By the year 2000, the focus of the Java platform shifted from graphical user interfaces, applets, and the web to serious server-side applications, confirming Java's readiness for enterprise adoption.

At JavaOne in 2000, Apple CEO Steve Jobs announced that Apple would bundle Java 2 Standard Edition with its new Mac OS X operating system. JDK 1.3 shipped and as per the new naming convention, it was bundled into the Java 2 Platform Standard Edition (J2SE) 1.3. To make it easy to launch GUI-based applications from the web browser, Java Web Start was announced, allowing Java applications to be launched by simply clicking a link within a web browser to download and run an application on the client desktop.

By the year 2000, hundreds of Java User Groups were established all over the world. The online developer community, known as the Java Developer Connection, had more than one and a half million members. While the overly anticipated issues surrounding Y2K never occurred, something far worse did: the dot-com bubble burst and investors suffered massive losses.

Subsequently, the web services phenomenon and service-oriented architecture (SOA) hype began to grow, driving interest from both developers and enterprises that used the Java platform. The Java Community Process (JCP) defined and incorporated Web Services standards into the Java 2 Platform Enterprise Edition (J2EE). There were now more than two million members as part of the Java Developer Connection and downloads of J2EE had reached one million. The release of J2EE 1.3 also included the specification for EJB 2.0, which addressed the API difficulties of EJB 1.0.

While the first Real-Time Java (RTJ) specification was released in 1999, it was not until 2002 that RTJ was thrust into the limelight. At the JavaOne developer conference in 2002, a battle waged between two Java-powered robots during a keynote. None other than James Gosling controlled one of the robots. This demo went on to showcase that Java technology could span applications running on enterprise servers, all the way to Java 2 Platform Micro Edition (J2ME) for consumer devices and to real-time Java applications.

Java reached a new level of stability with the release of JDK 1.4 (Merlin). This formed the basis of Java 2 Platform Standard Edition (J2SE) 1.4. Additionally, downloads reached more than two million for J2EE. To support web services development, Sun Microsystems released the Web Services Developer Pack 1.0.

The year 2003 became an under-the-radar kind of year for Java as far as major technology introductions. However, 2003 marked the official release of the new Java coffee cup logo and the release of Java 2 Platform Enterprise Edition 1.4. There were some new marketing-related events with the launch of the Java.com web site and the Java.net community-focused site. Various statistics released at the time indicated that approximately 75 percent of professional developers used Java as their primary programming language for development.

The use of Java technology by NASA for its command and control center applications that were used to study the images from Mars exploration rovers provided a significant boost to Java's already impressive image. The NASA Jet Propulsion Laboratory (JPL), in conjunction with Wind River Systems, developed the Mars rovers devices. They used the Java platform for the program, which controlled the rovers' operating system. The Java program used for the robotic rovers was nearly identical to the JPL's online program Maestro, which allowed site visitors to guide a simulated rover across a 3-D Martian terrain.

The Open Source movement and the Linux OS gained significant traction by 2004. The Apache Software Foundation received reverence by the open-source community and Java developers who adopted several libraries and components released under the Apache license housed under the Apache umbrella. The big push by open-source advocates, as well as the general awareness and adoption of open-source application builds by Java developers, sparked a debate at the 2004 JavaOne conference, and two differing camps emerged. IBM, Apache Software Foundation, and a significant portion of the developer community wanted Sun to embrace an open-source model for Java and its future evolution. James Gosling, Sun Fellow Rob Gingell, and others opposed the move, citing that this would lead to multiple, incompatible open-source implementations of Java, thereby affecting its interoperability.

The NASA/Java story continued as the *Spirit* Mars rover touched down to traverse Martian soil. Statistics revealed that the size of the Java developer community building Java applications worldwide at this time was four million strong, and the official count of the worldwide Java User Groups included about 550 members. Estimates also compiled that Java ran on one and a half billion devices and more than 600 million desktops.

Finally, in 2004, Sun Microsystems and Microsoft settled their differences after six years of complex litigation. The settlement amount charged Microsoft $1.6 billion for allegedly violating the Java license agreement by creating its own Java version and letting it break on non-Windows machines. While this was a victory of sorts for Sun and the Java platform, Microsoft had already strengthened its position with the launch of the .NET platform in February 2002 and the C# language had gained its own developer following. Nevertheless, the resulting outcome was good for the Java community—it ensured that Java stayed wholesome and interoperable.

Amid a lot of fanfare, 2005 marked the tenth anniversary of Java. At that time, the intent to drop the Java 2 moniker and call the platform simply Java Standard Edition or simply Java SE circulated. The venerable Java mascot, Duke himself, appeared at several birthday celebrations to serve cake! Sun reunited members of the original "Green" team during a keynote break session. The Green team's original work eventually led to the commercial Java offering.

Estimates involving Java technology showed that its usage had skyrocketed since its inception. An estimated four and a half million Java developers and more than two and a half billion devices enabled by Java existed by 2005.

The open-source debate around Java was finally settled in 2006. Sun released Java under the GNU General Public License (GPL), much against the wishes of IBM and the Apache Software Foundation, which would have preferred the release of Java under the Apache license. Sun offered all three editions of the Java platform—Java SE, Java EE, and Java ME—under GPL. Along with this release, Sun also altered the branding and nomenclature for the Java platform. What was previously called Java 2 Platform Standard Edition (J2SE) was now simply called Java SE. Sun also subsequently released the Java HotSpot virtual machine and compiler under GNU GPL as well. Figure 1 depicts the various releases of Java versions on a historical roadmap.

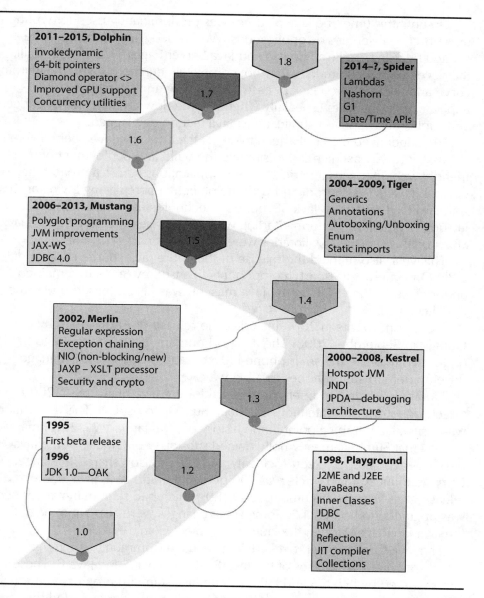

2011–2015, Dolphin
invokedynamic
64-bit pointers
Diamond operator <>
Improved GPU support
Concurrency utilities

1.8

2014–?, Spider
Lambdas
Nashorn
G1
Date/Time APIs

1.7

1.6

2006–2013, Mustang
Polyglot programming
JVM improvements
JAX-WS
JDBC 4.0

2004–2009, Tiger
Generics
Annotations
Autoboxing/Unboxing
Enum
Static imports

1.5

1.4

2002, Merlin
Regular expression
Exception chaining
NIO (non-blocking/new)
JAXP – XSLT processor
Security and crypto

2000–2008, Kestrel
Hotspot JVM
JNDI
JPDA—debugging
architecture

1.3

1995
First beta release
1996
JDK 1.0—OAK

1.2

1998, Playground
J2ME and J2EE
JavaBeans
Inner Classes
JDBC
RMI
Reflection
JIT compiler
Collections

1.0

Figure 1. *Historical timeline of Java releases from version 1.0 to version 8.0*

Up until this time, the Java platform was predominantly used for writing mission-critical server-side applications. Web-based user interfaces were created by using the Java Servlets and Java Server Pages technologies. Still, the development community was not completely enamored with the learning curve and the perceived lack of ease in designing and developing web applications using Java. Especially when it came down to creating UI widgets and supporting rich web applications, Java technology lagged.

Sun announced the JavaFX technology at the JavaOne developer conference in 2007. JavaFX was intended to simplify the build and deployment of user-friendly web interfaces and rich Internet applications across a broad range of devices. JavaFX was introduced with the objective of replacing Swing as the standard GUI library for Java SE, but both technologies have continued to be included in the Java platform. Starting with the release of JavaFX 2.2 and Java SE 7 update 6, the JavaFX libraries were bundled as part of Java SE.

This year also marked the release of the entire Java source code under GPL. Only a few third-party components licensed by Sun still remained under closed source. Duke, the Java mascot, was also released under the BSD license.

Significant events in 2008 included the release of Android 1.0 by Google in September 2008. The Android operating system would go on to revolutionize the smartphone industry and brought Java language development to smartphones in a big way.

Until 2009, Sun had been the steward for the Java platform. In 2009, Oracle announced its intention to acquire Sun Microsystems. This acquisition was a significant turning point in the history of Java. January 27, 2010, marked the day that Sun became a wholly owned subsidiary of Oracle. At the JavaOne developer conference, Scott McNealy and Larry Ellison shared the stage. Larry announced that Oracle was 100 percent behind Java. Java EE 6 was also released this year. At this time, Java FX 1.0, which had seen minimal adoption, was upgraded to Java FX 1.2. Some small changes were also announced to the Java language through the launch of Project Coin.

The Java Community Process (JCP) Executive Community approved the next two major releases of the Java Platform, Java 7 and Java 8. These were covered by JSR-336 and JSR-337. The Java standard progressed through the Java Community Process while the OpenJDK project provided the reference implementation.

The 2011 release of Java 7 provided several enhancements to the Java platform, including concurrency utilities, Strings in switch statements, Garbage-First collector, and JVM support for non-Java languages. JavaOne 2012 saw the surprise return of James Gosling to JavaOne and the community keynote.

Several sessions covered the upcoming Java technologies in Java SE 8. Oracle released Java EE 7 right before the 2013 JavaOne conference. The Internet of Things was a major theme of this event. The Java SE 8 roadmap was also a topic of discussion during a strategy keynote. Java SE 8 was ultimately released in March 2014. As of this writing, in the summer of 2017, Java SE 9 is slated for general availability release on September 21, 2017.

JDK Versions

The 2006 JavaOne conference retains a place in Java history as the event where Sun first announced that it would release Java under the GNU General Public License (GPL). The HotSpot virtual machine and compiler were released under the GNU GPL in November 2006. Then, in May 2007, Sun released the complete source code of the Java Class Library under GPL. There were a few components that remained closed source since Sun did not have the ownership rights to make that source code available. Over the course of the next couple of years, each such component was either released under open source or an alternative was provided. By December 2010, the entire JDK was available as open source without reliance on any binary plugs.

Release History

The year 1996 marked the inaugural release of JDK 1.0, referred to as the Java Developer Kit (JDK). This release included the developer tools and the runtime. A runtime-only package known as the Java Runtime Environment (JRE) was also made available. Even to this day, the name JDK has stuck and everyone refers to the Java platform by its JDK version. Java 1.1 (JDK 1.1) introduced inner classes.

Starting with JDK 1.2, code-named PlayGround, the release was renamed as Java 2 Platform Standard Edition. This was a significant release and tripled the size of the Java platform to more than 1500 classes in 59 packages. The Collections framework was introduced into Java and Swing now became part of the core platform. A Just-In-Time (JIT) compiler was also added.

Java 1.3 (JDK 1.3), named Kestrel, was released in May 2000. The HotSpot JVM was included with this release. A major addition to the Java platform was the synthetic proxy classes. These dynamic proxy classes allowed the creation of a proxy object for a list of interfaces without having to write that class at compile time. It offered the ability to provide a type-safe reflective dispatch to the underlying objects through their exposed interface.

Java 1.4 (JDK 1.4), known as Merlin, was released in February 2002. This release had some significant additions to the language and the APIs. Support of regular expressions and the addition of non-blocking I/O were fundamental improvements to the platform.

Starting with the next release, the naming convention changed yet again. The September 2004 release of Java SE 5 (JDK 1.5) was code-named Tiger. Generics, which provided compile-time type safety for collections and the annotations were major introductions in the release. Other significant additions included auto-boxing, static imports, the short form of the for loop, enumerations, and variable argument declarations. These features made Java SE 5 the biggest upgrade to the Java platform to date.

December 2006 marked the release of Java SE 6 (JDK 1.6), code-named Mustang. This release supported several new features, including support for scripting languages. It also provided the Java Compiler API. Java SE 6 saw significant adoption after its release. Even today, a large portion of the Java application code base is written in Java SE 6.

The next major release occurred in July 2011. Java SE 7 (JDK 1.7), also named Dolphin, saw the incorporation of elements from Project Coin. This was also the first release under OpenJDK.

Java 8 (JDK 1.8), released in March 2014, was the first version not assigned a code name. Eventually, Java 8 was code-named Spider, bringing a sigh of relief from the developer community that the historic naming convention will continue! This release introduced some significant features and improvements in the areas of security, performance, and tooling. Lambdas, the new Date and Time API, the Nashorn engine, G1 garbage collector, and other features made Java 8 the largest update to the language, surpassing those of JDK 5.0.

Java 9 (JDK 1.9) is the latest Java platform scheduled for general availability release, as of this writing, on September 21, 2017. This version has not yet been assigned a code name. At the time of this writing, a release candidate has been made available with all the features frozen in anticipation of the general release. The largest capability enhancement to the Java platform will be to its modular system, also known as the infamous Jigsaw Project. This significant feature has been the main cause of multiple delays to the Java 9 release schedule.

The goal of Project Jigsaw is to bring modularity to the Java platform by breaking the Java Runtime Environment (JRE) into smaller, interoperable, and modular components. This would enable the Java Platform to be easily scaled down to smaller computing devices and would have an immediate impact on the emerging Internet of Things (IoT) landscape. The modular system would also improve application security, performance, and maintainability.

The adoption of Java 9 will ensure that the management of large application portfolios or the maintenance of millions of lines of code will become far easier to tackle. I expect Java 9 to have a beneficial effect on enterprises that adopt application portfolio management strategies, modernize legacy non-Java applications, and migrate older Java applications to the new platform.

Summary

The history of Java has been quite eventful, filled with rapid advancements and additions to the language. As Java grew and matured with each subsequent version, the participation of developers at the annual JavaOne conference demonstrated the soaring popularity of the language and its fundamental platform. To date, no other programming language in history has experienced the same kind of growth and adoption as Java. In today's world, Java powers smartphones, wearable devices, machine learning software, big data analytics, and IoT platforms. As Java continues its journey, it must now co-exist with other dynamic and specialized languages. If history is any indication, the Java platform will continue to adapt and embrace new features to stay at the head of the pack.

CHAPTER
1

Java and the Enterprise

L arge-scale adoption of Java has emerged over the past decade with an estimated 90 percent of Global 2000 companies committed to a significant investment in the Java platform. Most enterprises today have developed a portfolio of Java applications that run business-critical processes, putting Java front and center of the enterprise's core functionality. As with any technology, the initial investment is never enough. It is important to remember that adopting a technology means also adopting its necessary maintenance and upgrades as well. As the Java platform continues to evolve rapidly, with new versions released every few years, businesses *must* enhance their Java applications regularly to remain competitive so that they can deliver modern functionality that is secure and provide the highest levels of performance.

Consider the quality of features, security, and performance improvements in Java Development Kit version 8 (JDK 8) alone, such as lambda expressions, several security enhancements, performance improvements for HashMaps, enhanced tools, and many other improvements. Enterprises wanting to retain their technological lead amongst their peers and those early adopters of emerging technologies will want to start preparing to modernize their applications by initially upgrading to JDK 8. If the enterprise plan is to modernize its Java applications during calendar year 2018, then upgrading to JDK 9 directly could also be a viable option.

Although the release of JDK 9 has had some delays, it will provide several additional improvements over JDK 8, including the modularity-related additions such as Project Jigsaw; JShell, which brings REPL (Read-Eval-Print-Loop) to Java; improved Java Virtual Machine (JVM) options; the Garbage-First (G1) garbage collector as the default; process API updates; and several other features. Although some commercial users may retain support for older versions, Oracle stopped public updates for JDK 7 in April 2015. Enterprises will have to enter into a commercial contract with Oracle to get continued support for JDK 7. Given that JDK 8 and the upcoming JDK 9 provide several major enhancements, it is prudent for enterprises to start formulating a modernization strategy for their Java applications.

Enterprise Adoption

Cloud computing. Big data. Mobile technologies. Social media. Gamification. Internet of Things (IoT). Unified communication. Collaboration. These are just some of the big trends currently being adopted by enterprises—many of which are incorporated in your own day-to-day project execution or planning activities. Although each trend promises the enterprise something different, they all share a common core: each is built on a technology platform that requires maintenance, upgrades, and forward thinking. In adopting the trend, you are also adopting the responsibility for its required maintenance and upgrade.

Companies, both large and small, have invested heavily in the Java platform and continue to build and enhance their Java application portfolio. In this chapter, we examine the adoption of Java in the enterprise and how the Java applications and the Java platform itself have evolved within enterprises over the past two decades. We also look at some of the challenges that enterprises are facing with respect to adoption of trends and carrying out successful modernization. Beginning the book with this appreciation of the Java platform's adoption in the enterprise will provide the insight, motivation, and direction regarding the investment and management of Java application portfolios that will be addressed in subsequent chapters. This chapter also briefly addresses emerging enterprise trends and the future usage of the Java platform.

Java's flexibility for enhancing and customizing functionality has made it particularly attractive for enterprise development, thereby making it the language of choice for building enterprise-specific customizations and applications. Java extends across popular open-source projects such as Apache Hadoop and its ecosystem of products for solving big data problems; open-source NoSQL products such as MongoDB, Cassandra, and HBase; products targeting artificial intelligence and machine learning applications; and many commercial products as well. Eclipse has released an open-source IoT stack for Java that simplifies development of IoT solutions. A variety of Platform as a Service (PaaS) options have emerged that support Java on the cloud. Java is used to develop mobile applications for Android. Because Java is flexible, Java is everywhere; it is especially embedded throughout the enterprise and has truly made the adoption of emerging technologies and trends a breeze in the enterprise environment.

Cloud computing, including hybrid cloud platforms, virtualized infrastructures, and software service platforms, are all extremely popular in enterprise IT departments. Cloud computing trends and enterprise cloud strategies revolve around defining the following:

- The benefits of adopting cloud-based solutions

- When to choose public versus private clouds

- Which applications should move to the cloud

- Security policies and concerns around the cloud

- Disaster recovery and business continuity policies for the cloud

Machine learning and big data analytics have boldly entered the mainstream world of technology. Previously, enterprises focused on building out data warehouses and data marts for reporting. Key performance indicators (KPIs) were established and then measured frequently to provide executive reports for performance tracking. Business intelligence reports were created against historical data to formulate a vast array of business decisions. The historical nature of the analysis most often resulted in reactive (rather than predictive) responses.

The advent of big data platforms has propelled a migration of workloads from traditional data warehousing infrastructure and software to distributed systems that run on commodity hardware. This has resulted in a substantial reduction of costs in achieving similar levels of insight and business intelligence. Moreover, with advances in real-time predictive systems, stream processing, and machine-learning algorithms, certain business decisions can be made in real-time based on models that can be created and trained against past data sets. Using these models, transactions can also be analyzed and scored in real-time to produce effective business decisions that were previously very cumbersome and time-prohibitive. Figure 1-1 shares many of the current trends adopted by enterprises.

Challenges to Enterprise Adoption and Modernization

Modernizing Java applications is an uphill task in most enterprises given the complexity introduced by dependencies, keeping the business running, regression testing, and estimating the cost and time involved in the modernization exercise with a fair degree of accuracy.

Although many enterprises have adopted Agile Development practices, test-driven development, and overall improvement of the actual software engineering approaches to application development and maintenance, we must keep in mind that many applications themselves have evolved over the years and pose significant challenges to their own future maintenance and interoperability with other applications in the enterprise.

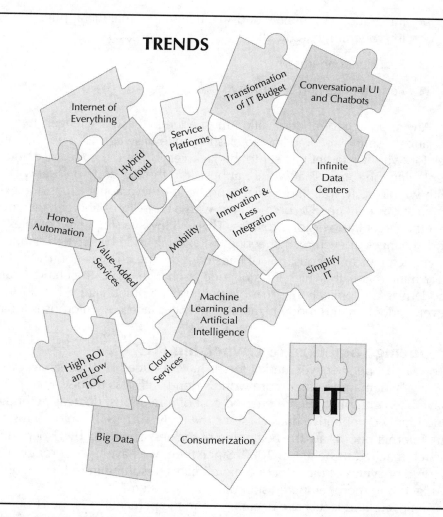

FIGURE 1-1.   *Trends in enterprise adoption*

As enterprises adopt the various emerging technology trends discussed earlier, specific challenges need to be addressed. Some of the key challenges faced by enterprises today include the following:

■ Reduction in the total cost of ownership (TCO)

■ Adaptation of legacy IT systems to service-oriented architecture and agile platforms to meet growing business demands

- Integration complexity and spaghetti code, making application interoperability difficult

- Security concerns

- Performance and scalability

Any approach to modernization must address these challenges. It is not a matter of simply recompiling an existing code base against a new compiler version with the target flag set to the Java version of the code base and deploying the same. That would, at best, run the old code on a new JVM with warnings. To truly modernize a portfolio of Java applications, the existing applications may need to be modified with new features and enhancements that the target Java version provides. This will involve simple to complex code changes or even reengineering the existing code base. With hundreds of applications and thousands of lines of code, the effort is not trivial. To determine manually which lines of code to change, make the changes, and modernize an application is feasible only up to a point. Figure 1-2 illustrates several adoption and modernization challenges faced by enterprises today.

Reducing Total Cost of Ownership (TCO)

From a cost perspective, market forces have reduced IT budgets over the last 15 years, demanding that more work is done with less money. Enterprises have been grappling with increased cost of operations, decreasing budgets, and highly competitive markets since the early 2000s. The mid-1990s and the Internet boom saw the beginning of reckless spending by IT departments, which reached its height in 2000. Since then, we have been through a couple of cycles of tough economic climates, resulting in reduction of IT budgets and more tempered spending on IT systems.

As overall budgets have decreased and the percentage of the IT budget spent on maintaining existing applications have increased, there is a renewed focus to reduce the TCO of existing systems, thereby freeing up a portion of the maintenance budget toward building new applications.

More than 80 percent of the IT budget is being spent on existing applications, in maintenance and keep-the-lights-on scenarios, with less and less budget available to invest in new applications and new technologies. This has resulted in advancement of Application Portfolio Management (APM), IT simplification, and rationalization methodologies. A whole discipline has evolved around APM, whereby entire application portfolios can be measured,

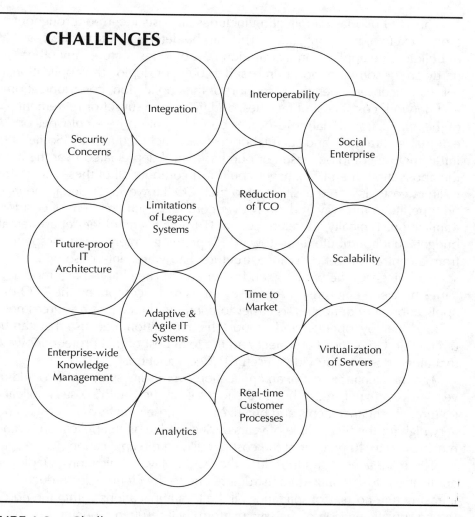

CHALLENGES

Security Concerns

Integration

Interoperability

Social Enterprise

Limitations of Legacy Systems

Reduction of TCO

Future-proof IT Architecture

Scalability

Adaptive & Agile IT Systems

Time to Market

Enterprise-wide Knowledge Management

Virtualization of Servers

Real-time Customer Processes

Analytics

FIGURE 1-2. *Challenges to enterprise adoption and modernization*

managed, tracked, and optimized to deliver the best possible results at the best price points. This reduces the TCO of the application portfolio and accelerates and maximizes the return on investment (ROI) from those portfolios. So rather than make specific application-by-application decisions, enterprises can look holistically at their entire application portfolio, or subsets of their portfolio, and make uniform business decisions and improve business outcomes.

The TCO of a Java application includes all costs incurred throughout the life cycle of that application. This can be determined from the cost of building the application, acquisition cost of infrastructure, any other hardware or software tools purchased to build or deploy the application, software licenses, operations, support of the application, communication and network costs, cost of facilities, and finally the sunset or retirement of the application. IT labor resources could be enterprise employees or external contractors, and such labor costs are included as well. Some of the infrastructure could be leased or purchased and depreciated over the life of the application. If an IT manager could just compute all of these direct and indirect costs, it would easily lead to the TCO. However, IT departments do not operate in this way and rarely ever compute each line item of cost for an application. Typically, there are central IT budgets and other departmental budgets that contribute funds toward IT spending. Enterprises also spend from a central budget on IT infrastructure, hardware, enterprise-wide software licenses, networking, and other areas. The charge-back model varies between enterprises. All these factors make computing the TCO of an application very difficult. It is easier to compute the cost of resources needed to build, deploy, operate, and support the application, because that can be directly tied to a specific project and the total cost of that project. However, that alone does not provide a useful TCO calculation.

The maintenance cost of an application over its life span can also add up year-on-year expenses. Although the focus is on the "build" costs, applications go through enhancements and bug fixes, and these maintenance costs can be very high for the first couple of years during the life of an application, even as much as 30 to 40 percent of the cost of building the application.

There are a few ways to reduce the TCO of Java applications. Deploying applications to virtualized infrastructure and to the cloud helps reduce infrastructure costs. Consolidating all the Java applications within the portfolio to one specific version of the Java platform will result in reducing support and maintenance costs. Rationalizing any third-party tools and software will provide further reduction. Lastly, investing in automation tools for the assessment and migration of Java applications to the most stable Java platform version will further contribute to the overall reduction of the TCO.

Legacy IT Systems

Existing application portfolios in large enterprises comprise heterogeneous technologies including mainframe applications, Java applications, Microsoft technology-based applications, hierarchical databases, proprietary languages and systems, and a variety of open-source and third-party systems. These portfolios most likely contain applications with redundant functionality in multiple places and could also contain redundant technologies from different vendors. I know of one company that had invested in 12 different reporting technologies over time. In this case, various reporting applications were built on a variety of these reporting technologies, resulting in avoidable licensing costs, lack of skill sets in their labor resource pool, and increasing support costs. This is not an isolated case. Enterprises that have been around for 20 or more years are guilty of proliferating multiple technologies, redundant functionality, and an aging and obsolete set of systems in their application portfolios.

Legacy IT systems that enterprises operate include mainframe applications, proprietary third-party systems, and Java applications still running on JDK 1.4.2, JDK 1.5.x, JDK 1.6, and JDK 1.7. I do not want to name any organizations here, but there are some applications today still running on JDK versions 1.2 and 1.3! It is truly amazing to see the longevity of some of these business-critical applications being used every day. Unfortunately, when it comes to supporting the new business requirements or necessary functional enhancements, these legacy applications are quite inflexible and not easy to modify. This can be attributed to several reasons: lack of proper documentation, departure of people who built the applications, monolithic application architecture, lack of in-house skills as in the case of the mainframe applications, difficulty in integrating with the legacy applications, lack of test cases and test harnesses, tight coupling between legacy applications, and a plethora of other similar reasons.

This leads to a very expensive support and maintenance budget to operate an application portfolio filled with legacy applications. The modernization challenges presented by such a portfolio are not easy to surmount and must be carefully considered to prevent adverse impact on the business itself. Thoroughly assessing the application portfolio, developing a well-researched roadmap, documenting the interaction between various systems, introducing new technology components, and reengineering some of the applications will pave the way toward modernizing a legacy application portfolio.

Some enterprises have resorted to legacy componentization techniques, in which the business logic in the legacy systems such as mainframe applications are exposed via a wrapper written in Java and exposed as an API to web applications or other Java applications. This is a temporary stopgap measure— all it does is increase the number of online transactions on the mainframe backend, since every call to the web application or the Java application will result in a call to the wrapper, which in turn will call the mainframe application and underlying database and then return the retrieved data through all the layers back to the calling application. This usually results in increased cost of mainframe usage. You can look into an architecture that caches the mainframe data closer to the web tier to avoid having to increase mainframe transactions. The main point is that such legacy componentization adds to the complexity and makes the enhancement and maintenance of such applications more difficult. Although this solution may be adequate for some scenarios, more often than not, completely reengineering the legacy applications to the Java platform will lead to ease of maintenance and will result in positioning the application portfolio for better ROI in the long run.

Integration Complexity and Application Interoperability

Java application portfolios have evolved over several years. Even specific Java applications within the portfolio have been enhanced since being built. As existing applications are enhanced, new applications are being introduced to enterprises, and these new application may need to integrate and interoperate with existing applications. Although some organizations have made an effort to implement a true service-oriented architecture right from the beginning, the reality is that no such architecture can anticipate every future need and be foolproof. Within a few years of an architecture-related exercise, functional and technical enhancements erode the architecture enough that the inevitable need for re-architecture becomes the new reality.

As applications evolve and need to communicate with other applications, project teams typically build point-to-point integrations between two or more applications. Enterprise Integration Patterns (EIP) are not typically followed. This results in spaghetti code and a faulty messaging and integration architecture. Complexity is a function of the number of services, interfaces, and application components, and the various connections among them. Complexity is also increased by the variety of data formats, richness of the data sets exchanged between application endpoints, throughput of transactions, peak loads, size of data payloads transmitted, low latency response, version mismatches between the communicating endpoints, and many other factors.

Increased integration complexity leads to increased risks to the business itself. There are more opportunities for failures, performance issues, and other runtime issues to surface. In addition, more costs and effort are required in adding enhancements to existing applications, testing the new features, and then releasing the application to production, since integration points have a tendency to fail or be affected adversely during application enhancements.

The same group in an enterprise does not necessarily own all the applications in a particular application portfolio. These applications could belong to multiple groups. Because of concerted efforts in defining a sound solution architecture, taking into account application requirements, integration requirements, and application interfaces, applications may initially integrate very well and interoperate perfectly at first. Application owners are typically concerned only about meeting the business requirements of their own applications and have to operate within their allocated budgets, deadlines, and available resources. The priorities and alignment of the application owners to their line of business will take precedent over cooperating with other application owners all the time.

Eventually, however, each application may evolve in its own direction based on the business needs of that application owner, and after a few years, interoperability issues will surface. Some of this can be addressed by having central architecture groups, proper governance, and a contract between application owners not to break advertised service endpoints and exposed APIs. But that level of sophistication is rarely found in many enterprises, and the lack of universal adoption among all applications tends to be the biggest hurdle. Basically, integration complexity and interoperability issues lurk in every application portfolio and surface at the most inopportune times, and tightly coupled applications often lead to increased complexity for support and maintenance obligations.

Some application portfolios have diverse integration technologies and paradigms that result in additional complexity, cost, and performance issues. Integration needs to be handled carefully with well thought-out strategies for data-level integration, application-level integration leveraging services and message bus architectures, business-layer integrations, presentation-layer integrations, and leveraging EIP.

Security

Java applications are typically complex and use several third-party and open-source libraries. It is incredibly difficult to keep track of every JAR file being used, every version of the open-source or third-party library, and every zero-day threat that may lurk within a Java application. Every year,

Oracle issues several patches and bug fixes to the underlying Java platform and eventually provides an update. Several security issues are tied to using Java in the browser. Use of Java in the browser via the Java plug-in has declined in popularity, and that definitely helps in reducing the exposure to possible security flaws; however, there are several vulnerabilities on the server side as well.

According to published reports, there were 58 Java vulnerability disclosures in 2010, and that figure rose to 65 in 2011. That tally increased to 68 in 2012 and skyrocketed to 208 in 2013. In a survey of other applications' vulnerabilities, Java was the most attacked technology, ranking at 50 percent, followed by Adobe Reader (22 percent), browsers (13 percent), and others (15 percent). In 2014, 36 vulnerabilities were reported in January, 37 vulnerabilities in April, and 20 vulnerabilities in July. As additional vulnerabilities become known, updates become available only for the supported Java platform versions. At the time of this writing, JDK 1.6 and JDK 1.7 are no longer supported, yet a majority of Java applications in enterprise environments are running on JDK 1.6 or even JDK 1.5. Only a small percentage of these enterprises are paying Oracle for extended support services. For a majority of the enterprises, this issue will most definitely rear its ugly head at some point. It is important to note that JDK 1.7 reached its end of life in April 2015, after which public support for JDK 1.7, which provided periodic updates, was withdrawn. It would be prudent for enterprises to migrate immediately to JDK 1.8 or JDK 1.9 and take advantage of all the fixed issues and new language features.

Performance and Scalability

The Java platform is very robust when it comes to building highly scalable, high-performance applications. Enterprise applications today are highly distributed architecturally and composed of loosely coupled technical components and/or services; they also integrate with several external services and are extremely mission critical. The typical approach to performance and scalability has been to build an application first and then approach performance issues by fine-tuning bottlenecks. This method works for performance tuning in general, but it fails to tackle the overall problem of scalability and performance at the portfolio level. Many people use the two terms interchangeably, but there is a distinction between performance and scalability.

Scalability is the ability of a system to respond in the same manner as load increases. For example, if the number of requests per second went up by 10 times, how would the system respond? If there is no perceived difference, the system has scaled to support the tenfold increase in requests. *Performance* is the ability of the system to maintain its response time when additional load is placed on the system's resources. The resources at the system's disposal include the number of CPU nodes, storage, I/O, memory, and so on.

No system is infinitely scalable, and there will always be a breaking point for any scalable architecture. Typically, enterprises do not anticipate Google-, Apple-, or Amazon-level traffic for their Internet-facing applications. Architecting for such scale would be cost prohibitive and unnecessary for most enterprises. What is important to understand is the breaking point for your own application architecture. The key determining factor for any enterprise is to ensure that expectations are met with more than adequate scalability and performance characteristics. If an enterprise needs to provide 200-millisecond response times and expects 100,000 requests a second, then that is the SLA that needs to be met! Although this expectation could change over time, you must architect for the right set of nonfunctional requirements that are pertinent to the use cases being addressed.

Typical performance and scalability issues that are faced by enterprises at the Java application level can be attributed to a few key areas:

- Poor capacity planning and workload estimation
- Not tuning the Java garbage collector
- Poor performance of the underlying database system
- Memory leaks

In addition to these Java platform–related issues, other plausible problems could arise such as network latency, integration to third-party systems, poorly written Java libraries that are used by the enterprise Java application, distributing application components across data centers, I/O related problems, and blocking threads.

NOTE
Modernizing to Java 8 will help alleviate several Java platform–related performance issues. Java 8 provides a more mature G1 garbage collector with dependable pause times, a consistent and configurable collector with command-line flags, and no need to tune the permanent generation. There are also performance improvements in some of the core classes, such as the HashMap class, for example. Previously, key collisions resulted in degrading performance on HashMaps. The Java 8 implementation of HashMap switches its hash bucket from a linked list to a balanced tree once the number of items in the hash bucket grows beyond a certain threshold. This ensures that the worst-case performance goes from O(n) for a linked list to O(log n) for the balanced tree to search and retrieve the key from the hash bucket.

Moving applications to a cloud infrastructure lends itself to easy horizontal scaling. Horizontal scaling, or scaling out, enables the addition of more nodes or machines to the current pool of resources dynamically on demand to increase compute capacity on the fly. Vertical scaling, or scaling up, is limited by the underlying size of the server. You have to add more resources in vertical scaling when the underlying server capacity is reached. In theory, horizontal scaling is limited only by how many nodes can be added successfully. But horizontal scaling has its disadvantages. Although it may appear to be a viable solution, you must also consider the operational costs, power, cooling, and larger data center footprint compared to a vertical-scaling solution. Some applications benefit from using distributed caches and in-memory databases. Processing data in-memory is faster than I/O operations to read and write data from disk or flash storage. Overall, application portfolios have a tendency to degrade in performance over time due to various factors, and it is important for enterprises to implement performance management tools to establish proper monitoring and management of enterprise applications.

Java on the Cloud

Infrastructure as a Service (IaaS) and Platform as a Service (PaaS) have both gained popularity in recent years. IaaS offerings were readily available, long before the PaaS model, as a viable option to traditional data centers for deploying Java applications. Oracle, Google, Red Hat, and several other service providers are focused on supporting Java with their PaaS offerings. Recognizing that millions of lines of Java code are being written today and the potential of the cloud, several major cloud providers have strengthened their Java cloud offerings. At the time of this writing, Oracle Java Cloud Service leads the pack in terms of tutorials, support, features, and a managed stack for deploying Java applications. Google, Amazon, and Azure also have dedicated portals that explain their Java cloud offerings.

Besides the well-known cloud vendors, several emerging vendors such as Heroku, Red Hat, OpenShift, Jelastic, CloudBees, and others also offer Java PaaS solutions. What developers find attractive is the ability to simply build and upload Java WAR or EAR files to the PaaS cloud. Developers can focus on the applications and the business functionality. The underlying platform automatically provides the infrastructure, resources (including storage and network bandwidth), compute units, and management and monitoring of the deployed applications. There are also options for load balancing, bursting, and auto scaling the applications to handle peak loads. Many enterprises have also implemented private cloud infrastructures to deploy their Java applications on their own.

An interesting emerging project, Eclipse Che, is bringing Java development to the cloud by providing features similar to the desktop Eclipse integrated development environment (IDE) as a service within the browser. This will enable developers to develop directly on the cloud rather than having to use an IDE such as Eclipse, develop on their local machines, and then deploy the applications to the data center environment. Eclipse Che will not only be a great option for developers, but it will also save time and resources by providing a familiar interface for developers to use from any location and any desktop or laptop.

The ability to build and deploy Java applications on the cloud very easily opens up the possibility of moving existing Java applications from an on-premises environment to the cloud environment. If the cloud environment is fully managed, this eases the burden of having to keep security patches up to date. The managed cloud stack provider will ensure that the entire environment is up to date.

There are some downsides to Java on the cloud as well. Depending on the application, there could be issues surrounding data privacy and the location where the data resides. There is no common standard for Java PaaS stacks. Lack of portability will tie an enterprise to a particular vendor, thereby causing the switch between PaaS platforms to be not as seamless as it should be.

Java on the cloud is here to stay, but before you adopt a Java PaaS solution, it is important to consider all the pros and cons. Whether you choose a private cloud or public cloud environment, a managed cloud service, or IaaS or PaaS will depend on the nature of the application and the particular business needs. The chapters later in this book address Java modernization in more detail, including various modernization techniques as well as the emergence and popularity of micro services.

Past, Present, and Future

For the purposes of this discussion, we will artificially divide the Java era into three separate segments: the *past* (Java 1.0 to Java SE 6 and Java 7), the *present* (Java 8), and the *future* (Java 9 and beyond). Figure 1-3 highlights the business and technology trends since 1995, with the technology trends specifically focused on the Java platform releases.

On March 18, 2014, Oracle released Java SE 8, a major feature release containing additions and enhancements in many functional areas. Java SE 8 includes 10 major feature additions in the Java language, compact profiles for customized Java SE platform for small devices, around 20 significant security enhancements, along with a host of other feature additions in areas such as JVM, concurrency, I/O and new I/O (NIO), internationalization (i18n), security, and performance, among others. Upgrading to JDK 8 often involves updates to the application(s) code and/or configuration(s) due to 29 incompatibilities, 11 API removals, and 14 deprecated APIs in the areas of JVM, Java language, and Java SE API.

There is widespread usage of Java 6 and Java 7 within enterprises. Some reports state that about 70 percent of Java installations in enterprises still run Java 6, or Java 7, even though Oracle stopped public support. A disturbing fact is that the majority of such Java applications do not have the latest security updates installed. Various security firms such as Bit9 (Carbon Black) have confirmed this. The last publicly available security update for Java 6, which was released in April 2013, is Java 6 Update 45.

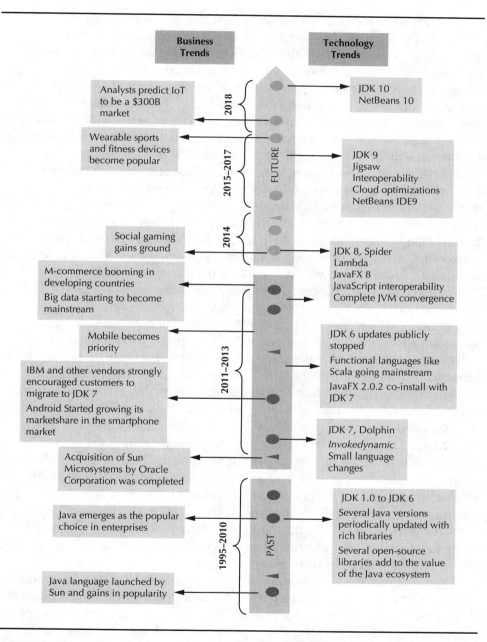

FIGURE 1-3.   *The past, present, and future of Java platform releases and business trends*

On average, enterprises have two or three major versions of Java concurrently deployed in enterprise IT environments, running various applications. If we also count the minor versions, including security updates, the number of minor versions of Java running could even be as high as 20 to 30 versions. Unfortunately, in reality, not all environments are kept up to date with security patches. Since the maintenance and upgrading of server environments fall on the IT administrators, enterprises are usually hard-pressed to keep their production environments upgraded with just the minor versions. As a result, enterprise Java application portfolios are typically littered with Java applications running in environments that are at vastly different minor version updates of the same Java platform. Industry reports suggest that this inconsistent practice tends to create IT security vulnerabilities, causing a greater risk to the enterprise as a whole. A comprehensive application modernization approach must bring true uniformity and eliminate the minor version discrepancies between the deployed environments. This approach should also focus on allowing a maximum number of two major versions that require continued support. Anything more than that will become an operational and technical drain for the enterprise.

According to a report from Carbon Black (a security-focused company formerly called Bit9), around 65 percent of enterprises had more than two versions of Java installed at the same time, and approximately 20 percent had more than three versions. Less than 1 percent of enterprises run the latest version of Java. You read that right—less than 1 percent. Enterprises have invested considerable capital and resources into their applications, which are compiled against a specific Java version. Enterprises cannot risk losing application functionality by simply upgrading the Java platform version to a new version—even an update to an existing version. Thus, there is proliferation of the minor updates of a particular Java version as well. Most of these enterprise applications are actively undergoing functional enhancements, so enterprises are forced to keep the specific Java version and the minor update version exactly the same for that particular application. Applications could lose some functionality or inadvertently introduce a bug if they were simply moved to run on a new Java platform version.

Oracle does have an auto-update process for Microsoft Windows and desktop computers that updates the latest Java Runtime Environment (JRE) on the system. However, versions that are other than the latest version will not be removed and replaced. This is done specifically by design, because enterprise users need more than one version of the Java platform. Unfortunately, these server-side upgrades are a major bane of the IT administrators in the enterprise!

Emerging Languages

The Java platform is no longer just about the Java language. A number of popular languages have emerged, including some that are gaining popularity in enterprises, such as Scala, Groovy, and Clojure. The Java SE 7 platform introduced the `invokedynamic` instruction to the language as a new bytecode. This made the implementation of compilers and runtime systems on the JVM for dynamically typed languages less cumbersome and improved the performance characteristics. Some JVM languages are interpreted, while some are compiled to Java bytecode that may be compiled just-in-time during execution to improve performance. JavaScript is also supported on the JVM by the Rhino and Nashorn (Java 8) JavaScript engines.

Scala adds functional programming abilities and can interoperate with existing Java applications since it can also run on the JVM. Scala's strength is in its focus on parallel computing. Groovy, another popular language for the Java platform, is a dynamic language and also interoperable with Java. Groovy, along with Grails, is becoming a popular choice for rapidly developing web applications. Clojure brings functional programming concepts and is basically a Lisp dialect. Although not as currently popular as Scala, Clojure is seeing a rise in use for specific areas such as analytics. JRuby and Jython round out the popular list of JVM languages.

So why do we even need other languages for the JVM when we have Java? The answer is simple. Just as a tool box has various tools besides a hammer to address specific needs, the programming world has multiple languages available to address specific types of problems and build applications. In fact, some languages are better suited to write front-end web applications compared to server-intensive multithreaded applications. Other languages may have ready-made libraries providing specific functionality that can be leveraged in an application. As such, being able to use an array of other languages for the JVM could be a matter of personal preference or the need to use a dynamically typed language as opposed to a statically typed language in the development environment.

How does the rise of other languages for the JVM impact Java modernization? One of the key benefits is that with support for many languages on the JVM, you can call libraries written in one language from another language without having to go through hoops. Although modernizing existing Java applications, enterprises can consider whether they would like to write enhancements in another language that is supported on the JVM or to incorporate libraries specifically written in a supported language. There could be advantages depending on the problem domain.

Addressing this topic further, languages implemented for the JVM typically fall into three broad categories:

- Many are languages for research and no one has heard of them outside of a small group working with that language.

- They are ports of existing languages to the JVM because they are gaining in popularity and porting the language to the JVM provides access to libraries.

- The languages have features that are currently not available in Java or have a perceived ease of programming compared to Java.

Oracle has addressed this topic in great detail and has published articles highlighting the features and usage of many JVM languages. Although this book will not go into detail on other JVM languages, we briefly discuss a few in the paragraphs that follow.

There has been a sudden surge and a rapid increase in the popularity of JavaScript and Node.js. Lots of new applications are being written in Node.js, especially real-time web applications, since Node.js is built with a focus on non-blocking event-driven I/O. Node.js is not currently built for CPU-intensive operations and heavy computation. An open-source project called Nodyn, which is sponsored by Red Hat, has implemented the functionality of Node.js APIs to the JVM. Node.js is not going to replace Java any time soon, but it is going to be a great complement to Java. Interestingly, Node.js will have an edge when it goes head-to-head with Java Enterprise Edition–based web applications.

In JDK 8, Nashorn replaced Rhino as the embedded JavaScript engine. Nashorn compiles JavaScript to Java bytecode using new language features based on JSR 292, including `invokedynamic`, which were introduced in JDK 7. The Nashorn engine can be called from the command line using the `jjs` command. Java classes can be called from inside JavaScript, and JavaScript can be called from within Java code. With the rising popularity of JavaScript on the server side—made even more popular by Node.js—enterprises will leverage both Java and JavaScript in their future application portfolios.

Scala has seen only a slow gain in popularity, but, nevertheless, several applications have been written in Scala and a parallel ecosystem has evolved around Scala and its libraries. The fact that Scala had lambdas and supported a functional programming style well before Java probably assisted in Scala's adoption and use. Some enterprise application portfolios contain both Scala code and Java code. Going forward, decisions need to me made about whether to convert the Scala code to Java or to maintain the Scala code and interoperate with Java applications.

Java developers are starting to get a taste of how other languages for the JVM are evolving to support a higher degree of concurrency and parallelism. Java 8's implementation of lambdas has brought new methods to the language and enabled Java developers to embrace a functional style. This has also allowed the Scala language to improve and standardize the bytecode emitted by Scala's compiler. Scala has built-in non-blocking I/O and asynchronous processing. The introduction of lambdas to Java has brought Java and Scala closer together and made each language a bit like the other. While modernizing Java applications, popular Scala frameworks can be more easily used from Java code. There is a ripe opportunity here for tools to evolve that will seamlessly build, integrate, and test combinations of Java and Scala code. One area where Java will still need improvement is in the immutable collections.

Groovy was designed from the ground up to bring productivity and tight integration to the Java platform. Groovy can be used to write anything from scripts to full-blown applications. Although Groovy is a dynamic language with features similar to other dynamically typed languages such as Python and Ruby, since Groovy 2.0, the language has also supported compilation and static type checking, thus offering type inference and performance closer to that of Java. Most of the code written in Java is compatible syntactically with Groovy. Several features of Groovy, such as closures, traits, functional programming with collections, and so on, have been addressed in Java 8. Many other features in Groovy are not addressed in Java. Given the ease of programming in Groovy, its richer feature set, its similarity to Java code, and its almost Java-like performance, many enterprises are building Groovy code bases. While modernizing Java applications, it is reasonable to look at Groovy to add enhancements to existing applications or write new applications that can integrate with existing Java applications.

Clojure has a focus on immutable value and developing multithreaded programs. It is also designed with an intent to work with the Java platform and help in concurrent programming. Clojure applications lend themselves to be easily packaged and deployed on Java application servers. Clojure makes it easy to call existing Java libraries from within Clojure. Tight Java integration is possible because Clojure is also designed for it to be easy to call from within Java applications. Clojure is lagging behind Scala in its adoption within enterprises. It will be interesting to see if enterprises make significant investments in Clojure. That will decide if the language will have a part to play in the future of Java modernization.

Jython is a Java implementation of the popular Python programming language. Jython programs can import and use Java classes and compile to Java bytecode. Jython has not gained that much in popularity to be considered as a threat to replace the Java programming language. It does, however, make it easy to integrate Java code into Python. Jython code can be more compact than Java code and can also be viewed as an alternative to JavaScript, for interacting with Java. As legacy Java code is modernized, it is not anticipated that enterprises will turn to Jython to replace Java code. It might be useful where Python-to-Java integration is necessary.

JRuby is an implementation of Ruby for the JVM. JRuby itself is written largely in Java. In principle, the purpose of JRuby is very similar to Jython. It is tightly integrated with Java, allowing two-way calling between Java and Ruby code. JRuby programs can be interpreted, compiled just-in-time or ahead-of-time to Java bytecode. JRuby 1.7 and later also make use of the `invokedynamic` keyword added to JDK 1.7. JRuby is not that popular in enterprises, and it is not anticipated to replace legacy Java code in enterprises. It might be useful where Ruby-to-Java integration is necessary.

As enterprises pursue a modernization strategy with respect to their Java application portfolio, they will need to look comprehensively at some of the other languages that are JVM-friendly. Enterprises have to weigh the advantages of adopting JVM languages other than Java. There needs to be a clear understanding of the benefits in a particular context. Learning curves and internal skills sets need to be factored into such decisions as well. Adoption of other JVM languages could lead to increased cost and development times in the near term. Regardless of the minor business challenges, many enterprises have already started using Scala, Groovy, and Node.js, and the other JVM languages will continue to play formidable parts in the future of Java modernization.

Summary

Whether you started your journey with Java and the enterprise from Java's early days or adopted the Java platform along the way, every Java enterprise developer shares one commonality—a need to build, manage, and update applications with an eye toward the future of Java. Sun Microsystems,

Oracle, IBM, and others, along with the Java developer community, have gone to great lengths to preserve the "write-once, run-everywhere" promise of Java and ensure that Java is the continued platform of choice for enterprises. Although Sun Microsystems is no longer in existence, Java has now become open source and the software has benefited greatly from consortiums such as Apache and Eclipse, which provide several popular open-source projects under their umbrellas. Trends shaping the future coupled with enterprise challenges have necessitated a rigorous approach for automation tools to protect and further enhance existing investments in Java application portfolios.

Recent Java platform releases have added many compelling features while improving performance and making the Java platform more secure. Java is now available on devices of every form factor and has progressed from mere server-side popularity to smart phones and beyond. Opening up the JVM to other languages has created an ecosystem in which "Java the language" and "Java the platform" have both forged their own identities. The adoption of the Java platform and the Java language are both on the rise, even after more than two decades of existence. It remains the most popular programming language and the preferred enterprise platform of our times.

CHAPTER

2

The Life Cycle of
a Java Application

The first public release of the Java platform was in 1996 with JDK 1.0. Since that time, Java has continually evolved to meet the changing needs of its users. It is highly unlikely that applications written in that initial release are still actively used by today's enterprises. These legacy applications, like the enterprises they serve, must evolve or be replaced. In the midst of continual evolution, is there any predictability in application development? Well, the guiding principles of development still remain true. Enterprises follow a process for generating an application. While the specifics of the process implementation vary among enterprises, in general this process begins with identifying a business need and securing budgeted funds. Once these have been addressed, a program is then created for the application's management and governance along with an identification of resources necessary to manage the program and ultimately execute the project. The project team, working under the program management umbrella, builds the application, tests it, and deploys it to the end user. After the successful deployment of an application, a different group within IT typically supports and maintains it. If additional budgets are procured, future programs could be created to enhance that application's functionality over time. Due to changing business requirements, enterprises routinely replace or remove applications based on their current needs.

Though the exact process and detailed steps may vary among enterprises, the analysis always starts the same way. Unless there is a compelling business need and a budget allocated to address that need, applications cannot be built or enhanced within an enterprise. This process also comes with its own set of challenges and business risks. Sometimes, projects are abandoned midway. Other projects are not estimated correctly from a cost or time perspective, thereby affecting the overall build and delivery of an application. Sometimes, enterprises, without even realizing it, build applications with certain functionality even though other applications already exist with that same exact functionality within the enterprise. This redundancy and wastefulness in poor application management happens more often than not.

The dynamics of an IT department within an enterprise is quite complex and in many cases has an effect on the success or failure of the enterprise itself. It is almost always the case that budget requests for technology upgrades are prioritized at the very bottom of the list, and enterprises often decide to stick with an existing technology platform version for another year to save costs. After a few years, these technology versions become obsolete and are no longer supported by the vendor. The decision not to upgrade or modernize applications ultimately puts the enterprise at greater risk if mission-critical platforms are affected.

This chapter explores several aspects of the application life cycle and the management processes associated with the application life cycle. We also present a viewpoint advocating the processes necessary to create a sound methodology that should be tailored to an organization's needs. An enterprise should develop an approach by using relevant products and tools to enable and customize its own application life-cycle management blueprint.

NOTE
The discussion of application life cycle in this chapter is not to be confused with application life-cycle events from a technical standpoint, in which an application deployed in an application server goes through life-cycle events such as startup, execution, and stop and shutdown in an application container such as a Java EE application server.

The Need for a New Application

Most organizations do not have a deep understanding of their portfolio of existing applications. At the level of each application, multiple owners and stakeholders are collectively responsible for the portfolio. However, stakeholders are concerned about the health of only the applications they own and focus their efforts on seeking budgetary support to maintain and operate their specific applications. Owners may have partnered with particular vendors to support their applications, and these service providers may change over time. Thus, it is rare for any one person or group to have deep hands-on knowledge of the application and how it evolved to where it is currently. Even at a functional level of understanding, application knowledge is typically fragmented across several people. To reconstruct this knowledge would be a futile exercise, because it would require several weeks to interview the various stakeholders across the organization. Nevertheless, enterprises must resort to this exercise when major enhancements are needed and insufficient information is available to the decision-making team. During this discovery exercise, the functional and technical understandings of the application are captured in a systems appreciation document, along with whatever background knowledge can be gathered regarding the application. Although it is better than nothing, this document still lacks a complete 360-degree understanding of the application, because it relies on a group of individuals, many of whom are relatively new to the application or possess only limited knowledge of its history.

After a couple of years, this knowledge document becomes obsolete as the application has been further enhanced without the knowledge base being properly updated. Once vendor resources have moved on to other projects, a few more enhancements are approved, and a new team steps in to take over the application, a new "systems appreciation" must be started again, taking into account all the historical knowledge that has been lost as a result of employee turnover and poor document retention.

Note that so far we have been discussing an individual application. If you raise this argument to the entire application portfolio, there might be nobody in the organization who could claim deep knowledge of all the applications in the portfolio. Over a period of 5 to 10 years, the applications in the portfolio all evolve in their own direction, and an enterprise is left with an application portfolio that siphons a good deal of the budget just to keep the lights on. When new applications are added to this portfolio, they will also succumb to the budget requests process and compete for allocation of support and maintenance funds. It may seem like a never-ending cycle.

Application portfolios that have evolved in this manner exhibit many of the following characteristics:

- Create huge business risks

- Provide poor return on investment

- Increase total cost of ownership every year

- Are rampant with functional redundancies

- Contain obsolete technology

- Hide lurking security issues

- Are bad investment decisions

- Contain old applications that can be sunset

- Involve increasingly higher maintenance costs

Application Life-cycle Management

During the active life of an application, it typically belongs to a portfolio of applications, integrates with other applications, serves a business unit with end users, goes through multiple enhancements and functional improvements, and in some cases undergoes re-engineering and new technology integration.

Eventually, it is renewed and replaced. Figure 2-1 illustrates the five major transition points in an application's life cycle:

1. Ideation & strategy

2. Requirement & design

3. Build & deployment

4. Maintenance & enhancement

5. Renewal & replacement

Application life-cycle management is a continuous process. Several products are available to aid comprehensive application life-cycle management, including tools that focus on program management, collaboration, software engineering process support, quality assurance and testing process, and governance.

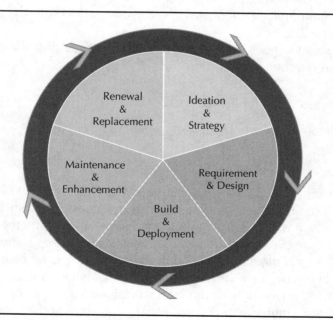

FIGURE 2-1. *Major transition points of an application's life*

> **NOTE**
> *These products or tools are beyond the scope of this chapter, but they may be used in your daily routine. This chapter also does not attempt to describe the software development or software engineering aspects of the application life cycle. Such topics are addressed in detail in other books dedicated to such topics.*

The application is managed as part of the program management that initiates, builds, and operates the application throughout its life cycle. In advanced organizations, the application life cycle is also subject to an application portfolio management process that enables the organization to manage the application as an individual asset that is part of a larger portfolio of applications. There are several advantages to this, which we will examine in subsequent chapters.

A governance process provides monitoring and management of the various application life-cycle stages. This process also manages other processes, including program management and application portfolio management, as shown in Figure 2-2.

Every application goes through the followings stages in its life cycle, which are covered in depth in this chapter:

1. Business case establishment

2. Application development

3. Operations

Although most of us wearing a software development hat or an IT administrator hat recognize and agree with the transition points of an application's life, it is also equally important that we understand the processes involved in the life cycle that are mapped to the stages of application evolution. This book draws a distinction between the transition points and life-cycle stages because the life-cycle stage view, employed by executives and application portfolio owners, is primarily driven by financials and the operational utility of the applications rather than delving into the details of application design, build, and deployment. Merely taking a technical and development-centric view of individual applications and application portfolios as a whole does not help to justify application modernization to senior enterprise leadership.

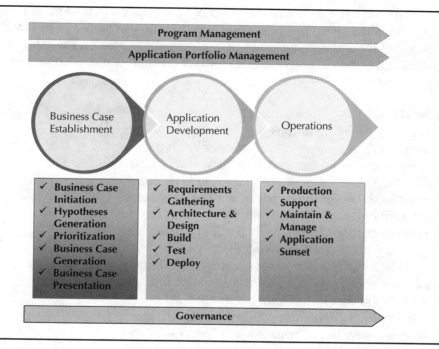

FIGURE 2-2. *The governance process monitors and manages an application and a portfolio.*

Hence, the contrasted yet similar process-centric view of the application life cycle at a high level is also important for us to understand. This will enable application teams to approach modernization programs with an emphasis on building business cases, justifying modernization, and demonstrating the business value of modernization. Addressing governance and operational aspects of the application portfolio, in addition to the development and deployment aspects, will also lead to the planning of application renewal and retirement, thereby completing the full life-cycle viewpoint of applications.

Business Case Establishment

Enterprises create different types of business cases at different levels of the organization. Business cases driving major business decisions can originate right from the CEO. As those decisions are beyond the scope of this book, we will primarily focus on the business cases at the IT department level, especially the need to justify the build of new applications to meet identified business needs. These business cases are sometimes solely created by the IT stakeholder and at other times by a partnership between the relevant business unit and IT stakeholder. External consultants may also be involved in this process.

NOTE
Business cases created as part of a larger business requirements definition and strategy are typically funded and executed in conjunction with a partner vendor. These projects aim first to build a sound understanding of the needs of the business before attempting to justify the realization of that business need to higher management. Such initiatives have a greater chance of success because it's not just a high-level business case established, but a well-thought-out business strategy and specific business requirements that would be fulfilled by implementing such initiatives. These strategy exercises attempt to provide a high-level understanding of necessary resource efforts and estimated timeframes for delivery of the initiatives, thereby making the requester's business case rock solid when it comes to seeking management buy-in.

Seasoned IT leaders and managers know how to build a business case with the right level of information, thus increasing their chances of getting the initiatives approved. They have also established good relationships with external service providers and know how to leverage the vendor's expertise to help deliver well-developed business strategies and business case documents to improve the chances of such initiatives getting funded. Even if you are not in the role of establishing or presenting a business case, it is important that you have a high-level understanding of these functions.

Technical resources may sometimes question this exercise and ask why they would need to understand a general business case. They live in a technical world totally apart from the business politics, right? That could not be further from the truth. If you objectively think about the business case, it serves four purposes:

- Provides management the opportunity to compare and prioritize projects with available funding and resources at the management's disposal

- Communicates business value and why a specific project should be undertaken

- Shares the project execution vision with a tentative high-level plan of time, effort, and cost

- Enables the team members to participate from the project inception stage and help systematically break down the project and articulate and substantiate the effort and time components of the business case

Projects that take this approach to business case creation have buy-in from the project team and a higher chance of success in getting approved, since the business case clearly captures the rationale for undertaking the project in the first place.

Establishing a business case consists of the following steps:

1. Initiating the business case

2. Generating the hypothesis for why an application is needed

3. Prioritizing the business needs against other stakeholder needs in an organization by mapping the relationship between building the application to the business objectives and goals

4. Creating a formal business case for sign-off

5. Presenting the business case to the key stakeholders for support and approval

Figure 2-3 illustrates the business case creation process. Let's take a deeper look at business case creation and the specific elements of the business case necessary to help procure funding for a new application.

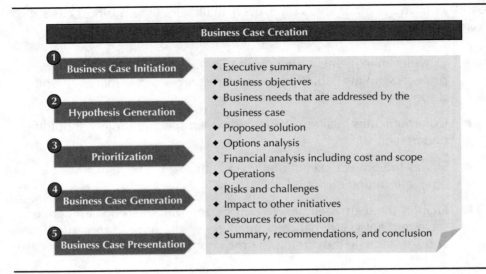

Business Case Creation

1. Business Case Initiation
2. Hypothesis Generation
3. Prioritization
4. Business Case Generation
5. Business Case Presentation

- ◆ Executive summary
- ◆ Business objectives
- ◆ Business needs that are addressed by the business case
- ◆ Proposed solution
- ◆ Options analysis
- ◆ Financial analysis including cost and scope
- ◆ Operations
- ◆ Risks and challenges
- ◆ Impact to other initiatives
- ◆ Resources for execution
- ◆ Summary, recommendations, and conclusion

FIGURE 2-3.   *Business case creation process*

Business Case Initiation

Which came first, the business need that sparked an idea or a good idea that sparked the invention of a business need? Regardless of the idea's origin, building an application to enable an idea requires several steps before that idea can materialize into a bona fide business case. The idea must first be outlined in a concrete document or presentation. It must also align to some business objectives that the organization has established for that financial year. The originator of the idea must rally others to support the idea, validate the idea, and further develop the idea. In enterprises, unless there is a clear business demand, ideas do not take flight easily. Ideas are typically strongly mapped to what business units need. Once a senior manager provides executive sponsorship, the requester must still figure out a way to gain the support of other stakeholders to build the business case and justify budgetary allocation for the project.

The typical questions surrounding the intent to build a new application are all about the business need, how strong the idea is, and who is behind it and shares in the vision of this application to meet the business objectives.

The questions raised during the business case justification analysis include the following:

- How much money will we make or save by creating this application?
- Why do we need a particular application?
- Is this application redundant to another similar application already owned?
- How much is it going to cost to build it?
- What is the effort?
- What resources are needed to build the application?
- What is the ongoing cost of support and maintenance?
- Do we have in-house skills, or do we need to bring in a partner?
- When will this application be delivered?
- What other applications will be impacted by this new application?
- Does it need to integrate with other applications and data sources?
- What type of infrastructure needs will this application have?
- Who is going to own the application going forward?
- Which team will be responsible for building and managing the application?
- What is the total cost of ownership?
- Is there packaged software available that we can implement instead of building the application?
- Will current packaged software that we have already implemented be able to provide this functionality?

Many other questions and variations usually come up for discussion.

Once these questions are answered in some fashion, the determined owner should assemble a small team to validate the need for this application and start to build a business case justification. Sometimes, it is just one unlucky individual who has an idea for a new application and must work on building this initial business case alone. Although this is not the final business case that ultimately wins approval and budget to build the new application, it is the starting point. This general process is known as *business case initiation*. It defines building the high-level rudimentary business case or business justifications of a new application. The approval process for seeking budget dollars for the new application requires a regimented and more detailed business case discussion at that time. However, at the business case initiation stage, the primary goal is to establish a very high-level business need for the application to justify the significant time commitment and allocation of resources.

The Necessity for a Business Case

Why is a formal business case even necessary? Is it not enough that business leaders meet for a few hours in a conference room and ultimately decide that they need to build a new application to meet a business need? Why create such an elaborate approval process? Well, unfortunately, this ad hoc approach does happen in some organizations. It may be that the business case is so obvious that a formal write-up is not necessary. Maybe a few handwritten pages of notes are enough to garner support and approval. There are stories of startups raising millions of dollars from venture capitalists with just some numbers scribbled on a napkin. But, as we all know, this is not the typical way projects are funded. Many unique business risks are associated with every project, and careful vetting of those issues are required and mandated by the formal business case initiation process.

In 2012, management consulting agency McKinsey & Company released a report that studied 5400 large-scale IT projects. In this study, McKinsey made the following conclusions about those IT projects: half of them had budgets over $15 million and a run rate of 45 percent over budget, 7 percent of projects were behind schedule, and 56 percent of the applications were ultimately delivered with less functionality than predicted. And other studies have reported a much larger percentage of projects delivered behind schedule. Compared to these staggering numbers, smaller projects appear to have better success rates than larger

IT projects. In 2012, researchers at Gartner published a similar report analyzing large IT projects with budgets in excess of $1 million. The study concluded that the failure rate for these large projects was almost 50 percent higher than for projects with budgets below $350,000. Several other reports have been published in the past few years by KPMG, IBM, and other leading IT services companies indicating that approximately 40 percent of all enterprise projects fail in some way. Forty percent! Key decision-makers within enterprises who follow these reports understand that they must adhere to stringent procedures to scrutinize the diligence process closely for all projects to justify the cost expenditure and resource allocation.

Two important criteria used to evaluate a business case are return on investment (ROI) and total cost of ownership (TCO). Although a TCO calculation includes cost, an ROI calculation quantifies both the costs and the expected benefits over a specific timeframe, typically five years. Lately, ROI metrics seem to drive more and more business case decisions. Infrastructure-related projects are usually measured by TCO, whereas projects that impact business value have a strong ROI story.

Organizations must have a well-documented process in place to apply a consistent standard uniformly to evaluate all business case creation requests. The business case creation and justification requirements are an integral part of funding new application initiatives.

In any organization, you can find stakeholders with competing interests jockeying to prioritize certain projects or to request certain limited resources, whether they be people resources or budgetary dollars. To distribute these finite resources effectively, enterprises must elevate and recommend only those projects that will provide the greatest returns; that means decision-makers need to depend on a well-structured process to guide them toward a successful result. A formalized business justification process also includes form templates and gating criteria to ensure that all proposed initiatives meet specific business needs and map to the overall goals and business objectives of the enterprise. A compelling business case, even during the business case initiation stage, should provide quantifiable metrics in addition to unquantifiable ones. This enables other stakeholders to advise the initiative owner or proposer whether to go ahead with the project or drop the proposal at the idea stage itself.

Start with a Hypothesis

It is important to decide very quickly whether the idea to build a new application has merit or not. Otherwise, valuable time will be spent pursuing an effort that will ultimately not get funded. To validate the business idea, start with a hypothesis. Why do you need this new application? Does it meet a set of critical business needs? Is there another way to provide the business need for the organization? What are the options to consider in meeting this business need? Does it make financial sense to build this new application? In a relatively short amount of time, these critical questions can be answered, at a high level, to justify continuing this analysis. This line of questioning also compels other individuals in the organization to provide their feedback to the idea initiator to validate the requested hypothesis.

Once the initial justification is documented, the requester can move on to building a detailed business case to garner support for the idea to build a new application. This exercise should be captured in a formal business case document for submission, review, and approval as part of the organization's guidelines and processes. The final decision will depend on the ranking priority of this initiative with other competing projects and the rallying level of support the proposed new application has gathered.

Prioritizing Business Needs

Every enterprise has more business requirements than available resources and budget. If an initiative does not address the most critical business needs along with a solid business case, it will most likely not receive funding. In most large and medium-sized organizations, documentation of the business case justification for project funding varies considerably. Although managers are urged to follow documented procedures as an overall compliance measure, in reality the results may not be consistent. As annual budgets are created and allocated for various anticipated and ongoing initiatives, organizations conduct key annual meetings and subsequent quarterly business reviews to prioritize and reprioritize departmental needs for budget allocation. This exercise enables an enterprise to score and rank initiatives based on relevance and urgency to the defined business objectives and overall vision of the company. The most critical needs are addressed first and receive the lion's share of the budget. The prioritization of business needs is sometimes carried out with the advice and participation of external business consultants.

Business needs prioritization should be conducted with the participation of all stakeholders from the relevant business units and departments. Although individual stakeholders may each believe that his or her project is of the utmost importance, a well-defined framework and methodology for prioritization can ensure objective selection of viable projects. Even then, the senior leadership is bound to have some degree of subjectivity or bias in their ranking of certain critical business needs over less prominent ones. They say that the squeaky wheel gets the grease. Perhaps the same is true in this selection process? The main point to note here is that flawed prioritization decisions will ultimately impact both the top and bottom lines of the enterprise's income statement. Hence, it is in everyone's best interest to make business needs prioritization a mandatory component for growth of the business.

So, what about small and medium-sized companies that do not have a defined process for business case creation and justification? How do they prioritize their business needs? Companies with relatively small application portfolios may not have as many projects in flight. However, these companies have a greater risk of going out of business if they do not properly manage their finances. For startups and smaller companies with limited resources, it is especially prudent that they institute an established process to prioritize their business needs and make critical decisions on how they will apportion budget dollars. In fact, annual meetings will not suffice for small companies. These organizations need to assess and justify their project investment decisions on a regular basis. Strict controls must be in place for these companies to recover quickly from bad decisions and redeploy resources to meet the demands of ever-changing competing priorities. Similar to setting up the initial business plan for a startup or small business at the corporate level, identifying the business case justification is just as necessary at the application level. Even though a company's revenues are not in the high eight figures, it does not mean that it can skip the need for business case justification. In fact, it is quite the opposite. The process for smaller companies may not be as long or as formal, but it is an important practice as part of the overall application portfolio management.

Going back to the context of large and medium-sized enterprises, a sound application life-cycle strategy coupled with application portfolio management and governance are essential to a truly successful company. This methodology ensures that the following items can be known or, at least, predictable:

- Making good investment decisions

- Building business functionality within the existing application portfolio

- Measuring the performance of the application portfolio to meet business objectives

- Minimizing risks associated with trying to achieve the prioritized business needs, thereby maximizing the success rate of the funded initiatives

Creating a Formal Business Case

Most enterprises have a formal business case template that standardizes and scales the request process. The relevant information and support provided along with the request form can greatly improve and maximize the chances of securing funding for that project. A typical business case contains the following topic areas:

- Executive summary

- Business objectives

- Business needs addressed by the business case

- Proposed solution

- Options analysis

- Financial analysis including cost and scope

- Operations

- Risks and challenges

- Impact to other initiatives

- Resources for execution

- Summary, recommendations, and conclusion

Going through the process of capturing a business case ensures that the stakeholder has researched the initiative, understood the pros and cons, collaborated with other experts in the organization, built the financial justification including TCO and ROI, identified resources needed for execution, analyzed risks, and developed a thorough overall knowledge and background about the proposed initiative. In a large enterprise, several people and departments may be involved in providing input to business case creation.

Presentation and Approval

The review and approval process for a business case should not be just one exciting event on a predetermined date. That type of approach to business case approval seldom ensures that a proper and well-analyzed business case has been created. In enterprises, the ideal process provides multiple dates and milestone targets for the business case creation and approval exercise. There may be an initial date to submit the business case initiation document with some basic information. If that submission is approved, additional meeting dates may depend on whether the proposed initiative meets certain criteria. There may be periodic reviews and information sharing sessions to gauge the progress of various business cases. Sometimes, a business case may require interaction and input from multiple departments and stakeholders or a steering committee may facilitate the business case development. These factors should be tailor-made to the individual company—there is no "one size fits all" approach. This business case creation process should align with the company's specific goals; it defeats the purpose if organizations view this process as additional compliance barrier or check-box requirement.

The budgetary cost allocation, the TCO analysis, and the models to predict ROI may be complex for some initiatives, and the review may require several interactions before the financial analysis can be completed. In other cases, the proposed application may have dependencies on other initiatives that are already in flight. In such a case, the exact nature of the integration between the two initiatives might still be in a state of flux and may necessitate a few stakeholder sync meetings to capture all the moving parts accurately.

The initial assumptions around the business requirements may adjust as the business case further develops. This will involve revisions to the business case solution approach or other areas, such as assumption of risk and available contingency options. It is also a good practice for the business case owners to socialize the case with key stakeholders within the organization on a periodic basis in the form of informal reviews and informal presentations so that they can build alliances and support. Stakeholders may be more open to sharing key information in a one-on-one setting rather than in a large group meeting in a stuffy conference room. Additionally, an hour-long meeting or an e-mail chain with 20 people copied might not be the appropriate forum for everyone to express their views and share their expertise or knowledge sufficiently. Some stakeholders may have questions for the business case owner to be taken offline for further debate and discussion in a more informal setting.

To avoid any issues, the business case owner should set up a series of meetings to review the proposal with one or two stakeholders at a time and allow for the natural refinement and improvement of the business case. It is also a good practice to present the material multiple times to become comfortable with all the elements of the business case.

Application Development

Once the business case for building an application is approved, the application has to be developed according to the project schedule. Although Agile methodologies are mainstream, most of the programs that receive funding want the best of all methodologies. These days, everyone wants to know the exact timeline, exact budget and resource needs, a well-defined set of functional requirements with a complete traceability matrix, well-defined technical architecture and detailed technical design, test cases built in advance, established application development and operations processes (DevOps), and an application deployed with zero defects. Although that works in an ideal world, a single hybrid of all methodologies such as Agile, waterfall, scrum, spiral, extreme programming, and iterative test-driven development does not yet exist.

In reality, what is necessary is the adoption of an application development methodology that makes sense for that particular project. The ability to infuse agility into the application development process and adopt the right set of tools to improve productivity ensures that a well-designed, QA-tested application will be developed.

In general, regardless of the specific software development methodology employed or the processes and tools adopted, the application development life cycle encounters five broad checkpoints before the application can independently spread its wings and fly. These steps are not sequential in nature and are interleaved and staggered throughout the application development life cycle:

1. Gather requirements.
2. Create architecture and design.
3. Build.
4. Test.
5. Deploy.

NOTE
This list does not advocate the waterfall model. In fact, one of the fallacies of the waterfall model is an assumption that the areas associated with application development are sequential. That method strictly imposes an arbitrary sequence with mixed results. It is important to reiterate that this section neither embraces the waterfall methodology nor suggests that the broad areas of application development processes are sequential in nature. Rather, we suggest that it is important to analyze application development in the context of its entire life cycle, both broadly within the five areas and specifically to the particular development needs, implementation requirements, and necessary processes and tools.

In summary, when it comes to application modernization, application development tools must be used in conjunction with other established processes and tools to garner a sound methodology. It should not be a process completed within a closed silo.

Operations

IT operations or application operations have evolved into an advanced field with strong processes and tools. Packaged applications and older applications are addressed by traditional IT processes by which they were previously operated. Not all applications in an enterprise can be created using a single, uniform methodology. Newer applications being built are the ideal candidates to be tested and managed under a comprehensive development methodology that incorporates continuous integration and embodies Agile principles.

Newer applications should ideally run in a virtualized environment, with proper capacity management, zero configuration, monitoring, and governance as part of an application portfolio. An application receives varying levels of production support throughout its life cycle until the application finally reaches sunset, when it is no longer needed or has been supplanted by another newer application. The three steps of operations are as follows:

1. Production support

2. Maintain and manage

3. Application sunset

Processes for Life-cycle Management

The three major application life-cycle stages are further divided into a total of 13 steps (depicted in Figure 2-2). These steps provide a more granular understanding of the stages. All three life-cycle stages are under the management of the three application life-cycle management processes:

■ Governance

■ Program management

■ Application portfolio management

Managing an application portfolio is an integral part of application life-cycle management. Applications that are built and deployed to support the business are never constant. They change on a periodic basis, are enhanced to support new business functionality, are modified to incorporate new technology, and are integrated with other applications to orchestrate business processes. Just as the applications are never constant, the business processes are also changing periodically. Enterprises have to ensure that proper policies are created to manage the ideation, creation, development, and management of an application and the larger application portfolio itself.

These applications exist in an enterprise to support the business. To ensure proper alignment of IT to business, the governance mechanism is extremely important. Governance mandates the compliance of standards and regulations, and it also identifies and measures the metrics and processes necessary to create a successful application life-cycle management strategy, tightly coupled with application portfolio management. Finally, well-designed programs should manage and govern all initiatives associated with the application life cycle and the overall portfolio. This is an incredibly vital step to the success of any enterprise initiative.

Challenges and Risks to Enterprises

In a recent Gartner report, analysts concluded that eight out of ten dollars spent by an enterprise on its IT initiatives is essentially wasted money. These dollars were spent to keep the lights on rather than meaningfully contributing to the increase in business value, business growth, and better market positioning for the enterprise. Many of these IT applications are highly business-critical ventures that devour additional spending and resources; business will grind to a halt if budgetary support is cut off. If these applications are not expendable and they require such a high level of commitment from the enterprise, what should the organization do?

Poor application management results in a significant loss of competitive advantage, rendering a company unable to contribute to the bottom line quickly and steadily. If businesses can identify and reallocate approximately 10 to 20 percent of their budgets to fund new application builds or technology-led business innovation ideas, they can successfully begin to modernize their existing applications and ultimately drive business growth.

Application Development and Operations (DevOps)

Traditionally, application development and operations unilaterally resided with IT departments. However, the last few years have seen the rise of a phenomenon called *DevOps*, where development teams and operations teams work together to deliver software products and applications rapidly. DevOps establishes a culture in which organizational processes and software development tools harmoniously coexist.

The following functions are impacted by DevOps:

- Application development
- Quality assurance and testing
- Release management and deployment
- Production support and maintenance
- Administration

- Infrastructure and application monitoring
- Application management
- Rapid response for critical business issues
- Disaster recovery and business continuity

Although it is beneficial to adopt DevOps, it is not wise to make drastic wholesale changes to the way an enterprise has set up its processes around these IT functions. Migration to an integrated DevOps solution takes time, planning, and a commitment to change the fundamentals of certain archaic processes.

Although we can read about ideal DevOps approaches and descriptions of how DevOps should be rolled out and executed, many of those suggestions are not applicable to large and medium-sized enterprises. Effecting a cultural change around established processes is not a trivial exercise. To institute a better approach, the change management requirement for development and operations to meld current processes successfully into DevOps will take 18 to 24 months.

For smaller organizations, especially product companies that are more nimble, setting up a DevOps team from the ground up is possible in a shorter amount of time. The blueprint for gradually building out a DevOps culture is especially relevant for large and medium-sized enterprises with an existing methodology and a current set of processes and tools in place. These organizations could have other programs in flight that would be jeopardized by abruptly introducing this culture shift; this change could also be met with resistance from some teams that prefer the status quo. It is clear that it would be nearly impossible to change the course of that ship suddenly without incurring massive repercussions!

Next, it is important to identify specific applications and specific programs that will be able to work within the new DevOps blueprint. Some of the anti-patterns around introducing DevOps into enterprises include these:

- Setting up a Dev team and an Ops team in separate silos
- Setting up a separate DevOps team
- Trying to create a single unified team by getting rid of the Ops team

If you are new to DevOps, you might assume that the easiest way to get started is by setting up two separate teams—one for development and one for operations—and then establishing rules of engagement and governance between the two. With two separate teams, it may appear easier to introduce some new tools and request the teams to work together under a new set of processes. An entirely different approach creates a third team in the middle, separate from the existing Dev and Ops teams. This additional team adds more confusion and an unnecessary barrier in between Dev and Ops. An even riskier approach is to scrap the existing development team and operations team and instead create a single, unified team, hoping that the newly merged team will magically be able to tackle DevOps. This is an unrealistic expectation that assumes that operational skills are interchangeable with developer skills; this is rarely the case. Cost-saving decisions like this will ultimately lead to a noncohesive team structure.

The ideal DevOps adoption will institute a continuous delivery process in which the development seamlessly moves through automated QA to production. The automation process is live end-to-end and enabled with a set of tools that everything is first time final. This essentially means that it is possible to modify application code, test it, and deploy the modified application in a completely automated fashion and having the confidence that there would be no new bugs introduced as a result of this modification. Code goes live the first time it is introduced into an existing application! Software bugs and functional anomalies are uncovered during automated testing and then automatically flagged and sent back to development for fixing. In production, there is complete end-to-end monitoring. In fact, every application component or service that is deployed to production will implement a management and monitoring interface as part of the application code itself. The application can self-heal. The ultimate intent behind DevOps is to create a continuous delivery process and automated deployments of the product or application. This on-demand automation and management, however, is easier said than done.

DevOps is not just about development tools. There are debates about using tools like Git versus SVN, Java versus PHP, Puppet versus Chef versus Ansible, Capistrano versus Fabric, Jenkins versus Gradle versus Maven. Rolling out these tools on projects does not necessarily mean that a DevOps culture has been created and adopted. Integrating processes into the fabric of the teams and enabling those processes with the right tools is incredibly important, but it's still not enough. It is equally essential to define the metrics to be tracked at both the application and portfolio levels.

As you introduce the DevOps culture, examine your application portfolio. Start with a general assessment of your portfolio to figure out where it would be best to introduce DevOps processes and tools. If you have recently added an application, that project might be a good candidate for portfolio modernization, especially if some applications are not very amenable to automation.

Creating an Application Portfolio

Before creating an application portfolio, an organization must identify what exactly constitutes an application. In many enterprises, the term "application" is loosely used. Applications can be a granular service in one instance and a collection of services, databases, and reports in another instance. In some cases, packaged enterprise resource planning (ERP) software or an Excel sheet with macros are called applications. Regardless of the exact definition, a collection of software services used to deliver a set of business functionality is a good way to interpret the term "application." It does not matter if this application is monolithic or is composed of several granular services. As long as a collection of source code or a set of services can be identified and a boundary can be drawn around it to indicate that all the components belong together as an application, that will suffice for the purpose of managing the life cycle of that identified application.

An application portfolio is a collection of such applications. The application portfolio is analogous to a financial investment portfolio, which also requires continuous governance and management of its contents.

Application Characteristics

In an application portfolio, each application should have the following defined characteristics:

- Comprehensive documentation
- Well-known business functionality
- Fairly accurate knowledge of the cost to build and maintain the application
- Derived business value
- Technical quality
- Total cost of ownership

- Return on investment (ROI)
- Dependencies and integration points to other applications
- Performance characteristics
- Life expectancy and its functional replacement

Typically, an enterprise will have multiple application portfolios. Each business unit may have its own set of applications. Sometimes, applications built using specific technologies are owned and operated by one group or a few overlapping groups. There is no one specific way to define and operate an application portfolio.

If an enterprise has not defined an application portfolio strategy and consolidated a set of applications under one umbrella for management, it is imperative that it do so as soon as possible. There are several advantages to managing applications as a unified portfolio rather than dealing with each application on its own. An economy of scale results from creating an application portfolio.

Portfolio Creation Process

The process to create an application portfolio requires three simple steps: collect, select, and define. The ultimate goal is to ensure that a set of applications is appropriately managed and monitored to deliver the best business value possible, thereby meeting the objectives of the application portfolio, leveraging the best technology, maintaining the highest technical quality, all the while keeping business risks low and optimizing spending. Managing each application individually without regard to other applications in the enterprise will not provide the operational scale necessary to achieve the ultimate goals.

Without an effective application portfolio strategy, program costs and project risks will exponentially multiply, resulting in the development of numerous redundancies across application boundaries. Most established enterprises witnessed this during the 1980s and early 1990s as several emerging technologies manifested in many custom and packaged applications. Within a few years, IT budgets came under heavy siege as these applications started to siphon dollars away from new development. The inception of application portfolio management strategies resulted directly from the need to identify and organize enterprise applications into a cohesive collection. Figure 2-4 illustrates the application portfolio creation process.

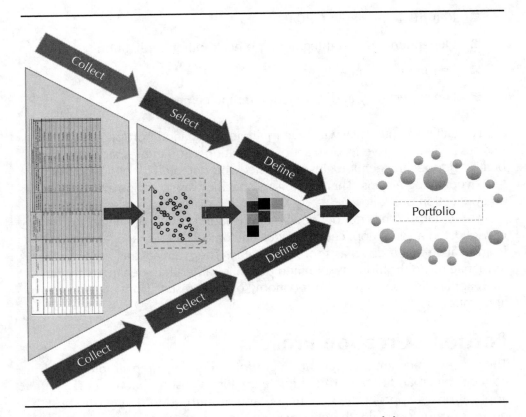

FIGURE 2-4. *The process to create an application portfolio*

Collect

The first and most important step in creating an application portfolio is application identification and collection of various data points and attributes about those applications. This is also probably the most difficult step. Depending on the maturity of an organization, legacy knowledge repositories may have been built during past data collection exercises, and chances are that the some of the data might already be stale. If an enterprise has an active application portfolio management practice and sound governance principles in place, then the application portfolio creation process can be skipped or drastically shortened to reflect that all applications are part of an existing portfolio and that the knowledge base is current. If that is not the case, enterprises will have to undertake this data collection exercise.

Most organizations approach this process by identifying applications owners, business analysts, enterprise architects, developers, database administrators, and other stakeholders who may be knowledgeable about a particular application. Interviews are conducted and application data is captured through a uniform template so that the collected data can be compared. The templates are typically built in Microsoft Excel. Some enterprises go beyond the Excel worksheet to create a database that houses the collected data. Others may invest in third-party tools to help collect and manage the application data.

This collection method relies on the people who were interviewed and who collectively possess the relevant data about an application. Depending on the age of the application, complexity of the application, and the length of time the various stakeholders have been associated with the application, the data collected through interviews may be immensely incomplete. The collection method relies heavily on an experienced interviewer who is skilled in extracting information through a series of leading questions. The interviewer must then drill down and ask detailed follow-up questions on the fly based on the initial set of responses. This method also assumes that the template used for data collection addresses all the possible attributes about an application; in reality, it does not. Typically, templates are built to address specific objectives. They primarily focus on collecting distinct attributes that can be analyzed to yield insights into the particular context for which they were collected.

The collection method never takes into account the actual source code, configurations, environment, or other development variables. To augment the data collected through this interview process, it is important to leverage tools that can analyze the source code of the application, the various libraries used, open-source components used, configuration files, and the environment in order to construct a detailed and thorough knowledge base for the application. Ultimately the data collection exercise should span multiple areas, including finance, operations, business, and technology. Once data is collected, various filters and comparisons can be applied to determine which applications can be categorized into an application portfolio. Large organizations can build multiple application portfolios based on different product lines, functional areas, or technologies.

Select

Once exhaustive data on the identified applications has been collected into a knowledge base, the next step is to select a set of applications that meet some established criteria to build an application portfolio. Building an application portfolio creates a baseline from which to start managing that portfolio. Although the selection criteria can vary, the overall drivers for creating the application portfolio need to be examined. For example, all applications owned by a particular business unit may be grouped into one application portfolio. In this case, the data collection exercise is not particularly beneficial for the application selection process but would prove useful later on for the actual management of the application portfolio. In another example, if the selection criteria analyzes all applications that run on JDK 1.6, several data points would need to be analyzed to collect all applications that meet this set of criteria, such as the following:

- Support for a particular set of business processes
- Integration with specific applications
- Active engagement in functionality enhancement
- Expenditures of dollars to maintain the portfolio
- Frequency of active trouble tickets

Within three to five years, it would be apparent if applications in the portfolio had evolved in different directions or deviated significantly from the initial set of criteria that classified the portfolio. The analysis is similar to the building of a financial portfolio. After a number of years, the performance of the instruments within a particular financial portfolio becomes diversified. At periodic intervals, one would balance the financial portfolio and adjust the underlying instruments to meet a new set of objectives. Equivalently, this process also occurs within an application portfolio. After a number of years, the application portfolio performs lower than its intended level, most likely due to objectives that have morphed over time. It is essential to analyze and manage the portfolio on a continuous basis.

NOTE
Application portfolio management is discussed in more detail in Chapter 3. At this time, the focus is on selecting a set of applications that meet certain predefined criteria to create an application portfolio strategy.

Define

Once the set of applications that belong to an application portfolio
have been selected, it is important to define the following criteria in the
definition step:

- Definition of the objectives

- Metrics for measurement

- How the portfolio will be managed

- Governance for that application portfolio

- Dashboard to monitor performance continuously

Although many large and mid-sized organizations believe that they have
already defined and operationalized application portfolios, typically that is
not the case. Realistically, many enterprises do not entirely empower their
application owners with well-defined application portfolios. Rather, portfolios
generally list the owners of applications, budget line items, and a few other
basic pieces of information. (I have come across several instances in which
even this limited information is not readily available and a scavenger hunt for
clues is necessary to gather relevant data points.)

If an enterprise already has a portfolio with application data that it has
captured and analyzed, you need to ask a few questions: How well-defined
and governed is the application portfolio? What metrics are being collected
and how often is the application portfolio rationalized and measured for the
business value it delivers? That will be the topic for the next chapter, where
we will discuss application portfolio management.

Summary

All applications follow a specific life cycle in terms of how they are
conceived, funded, built, deployed, supported, and finally retired and
replaced. These applications could be Java, or non-Java such as legacy
applications, mainframe applications, and applications in other languages,
residing sometimes within the same portfolio.

Java applications have a well-defined life cycle in most enterprises as the
Java platform and the technologies surrounding it are universally supported

and understood. There are significant challenges to funding brand-new initiatives in enterprises since 80 percent of budgets are consumed by existing applications to keep mission-critical business functions running. Creating a formal methodology and a set of processes to manage the application life cycle will yield optimum use of budgetary dollars to maintain and support the application portfolio.

Many large enterprises follow a formal business case justification exercise for supporting application enhancements and modernization. Understanding the life cycle of an application and the application portfolios, as a whole, will ensure that the business case is also properly vetted and justified. The absence of an application portfolio strategy puts an enterprise at increased risk for revenue leakage and strained IT resources. The processes outlined in this book will ensure that application characteristics can be identified and documented, as well as tracked and measured via relevant metrics. The relevance of DevOps in recent years has positively impacted application modernization initiatives. The governance of application portfolio strategies and project execution methodologies will ultimately result in cost savings that can be redirected toward new initiatives within the enterprise.

CHAPTER
3

Application Portfolio
Management

Application portfolio management emerged as a practice during the early to mid-1990s to provide a way for enterprises to measure and compare the business value and quantifiable benefits of applications to the operational and maintenance costs. This discipline helped IT departments to discover, understand, segment, categorize, and manage the various applications under their control. During that time, the impending threat of application failure due to the Y2K bug was a concern for all organizations, both large and small. Several legacy applications were especially considered to be at risk. This prompted many organizations to document their applications thoroughly, develop a comprehensive database of application knowledge, analyze the available budgets, monitor the spending on applications to fix the Y2K issues, and thus develop the beginnings of a knowledge repository. This led to the accelerated establishment of application portfolio management as an IT discipline. In the previous chapter, we defined what an application is and discussed how to create an application portfolio if one did not yet exist within the organization. In this chapter, we explore applications, application attributes, analysis of the created application portfolio, and management of the application portfolio.

Until the proliferation of the Internet and the widespread availability of the World Wide Web to the public in the early 1990s, a majority of organizations had neither elevated the role of information officer to the C-suite nor required well-defined IT department policies and procedures. As a result, there was little to no governance of the mostly mainframe and client-server applications. The wide popularity of the Internet and the sudden increase in consumer-owned PCs created a proliferation of enterprise applications. Employee portals, partner extranets, and company-wide intranets led to more applications being built and owned by enterprises. With the introduction of Java and other related technologies, building and deploying enterprise-class applications became easier than before. To manage the process of investing in applications, maintaining and managing the applications, and deriving maximum value from the enterprise applications, a management discipline emerged that combined business, operational, technical, and financial skills. This discipline was complemented by the emergence and advancement of another discipline called *Enterprise Architecture (EA)* that combined the ability to understand technical architecture and domain functionality and align IT to business strategy and business needs. This led to the definition of processes, metrics, and tools to manage the portfolio of applications. Thus, the discipline of Application Portfolio Management (APM) emerged and grew into a sound practice through the early 2000s.

As the discipline of APM was getting rooted into an established process, the nature of the application portfolios also evolved. From being mainly mainframe applications and client-server applications, limited to a few specific technologies and technology vendors, the application portfolios of today are very diverse in the breadth and depth of technologies, platforms, programming languages, off-the-shelf vendor products, and custom applications. The complexity of the application portfolios that need to be managed has also resulted in an evolution of the APM discipline itself, the advent of new tools, invention of methodologies and processes, and retraining of resources on specialized skills to implement APM within the enterprises. Most enterprise application portfolios contain a liberal amount of Java applications. When managing an application portfolio, one cannot just manage the Java applications or just the older legacy applications; it must be a holistic approach.

This chapter explores application portfolios in general. The methodologies and techniques discussed here are relevant to all application portfolios regardless of whether the applications are built on the Java platform or not. The interdependence of legacy applications with both Java and non-Java applications necessitates the need for the APM discipline to work seamlessly across technologies within an enterprise.

NOTE
The Y2K bug was not just a computer programming–related bug associated with the formatting and storage of calendar data. The practice of representing the year with two digits did cause problems with programming logic–related errors when going from 99 to 00. But another problem was hidden as well. Some programmers had misunderstood the Gregorian calendar rule, where years exactly divisible by 100 are not considered leap years. What they forgot was that this rule is true except for years that are divisible by 400. Thus, the year 2000 was a leap year.

What Is Application Portfolio Management?

APM is an IT discipline that inculcates strategic decision-making to govern, manage, measure, and monitor the entire set of applications within an enterprise. The field of Application Portfolio Management focuses on transformation and modernization of a set of applications, optimizes the spending on the applications, manages complexity and risk, figures out enhancements, and also makes decisions on which applications to keep and which applications to sunset. APM is an integral part of the planning activity within IT departments and is closely related to project portfolio management (PPM). A concise yet accurate definition of APM would be, "APM is a discipline that focuses on continuous improvement of an entire portfolio of IT applications to maximize the return on investment from that application portfolio while ensuring that the applications meet the business needs of an enterprise."

To execute APM continuously in an organization, specific steps need to be performed periodically. Data needs to be collected on all applications that are brought within a portfolio for management. The collected data needs to be formulated into sets of attributes and a knowledge base. The formulated application data needs to be analyzed. A set of hypotheses needs to be generated that are in line with the business objectives for the portfolio. Metrics of interest need to be established and a process for continuously collecting the metrics needs to be implemented. The analysis will lead to validating or invalidating the hypotheses. Finally, a roadmap is generated to transform and modernize the applications in that application portfolio so that the portfolio is fully optimized with respect to the key business drivers. Once this exercise is undertaken, a baseline is established and a knowledge base is built. From that point on, the process can be continuous with respect to data collection and metrics collection on the application portfolio.

Typical business drivers are reduction of cost, identification and mitigation of business risks, elimination of functional or technical redundancies, and optimization of investment decision-making regarding the application portfolio to reduce TCO and improve ROI. APM execution strategies to meet the business drivers include rationalization of the application portfolio, introduction of new technologies into the portfolio, transformation of the business process, application re-engineering, replacement of custom applications with packaged applications, decommissioning and retiring applications, modernization and enhancement of applications, introduction of new business capabilities into the portfolio, introduction of new technical capabilities into the portfolio, migration of applications to new technology platforms, upgrade of applications to new versions of technologies, movement of applications to a cloud infrastructure, and sometimes even a status quo decision to maintain the applications.

Why APM?

Current critical challenges faced by enterprise IT include the following:

- Many applications have evolved over time in an unplanned manner and pose architectural and design challenges to maintain and enhance.

- A large number of applications are spread across various business units without clear ownership and operational insight.

- Functional redundancies exist in many places that departments may not even be aware of.

- Cost reduction is an important goal for IT departments as budgets dry up for new initiatives.

- Knowledge of existing applications is fragmented at best, and many applications pose a business risk by not having subject matter experts knowledgeable about the inner workings of the application.

- Time-to-market is very slow for enhancing and introducing new business capabilities into existing applications.

- Technical components and vendor products are redundant within enterprise application portfolios.

- Tight coupling exists between monolithic applications, causing integration and interoperability nightmares.

- Obsolete technology, proprietary technology restrictions, and the lack of adequate skill sets exist among existing IT resources to manage and service these applications.

APM aims to address these challenges and ensure that such issues can be controlled and eventually eliminated.

The Peer Disciplines of APM

APM should be tightly coupled with a few other disciplines to help strategize and operate the IT department. When it comes to envisioning the acquisition of new business capabilities or building new technical capabilities, significant resources are needed. There is a fundamental need for the right mix of people, processes, and technology to execute any IT project successfully. The availability of time, resources, and budget are some of the key variables that need to be evaluated and mitigated in any APM strategy.

Most enterprises have established groups around project management or program management, investment risk management, and workforce management. Enterprise Architecture (EA) is another established discipline that looks holistically at all the architecture layers of the enterprise in the context of application development and APM. This discipline makes recommendations regarding architecture best practices, prioritization of business capabilities and technical capabilities, resources needed to execute projects, and technical architecture and design decisions.

Critical projects within enterprises are trusted to enterprise architects who typically oversee the life cycle of application development and management. Some enterprise architects may specialize in infrastructure, technology, or specific functional domains, while others may be general solution architects. Enterprise architects help create IT- and architecture-related governance processes and actively participate in application development projects and strategic portfolio management.

To practice APM as a strong discipline within an enterprise, APM needs to be established from the beginning with a strong nexus between APM, PPM, and investment risk management (IRM). APM is application-centric, PPM is project-centric, and IRM is investment-centric. Additionally, strategic involvement of EA to this nexus of APM, PPM, and IRM will provide continuity across all three peer disciplines to monitor and manage architecture decision-making, projected funding, and available resources. APM exercises lead to well-established roadmaps that identify initiatives over a three- to five-year timeframe. Such initiatives generated through APM serve as inputs to PPM and IRM. Figure 3-1 depicts the relationship between APM, IRM, and PPM and shows how EA acts as a glue to ensure that the three disciplines are aligned.

Initiatives selected through proper understanding and analysis of APM, PPM, and IRM stand a much higher probability of staying on time and within budget, thereby successfully achieving their stated objectives.

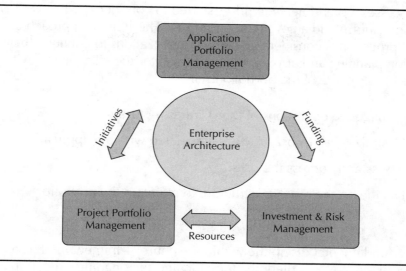

FIGURE 3-1. *APM and its tightly coupled peer disciplines*

APM Magnified

Although we have discussed APM and its relationship to its peer disciplines within an enterprise, at a much deeper level, APM has links to many fundamental processes within an enterprise. One of the fundamental precepts of the IT department within an enterprise is to align business and IT successfully so that technology is leveraged as a competitive advantage to achieve business objectives. The past 15 to 20 years saw a shift in the objectives of the IT department and the role of IT itself. Apart from business–IT alignment, the IT department has faced considerable pressure to prioritize and manage its funding to maximize business value. Resource alignment is a key critical task, balancing a finite set of resources in terms of people, skills, and other assets. Last, but not the least, all successful IT departments have implemented a thorough and well-managed governance process to manage projects, manage investments, manage application portfolios, manage their workforce, or manage and mitigate operational and technical risks.

Enterprises originally adopted APM with the intent of using it as a planning activity for their application portfolios. In the course of such planning, several business departments were impacted either upstream or downstream of the

APM processes. Over time, enterprises started to consider APM as both an execution platform and a governance platform. This holistic approach to the APM process has considerably helped organizations to continue their application planning and also continuously monitor the following activities to optimize the structure of the portfolio itself:

- Manage the operations of the IT infrastructure.

- Optimize the IT cost structure associated with the applications.

- Assess and address the risks.

- Decide on the resource structure to maintain the portfolio.

Scope of APM

APM is a fundamental discipline within the entire IT framework. It is a part of both the strategic planning function and the ongoing execution and operations function. Some organizations incorrectly incorporate APM only into the planning function. When APM is integrated into the operational aspects of IT, in the day-to-day execution, and leveraged in a continuous manner, it also boosts the effectiveness of the other IT disciplines.

APM is not a separate entity or group of people established to manage applications. APM is a function of the entire IT department, and as such, the owners and stakeholders of the APM function need to be established from the various lines of business and from enterprise architecture. APM should also have representatives from the peer disciplines. The APM core group should report to a chief information officer (CIO) Council, which can be thought of as a group that helps the CIO make key decisions regarding strategy and policy for the enterprise, since APM fundamentally works to maximize the business value of an application portfolio while reducing business risk. From a financial perspective, APM works to optimize the TCO and maximize the ROI. It is almost impossible to achieve complete, simultaneous harmony among cost, risk, ROI, and business value. There will always be compromises and unknown variable prioritizations to contend with to ensure that certain thresholds are maintained. It is a very delicate and complex balancing act. From a cost focus, clear APM alignment within the enterprise can effectively reduce the IT cost run rate, a desirable goal for any enterprise.

An organization that has never managed to establish APM as a discipline, or that has not had the opportunity to execute APM effectively for several years, can benefit greatly from APM to reduce the costs associated with IT execution and operations. Mature organizations that have established APM and already optimized significantly on operational costs can use a continuously integrated APM function for strategic planning, prioritization of future business capabilities, governance of the application portfolio, and for many other strategies to ensure optimal deployment of funds and resources into the application portfolio. As the APM discipline becomes integrated within the organization, APM would serve as the source of future proposed initiatives, and these inputs would feed into PPM and IRM disciplines. APM would also serve to develop business case elements, prioritize business capabilities, identify necessary technical capabilities, eliminate functional redundancies, consolidate IT assets, and provide an effective cost-versus-benefit analysis to support ease of implementation.

The governance process associated with APM would help to establish various metrics of interest to the organization. In addition to defining the metrics, APM would be involved in the continuous measurement, analysis, and reporting on these metrics. Successfully deploying APM within an enterprise would allow for a data-driven, analysis-centric management of application portfolios that thrive and maximize the execution capability of a business.

Figure 3-2 shows the IT landscape from the point of view of APM. As a discipline that spans the entire planning, development, and operations processes, APM is a holistic and integrated approach to optimizing and managing the application portfolio. This is depicted in the figure as Conceive, Build, and Operate, with DevOps being relevant in the Build and Operate phases. Although APM is integral to the Conceive phase, it is very effective to integrate the APM discipline throughout the full life cycle of an application. Every application that receives approval to be built must be owned by a particular line of business or business unit. To build, maintain, enhance, and operate an effective and comprehensive portfolio, an application owner needs to be identified for the day-to-day oversight of projects, management of the budget and resources, and the responsibility to keep the information about the application current. Such application owners are critical to the success of the overall APM process.

Compliance is a key aspect of governance. If any of these responsibilities are not fulfilled, the overall IT governance process could be affected by these noncompliant applications. Once an enterprise has established comprehensive

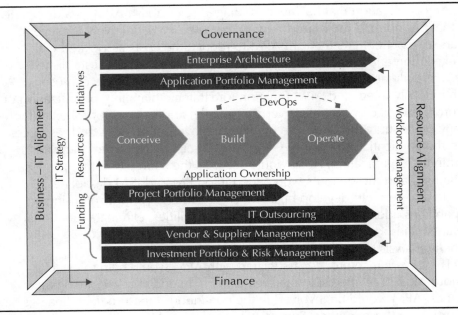

FIGURE 3-2. *Dynamics of the IT strategic and operational landscape*

compliance policies, guidelines, and standards, the organization runs the risk of having inaccurate or inadequate information as a result of relying on those noncompliant portfolio applications. Moreover, any decision-making with respect to APM could be flawed. One way to manage compliance would be to ensure that there is effective communication to all the application owners, application groups, and lines of business. The risks need to be clearly communicated as well. If there is buy-in from executive management, an escalation path could be established to ensure that noncompliant applications are soon brought under the governance umbrella.

IT Strategy and Workforce Management are two significant processes that also interact with APM. Some enterprises undertake the management of IT Strategy as an annual exercise to prioritize IT needs. Other enterprises have an established IT Strategy group that manages IT Strategy as an ongoing process. In such cases, there is a tight coupling between IT Strategy and APM. Many applications might be outsourced for maintenance and operations. APM can analyze such portfolios and decide whether other applications can benefit from outsourcing and whether certain applications can be consolidated or ultimately shut down. An outsourcing vendor is typically not motivated to suggest such options for the application portfolio that they maintain, since that would impact their overall business. APM governance can also closely monitor the performance of such vendors in maintaining and managing the outsourced applications within the application portfolio and maximize the cost allocation of such outsourced portfolios.

Identification of most, if not all, major IT initiatives would have been the outcome of developing a roadmap from application portfolio analysis and the process of continuous management of the application portfolio. This would positively impact the TCO, improve the ROI, and bring better alignment to the business needs.

What Is Not APM

Now that you have a general understanding of how APM operates, it is also important that you understand what is not included in the definition of APM. Many IT departments are starting to use the term "APM" very loosely for all routine IT activities. Activities that are performed on individual applications or activities that are performed in a silo without regard to the entire application portfolio or its impact on the portfolio are truly not considered to be APM-related activities. Similarly, the day-to-day management of an application and project planning necessary to perform maintenance and upgrades on the hardware infrastructure or software licenses of an application is not considered to be APM-related activity. Additionally, project planning to develop an application using release and configuration management or resource planning is not APM activity. Funding projects in a standalone fashion or funding special projects to solve specific issues or bug fixes is not related to APM. Developing and maintaining an application, supporting an application, introducing new functional improvements into an application, and integrating two applications in a point-to-point fashion are not related to APM. It is generally important for IT to undertake such projects to keep the lights on, but these projects are not, in and of themselves, APM. APM cannot conceive and originate every single project executed by an IT department. It is important to note that these activities are not the specific intent or purpose of APM.

To summarize, APM is not

- A software development methodology

- A standalone process owned and operated by a separate group within IT

- A funding process or approval process for identified initiatives

- A process that is completely automated
- IT Strategy, DevOps, PPM, IRM, or EA
- A replacement for an application owner
- A fully objective exercise, especially with respect to recommendations
- APM, in fact, generates hypotheses and employs subjectivity to score applications.

Continuous and Integrated APM Discipline

Although there is no single way to approach APM, a few fundamental building blocks are required to craft an enterprise's approach to the management of its application portfolio. The application portfolio is managed in principle similarly to an investment portfolio. Key objectives and drivers need to be identified, investment and funding decisions have to be made, the portfolio has to be balanced with respect to the objectives, and an overall understanding of the tactical and strategic aspects of managing the portfolio needs to be in place.

You may wonder what drives enterprises to consider and ultimately adopt APM. Here is a sample list of key business and IT drivers that lead to the adoption of APM in enterprises:

- Transparency to IT investment
- Communication of business value of applications
- Prioritization of IT assets
- Greater visibility for leveraging existing IT assets under management
- Methodology for managing and providing maximum value of new IT assets
- Understanding usage of applications and value for business users
- Determination of latent business risks in the application portfolio
- Determination of outsourcing opportunities for applications
- Reduction of TCO and increase of the ROI

Some of the decisions made regarding the application portfolio will be IT-centric and other decisions will be business-centric. IT-centric decisions identify application rationalization and application simplification opportunities within the portfolio. Applications are analyzed to determine their overall business value and alignment to current business processes. Technical quality and health of the applications also need to be assessed. The IT-centric decisions look at cost reductions and quick wins for application portfolio rationalization.

Business-centric decisions to APM take a more strategic and longer term view of the application portfolio. Existing business capabilities are identified for modernization. Future-state business process models are considered. Managing the application portfolio involves understanding the business requirements for the future and determining what business capabilities will need to be built into the application portfolio. In essence, there is a transformation of business processes to support evolving business models.

Whether an organization is making decisions that are IT-centric, business-centric, or a hybrid of the two, the business and technical capabilities inherent in the application portfolio need to be well understood. The complete enterprise architecture stack should be well documented and the applications themselves need to undergo functional and technical decomposition. This is covered in detail in the next chapter.

We can all relate to living in the same residence and accumulating several possessions over a long period of time. After several years, it can be hard to understand why we purchased most of those things in the first place. Many times, we often forget that we even own a certain item—which is why many of us own two or three can openers! And, ironically, when a can needs to be opened, we may not be able to find even one of them! I have used this analogy in the past to describe the need for APM in enterprises.

In any real scenario, all organizations are continuously balancing their application portfolios and engaging in a combination of IT-centric and business-centric modifications of the application portfolio. A uniform methodology can be applied to IT-centric and business-centric analysis of APM. This approach essentially consists of three pillars:

- Renovate

- Integrate

- Manage

All enterprises are in a constant state of renovation, integration, and management of their applications. These three pillars are not sequential steps, nor do they have a finite start and end. All enterprises are in some stage of maturity with respect to these three pillars. Understanding the dynamics of these three pillars and applying a sound APM framework with the right set of tools and APM governance will ensure that an enterprise can continuously optimize each of the three pillars with respect to the others and maximize the value of the application portfolio. Figure 3-3 illustrates what is to be expected in each of the three pillar, from tasks performed to the output that is generated.

Large enterprises have been around for many years. Their limited space is overflowing with existing hardware, software, and applications. Every year, more assets are added to the mix. In these environments, it is highly unlikely

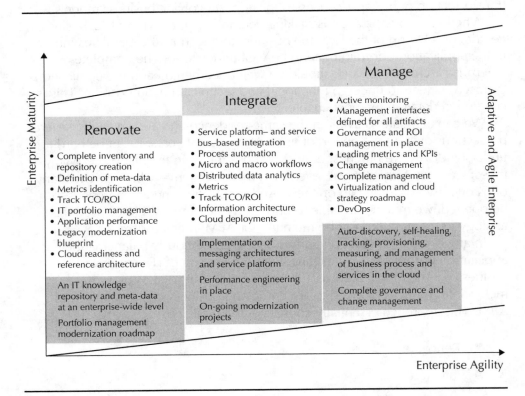

FIGURE 3-3. *Continuous APM and integrated discipline: renovate, integrate, manage*

that existing assets and IT systems are consolidated or eliminated. When new technology components or new applications are introduced into an enterprise, someone needs to ask how they will work with existing applications. Enterprises must optimize their IT resources; they cannot afford to accumulate assets and create unnecessary organizational chaos. They have to figure out a way to create an inventory of assets and then track and keep that inventory current. Eventually, the inventory will become more than just a collection of data; it will evolve into a knowledge repository. Managing applications and tracking the associated operations and finances will help enterprises realize the much sought-after ROI. Renovation, integration, and management are the three pillars needed to organize an enterprise's IT portfolio.

Renovate

In the renovation stage, an application inventory and knowledge repository must be created if one is not already available. The existing repository also needs to be refreshed periodically. Some automation tools can be leveraged to ensure that certain application attributes are tracked automatically. Understanding the various architecture layers including the business architecture, functional architecture, technical architecture, and the infrastructure architecture will provide insights into the knowledge base. Application architecture and information architecture are outcomes of the business and functional architectures. The architecture decomposition will enable an enterprise to understand the business capabilities and the technical capabilities already present in the applications. This will ensure that all redundancies in application functionality are understood. It is highly likely that certain business capabilities and functionalities have been built into more than one application. Similarly, certain technical tools and technical components may also be redundant, especially in some applications that are no longer actively used.

The renovation stage also involves considerable manual effort to sift through the IT landscape, leverage application owners and other stakeholders, and compile the knowledge base. During this stage, it is not uncommon to discover applications that are no longer being used or applications of very poor technical quality with limited business value still being supported in production. A catalog of applications, components, and services needs to be created with an enterprise-wide metadata repository containing attributes about these services. The repository also needs to include policies, standards, best practices, and guidelines for building or buying new applications or other IT assets.

After an analysis of the portfolio, an implementation roadmap for renovation emerges. Once the renovation stage has been completed, a consolidated, enterprise-wide knowledge repository with application attributes and meta-data will exist. Some key outcomes of renovation include an understanding of the following areas:

- Application portfolio and application attributes
- Operational, financial, and technical performance of the application portfolio
- A blueprint to modernize legacy systems
- Cloud readiness of the application portfolio and a reference cloud architecture
- TCO and expected ROI

Integrate

When an organization is able to execute the integration pillar, that means the APM discipline has reached a certain level of maturity and enterprise architecture has also integrated into the core APM processes. To be highly successful in developing a well-integrated application portfolio, the business architecture needs to be well understood. The integration stage involves making architecture decisions with a deep understanding of business processes and associated workflows. Architecture decisions are made around integration patterns, message formats, data formats, and protocols. Enterprises in the integration stage treat information architecture as a fundamental part of enterprise architecture.

From a technology perspective, the Java technology platform has strong support for messaging and web services, including service description and discovery, security, and distributed computing. Several open-source and third-party vendor products are pure play, multi-protocol enterprise service bus platforms based on Java technology that enable integration in a heterogeneous IT environment. The Java Connector Architecture (JCA) is an integration standard that is part of the Java 2 Platform, Enterprise Edition (J2EE), specifications to integrate with enterprise information systems. The enterprise service bus (ESB) platforms are branded as business integration platforms. They support various messaging architectures and include support for Java Message

Service (JMS), Java Connector Architecture (JCA), Simple Object Access Protocol (SOAP), and Representational State Transfer (REST).

As an enterprise continues to achieve maturity along the integration pillar, some of the modernization initiatives identified as part of renovation start to become implemented. Application performance measurements and other metrics are now in place. The ability to track TCO and ROI are now entrenched into the enterprise. The cloud readiness achieved after the renovation stage gives way to actual cloud deployments.

Enterprise Integration Patterns

The earlier types of legacy business applications used to live in a silo, where each application had its own database, screens, and usually a dedicated set of end users. Such monolithic applications gave way to business applications and services that increasingly needed to access the business functionality exposed by other applications and services and their underlying data. Authorized business end users in enterprises expected easy access to the business functionality made available to them. To connect applications to one another, message-oriented middleware products started becoming popular and soon evolved into ESB technologies. Such products provide the plumbing needed for application and service integration and address the transport protocols, data formats, routing, and data transformation. While messaging could be synchronous or asynchronous, the trend and direction has been to adopt asynchronous messaging architectures and REST-based services. In web-centric application architectures, with distributed services and components that are loosely coupled, this approach has provided maximum flexibility and ease. Enterprise Integration Patterns (EIPs) document a proven way to implement a solution in a repeatable manner. Patterns incorporate the experience from several attempts to build the same type of solution repeatedly and provide observations from actual practice, including mistakes that were ultimately corrected. Many Java implementations of the popular EIPs exist today. Apache Camel is an example of a popular open source implementation.

Manage

There are two key aspects to managing an application portfolio: governance and enablement. The governance aspect consists of processes and controls to ensure that the portfolio is managed like an investment portfolio. The second aspect is the enablement of the processes with technical tools and automation so that management and monitoring of the applications happen continuously. To implement automation, an enterprise needs to factor in management of its components and services early on in the architecture and design phase.

The Java platform provides Java Management Extensions (JMX) as a part of its core APIs. I have seldom seen an enterprise create an architecture design of its software components and services that includes a management interface in addition to the business interfaces that have already been implemented. The trend today highlights how enterprises are now creating reusable application frameworks and then using those frameworks to build their applications. If inclusion of a management interface to software components and services becomes instilled into the development life cycle, it will ensure that the applications will be clean, organized, well integrated, and well managed.

Additionally, an enterprise reaching its maturity along the manage pillar will have well-defined KPIs and leading metrics in place. Active monitoring and management interfaces will be in place for all artifacts. Portfolio governance and ROI management of the application portfolio will also be integrated into the core of the enterprise. As the three pillars—renovate, integrate, and manage—continue to mature at their own rates, an adaptive and agile application portfolio will have in place auto-discovery of application components, self-healing, tracking, provisioning, measuring, and management of business process and services in the cloud.

Application Portfolio Analysis

Before embarking upon the renovation of the application portfolio, the application portfolio needs to be assessed and analyzed thoroughly. Then, periodically the process has to be repeated. A three-step process can accomplish this assessment:

1. Discover

2. Analyze

3. Recommend

The first step involves collecting data and meta-data about the applications in the portfolio. Most enterprises have collected some data in the past, but there is a danger of that data being stale, especially if it is not kept current, not properly governed, or not adequately managed. Also, most of the time, such available data is only partially complete. It is best to validate the available data and then identify the gaps in the existing inventory. Once this comprehensive data has been identified, an analysis of that data needs to take place. There are several dimensions along which the application data can be analyzed, leading to insights and hypotheses around the application portfolio. At this stage, business and technical capabilities that need to be built into the portfolio must also be identified and prioritized. Finally, these analysis and prioritization exercises will yield a roadmap of initiatives factoring in the costs, risks, dependencies, and business cases around these initiatives, all of which need to be properly understood for a successful assessment. Figure 3-4 provides a view of the three-step process to assess and application portfolio, what activities are undertaken within each step, and what the outputs are from the execution of the activities.

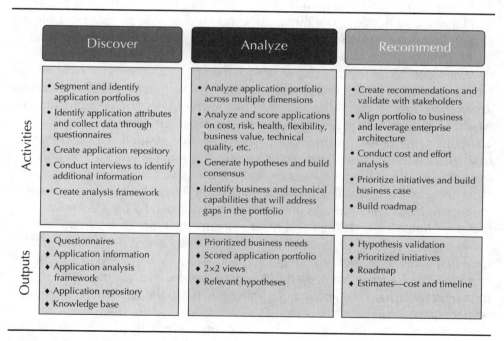

	Discover	Analyze	Recommend
Activities	• Segment and identify application portfolios • Identify application attributes and collect data through questionnaires • Create application repository • Conduct interviews to identify additional information • Create analysis framework	• Analyze application portfolio across multiple dimensions • Analyze and score applications on cost, risk, health, flexibility, business value, technical quality, etc. • Generate hypotheses and build consensus • Identify business and technical capabilities that will address gaps in the portfolio	• Create recommendations and validate with stakeholders • Align portfolio to business and leverage enterprise architecture • Conduct cost and effort analysis • Prioritize initiatives and build business case • Build roadmap
Outputs	♦ Questionnaires ♦ Application information ♦ Application analysis framework ♦ Application repository ♦ Knowledge base	♦ Prioritized business needs ♦ Scored application portfolio ♦ 2×2 views ♦ Relevant hypotheses	♦ Hypothesis validation ♦ Prioritized initiatives ♦ Roadmap ♦ Estimates—cost and timeline

FIGURE 3-4.   *Three-step process to assess an application portfolio*

Discover: Application Inventory and Data Collection

The discovery process, especially the data collection exercise on the application portfolio, is one of the most fundamental activities. Without data, there can be no analysis. If there is insufficient knowledge of what an enterprise owns, then how can that enterprise make the right decisions? In large enterprises, there may be hundreds or even a few thousand applications with extremely fragmented management and ownership. Knowledge of the application cannot be taken for granted. The age of the various applications in an application portfolio could vary and in some cases vary greatly! There could possibly be large gaps in the knowledge and understanding of those applications that are among the oldest in terms of age and existence within an enterprise. This has been observed to be especially true regarding the details and nuances of the business processes supported by the application and the internal code and quality of the application. Over time, it is natural that legacy knowledge about the application erodes away as fewer people know about the internals of older applications.

Most enterprises have an established process around their software development life cycles (SDLCs). As part of the SDLC, an enterprise typically creates functional and technical documentation as well as design documents for applications designed and implemented by the enterprise. Such documentation would be current only at the time when the applications were conceived and built. Over time, documentation becomes stale as applications go into maintenance mode. Also, many enterprises may not maintain financial and operational data at the level of granularity of an application. That data would most likely be tracked at the project level or at an overall budgetary standpoint for departmental resources. As anyone who has managed a project knows, budgeted funds are reclaimed and repurposed all the time. Doing more with less is a motto we can all relate to. Another challenge is that resources could be used in a general manner but not tracked and correctly attributed to a particular application. As a result, some of the data associated with an application would then be stale or incorrect, oftentimes unbeknownst to the application portfolio owner and manager.

As part of APM, the discover phase should be carefully planned to validate data quality of the applications, and all efforts should be taken to build a good baseline application repository. All the stakeholders should be involved, and methodical interviews using uniform templates and questionnaires will help collect relevant application-related data. Operational and financial data may need to be further dissected, to better understand the association of such data at the application level. As APM governance processes are set up and data collection becomes more automated, the underlying assumptions will yield higher quality operational and financial data. Automation tools should also be leveraged to analyze source code and conduct discovery on application source code and the application environments. This will result in an accurate application repository with a wealth of information about the applications. This should not be viewed as a one-time exercise. There should be periodic refresh of the application repository and the data should be tracked and captured continuously.

Application attributes can be generated from the application repository after successful completion of the discover phase. The "Application Attributes" section that follows identifies several common attributes that are useful to generate. Some of the attributes are directly available from the collected data, and other attributes are derived from the collected data. These attributes can be used to segment and group applications into subsets and to categorize applications into multiple groups. This is especially useful if the enterprise application portfolio is very large. This segmentation enables the analysis to filter and view applications that are of interest, instead of having to review all of the applications all at once. Experience has also shown that it is typically difficult to manipulate groups of applications that exceed 25 to 30 in number.

The discover phase does not stop here. Although discovery implies finding and collecting data only into an inventory, the proposed methodology also does some degree of analysis on the application repository to create an application knowledge base. Figure 3-5 shows a detailed view of the discover phase, including the creation of the application repository and the subsequent transformation of that repository to an application knowledge base. Various types of rules and policies can be defined. Some rules could be related to upgrading the technology versions of the applications; other rules could focus on the threshold values of certain attributes. There could be policies related to integration, ownership, documentation, consumption of services, and a variety of other areas. These rules can be created and housed within the same repository. The rules and policies can also be applied to the automated source code analysis to build further data points that provide additional insight into the applications. Part of the discover phase is to transform the passive data collection exercise into a more active knowledge base that can be leveraged to derive insight and make informed decisions.

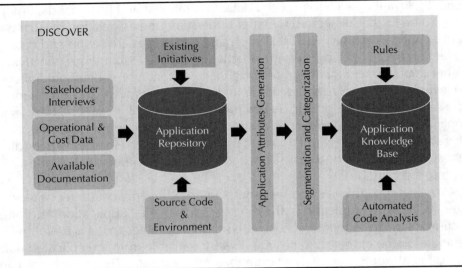

FIGURE 3-5. *Discover phase: creating an application knowledge repository*

Application Definition

Most organizations have a defined architecture practice that looks at the entire enterprise architecture to align business strategy to technology strategy. Applications are built that encapsulate the functionality, taking into account business processes, information and data flow, business functionality, and technology necessary to execute the business strategy. The actual definition of an application is nebulous at best and varies from one organization to the other. At one end of the spectrum, there are monolithic legacy applications that are presumed to contain the entire code base along with the database and other files necessary for execution. At the opposite end of the spectrum, some organizations classify a web site or a web service as an application.

For the purpose of executing APM exercises within an enterprise, it is important to reach a uniform and well-understood definition for an application. This definition is easier to grasp when it is a monolithic client-server application that includes the screens, business logic, and database. Many earlier Java applications were also monolithic, using the Abstract Window Toolkit (AWT) or Swing and sometimes even forcing business logic into such presentation layer components. Eventually, with the introduction of JavaServer Pages (JSP) and servlets, that client-server architecture evolved to a multi-tier Internet application architecture. As application architecture evolved to distributed multi-tier models, several components, especially technical components, were beginning to get reused.

In addition to such monolithic applications, a set of web services or software components that orchestrate together to deliver a series of business functions can also be called an application. In this case, it is important to assign each service or component to one logical group for the purpose of belonging somewhere so that another application does not contain that same service or component. Each application should have a specific functional and process boundary. Once this is established, it becomes easy to define what constitutes an application. An application can also be considered a unit for budget allocation, resource allocation, maintenance purposes, enhancement purposes, and for the purpose of ownership within an organization. Such a unit, which is a collection of business functionality, also fits within the definition of an application.

Defining application units and application boundaries clearly enables organizations to manage the lifecycle of an application effectively and easily leverage and reuse the application functionality across the organization. Lack of application definition, lack of application ownership, and an absence of the APM discipline may manifest in functional and technology redundancies in an application portfolio. Through this analysis, it is not uncommon to discover that four or five applications provide very similar functionality in various business units, and sometimes even within the same business unit. It is also not uncommon to see similar technology products from several vendors being used to build various applications rather than leverage the skills, knowledge base, and vendor product licenses that are already available within an application portfolio. The APM discipline coupled with an established enterprise architecture practice and clear application definition ensures that redundancies within application portfolios can be minimized.

Application Attributes

As part of the renovate pillar, when information is gathered about the applications existing within an organization, an enterprise should commit to establishing an APM practice and define its application portfolio strategy. For the purpose of governance and management of the application portfolio, this information gathering spans various practice areas, including business, operations, finance, technology, infrastructure, and compliance. The gathered information is organized into a set of attributes. Some attributes are directly discernable or measurable, whereas other attributes must be derived or analyzed from observations or calculations. It is important to note that not all attributes are derived from observations or calculations. In fact, these attributes are somewhat subjective and interpreted according to a scoring framework using a scale to measure the application. For example, Application Maintainability is an attribute, but how is this attribute measured? Based on a baseline agreed upon within the enterprise as to what constitutes Application Maintainability, this attribute can be periodically observed and captured for each application in the portfolio to track whether the maintainability of the application is getting better or worse.

Following is a common list of application attributes, categorized by area, that are useful to collect and track on a continuous basis:

Business Functionality

- Number of critical business processes supported
- Criticality to business
- Number of business units supported
- Business priority

Architecture and Design

- Application complexity
- Technical capability
- Technology risk
- Functional redundancy
- Technical redundancy
- Extensibility
- Reuse
- Deployment
- Security
- Documentation
- Software and hardware platforms

- Conformance to standards/architecture
- Software and hardware platform specification
- Number of languages, technologies used

Integration and Workflow

- Workflow complexity
- Configurable workflow
- Distributed transactions
- Measurable transaction delays
- Real-time/batch
- Business rules
- Integration dependencies
- Enterprise integration patterns
- Data formats
- Data interchange
- Data transformations
- Integration dependencies
- Number of internal interfaces
- Number of external interfaces
- Type of interfaces

Administration and Support

- Application maintainability
- Skill set availability
- Technology obsolescence
- Technology maturity
- Monitoring

- Number of releases in the past year
- Change in size of the application due to the releases
- Function points
- Percentage change in function points
- Life cycle of the technology
- Number of lines of code
- Number of services
- Risks
- Defect tracking and documentation
- Backlogs
- Number of failed fixes
- Support team size and characteristics
- Level of customization

Performance and Resiliency

- Scalability
- Availability
- Reliability
- Recovery time objective
- Peak load performance degradation
- Performance service level agreement (SLA) deviation
- Availability SLA deviation
- Current recovery capability
- Support window requirement
- Elapsed time
- Defects per line of code

- Number of failed bug fixes
- Number of outages
- Average downtime
- Disaster recovery
- Number of network domains
- Usage pattern and interfaces
- Number of users and concurrent users

Usability

- User satisfaction
- Personalization
- Approvals
- Multiple form factor devices
- User complaints

Finance and Operations

- Percentage productivity improvement
- Total cost
- Percentage change in budget
- Cost of consolidation
- Run labor costs
- Potential savings in labor costs through outsourcing
- Maintenance costs
- License costs
- Hardware costs
- Operational costs

Analyze: Application Assessment and Analysis

The strategic decision-making process associated with APM is dynamic and continuous and uses methodologies, processes, and tools to enable applications to meet key enterprise objectives by analyzing applications along several key areas, including the following:

- Business value
- Technical quality
- Application health
- Risks
- Investment decisions
- Architecture decisions
- Resource allocation
- Functional redundancies
- New technology introduction
- Application decommission decisions
- Outsourcing
- Business requirement prioritization

These areas represent some typical application dimensions of interest to APM. These dimensions are themselves constituted from one or more application attributes that were either collected or derived as part of the discover phase. Enterprises are making decisions continuously on which applications to invest in, how to build new business functionality, which applications to retire, and how to budget the maintenance of several disparate applications.

Application portfolios are tightly connected to the business strategy and technical strategy of an organization. Hence the analysis of the application knowledge base created in the discover phase will align the analysis to the business objectives. The analysis will result in the generation of several hypotheses that need to be validated. The generated hypotheses should also be mapped to business objectives to ensure that effort is not spent in areas that are not of importance to the business.

One aspect of the analysis will focus on scoring the applications along various dimensions and then generating 2×2 matrices that select, plot, and compare the two selected dimensions against each other. At this point, an interpretation of the hypotheses can be formulated. Based on the theme of the analysis, the specific 2×2 views of interest can be listed and the relevant application attributes that constitute the dimensions of analysis can be extracted from the knowledge base.

Some of the 2×2 views of interest to the analyze phase are listed next:

- Business value versus cost

- Business criticality versus technical quality for risk reduction

- Technology obsolescence versus performance SLA deviation for understanding application health

- Application criticality versus business capability

- Cost versus sourcing

- Business criticality versus SLA deviation for understanding risk reduction

The analysis ultimately results in a report that is used as input into the recommend phase.

The second aspect of the analyze phase involves understanding whether any new business capabilities or technical capabilities need to be built into the portfolio. If any initiatives are already in progress or upcoming initiatives are in the pipeline, this phase should be used to analyze and prioritize the capabilities that need to be built. If such capabilities are already available, a redundancy analysis can be completed to determine whether existing capabilities can be either enhanced or reused. The output of this analysis exercise will be a list of capabilities that can be prioritized along multiple dimensions—for example, the cost of building the capability versus the ease of its implementation. Prioritization and planning will also contribute to the analysis report to help understand prioritized business needs and the implementation cost, complexity, and risks of attempting such an implementation. The output of the analyze phase is now used in the recommend phase. Figure 3-6 illustrates the details of the analyze phase.

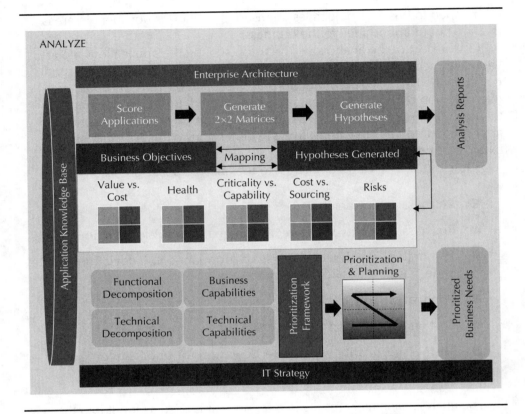

FIGURE 3-6. *Analyze phase: application analysis and hypotheses generation*

Recommend: Initiatives Prioritization and Roadmap Definition

This phase starts with the analysis report and the prioritized business needs, which were the output of the analyze phase. The hypotheses that were generated and mapped to business objectives need to be validated. The prioritized business needs and the validated hypotheses are used to generate initiatives that need to be implemented. Depending on the goal of the analysis exercise, the initiatives could be used to reduce cost of operations of the application portfolio, rationalize the applications, eliminate redundancies, and transform the portfolio to acquire new business capabilities and other goals. The hypotheses and the initiatives identified will vary greatly depending on these goals. Figure 3-7 shares a visualization of how initiatives are prioritized and an implementation roadmap is generated.

Once the initiatives are identified, a cost model needs to be built and the benefits need to be examined. Complex and expensive initiatives will need a strong business case before they can be launched. The APM discipline has business case development built into it as part of the governance process. Investment Portfolio and Risk Management disciplines as well as the PPM disciplines are tightly integrated into the process of recommendation, since funds and resources are provided and managed under the auspices of those disciplines.

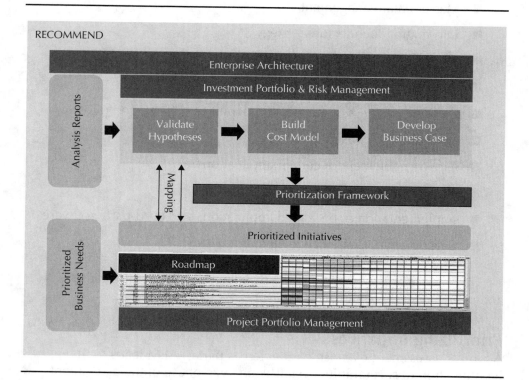

FIGURE 3-7.   *Recommend phase: prioritize initiatives and generate an implementation roadmap*

Business Case

Chapter 2 included a detailed section on business case creation, in the context of building a business case to create a new application. Building a business case for an initiative identified as part of APM is very similar. It is just that the initiative identified may not necessarily be that of building a new application or even enhancing an existing one.

The initiatives that need business case development could include any of the following:

- New application development or enhancement of existing applications

- Business process re-engineering

- Master data management

- Information architecture strategy

- Elimination of functional redundancies

- Introduction of new technology

- Building business or technical capabilities into the portfolio

- Infrastructure consolidation

- Cloud enablement of certain applications

- Decommissioning applications

- Implementation of packaged applications and third-party software

- Several other types of IT related initiatives

The business case creation process outlined in Chapter 2 is directly applicable to all these situations.

Prioritizing Initiatives

A typical assessment exercise conducted as part of APM leads to the identification of several initiatives. The analyze phase of the assessment exercise results in several hypotheses being generated to address the business objectives. The resulting detailed analysis and hypotheses validation will yield initiatives that need to be executed to achieve the business objectives. Prioritizing the identified initiatives involves understanding the following items:

- Identify whether any fundamentally new business capabilities need to be built.

- Identify whether any new technology capabilities need to be built or new technology introduced.

- Estimate the rough order of magnitude cost of the initiative.

- Estimate the resources needed and a timeline with ramp-up and ramp-down of resources.

- Document all dependencies required to execute the initiative.

- Document all the risks associated with executing the initiative.

A simple framework to prioritize the initiatives involves computing four distinct parameters—cost, risk, ease of implementation (EOI), and business value—with scores for each initiative. Although a two-dimensional plot will take into account only two of the four identified parameters, it is still possible to include three or all four of these parameters in a plot. The values of the four parameters can be plotted to compare the initiatives. All four dimensions, or a subset of the dimensions, can be compared, and then decisions can be made regarding which initiatives will take priority. Figure 3-8 illustrates this plot based on a hypothetical set of initiatives identified within an enterprise. The y axis represents the business value, and the x axis represents the cost, as indicated by the effort and investment required. The size of the bubble indicates the EOI, with a small bubble indicating that EOI is high and a large bubble indicating EOI is low. Finally, the risk is captured by the patterns of the bubble, with no shading highlighting low risk, dots indicating medium risk, and dark shading signifying the highest risk. Thus, all four parameters are conveyed to allow for a thorough comparison and prioritization of the initiatives.

Designing the Roadmap

The roadmap is a high-level plan that accounts for timelines, dependencies, and resources needed to execute the initiatives. It provides a staggered view of the initiatives over a time period, with approximate start and end dates.

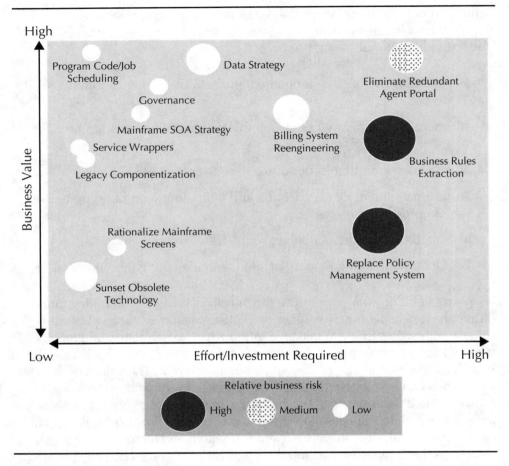

FIGURE 3-8. *Illustration of a plot to prioritize initiatives*

The granularity of the time period can be quarterly or monthly, depending on the availability of resources and the accuracy of the information. Typical roadmaps span three to five years. Every year, the roadmap needs to be revisited and updated based on the new information available, taking into account that business priorities might have changed from the original basis upon which the roadmap was generated. Certain initiatives can be delayed or completely shelved due to changing business conditions, a different business direction, or even lack of funds.

A roadmap should never be set in stone. It is a living document that comes under the ownership of the governance process and the APM discipline.

Measuring Portfolio Performance

The simplest way to measure the performance of an application portfolio is through a method that is similar to the balanced scorecard approach. The balanced scorecard approach expands traditional financial measures to three other areas—namely, customer, employee, and operations—to measure the performance of an organization. In the context of APM, our approach to measuring application portfolio performance looks at areas such as IT operations, business perspectives, sustenance of APM, organizational perspective, and finally the financial perspective. Metrics have to be identified and measured that will help determine excellence in operating the application portfolio and the business value of the applications contained within the portfolio.

The IT operations perspective reviews the APM processes that were developed and implemented to manage the application portfolio. This area would take into consideration the dependencies and coupling between the peer disciplines of PPM and IRM to operationalize APM successfully and efficiently.

The business perspective measures the business value of the applications in the portfolio, technical quality, functional and technical health, and the ease of developing or enhancing business capabilities within the portfolio.

Sustenance provides a view of the resources needed to sustain the APM discipline and APM governance within an enterprise. It also provides a prioritization framework to score, compare, and prioritize necessary business requirements as well as recommend future initiatives to optimize and rationalize the application portfolio, thereby improving ROI.

The organization perspective spotlights the valuable viewpoint of how stakeholders across an organization are engaged, how the core group owns APM, how APM metrics are consumed, and how decisions are made by users interacting with the application portfolio.

The finance related perspective enables tracking the TCO and ROI of the application portfolio, the cost of introducing new capabilities and enhancing existing applications, the actual cost of labor, and other financial metrics of interest.

Metrics Definition

Multiple types of metrics can be created depending on the interests of various stakeholders in an enterprise. Many metrics are role specific. Certain stakeholders may be interested in granular metrics only, whereas others may want to understand an entirely different type of metric. For example, an enterprise architect has a different view of APM metrics compared to an application owner. The specific application maintenance and production metrics may be of interest to the application owner, whereas the quality and health of the application may be of interest to an application architect.

Broadly speaking, metrics can be classified into four categories:

- Application metrics
- Application portfolio metrics
- APM process metrics
- APM effectiveness metrics

These metrics can also be classified into specific types, such as technical metrics, business metrics, operational metrics, financial metrics, and so on. However, these categories do not reflect the interrelatedness of the metrics. For example, a cost-related metric is a type of financial metric, but it can also occur in more than one of the four categories. The metrics that are measured at the category level can quickly reveal the success of the APM discipline with respect to individual applications, application portfolios, the APM process itself, or the APM discipline effectiveness. To have a broad overview of APM governance and the APM discipline, one needs to look at these metrics at the category level.

Application Metrics

Application-level metrics represent data that provides a view of how well the application is managed within the APM processes. These metrics are of interest to application owners, application architects, and stakeholders at the individual application level.

Application Portfolio Metrics

Application portfolio metrics represent aggregation of application data at the application portfolio level. These metrics represent specific facets of interest to portfolio owners in identifying problems, opportunities, and types of applicable action. This would also be of interest to enterprise architects and key IT stakeholders.

APM Process Metrics

APM process metrics measure the compliance and coverage of the APM process itself. These metrics are of interest to management and business stakeholders in addition to key IT stakeholders.

APM Effectiveness Metrics

APM effectiveness metrics are of interest to the core APM group as well as the core groups of the other APM peer disciplines. Senior management may also be interested in the performance and efficacy of the APM processes.

Success with Metrics

Merely setting up metrics or successfully measuring their results does not guarantee APM success. To achieve success and sustain that success in the context of APM, one must follow certain practices. First of all, metrics should be well defined and clearly understood. All metrics should have meta-data associated with them that provide the following:

- **Objective**   Why the metric was defined in the first place

- **Acquisition**   Source of the metric and how the metric is measured

- **Frequency**   Frequency of measurement and frequency of consumption of the metric; these two need not be the same

- **Stakeholder(s)**   Metric owner and other interested parties

- **Measure**   Baseline value, range values, thresholds, aggregates, and other measures associated with the metric

- **Movement**   Trends, status, alerts, reporting, sliding windows, and similar activity associated with the metric

Metrics can appear in a dashboard, and they can be leading, lagging, or a part of the key performance indicator (KPI). Understanding a metric in this manner ensures that the metric will be used in good decision-making, thereby making the metric a success to the APM discipline.

Metrics Gone Wrong

So, an enterprise has reached the stage where APM governance has been established and the relevant metrics have been defined. The process is still not quite complete. Establishing metrics and measuring them is not sufficient. Most enterprises typically run into some metrics-related problems at this stage, including the following:

- The data collected could be too complex to derive meaningful metrics.

- The timeline over which the data is collected might be too long. The actual metrics of interest might be available within a tight window and any decision-making based on the metrics might be effective only if done within that particular window. However, the data upon which you rely for the metric and subsequent decision-making might get diluted during the long timeline and render the metric ineffective.

- There could be stale or poor quality data in the midst of good data, which can cause the entire data set used for metrics generation to affect the metrics quality.

- The stakeholders may not know how to interpret the metrics for proper decision-making.

- Stakeholders may be looking at the wrong metrics.

- Management may not have bought into the process; even though relevant stakeholders made informed and factually supported recommendations, executive management may not follow that plan.

Stakeholders and Metrics

The metrics by themselves will not create any meaningful impact to the enterprise. Metrics are only as important as the stakeholders who are interested in them, who leverage the metrics to make the right decisions, and who make the right recommendations to the enterprise. If metrics are collected but not used in the decision-making process, it is a wasted effort. Stakeholders need to understand the APM discipline and develop a strong understanding of what the metrics mean and how metrics are computed. If there are measurable gaps in the metrics, stakeholders need to propose and establish additional metrics that would be of use to them. As the discovery process associated with APM collects and builds a knowledge base of application data, the relevant attributes are collected to measure and manage the applications. Once a baseline is established, the process should ensure maintenance of that baseline data and enhance the quality and quantity of the data to make metrics more meaningful.

Expected Outcomes from APM

Implementing and institutionalizing APM within enterprises will lead to tremendous benefits over time. From a business perspective, APM will lead to the following outcomes:

- Business risk reduction in the application portfolio

- Reduction of application maintenance and support costs from full-time equivalent (FTE) reduction

- Reduction of infrastructure costs

- Rationalization of the application portfolio and reduction in the number of applications

- Reduction in costs directly tied to cloud adoption

- Cost savings resulting from shutting down or phasing out (sunsetting) some applications

- Direct financial benefits, reduction in TCO, and improvement of ROI

- Improved business-to-IT alignment and superior governance and management of projects and project portfolios

- Leveraging peer disciplines such as PPM and IRM to better forecast resource needs

Sustaining APM

Sustaining APM is easier said than done. Although there is a steep curve to implement APM successfully in an organization, a strong commitment is needed if an enterprise wants to sustain APM beyond a three- to four-year horizon. One of the biggest challenges to sustaining APM is that business processes are susceptible to many influences, some of which can force business models to change suddenly. Competitive business dynamics, market forces, and changing business needs all result in enhancements and modifications to existing applications. Newer applications may also need to be built. Technology advancements will force enterprises to leverage new technology stacks, newer versions, or APIs to build the new business functionality. Portfolio management has to keep up with the speed of business!

Strong APM governance along with continuously integrated APM processes enabled by automation tools will safeguard the knowledge base leveraged by APM by keeping it current. This source of application attributes and metrics will ensure that the portfolio stays optimized and aligned with other enterprise initiatives. It is vital to resolve all ambiguities swiftly and never to allow the application inventory to fall behind. The quality of information in the application repository should be complete without any gaps.

The APM discipline and the processes instituted to support it need to be evaluated on a regular basis. APM process metrics and APM effectiveness metrics should be analyzed frequently to ensure that APM is performing well. If APM is not performing well, it needs to be refined quickly through a defined change-management process. The analysis framework and prioritization framework should also be visited periodically to ensure that they are also current.

Guiding Principles for APM Implementation

Following are some basic principles of effective APM implementation:

- As part of the recommend phase, identify quick wins and launch pilots for the quick wins.

- APM decisions should be accompanied by a high-level business case and roadmap to justify the initiatives.

- All recommendations should meet the organization's key business objectives.

- The suggested roadmap and length of the overall journey should consider the organizational culture, resistance to change, and pace of change desired.

- The application portfolio rationalization should generate savings for self-funding future waves of application rationalization.

Summary

All enterprises have accumulated applications, technology components, and other assets. They have all built business and technology capabilities to deliver business value. These application portfolios employ not only Java applications but also a variety of other heterogeneous platforms. Application portfolio management can be instituted as a discipline to manage the entire application portfolio continuously. This needs a well-defined methodology, a set of processes that make up the APM discipline, and a set of tools that can institutionalize APM within an enterprise. APM cannot exist without investment risk management, project portfolio management, and enterprise architecture. Enterprises are in a constant state of renovation, integration of the applications, and management of the application portfolio. Thorough governance along with periodic discovery and analysis of application-related data will ensure that the application knowledge base stays current. This will result in proper decision-making and support for the necessary initiatives to propel and meet ongoing business objectives.

CHAPTER
4

Architecture
Decomposition

The IT discipline of application portfolio management (APM) positively impacts organizations and helps ensure that IT budgets are spent wisely on relevant and functional applications rather than redundant or unnecessary ones. However, APM cannot achieve this objective single-handedly. As you saw in the previous chapter, the relationship between APM and the peer disciplines of project portfolio management (PPM) and investment risk management (IRM) are immensely intertwined, and an even stronger relationship exists between APM and enterprise architecture (EA).

The EA approach engages business and IT stakeholders, aligns business objectives to technology projects, and channels the execution of enterprise projects toward business outcomes that support the desired business vision and objectives. The enterprise architect role has evolved to become a central figure in the IT strategy and the alignment of business to technology.

How does the EA discipline capture the attention of business and IT stakeholders? How are IT projects aligned to ensure that they meet business objectives? These are some of the questions that will be discussed in this chapter as we delve into the nature of EA and what constitutes EA, and distill the various layers that form EA. The decomposition of the various architecture layers enables the applications to be completely dissected and understood from a business, functional, and technical perspective. Hypotheses can be generated regarding which areas of the application portfolio are strong and which areas are weak, enabling enterprises to make effective business decisions. Through the process of architecture decomposition, the discipline of EA can be viewed from a nontraditional sense to highlight the impact of EA on APM as a whole.

Enterprise Architecture Distilled

Enterprise architecture has been a rising force within every IT department. Although this field existed in some shape or form since modern business processes were adopted, EA was not formalized or accepted as a discipline until about 25 years ago, when enterprises started to leverage information technology (IT) to execute the business vision and create a competitive advantage. To be precise, in 1987, J.A. Zachman published an article in the *IBM Systems Journal* titled "A Framework for Information Systems Architecture," which highlighted the challenges faced by enterprises that manage the complexity of distributed IT systems and the vision of EA as it aligns business to IT. This revolutionary article guided the evolution of the EA discipline over the next two decades.

As a result of this new revelation, enterprises soon realized that they were spending more and more money to build IT systems that were becoming unnecessarily complex and increasingly unwieldy. These IT systems were evolving in their own direction without regard to actual business requirements, causing a gross misalignment of business and technological objectives. This divergence led to the development of two specific methodologies that created and defined an approach to EA initiatives:

- The Zachman Framework

- The Open Group Architectural Framework (TOGAF)

Standard Approaches to EA

Although there are several approaches to EA, many follow the same guiding principles. Many technology companies, systems integrators, and IT outsourcing vendors provide their own monogramed version of EA and provide individualized methodologies, approaches, and frameworks. All of these approaches provide the ability to create and implement the required processes, identify and establish the necessary roles and responsibilities, and establish the governance and best practices necessary to sustain a successful EA program in an enterprise.

A mature EA framework defines the principles and best practices that establish a layered view of a particular organization. It also abstracts the business processes and business capabilities from the business functionality provided by applications, as well as the technical capabilities from the actual technology and software components in place. EA also formalizes the information architecture that extracts all data and information residing within an enterprise to support the execution of applications. This is true of all EA approaches.

Zachman Framework

The Zachman Framework is probably the oldest EA framework in existence. It provides a structured way to define the fabric of an enterprise. The usefulness of the Zachman Framework and the application of its structure can be applied universally to other disciplines as well. In fact, the Zachman Framework was initially implemented for empirical observations in the descriptions of buildings, airplanes, and other complex arenas.

The framework consists of a classification matrix (6×6 matrix) that addresses the following: who, what, when, where, why, and how. The answers are plotted along one dimension, whereas the other dimension transforms the abstract idea into an instantiation. The Zachman Framework is more of an ontology or classification system that helps to organize detailed enterprise artifacts. It is not an actual methodology or process to define EA. Since the Zachman Framework is quite abstract, several other approaches to define an EA framework have customized and enhanced the basic Zachman structure into more universally applicable principles.

The Open Group Architecture Framework

The Open Group Architecture Framework, best known by its acronym TOGAF, is an approach to defining, implementing, and governing an EA. It describes an EA as consisting of four architectural layers: business architecture, application architecture, data architecture, and technology architecture. The TOGAF we know today had its origins in a methodology that was used to describe technical architectures. Since its inception in the 1990s, TOGAF has evolved into a mature full-fledged approach for EAs. It has emerged to be the global standard. The Open Group Architecture Forum develops and maintains TOGAF. Comprising a couple hundred enterprises, the forum regularly revises and improves upon the standard. Figure 4-1 depicts TOGAF's representation of the architectural layers in an enterprise.

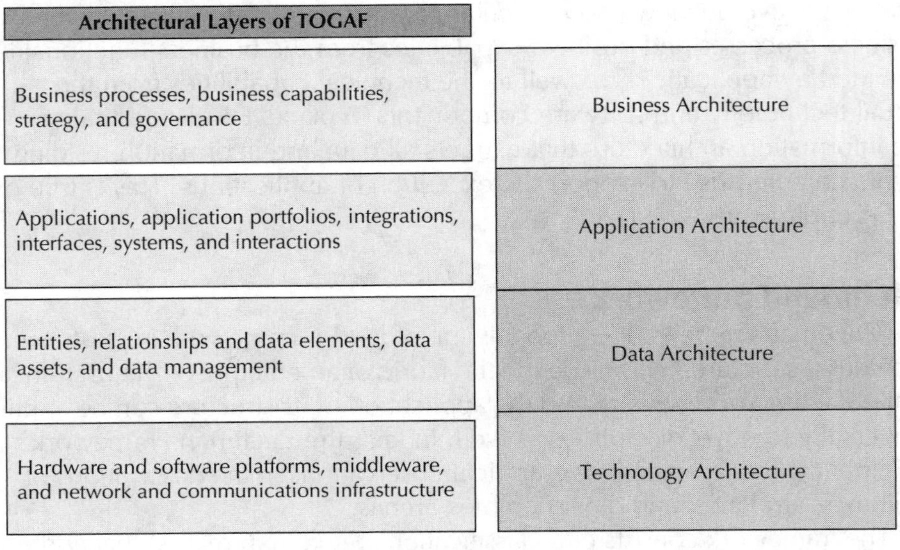

Architectural Layers of TOGAF

Business processes, business capabilities, strategy, and governance	Business Architecture
Applications, application portfolios, integrations, interfaces, systems, and interactions	Application Architecture
Entities, relationships and data elements, data assets, and data management	Data Architecture
Hardware and software platforms, middleware, and network and communications infrastructure	Technology Architecture

FIGURE 4-1. *TOGAF representation of the architectural layers*

Other Approaches to EA

In addition to the Zachman and TOGAF frameworks, several industry analysts, such as Gartner and Forrester, regularly publish various approaches, articles, reports, and tools to improve upon EA. Several large IT outsourcing providers, such as IBM Global Services, Accenture, TCS, and Infosys, have also created custom methodologies and frameworks to tackle EA. Although their naming conventions, terminologies, and solution branding may appear to be different, their approaches all share several common traits. In reality, most customized EA frameworks are conceptually similar, although the owners of those frameworks monopolize and capitalize on their unique differences.

The Architectural Layers in the APM Context

While TOGAF created the architectural layers of business, application, data (information), and technology (technical), from the point of view of application portfolio modernization one has to adopt a slightly different view of these architectural layers. The TOGAF view focuses on EA from a domain perspective, drawing a distinction between the layers based on the skills and subject matter expertise. TOGAF provides the methods and tools to assist the creation, use, maintenance, and governance of EAs. The TOGAF Architecture Development Method (ADM) provides a reliable and repeatable process for architecture development.

The purpose of an APM-centric architecture view is not intended to be a replacement for TOGAF at all. In this light, TOGAF can continue to serve its purpose from an EA perspective. The APM-centric view is driven by the management and modernization of an application portfolio through the adoption of a functional view of architecture.

Figure 4-2 illustrates an APM-centric view of the enterprise architectural layers. In this picture, the architectural layers are depicted as business architecture, functional architecture, technical architecture, and infrastructure architecture. It is important to understand that the functional architecture, which is also referred to as logical architecture, encapsulates and breaks down the application functionality into logical components that collectively embody a particular business function.

Although application architecture and data architecture are important, they are addressed within the context of the business and functional architecture that monitors all the business capabilities and application functionalities provided by an application portfolio. From an APM perspective, the TOGAF technology architecture can be thought of as a combination of the APM-centric technical architecture, which addresses the software components, and the

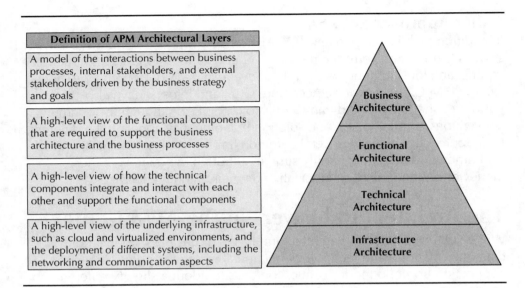

Definition of APM Architectural Layers

A model of the interactions between business processes, internal stakeholders, and external stakeholders, driven by the business strategy and goals
A high-level view of the functional components that are required to support the business architecture and the business processes
A high-level view of how the technical components integrate and interact with each other and support the functional components
A high-level view of the underlying infrastructure, such as cloud and virtualized environments, and the deployment of different systems, including the networking and communication aspects

Business Architecture

Functional Architecture

Technical Architecture

Infrastructure Architecture

FIGURE 4-2.   *APM-centric view of the architectural layers*

infrastructure architecture, which addresses hardware, virtualization, and the cloud. This granularity and separation is important in the context of APM. So, for the purposes of APM, it is important to disrupt the traditional approach to EA by introducing the notion of a functional architecture and also to separate TOGAF's technology architecture further into technical architecture for software and infrastructure architecture for hardware.

A simple analogy can illustrate this scenario: Consider a potluck invitation. Each guest is asked to bring a dish using a specific list of ingredients. Several different ingredients must be incorporated into the various dishes. When people sign up to make a dish, they are given a list of ingredients to use. People who have been provided with similar lists of ingredients for their dishes are grouped together and given those ingredients. Then, at the time of the potluck, the dishes are brought to a room and organized on tables into categories based on the type of course each represents: appetizer, salad, soup, entrée, or desert. The dishes that originally shared a commonality with a similar ingredient list now belong to an entirely different group, as a prepared dish based on its consumption characteristics. So, although similarities existed in the ingredient lists, after transformation into the end dish, many of those similarities were no longer evident. In the same way, business processes, functional requirements, data elements, technical components, infrastructure, and the like, are the "ingredients" used to create applications. The EA viewpoint enables us to consider the application landscape in a slightly different way than we would from the point of view of APM.

To reiterate, the TOGAF model has four architectural layers: business architecture, application architecture, data architecture, and technology architecture. With the advent of SaaS-based platforms running on highly distributed, virtualized cloud infrastructures, where REST and web services can be deployed for consumption, from anywhere at any time, one can no longer continue to take the traditional view of the EA layers. Although the business architecture definition between TOGAF and our APM-centric architectural layers is aligned, the other architectural layers in TOGAF need to be dissected a bit differently. The application architecture requires a segmentation and analysis from the vantage point of functional and technical architectures. The data architecture must now be viewed from the perspective of information architecture, which has dependencies on the business and functional architectures. For the purpose of analysis in the context of APM, the previously defined technology architecture needs to be separated into two layers: technical architecture and infrastructure architecture.

Business Architecture

Although there are several definitions of business architecture, a simple but effective one characterizes business architecture as a blueprint for business processes and business capabilities, with a governance structure baked into its fabric, to create and execute the business strategy. The Object Management Group (OMG) specifically describes business architecture as an integrated perspective of the enterprise across five specific views:

- Business strategy

- Business capability

- Business value stream

- Knowledge management

- The organization

The descriptions of the five views that follow provide a good primer on business architecture.

Business Strategy   The business strategy view represents the business objectives of the organization and the business drivers. The objectives are mapped to strategic and tactical approaches for realizing the business vision. Key performance indicators (KPIs) and other metrics are used to track the progress and success of the enterprise in achieving its business goals. Business strategy is not a static representation, but rather a view that reflects market forces, competition, innovation within the enterprise, mergers and acquisitions, and the customers of an enterprise.

Business Capability   The business capability view can be defined as an atomic unit representing a collection of business functions. These business functions typically describe the interactions and orchestrations of a business process and the departments or business units impacted by those business functions. Business capabilities can impact a wide range of entities spanning the entire enterprise, including employees, customers, suppliers, partners, and executives.

Business Value Stream   The business value stream view captures both quantifiable and intangible values that arise from the activities within an organization. The recognized value is delivered to the internal and external stakeholders, who are served by the business capabilities. Value streams are distributed across departmental and organizational boundaries; they are used to measure and quantify the value derived from the execution of business processes.

Knowledge Management   The knowledge management view recognizes that every domain cultivates its own terminology and every business within that domain evolves its own set of semantics and understanding of the larger industry vocabulary. This view establishes that enterprises use this customized language to structure their operational processes. These semantics are shared across an organization and a collective understanding of its etymology is necessary for the successful execution of business processes at the business unit level. This is one of the reasons why new employees require a bit of time to "get their feet wet" before they understand the company culture and lingo, even if they have worked in the industry for quite a while. The new employee needs to understand how things get done at the new company. Simple tasks such as how customer orders are defined, which attributes are captured, and how the order is fulfilled will differ between organizations, even within the same industry. The taxonomy and ontology for the business are an important part of the knowledge management view.

The Organization   The core structure of an organization forms an important view of the business architecture. This perspective examines the following: how roles are defined within a company and the interrelationships of those roles, the structure of the business units, the mapping of capabilities and business functions to those units, and the decomposition of business units into smaller teams. These aspects all define the individuality of an organization. From time to time, organizations undergo restructuring when they realize that the business strategy and the execution of the business capabilities are not optimized under a particular organizational structure. The management functions, and their interactions with business units, are also captured within this organizational view.

Conceptual business architecture is shown in Figure 4-3 for a segment of the transportation and logistics industry. In the figure, the core business process areas such as logistics, equipment management, rail and dray, finance, and business management are identified. External partners and vendors interact with the core business processes. Business operations, analytics, integrated marketing and communications, and other departments support the core business architecture of this hypothetical company.

Significance of Business Architecture to APM   Identification and prioritization of business capabilities is central to the success of APM within an enterprise. Although other views are important, to create an application portfolio, applications have to be identified and their business capabilities understood. To analyze and rationalize an application portfolio, the business processes have to be well understood and the application functionality has to be broken down into granular logical blocks and decomposed and mapped to the business capabilities that are supported within the application portfolio. Hence, the understanding and creation of the business architecture blueprint is an integrated task with the APM discipline.

Functional Architecture

Functional architecture is known by many different names, including domain architecture and logical architecture. While business architecture captures

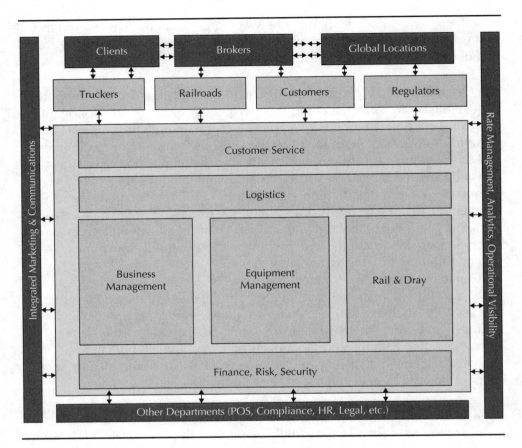

FIGURE 4-3. *Sample business architecture*

the necessary business processes, in order to execute those processes, several discrete pieces of functionality must first come together.

This functionality can be mapped to lines of business and business processes. To execute the business processes described by business architecture, the processes have to be broken down into level 2 and level 3 subprocesses. To execute the subprocesses, functional requirements are written, including use cases and the behavior of a system.

Figure 4-4 further develops the business architecture from Figure 4-3 and shows how each business component of the business architecture is broken

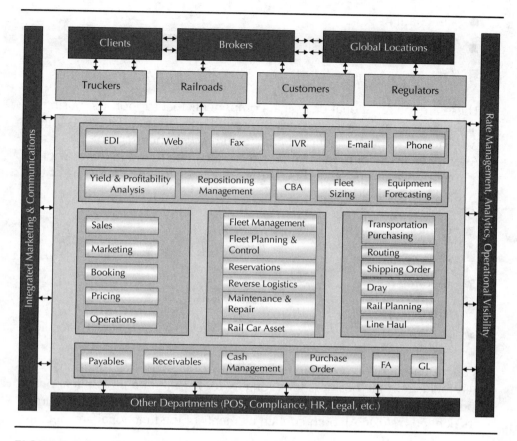

FIGURE 4-4.   *Sample functional architecture*

down into its constituent functional architecture components. For example, if you take the business architecture for the logistics and transportation industry and, within that, the specific business area of rail and dray, you can identify a functional architecture that consists of high-level functional blocks such as the following:

- Rail planning
- Rail billing

- Line haul
- Transportation purchasing
- Drayage

These are the functional or logical components that support the business architecture and the business processes around rail and dray. Figure 4-4 also shows other conceptual functional architecture components.

Another example of functional architecture can be found in the area of order management, represented by a functional architecture consisting of the following functional blocks:

- Contracts
- Pricing
- Quoting
- Collections
- Billing and receivables

Functional architecture is an essential layer that captures functional requirements and the business functionality to be built into an application to support business needs. The application architecture and data architecture layers defined by TOGAF both contain elements of the functional architecture.

Technical Architecture

The technical architecture layer of EA presents the technical components necessary to implement the functional architecture identified in the previous section. This specific definition of technical architecture limits the scope to software components. The hardware and networking components, the physical architecture, and deployment architecture all fall under the infrastructure architecture layer.

The particular separation of infrastructure architecture from the traditional definition of technical architecture specifically allows for a thorough analysis of an application portfolio. By separating out these concerns from the overall application portfolio during the analyze phase, a greater focus can be placed on the following topics:

- Infrastructure server consolidation
- Virtualization
- Cloud adoption
- Cloud readiness

In the traditional TOGAF specification of EA, technology architecture includes the hardware infrastructure. However, for the purposes of our definition, the application and data architecture elements span the functional and technical architectural layers. This allows for an easier APM analysis, especially to identify redundancies in functional and technical components and to rationalize these architecture layers independent of one another.

If you were to apply the traditional EA approach to analyze application and data architectures, you would not have visibility into the functionalities that exist in multiple locations within the portfolio. With a modernized approach, you can easily create a matrix that maps and identifies repeated occurrences of a particular functional block in more than one application within the application portfolio. Figure 4-5 illustrates this mapping of functional components to the applications within a portfolio. The functional blocks appear along the rows and the applications appear along the columns. The checkmarks indicate all the functional blocks supported by an application, making the redundancies distinctly visible in this application portfolio.

Similarly to this approach, a matrix can be used to map technical components against the applications. This exercise can discover redundant technical components purchased from various vendors to build new applications rather than leverage previously custom-built or purchased technical components providing similar functionality. Figure 4-6 depicts the mapping of the applications to the technical components.

Technical architecture captures software components, reusable services, software frameworks and products, messaging architectures, protocols, and custom components. For the purposes of this discussion, we can simplify the technical architecture stratum to be represented as a multi-tiered layer comprising Presentation & Communication Services, Business Application Services, and Enterprise Information Services. There could also be framework

Existing Applications

Logical Components		Warehouse	Integrated Management	Equipment Manager	Equipment Logistics	Equipment Management	Sales, Marketing and Planning	Business Management	Logistics and Rail	Equipment and Finance	Logistics and Finance	Receivables	Rail Planning	Excel Reports	Expediting System	Rail and Shipping	Pricing	Equipment Tracking	Rail Planning	Rail Billing	EDI Manager	Misc Functions	Cargo and Space
LC1	Logistics	✓	✓	✓	✓	✓	✓	✓	✓		✓			✓									
LC2	Business Management		✓	✓			✓	✓															
LC2.1	Sales	✓	✓	✓			✓	✓															
LC2.2	Marketing	✓	✓				✓																
LC2.3	Pricing	✓												✓			✓						
LC3	Customer Service		✓	✓												✓					✓		
LC4	Rail & Dray	✓	✓	✓			✓		✓				✓	✓		✓			✓	✓	✓		✓
LC4.1	Rail Planning		✓	✓			✓						✓	✓		✓			✓		✓		
LC4.2	Shipping Order (Rail-Billing)		✓	✓									✓	✓		✓*					✓		
LC4.3	Line Haul		✓	✓										✓		✓							✓
LC4.4	Transportation Purchasing	✓	✓				✓		✓		✓		✓			✓					✓		✓
LC4.5	Drayage		✓	✓																			
LC6	Equipment Management		✓	✓			✓	✓							✓			✓					✓
LC6.1	Equipment - Fleet Management		✓	✓		✓																	
LC6.2	Equipment - Fleet Planning & Control			✓																			
LC6.3	Equipment - Reservations		✓	✓		✓								✓									
LC6.4	Equipment Maintenance & Repair									✓				✓				✓					
LC6.5	Rail Car Asset Group		✓	✓																			
LC6.6	Per Diem											✓		✓				✓					
LC7	Finance		✓	✓			✓			✓		✓	✓						✓				
LC7.1	Payables		✓	✓			✓	✓						✓							✓		
LC7.2	Receivables		✓	✓			✓	✓								✓					✓		
LC8	Ocean Carrier Services (OCS)		✓	✓																			

FIGURE 4-5. *Mapping of functional components to applications*

Application	IDMS	IDMS-DC	ADSO	APCA (Custom M/F UI)	Cobol	JCL	CICS	MQ	DB2	Oracle	Nomad	Teradata	CGL/BIQuery	Holos	EasyTrieve	Informatica	Excel	MS-Access	Actuate	Crystal Reports	Web-Focus Reports	Power-Builder	Java-Swing	Pro-Cobol	Pro*C	FileNet	NDM (Network Data Move)	Gentran	FaxSys	EasyTrieve (Cobol Like)	Endeavor(SCC)	Mainframe	Windows NT	RS 6000
Warehouse	✓	✓	✓	✓	✓	✓					✓	✓	✓														✓					✓		
Integrated Management	✓	✓	✓	✓	✓	✓	✓	✓										✓														✓		
Equipment Manager	✓	✓	✓	✓	✓	✓	✓	✓																							✓	✓		
Equipment Logistics	✓	✓	✓	✓	✓	✓																				✓					✓	✓		
Sales and Marketing	✓		✓	✓	✓																										✓	✓		
Cargo	✓	✓							✓																									
Trucking and Fleet Management	✓				✓				✓																	✓								
Pricing										✓				✓		✓			✓			✓		✓	✓		✓				✓		✓	
Receivables																	✓	✓				✓		✓						✓	✓		✓	
Rail Planning										✓		✓	✓				✓	✓								✓	✓							
Finance Application																					✓				✓									
Payables										✓												✓												
Management Screens																																		
Equipment Management										✓																✓							✓	
Equipment Leasing	✓	✓			✓	✓			✓	✓	✓			✓																	✓	✓		
Expediting System				✓	✓	✓				✓	✓																			✓				
Logistics																																		✓
Equipment				✓		✓					✓																				✓	✓	✓	
Business Management				✓							✓																							
Misc Functions																							✓					✓		✓	✓			✓
EDI Manager	✓			✓	✓																										✓			✓

FIGURE 4-6. *Mapping of applications to technical components*

components and enterprise service bus components distributed throughout this conceptual tier, thus implementing this technical architecture as an N-tiered architecture.

The high-level tiers of the sample technical architecture described previously are shown in Figure 4-7. In this conceptual technical architecture layer, the Presentation & Communication Services layer could contain the following technical components:

- Portal server

- Mobility services

- Content management system

- Operational reporting

- Interactive voice response (IVR)

- Fax server

The argument could be made that a reporting component may have to receive data from a database or that a content management system would have a front end user interface and a backend repository where versioned content would be stored. In that case, wouldn't these technical components span the business services or information services tiers as well?

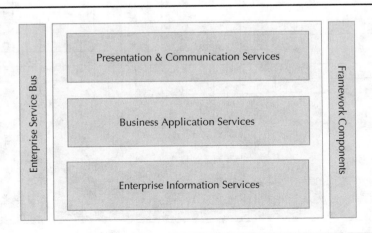

FIGURE 4-7. *Sample technical architecture*

From an architectural perspective, all of these components are technical components and can be associated with technical architecture in our layered architectural model. From a convenience standpoint, we represent the technical architecture as a multi-tiered architecture and assign components to a particular tier. Some components may have a major part of their usage associated with the presentation tier and other components with the business tier. Because of this, we chose to associate technical components with that tier where we feel they belong based on the major functionality. In the current distributed architecture world, many technical components are composed of loosely coupled subcomponents and most of them provide a UI and access some kind of a data store. The primary function of the technical component should dictate where you would place them in a tiered technical architecture.

Infrastructure Architecture

The traditional focus of EA has always been on the business and application architecture layers and, to a minor extent, on the information architecture layer. Infrastructure architecture was included within the technology architecture layer and was largely assumed to be available in a data center. This resulted in a larger focus on business and functional requirements and a lesser focus on nonfunctional requirements. This is the case in the execution of most projects today. While we discuss business-to-IT alignment and applications supporting business functionality, none of this can really work without the infrastructure upon which the applications run.

Today's infrastructure architecture has evolved into a complex layer that emerges beyond a group of servers on which applications are deployed. Collaboration and unified communications have taken enterprises by storm. Applications are being deployed on private, public, and hybrid clouds. Enterprise mobility is a central theme in most IT departments. Distributed storage solutions and software-defined networking have influenced fundamental shifts to how we approach infrastructure design, provisioning, and management. It is finally time for the traditional view of EA layers to transform and manage modern application portfolios effectively and more efficiently.

Solution Architecture

Solution architecture characterizes and defines a specific solution to a set of business requirements. Solution architecture should not to be confused with enterprise architecture, although the two are closely related. Solution architecture combines all four of the architectural layers—business architecture, application architecture, information architecture, and technical architecture—into a single structure by identifying specific components in each of the layers necessary to meet the scope and business requirements of the solution.

The focus of solution architecture is as follows:

- To build or enhance applications to meet the functional requirements

- To understand the details of the business processes and the subprocesses that are impacted by the application

- To design the information model, data flow, and data transformations necessary

- To define the technology components needed to build the application functionality

- To ensure that the final solution design will meet all nonfunctional requirements

You are probably wondering why we introduced yet another architecture at this juncture? Haven't we already analyzed four separate architectural layers? How is this one different? Solution architecture operates at a tactical level in the context of a specific business solution, whereas the EA is more strategic and does not focus on a specific business solution. The roles within enterprise IT have evolved to feature a solution architect who associates with a particular implementation or project. Only as we get deep down into a solution architecture can we begin to understand the specific functional and technical components that must be implemented for that business application. So there is a direct relationship between the solution architecture and the functional and technical decomposition of an application and the application mappings to the functional and technical components. Architecture decomposition is addressed in more detail in the next section of this chapter.

Depending on the scope of the solution and which business areas will be impacted, the key solution architecture stakeholders include business owners, process owners, and application owners who are responsible for ensuring that the solution is built, deployed, and maintained. We covered business and technical architecture layers earlier in the chapter; here we will describe the application architecture and information architecture layers that are relevant to the context of solution architecture.

Figure 4-8 shows how the application and information architecture layers are related to the architectural layers from an APM perspective, as was discussed earlier in this chapter. When we view the architecture stack from this vantage point, information architecture spans the business and functional architecture layers, whereas application architecture spans the functional and technical architectural layers. As we go down the architecture stack, it becomes highly technical, and as we go up toward the business architecture layer, the focus completely shifts to business processes and business capabilities. The solution architecture can be viewed as a contained framework, focusing on a particular set of business requirements and business capabilities. On the other hand, an EA stack takes a holistic view of the enterprise, focusing on best practices and industry standards that the enterprise should adopt. In the end, it is important to note that solution architectures need to be compliant within the framework and best practices established by EA.

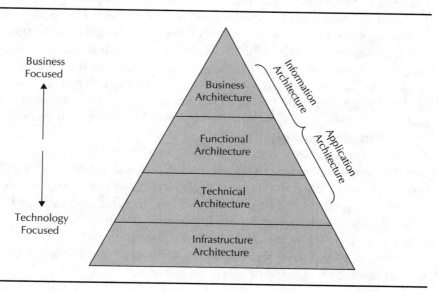

FIGURE 4-8.   *The relationship of application architecture and information architecture layers to the APM view of the architectural layers*

Application Architecture

The application architecture describes the structure, design, workings, and functionality of an application to support a set of business requirements. This architectural layer also describes how applications interact with one another, what databases and third-party components are accessed, any messages that need to be sent, and how the applications are built leveraging the technical components.

Applications are the central focus of the application architecture. An application portfolio will contain several applications, related in some fashion, by either a line of business, a specific business process, or a technology stack.

Projects and budgets are typically allocated to support, enhance, and maintain existing applications or to build new applications. This has compelled EA to focus heavily on the application layer. Most software development life-cycle processes are designed to build, test, release, and support applications. There has been a steady paradigm shift in the base definition of an application. The past few years have seen the evolution of loosely coupled services that orchestrate to support a business capability. An application boundary can be established to state that a set of related business functionalities, supported by the creation of business logic, will be called an application. The application can comprise select services, some of which may be used by other applications. Hence, the traditional definition of an application architecture layer within the EA stratum needs to be revisited, at least in the context of application portfolio analysis.

As organizations strive to reuse business functionalities exposed via services, applications will need to be analyzed with the view to componentize the functionality encapsulated by an application logically so that hidden services within the application logic can be identified and eventually reused. The analysis will also reveal an understanding of the technical components that are used by the application. Hence, application architecture spans the functional and technical architecture layers in our view of the EA layers, as geared toward an application portfolio analysis.

Information Architecture

In the 1960s and 1970s, IT and computer systems basically represented what we refer to as *information technology* and *information systems* today. During the 1990s, the emergence of the Internet and the World Wide Web changed the view and the scope of information architecture. With the advent of big data tools and the eruption of social data, public data, and end user data generated by transactions with enterprises, information architecture has become a complex field. The proliferation of media has resulted in images, videos, and sound files being created in copious amounts, adding to information complexity and proliferation.

Information architecture, previously called data architecture, is interpreted quite broadly today in the context of the EA layers. Some of the elements of information architecture in a broad interpretation include the following:

- Data flows
- Inputs and outputs of process elements
- Data in databases
- Content in content management systems
- Message formats
- Data formats
- Data transformations
- Taxonomies
- Ontologies
- Business rules
- Reports
- Documentation
- Canonical data models
- Entities and entity relationships
- Schemas
- Master data management

Information architecture spans and supports the business and functional architecture layers in our view of the EA layers, as geared toward application portfolio analysis.

Architecture Decomposition

Architecture decomposition is the process of individually deconstructing the EA, and all its architecture layers, into their constituent pieces. We have seen the TOGAF model for EA that embodies four distinct layers—business architecture, application architecture, data architecture, and technology architecture. With respect to our approach to modernization of IT systems and APM, the four layers of EA should be viewed from an architectural perspective—namely, business architecture, functional architecture, technical architecture, and infrastructure architecture.

Each layer could be further dissected into tiers or sublayers. For example, the technical architecture layer could be broadly categorized into four tiers:

- Presentation
- Business services
- Integration
- Information services

This tiered representation provides a way to organize the technical components. You might notice that integration occurs between components in all the tiers, but the adapters and integration-related components are conceptually associated with the integration tier.

The business architecture layer could be composed of level 1 process descriptions to communicate the processes at a high level. In addition, this layer could also provide a drill-down of the same processes at a more detailed level 2 and level 3 understanding. The functional architecture layer could be composed of very high-level descriptions of functional components, also called logical components, which encapsulate business functionality to support the business processes. Those high-level functional components can be examined at a more granular level, represented by lower level functional components that collectively make up the higher level functional component. The level of granularity would depend on the abstraction at which the functionality needs to be understood.

The infrastructure layer can be composed of the bare-metal hardware, virtualization layers, management and monitoring layers, networking layer, cloud fabric, and the like, to address the resource needs of the components in the other layers.

The specific components that make up a particular layer are not a tangible physical asset or block of code running on a particular server. The components are conceptual for the purpose of abstracting their functional or technical nature. It is not that these components are running on one physical server. In fact, the underlying blocks of code that execute to provide the functionality of a component are most likely distributed across application boundaries and across server boundaries. That same block of code could be running on multiple virtual machines and could be used by multiple applications.

The layers provide the abstractions to demarcate the following: what is relevant to the business to meet business objectives, what is relevant to understanding the business functionality, what is relevant to the technical software components and frameworks necessary to build the business functionality, and where and how all these will ultimately execute. The act of representing EA in a layered manner is itself a decomposition of sorts. Further decomposition of each individual layer into tiers and sublayers enables us to decouple self-contained and modular units of that particular layer for further analysis in the context of the application portfolio, to show us the relationship of that modular unit to the functioning and existence of an application.

If we assume that we can identify modular units representing a level of acceptable granularity for each of the architecture layers and its sublayers, then the modernization of IT systems boils down to the modernization of the modular units themselves. The application portfolio then essentially becomes a collection of these modular units working together to form an application. The modular unit can be a part of a business process, a granular functional component providing some business functionality, a technical component or service, or some representation of a piece of the infrastructure. The purpose of architecture decomposition is to understand the following:

- Similar occurrences of a modular unit in multiple places within the application portfolio

- The point of coupling between the modular units

- The level of cohesion and integration between the modular units

- The functionality contained within a modular unit

- The cost of operating the modular unit

- Frequency of change or enhancements introduced

- Skills needed to maintain and support a modular unit

The most difficult piece of information to collect from this list is the cost of operating the modular unit. Project costs and budgets are usually managed at the level of the application. One would have to collect application-level finance and operational data to interpolate and extrapolate data points to arrive at cost calculations of high-level components or lower level modular units within the architecture layers. In most cases, however, it is sufficient to develop an understanding of cost looking at the higher level components within the architecture layers.

Architecture decomposition is an extremely valuable evaluation in the context of mergers and acquisitions (M&A). When two enterprises desire to merge and consolidate their IT systems, a thorough understanding of the application portfolio and decomposition of the architecture into its constituents at a granular level are vital to the analysis. This exercise will uncomplicate the decision of how to integrate the applications and even identify which applications should be discarded as redundant or nonessential.

Functional Decomposition

Functional decomposition breaks down the functional architecture layer into a set of high-level blocks that describe the line of business or the business area that is supported. At this level of decomposition, the understanding of the business functionality will be at a high level. There will be little knowledge of which applications provide valuable business functionality. Typically, groups of applications that provide that business functionality will be identified. The decomposition of that first level of identification into the next level will result in a more granular understanding of the business functionality for that business area or line of business.

In our example of the rail and dray business area, the first level of decomposition of the functional architecture layer gives rise to the next level of granularity. For illustration purposes, further decomposition would reveal that rail and dray is additionally composed of the following:

- Line haul
- Rail billing
- Drayage
- Rail planning

- Purchasing

- Routing

- Shipping order

As a natural evolution of IT systems over the past couple of decades, these functional components, identified as logical components that make up the functional architecture, are implemented in more than one part of the application portfolio. Several distinct business units might have a need for similar functionality over time. As is the case with most companies, the business units build an application or enhance one of their existing applications to provide the functionality they need within the budgets they have. Where APM is not an established discipline and where EA does not closely integrate with APM, PPM, and IRM, there is a proliferation of similar pieces of business functionality throughout the application portfolio. In an ideal world, before building any new business functionality, we would investigate whether such functionality exists elsewhere within the enterprise to leverage those components.

The dynamics of modern enterprises do not easily lend themselves to such reuse, especially considering how applications are conceived, designed, built, and deployed without a functional knowledge of other applications within the portfolio. To illustrate this further, a particular business unit may require additional functionality for its application. Before such an undertaking, there are integral questions to ask: Who will take the responsibility of enhancing the existing functional component with this additional functionality? Who will test it? Who will provide support for the application? Who will assist the business unit with additional enhancements over time? In most organizations, no one person or group ever proactively steps up to offer their services and, as a result, each business unit ultimately decides to build and own the particular applications that it currently lacks.

There have been attempts to provide functional components centrally. It has mostly resulted in partial success. Enterprises have been more successful in providing technical components, frameworks, and libraries centrally with reuse in mind. EA and governance has also seen success in the enforcement and adoption of common technical components and frameworks within the enterprise. I have been a part of building such service platforms and I have led and participated in several decomposition exercises to develop an understanding of application portfolios to eliminate redundancies and promote reuse.

With the advent of service-oriented architectures and services platforms, the enterprise landscape is beginning to see a significant transformation. We will visit this topic in more detail in Chapters 10 and 11 of this book.

Technical Decomposition

Technical decomposition breaks down the technical architecture layer into a set of high-level technical components. These components support building the application functionality represented by the functional components identified in the functional architecture layer. The relationship between the technical and functional components is many-to-many and can be easily represented by a matrix. Since most enterprises view IT systems from a technical viewpoint, it is far easier to understand which applications are built leveraging particular technical components. High-level technical design and description of technical components are typically available and documented within an enterprise. Although mapping and reuse of technical components may not be available, that aspect can be created as part of the assessment phase during the initial application portfolio analysis.

To explain technical decomposition further, we represent the technical architecture layer as a multi-tiered architecture composed of the following:

- Presentation
- Business services
- Integration
- Information services

Presentation Tier

The presentation tier represents the user interfaces; user experience; content; personalization; views; rendering for various form factors and devices; repurposing content; interfacing and user interaction with mobile, web, and wearable devices; user session management; and services used at the business services tier.

Business Services Tier

The business services tier can also be referred to as the application services tier. This tier contains business logic within applications or exposed as business services for consumption by a variety of consumers. Some typical examples of high-level technical components existing in the business and applications services tier include these:

- Business rules engine
- Workflow component
- Analytics services
- Legacy wrappers
- OLAP servers
- Application servers
- Document management

This is just a sample of the high-level components. These components can be further deconstructed into specific technical components. Custom and third-party frameworks and library components are also represented in this business services tier of the technical architecture layer. Some examples of such framework components include these:

- Logging and tracing
- Alert notifications
- User profile management
- Security and encryption services
- Systems management utilities
- Data persistence components
- Business exception management

Again, this list is just a representative sample. The data persistence components could be considered as a business service or, in some architectures, could reside at the information services tier. It is a matter of convenience and preference for how this component is viewed. The business services tier is incredibly dense with rich data to be leveraged by the specific needs of an enterprise.

Integration Tier

The integration tier is responsible for all the integration needs of an application. The business services tier contains all the business logic to realize the functionality of an application. To perform, business services need to access enterprise information systems such as databases, content, repositories, third-party components, and the like. This operation is achieved through the integration tier, which essentially consists of message-oriented middleware, enterprise service bus, adapters to access other systems, and any proprietary integration technology necessitated by third-party technical components. A representative sample of the technical components and framework components in the integration tier includes the following:

- Transport layer
- Messaging layer
- Content routing
- Legacy adapters
- Adapters to enterprise resource planning (ERP) systems
- Business activity monitoring
- Business process management
- JCA components

Information Services Tier

The information services tier abstracts access to enterprise information systems. This tier is not to be confused with the data (information) architecture layer as defined by TOGAF in its model for EA. The enterprise information services tier is the backbone of an enterprise. It is closely intertwined with business processes, since data and process are interrelated functions. There is an overlap of the information services tier with the representation of the information architecture layer and its sublayers. The main thing to note is that, as part of the information services tier, the focus is on the technical nature of the services—namely, how the data is exposed to other systems and how the data is stored and managed from a technical point of view. The focus is also on the actual technical software used to store, manage, and expose the data. A representative sample of the technical components and framework components in the information services tier include the following:

- Operational data stores

- Relational databases such as Oracle databases

- NoSQL databases such as Mongo, Aerospike, and Cassandra

- Data warehouses

- Mainframe systems

- ERP and customer relationship management (CRM) systems

- ETL (extract, transform, and load) processes

- Financial systems

- Human resources systems

- Master data management software

- Custom services and queries for extracting data

For this analysis, we have included CRM, financial, and HR systems in the information services tier. These systems are leveraged by many other systems for the information they contain and manage; these systems, by themselves, are end-to-end. Some viewpoints might classify these systems within the business services tier; either way, it is more a matter of convenience rather than a functional categorization.

In general, enterprise software that houses valuable enterprise data falls under the information services tier. The actual data center in which they are housed is part of the infrastructure layer. Additionally, the definition of entities, data and message formats, the flow of data between the nodes of the processes and workflows, schema definitions, policies, and the information fabric itself all fall within the information architecture layer.

Technology Redundancy
The technical architecture layer carries a lot of importance within IT departments. The roles such as business analyst, functional analyst, domain

architect, business architect, and subject matter expert tend to focus on the functional components, functional requirements, business requirements, business capabilities, and business processes within an organization. Typical technical roles such as developer, technical lead, and IT manager engage with various technologies, libraries, technology platforms, third-party software, and tools to build applications to meet expected functional requirements. These roles typically focus more on the application functionality to be built using the technical components at their disposal rather than focusing on the understanding of business capabilities and functional components.

The technical architecture layer is also where typical IT budgets are consumed to build or buy additional technology components and third-party vendor software without attracting a lot of attention—especially from the business folks who authorize the budget or the senior IT managers focused on delivering the functionality to their business counterparts. Since everyone collectively wants to deliver the business functionality, if the technical roles demand the procurement of certain technology components, more often than not, it will happen. With several enterprise-grade open-source components available today, there has been a proliferation of these components, sometimes with redundant functionalities, being adopted by an enterprise; this is primarily due to familiarity or preferences of a team for one component over the other. Eventually, enterprises are left maintaining and managing multiple technology components with similar or overlapping functionalities used by different applications.

Figure 4-9 shows a matrix that maps functional components to technical components within our conceptual functional and technical architectural layers. This mapping illustrates which technical components are needed to support a particular functional component and realize that functionality. For example, almost all functional components shown at the level of granularity in this figure require some form of reporting. What is not clear from this matrix in Figure 4-9 is whether the reporting component depicted here for various functional components is the same third-party reporting software or something else.

It is natural that over time, an enterprise will accumulate a group of technologies, many with redundant capabilities. To illustrate this point, we can use a reporting component example. Operational reporting can be employed by multiple applications, as shown in the mapping in Figure 4-6. Upon further

Technical Components

Logical Components		TC1 Reporting/BI/DWH	TC2 EDI	TC3 Mobility Services	TC4 Alert Notification	TC5 Document Management*	TC6 Data Transformation - ETL	TC7 Work Flow	TC8 Fax Server	TC9 Email Server	TC10 IVR	TC11 Enterprise Service Bus (Messaging bus)	TC12 Rules Engine	TC13 Imaging*	TC14 User Interactions	TC15 Error Corrections	TC16 Content Management	TC17 Portal Services	TC18 Persistence	TC19 Profile Management	TC20 System Management	TC21 Security
LC1	Logistics	✓						✓				✓			✓	✓			✓	✓	✓	✓
LC2	Business Management																					
LC2.1	Sales	✓		✓		✓						✓		✓	✓	✓		✓	✓	✓		✓
LC2.2	Marketing	✓			✓							✓			✓	✓	✓		✓	✓	✓	✓
LC2.3	Pricing	✓	✓		✓							✓	✓		✓	✓	✓		✓	✓	✓	✓
LC3	Customer Service	✓	✓		✓				✓	✓	✓	✓		✓	✓	✓			✓	✓		✓
LC4	Rail & Dray	✓	✓									✓			✓	✓			✓	✓	✓	✓
LC4.1	Rail Planning	✓	✓						✓			✓	✓		✓	✓			✓	✓	✓	✓
LC4.2	Shipping Order (Rail-Billing)											✓			✓	✓			✓	✓	✓	✓
LC4.3	Line Haul	✓										✓			✓	✓			✓	✓		✓
LC4.4	Transportation Purchasing	✓	✓									✓			✓	✓			✓	✓	✓	✓
LC4.5	Drayage	✓	✓		✓							✓			✓	✓			✓	✓	✓	✓
LC6	Equipment Management	✓										✓			✓	✓			✓	✓		✓
LC6.1	Equipment - Fleet Management				✓	✓						✓		✓	✓	✓			✓	✓	✓	✓
LC6.2	Equipment - Fleet Planning & Control	✓							✓			✓			✓	✓			✓	✓	✓	✓
LC6.3	Equipment - Reservations											✓			✓	✓			✓	✓		✓
LC6.4	Equipment Maintenance & Repair	✓					✓					✓		✓	✓	✓			✓	✓	✓	✓
LC6.5	Rail Car Asset Group	✓			✓		✓					✓			✓	✓			✓	✓	✓	✓
LC6.6	Per Diem	✓			✓		✓					✓			✓	✓			✓	✓		✓
LC7	Finance	✓																				
LC7.1	Payables	✓				✓	✓					✓	✓	✓	✓	✓			✓	✓	✓	✓
LC7.2	Receivables	✓				✓	✓					✓	✓	✓	✓	✓			✓	✓	✓	✓
LC8	Ocean Carrier Service (OCS)	✓					✓					✓			✓	✓		✓	✓	✓	✓	✓

FIGURE 4-9. Architecture decomposition and mapping functional components to technical components

analysis, we would discover that reporting is accomplished by eight different reporting technologies:

- Holos
- Crystal Reports
- Web focus
- Hyperion
- Excel reports
- Visual Basic reports
- Pentaho
- Custom SQL queries

It is quite conceivable that all of these reporting technologies are very important to the enterprise. However, in reality, it is more likely that one business group prefers a particular reporting technology over another one. Decisions to purchase technology components must be rooted in deliberate analysis rather than happenstance. If not, the necessary checks and balances to justify project spending will wither away to make way for wasteful corporate spending.

Future State Architecture

In the quest to transform and modernize portfolio applications, one of the key activities performed is the identification of the current-state architectural portfolio and the future-state architectural components to be acquired. This exercise enables an organization to determine a baseline for the application portfolio, with respect to the business objectives that need to be met and the business and technical capabilities that need to be acquired for the strength of the portfolio. EA is an integral part of this process, which works interdependently with APM to envision, create, and achieve the future-state architecture. The details of the EA discipline and the creation of the future-state architecture is beyond the scope of this book and could be a few chapters in and of itself. Hence, we will just touch upon a few key pertinent points in this section.

The development of the future-state architecture for an enterprise is a complex and detailed exercise that results in the identification of numerous gaps between the as-is state and the to-be state an enterprise wants to achieve. This is known as the *gap analysis*. After the gaps are identified, a root cause analysis will reveal the fundamental pain points that have resulted because of these gaps. This analysis can be performed on any of the architectural layers that we have discussed in this chapter. The inquiry is not limited to any one particular architecture.

Once the gaps are identified and the root causes are understood, the various architectural layers will need to be constructed to address those gaps. In the process, existing capabilities within each of those architectural layers will be used. This is not a "from the ground up, clean slate" building of the architectural layers. Rather, it leverages existing components in each layer and determines whether any of the components can be enhanced or modified to mitigate the gaps. Sometimes new capabilities are built that cannot leverage existing components. In those cases, capabilities will be built from scratch as part of the identified initiatives. This gap analysis, coupled with a leverage analysis, will provide a clear picture of capabilities that need to be acquired to modernize the existing application portfolio.

In conjunction with the EA team, the APM team will build a roadmap to achieve the capabilities to remediate the gaps. There will also be input from the PPM and IRM peer disciplines. Typically, these capabilities are not built in a "big bang" approach. It is a methodical process that accounts for several competing variables. There are several justifications for this:

- All capabilities may not be equally important.

- Resources needed to build the capabilities will not be sufficient.

- Budgets may not be able to address all capabilities.

- The business value of some of the capabilities may be more than others.

- Some capabilities may be low hanging fruit that can be achieved with minimal effort.

There could be many other reasons depending on the circumstances and the organization. At this point, a prioritization exercise would need to be conducted to rank the business capabilities to ensure optimal use of available resources, budgets, and time to market, to maximize business value.

Necessary technical capabilities to support the business capabilities can either be built or procured from a vendor. This process of identifying the future-state architectural components is visually depicted in Figure 4-10. It is a three-step process:

1. Envision

2. Analyze

3. Decide

During the envision step, a gap analysis is conducted between the existing, as-is architecture and the future-state, to-be architecture. Participation in a series of workshop-driven stakeholder meetings can successfully identify the desired set of business capabilities for this gap analysis. Business drivers are then mapped to business capabilities that need to be built. The business value of each business capability is articulated. Technical gaps and pain points are addressed by identifying technical capabilities that also need to be built.

During the analyze step, the desired business and technical capabilities identified during the envision step are created and customized as part of this framework. Future-state, to-be processes for functional and technical architectures are also rationalized based on the gap analysis from the envision step. Functional and technical decomposition exercises are applied and mapped to identify redundancies, and these findings are input into the to-be, future-state architecture visualization process.

Finally, during the decide step, the prioritized list of business and technical capabilities are mapped to specific business and technical architectures. The architectural components are justified in the context of business drivers. The prioritized capabilities form multiple scenarios that need to be analyzed. Chapter 5 will discuss this process in more detail.

Business Capabilities Prioritization

Prioritizing business capabilities starts with identifying a list of desired business capabilities that need to be acquired by the application portfolio to meet the future business needs of the enterprise. Gap analysis and root cause analysis lead to a better understanding of the current business architecture and the other architectural layers. Business unit stakeholders and domain architects should collectively identify the missing business capabilities in the

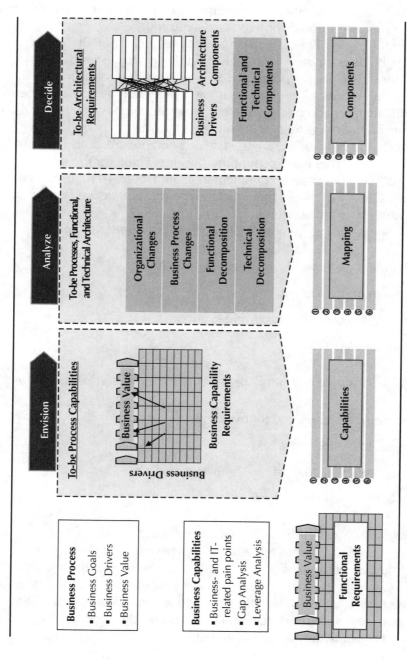

FIGURE 4-10. *Process to identify future state architecture components*

existing portfolio. To reach the to-be, future-state architecture, these business capabilities will need to be prioritized and acquired.

Given budgetary challenges and organizational risks, not all desired business capabilities can be immediately built. Even shortlisted business capabilities should be prioritized to provide a full understanding prior to the build phase. The prioritization of business capabilities can be accomplished via the "envision, analyze, and decide" methodology, encompassing the creation of future-state architecture. In fact, the business capabilities prioritization exercise rests at the heart of the future-state architecture creation. This simple analysis framework takes into account the business value for the desired business capability and its ease of implementation. Figure 4-11 illustrates a simple prioritization framework that ultimately results in a defined roadmap to create the future state architecture.

Here are some sample parameters to score the business value:

- Alignment to a specific business objective

- Increase of productivity

- Measurable benefits to top-line growth

- Quantifiable savings

Similarly, here are some sample parameters for ease of implementation:

- Technology complexity for building this capability

- Impact to business process

- Ability to leverage existing components

- Impact to end user and retraining

We could also weight the scoring factors by using a scale of 1–4 to compare the business value to the ease of implementation. Plotting this data for all desired business capabilities will result in the identification of capabilities with high business value and easy implementation. Once this objective analysis framework has been applied to the business capabilities, and relevant stakeholders have ratified the decisions, the process will yield a prioritized list of verified business capabilities.

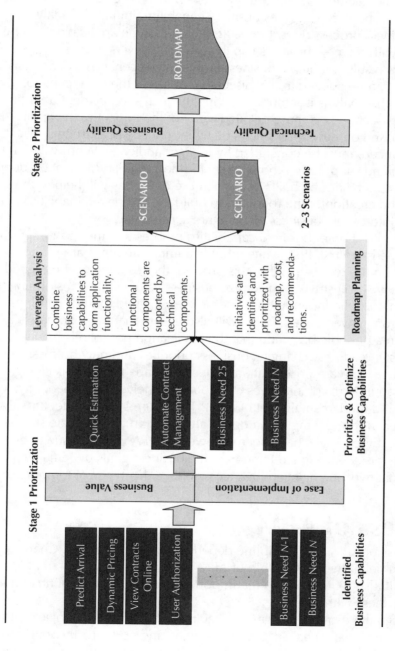

FIGURE 4-11. *Business capabilities prioritization*

During the decide step, several questions may emerge during stakeholder workshops. Where exactly does business capability fit in to the analysis? Which business process does it impact? Which existing application can be enhanced with the new business capability? The answers to these types of questions result in multiple business architecture scenarios. An analysis framework can be applied to this discussion to select the best scenario. Sometimes the analysis is informal, leaving the teams to decide. Other times, for complex scenarios, a more detailed study of the impact to the application portfolio, based on new applications being introduced or existing applications being enhanced, must be concluded by a larger audience. Who will own the application and support it? Who will pay for the capability? In what sequence should the capabilities be built? Some of these questions will help in the planning and creation of the roadmap to build the business capabilities and create the future-state business architecture successfully.

The prioritization of business capabilities ensures that the most important business needs are met first, while other less important ones are pushed farther out on the roadmap. After this process, the resulting well-designed set of initiatives will strive to maximize business value while transforming the application portfolio into one that is completely aligned to future business goals. A strong governance process will also ensure that the roadmap is revisited on a periodic basis and that the application portfolio is managed continuously to address changing business priorities and new business needs. This could result in a reprioritization of business capabilities, thus changing the roadmap in terms of initiatives that could be shelved, modified, or newly built. This is a fundamental tenet of APM. The future-state architecture always starts with a vision looking forward; it is always in an intermediate state of realization. If these steps have been followed, the EA will continue to evolve in the right direction, aligned to address the business goals by remaining flexible, adaptive, and agile enough to undertake the needs of tomorrow.

Success of APM

The success of APM as a discipline depends on several factors. Chapter 3 covered in detail the relationship of APM to its peer disciplines of PPM and IRM. It also touched upon the importance of the EA discipline and its interrelatedness with APM.

Although there are challenges to establishing APM methodologies within an enterprise, the greater challenge is in sustaining and nurturing the longevity of the APM discipline. In fact, a prerequisite to a successful APM practice within an enterprise is the success of the EA discipline. A successful EA discipline safeguards that the necessary maturity and thought processes are already equipped to welcome APM. It also ensures that stakeholders are capable of aligning IT systems to business capabilities using principles of project governance and industry best practices.

The acceptance of APM is important to establishing successful modernization and transformation programs within an organization. One cannot have collaborative modernization as a standalone strategy. Successful modernization of IT systems depends upon a comprehensive and detailed understanding of the application portfolio at the granular level.

Successful APM with EA

Successfully sustaining APM largely depends on the success of the EA discipline. Although short-term success can be achieved by narrowly looking at the infrastructure architecture, at the consolidation techniques applied to that layer, or at the subset of applications to rationalize a portfolio, that is not enough. To reap the full benefits of APM, an organization must be able to optimize cost, mitigate risk, eliminate redundancies, modernize and transform business and IT, and enhance future investments in the application portfolio. Long-term advancement of APM is dependent upon an organization having a vision for its business architecture. To sustain APM, an organization must have an established EA discipline. The EA provides a blueprint for the enterprise to realize and align strategic business objectives to future programs on the roadmap. The EA discipline also involves a tactical execution of programs, influencing the prioritization of future business and technical capabilities integral to achieving the business vision.

EA Stakeholders and APM Stakeholders

The stakeholders for EA are varied and come from all parts of an organization. The stakeholder groups span project teams, senior business executives, senior technology executives, developers, operations and support, partners, customers, end users, internal business departments, and the like. It is also possible that the individual stakeholders may belong to more than one stakeholder group. Some of the legacy groups may be permanent, established as part of the formal organizational structure, while other teams may be temporary, informally created as a special interest group in the context of a specific program. Stakeholders in informal groups cannot be ignored, since they may be subject matter experts or may wield power and influence over some of the stakeholders in the formal organizational group.

Individual stakeholders and stakeholder groups that are part of this sphere of influence are crucial to the endurance of APM and its modernization endeavors. Although each individual and stakeholder group has differing roles with respect to APM, their collective contributions are incredibly vital to its success within an enterprise.

For the APM discipline to succeed within an enterprise, it is extremely important that the core APM group identify the key stakeholders relevant to APM and engage them using active stakeholder management principles. The APM core group is tasked with identifying the key stakeholders not only by role but also by name; they must engage and meet with them in order to get their perspective and feedback on key events. A compelling APM value proposition and benefits analysis must be conducted by the relevant collaborators, including sponsors, executives, supporters, and opponents, in order to understand the dynamics of the stakeholders and their positions with respect to APM. As APM evolves as a discipline, its application to achieve business objectives is contingent upon garnering the support of these key stakeholders and requiring their continuous, active engagement throughout the entire life cycle of the application portfolio.

Roles in the Organization

Table 4-1 captures a subset of the typical roles in an organization that support applications within the enterprise portfolio.

Sustaining APM Through the EA Discipline

The positive influence of the EA discipline upon APM ensures that APM can be sustained. Some of the EA stakeholders will likely be part of the core APM group as well. For the long-term success of APM, involvement of EA in the following aspects of APM is a priority:

- Identifying the portfolio

- Creating APM governance

- Creating well-defined APM processes

- Using tools to implement and execute the APM processes

- Defining APM metrics

- Analyzing and prioritizing frameworks

Role	Description
Senior executive / business leader	Sponsors the initiative and is part of the steering committee guiding the process. Approves funding and scope.
Application portfolio owner	Owns the portfolio and is part of the steering committee. Provides leadership and guidance.
Enterprise architect	Defines the business and functional architecture. Influences decisions and reviews deliverables. Ensures alignment to business objectives. Member of architecture governance.
Application owner	Owns one or more applications and is a key contributor to all engagements that impact applications owned.
Business analyst	Gathers and analyzes data. Owns some of the business processes and business capabilities. Understands the functionality of the applications and contributes to the business architecture and functional architecture.
IT manager	Manages projects and development of applications. Contributes to various engagements.
Technical architect (application architect)	Defines the technical architecture and application architecture.
Business user (application end user)	Uses the applications and also requests enhancements and additional functionality. Requests can result in the identification of business capabilities that need to be acquired.
Maintenance and support engineer	Supports applications, technical components, and infrastructure. Responsible for bug fixing and general application maintenance and support.
Financial analyst / risk analyst	Recommends investment decisions and understands costs and budgets. Part of risk assessment and risk mitigation.
System administrator	Administers various system components. Has ownership of infrastructure and supports the technical team.

TABLE 4-1.   *Typical Roles in an Enterprise Supporting APM*

As the EA discipline attains maturity within an organization, it will provide a visualization of the future, to-be state necessary to meet business objectives. This future-state architecture captures the expected business and technical capabilities that need to be acquired by the business. This has a direct effect in the application portfolio and influences its direction and evolution. EA aligns APM to the business needs for the development of a comprehensive roadmap. EA is also closely intertwined with the APM, PPM, and IRM disciplines to estimate budgets, identify and mitigate architectural risks, and participate in the governance of identified and approved programs.

EA is a natural partner to APM. APM focuses on reducing and optimizing overall costs incurred in operating an application portfolio. EA participates in budget planning exercises and identifies applications that are operating suboptimally, from both a business and a technical perspective. This exercise will naturally lend itself to eliminating poorly performing applications from the portfolio.

EA and APM Interaction

EA and APM are joined at the hip. The stakeholders from both disciplines interact with other common collaborators. To benefit from EA and APM, and to ensure the realization of enterprise business value, one must adhere to a few simple principles. The advancement of both disciplines relies on clear communication to all relevant parties and the capturing of organizational benefits to be shared with company executives.

Guiding Principles for EA and APM Interaction

Although EA and APM can be viewed as complementary disciplines that share similar stakeholders and budgetary resources, some guiding principles are imperative for their interaction to function efficiently without clashing. These assumptions will warrant that EA and APM can function in their own right and unite in alignment:

- All the recommendations made in the context of a strategic engagement, and the scope of such recommendations, should map back to specific enterprise objectives, and both the EA and APM processes must be aligned with respect to those recommendations.

- All key APM decisions that result in initiatives should be supported by a high-level roadmap and business case to justify the initiatives identified in the roadmap. EA should be a part of the roadmap definition and business case justification.

- All recommendations and roadmap definitions must identify quick wins to ensure that the journey to the roadmap realization begins smoothly with fewer roadblocks. EA should be closely involved in launching pilots for the execution of the quick wins identified.

- The suggested roadmap and the duration of the roadmap should take into account business risks, business outcomes, culture, change management, and the speed of change.

- If a rationalization exercise is conducted, EA should be a close part of such portfolio rationalization initiatives. APM and EA disciplines should look to create self-funding opportunities from cost-saving portfolio rationalization exercises.

Benefits of EA

Although the focus is on APM and its impact on driving enterprise modernization, EA does merit a detailed discussion because of the dependence of APM on EA for its success. EA contributes directly to the business objectives by deriving and participating in business strategy to IT strategy alignment. EA also contributes indirectly to the enterprise by participating in APM and its peer disciplines. Some of the observed benefits include the following:

- Support of EA to APM peer disciplines assists with investment decisions, risk mitigation, investment support, and risk management, influencing decisions at the program and program portfolio levels by supporting PPM initiatives.

- Resource prioritization includes people, budgets, and IT system resources.

- Solution architecture and project management activities are provided by enterprise architects. These architects facilitate decision-making, determine the scope of the project, collaborate between the solution and project team members, and build consensus among project stakeholders. They also participate in the creation and review of quality deliverables.

- During M&A activities, architectural layers can be impacted, requiring the consolidation of application portfolios. EA plays an important role in M&A.

- Enterprise architects are the stewards of standards and best practices. It is difficult to enforce such practices by control. Enterprise architects wield considerable clout and influence the adoption of such standards and best practices across the enterprise.

- Risk management and investment decisions in the application portfolio are critical to increasing business value to the enterprise. EA plays a central role in this process.

Summary

For the APM discipline to be successful, interdependence with the mature processes of the EA discipline is necessary. There are several ways to institutionalize EA. A popular and comprehensive standard for defining EA is TOGAF. Although TOGAF meets a specific need, we must also consider the APM-centric view of the architectural layers to carry out successful modernization and management of an application portfolio.

Architectural decomposition is a technique used to dissect and deconstruct each architectural layer into its constituent components. Solution architecture is a tactical realization of the EA in the context of a specific set of business processes and requirements. It provides a way to understand the process and the functional and technical details of an application, and it assists with decomposition efforts.

Within an application portfolio are possible redundancies in functional and technical components used by different applications. Modernizing an application portfolio will involve envisioning a future-state architecture. Several stakeholders in EA are also potential stakeholders for APM. EA also assists APM in the prioritization of business and technical capabilities by providing input into the creation of such analysis and prioritization frameworks and by applying those frameworks to identify prioritized business capabilities and technical capabilities to meet future, to-be state architectural needs.

CHAPTER
5

Legacy Java
Modernization

Enterprises that have weathered the recessions of the past two decades have discovered the power of leveraging information technology systems to enable and advance their business interests. The longer a company has been in existence, the more heterogeneous its information technology systems tend to be. Since the advent of Java, almost all medium-size and large enterprises have built systems based on the Java platform as part of their information technology landscape. Once a Java application has been built and introduced to the business, it does not stop there. The application will need enhancement from time to time based on new business requirements, and it will also need to integrate and interoperate with other applications.

The consideration of budgetary allowances for new functionality requirements is not enough. Decision-makers must consider several aspects before an application is built or procured for the portfolio. If portfolio determinations are made in a silo, without informed awareness of any other duplicative or obsolete applications, the process is flawed. This results in application portfolios that are varied, complex, and poorly optimized with regard to operations, cost, business risk, technical quality, and future investment decisions. Even in the case of application portfolios that are predominantly based on Java technologies, the applications span a variety of JDK versions, third-party components, open-source components, and other libraries. This leads to a situation in which the application portfolio becomes a legacy that starts to tax the efforts of the IT department to keep things functioning at status quo.

This chapter explores legacy application portfolios and discusses various approaches to addressing the quintessential issues. Chapter 4 reviewed the concepts of architecture decomposition and the functional and technical components that make up the application portfolio. Based on this knowledge, organizations will be equipped to make informed decisions to refresh legacy portfolios and position themselves to optimize their investments and reduce complexity in terms of operations and integration.

Modernization of an application portfolio is a holistic exercise, not just an activity restricted to the application layer and the application code. Modernization occurs across all architecture layers. Figure 5-1 depicts the high-level process flow with respect to modernization decision-making and shows a sample of modernization options that exist within each architecture layer. In the figure, the architecture layers depicted show the TOGAF (The Open Group Architectural Framework) architecture model. (TOGAF and its architectural layers were discussed in Chapter 4.) This chapter will conduct a detailed examination of the application modernization options.

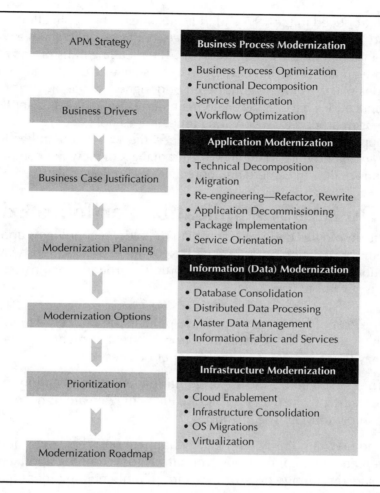

FIGURE 5-1. *Modernization across architecture layers*

Legacy Application Portfolios

Before we can discuss modernization options, we first need to define what constitutes a legacy application portfolio. Is it the type of technology used for implementing the applications, is it the age of the applications, or is it some other factor? Does a legacy application portfolio immediately imply obsolescence and the need for replacement? To answer these questions, you must understand the first use of the term. The concept of legacy applications was first introduced in the 1970s to indicate all existing applications. In the 1980s and 1990s, the word "legacy" underwent a semantic change with regard to information technology systems. The meaning transformed to imply those applications that have been in existence as compared to new applications that were being considered or designed. Since the era of Y2K, legacy applications have represented mainframe applications or applications that have been around for a very long time. It does not necessarily suggest that the application is out of date, but it does imply a level of inflexibility and unnecessary expense for maintenance and management when compared to applications built using emerging, more agile technologies.

Why Do Legacy Application Portfolios Exist?

If newer technologies perform better than the older technologies upon which some application portfolios are based, the real question is why do organizations keep legacy application portfolios around? The answer to that question is several-fold:

- The cost of replacing the legacy applications can be prohibitive and the return on investment (ROI) from the replacement applications may take too long to justify a proper business case.

- The perceived business risk of retiring legacy applications and replacing them with new applications may create unnecessary panic within an organization.

- End user familiarity with legacy applications, their opposition to replacement applications, and efforts for retraining application users discourage organizations from implementing ideas to replace legacy applications.

- Lack of documentation or deep knowledge of the functional workings of legacy applications prevents a detailed understanding of its business capabilities. These legacy applications function as a "black box," and organizations come to rely on them without knowing how they truly work.

- Legacy applications may perform effectively and may not be that critical to the organization. In this case, it may be best to keep operating the existing application as is.

- Contracts with existing vendors and infrastructure providers may not be easy to terminate, and organizations may have to wait three to five years to reconsider any modernization of the application portfolios. By that time, other priorities take over and new employees join the company or are promoted into other roles. With this new perspective, an organization may choose to renew existing contracts rather than pursue a large-scale endeavor to modernize the legacy portfolio.

Reasons to Modernize Legacy Application Portfolios

In several situations, a thorough business case analysis could indicate that opting for newer technologies can substantially reduce the total cost of ownership (TCO) of a legacy application portfolio. Although the cost of replacing an existing legacy application may be higher than the cost of maintenance, if the costs can be recouped within five years, this is worth considering.

Sometimes, the lack of resources and lack of skills for the legacy technology will pose business risks to an organization. What if no timely maintenance support is available? What if the resources supporting the application lack sufficient skill sets to maintain the technology? People who have taken over maintaining the legacy applications could inadvertently introduce system defects because they lack the deep knowledge of these applications, and the original authors may have moved on to other positions or may have left the company altogether. In the long run, the business risk posed by continuing to operate legacy applications might outweigh the additional cost of building replacement applications.

There is a constant discovery of security holes and vulnerabilities in technology platforms, libraries, and APIs. Without sufficient vendor support and community involvement, it is almost impossible to thwart the attacks that leverage such vulnerabilities. Newer versions of technologies and emerging technologies will have better support capabilities and patches for known threats and discovered vulnerabilities.

The effort and complexity of integrating older applications into newer ones may result in the rebuilding of similar functionalities in the consolidated application portfolio, leading to functional redundancies both within a portfolio and generally across all portfolio applications. This problem of inflexibility and lack of legacy application agility will prevent such applications from being leveraged by the newer application portfolios built within enterprises.

Although there are several reasons to modernize legacy application portfolios, it is important to note that these reasons apply not only to older mainframe applications, but also to Java applications, PHP applications, and Windows applications. Older applications, generally those eight to ten years old, suffer from symptoms that indicate they need to be modernized.

Enterprises should position themselves so that they can manage their application portfolios effectively and ensure that they modernize those applications at the right time. This is not an easy task. Modernization efforts need effective application portfolio management (APM) coupled with established enterprise architecture (EA) practices to transform application portfolios successfully.

Business Drivers

Any modernization efforts for existing legacy application portfolios must be supported by business drivers that validate and justify an organization's future direction and business strategy.

The reasons organizations seek modernization typically fall into a few broad categories:

- Reduce TCO
- Gain competitive advantage
- Identify and mitigate business risk
- Optimize investments
- Eliminate redundancies
- Innovate portfolio capabilities
- Increase agility and adaptability

The business drivers can be mapped to one or more of these seven broad categories. It is difficult for an organization to execute a business strategy and optimize a portfolio while simultaneously advancing all the seven levers. Typically, only one or two leading factors play a dominant role in the modernization exercise. The decision-making processes influencing legacy application portfolio modernization efforts are mainly guided by the business drivers that map to those dominant categories.

Modernization Options

Modernizing a portfolio consisting of legacy Java applications and other legacy applications can be complicated. The applications are closely connected and work together to support a set of business processes. Any modification to one application in the portfolio can set off a cascading effect. An approach involving architecture decomposition allows for a complete understanding of the functionality, business capabilities, and technical capabilities of the portfolio. Based on a complete portfolio analysis of the resulting business drivers, a set of recommendations can be derived regarding the necessary action items for each application in the portfolio.

Figure 5-2 depicts the key business drivers that influence portfolio modernization. The diagram also illustrates the typical prioritization parameters that are quantified and considered within the context of a portfolio analysis. The modernization options for applications in the portfolio are derived as an outcome of the detailed analysis. We have already discussed the details of APM and the analysis frameworks in previous chapters. The prioritization parameters shown in Figure 5-2 act as a summary of the total analysis framework.

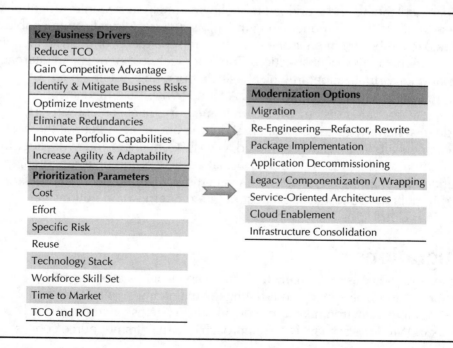

FIGURE 5-2.   *Arriving at modernization options*

There are several modernization options to consider prior to launching a modernization exercise: applications can be left untouched, migrated over to newer libraries, reengineered on the same technology platform used currently, reengineered to a completely different technology platform, eliminated from the portfolio through decommissioning, or replaced by a packaged off-the-shelf vendor product. As Figure 5-2 illustrates, legacy componentization, also known as legacy wrapping, and service-oriented architecture are two types of reengineering exercises. Infrastructure-related modernization options such as cloud enablement and infrastructure consolidation are also shown as possible options, since it is equally possible to modernize an application purely at the infrastructure layer without any large-scale application-level changes to the code base. Any decisions regarding a specific modernization pathway should be purely driven and supported by the analysis exercise.

When an application portfolio is modernized, it is not only the application logic that is altered; the modernization also affects the database and the application infrastructure. Thus, an upgrade of the underlying database to newer versions or a migration of the database to newer database technologies may be necessary. Similarly, database consolidations may also be possible. Infrastructure needs of applications are also subject to change. Capacity planning and workload modeling can help to size infrastructure needs and assist with modernizing the infrastructure. Virtualization enables workloads to be run in environments that are separated from their underlying hardware by a layer of abstraction. Container technology offers an alternative method for virtualization, in which a single operating system on a host can run many different applications. A cloud VM (virtual machine) has a complete operating system with its own memory management, drivers, and file system, whereas containers share the operating system of the host. Containers are lightweight compared to VMs. Containers and VMs differ in their approach because containers virtualize the OS and help run multiple workloads on a single OS instance, while the VM virtualizes the hardware to run multiple OS instances. Infrastructure modernization options need to consider cloud VMs and containers.

Migration

If the portfolio consists of many mainframe applications, one migration option could involve lifting and shifting the mainframe applications out of the mainframe environment to run on an open systems environment such as Linux or Windows servers. In this approach, the mainframe source code is recompiled on technology platforms that emulate the mainframe environment on another operating system. This is not a rewrite of the mainframe code base to a newer technology such as Java; instead, this approach uses emulation of mainframe code on Windows or Linux operating systems. If such mainframe applications have any assembly code, that will need to be replaced by COBOL. Additionally, there might be minor modifications needed to a COBOL code base to support the COBOL compilers used to consolidate the mainframe applications on the emulated environment. This option has been very successfully executed by several large enterprises. The approach carries very little business risk because the end user still interacts with the applications through a green screen. In essence, the mainframe application has been "lifted and shifted" to a Windows or Linux environment without any functional or major technical changes.

Although eliminating all mainframe applications is a long-term effort, several candidate mainframe applications can be migrated in this manner. This approach also provides an immediate reduction in the operating costs of the applications. You might ask, Why not re-architect and rewrite the application logic in Java? If the cost versus benefit is not readily apparent, it may not be prudent to engage in such a reengineering exercise to convert the mainframe application to Java. The cost of maintenance might be very small compared to the cost of modernizing the entire mainframe application to Java. There are several trade-offs to consider: The skills to support the applications would require COBOL and mainframe expertise. The code itself could be difficult to enhance and maintain. However, if the mainframe application logic needs to be substantially modified, the benefits of reengineering to Java from the ground up could be justified.

If the legacy applications are written in other languages, such as C / C++, PHP, or Java, the migration would involve making appropriate modifications to the source code to incorporate any new features or API changes in the language of the application source code. Some people argue that if Java is the base, then merely changing the code in a few places and testing it to ensure functional compatibility would be enough for migration. However, in reality, test cases are sparse and do not encompass all the use cases. Unit test cases do not even exist in many situations. If the source code runs into hundreds of thousands of lines, it becomes more challenging, making it an onerous task to identify all areas in the code base where changes need to be made. Automation could help to solve such source code analysis issues, making it no longer a manual task. Regression testing and functional testing would also be required to address any defects that may have been introduced into the application during migration.

Migration involves software components as well as the hardware itself. Applications can be migrated to commodity hardware or to a cloud-based architecture. In the case of Java, at a minimum, a simple upgrade of the JDK/JRE to run the test cases and ensure functional compatibility should occur. Incorporating a new API could enhance performance, stability, or maintainability. This upgrade could happen at a later stage of the more comprehensive modernization exercise.

Reengineering

Reengineering a legacy code base involves leveraging object-oriented concepts and service-oriented architectures. If an organization wants to retain the same legacy technology and perform only necessary minor enhancements, there would be no business justification for reengineering. In that case, as-is maintenance would be the only action required. If the application functionality is critical to an organization and requires major functional enhancements to the application, a stronger case for reengineering could be made at the time of introducing those new improvements.

Any exercise in reengineering must ensure that the application becomes more architecturally flexible for easier integration with future technologies. A reengineered solution adhering to service-oriented architecture (SOA) principles provides the resilience and elasticity needed for the seamless introduction of new business and technical capabilities into the application portfolio. Reengineering can involve both forward- as well as reverse-engineering. Additionally, parts of the application functionality could be reengineered or completely rewritten from scratch. Although tools are available on the market that claim to convert any existing COBOL or other legacy code base to Java, the reality is that the resulting source code will leave much to be desired. It is rather risky to allow critical business applications to be reengineered to Java via automatic conversion from COBOL. Moreover, in addition to their risks, these tools are quite expensive for use only on noncritical and low-business-value applications.

Another approach could involve extracting business rules from existing legacy applications. There are tools available to extract the business rules, but the specific context of those rules and which business processes they impact cannot automatically be known. Both domain and functional experts, knowledgeable about the business process, would need to contextualize the business rules that have been extracted from the legacy applications.

This process would require additional resources that can extensively increase the time, cost, and scope of the original modernization exercise.

In the end, the implementation of the reengineered application is tasked with ensuring that these business rules are properly implemented within the new application in the correct context. One best practice includes collecting all the old tests and rewriting these to test the new code. Often, business rules remain hidden in legacy code. Therefore, the choice to reuse old tests significantly increases the chances of uncovering this undocumented knowledge.

The underlying database and records are another area of concern when reengineering legacy applications. Legacy applications, especially mainframe applications, could store data in hierarchical databases such as Information Management System (IMS) or file stores such as Virtual Storage Access Method (VSAM). Conversion of such databases to a relational database is complex. There could also be other applications that consume such mainframe data; therefore, any reengineering effort must safeguard and preserve the data formats expected by those interfaces, adopt a new data format, or expose the data via a new service. In essence, consumers must update their applications in conformance with the new data format or service interface. Upgrading relational databases and NoSQL databases to newer versions is also an essential task to take advantage of security fixes, feature additions, and performance. This is another area where companies lag behind.

Legacy systems contain a lot of batch processes that run jobs at certain times, very much like CRON jobs on UNIX and Linux systems. Conversion of Job Control Language (JCL) scripts, static batch jobs, and dynamically generated batch jobs should also be addressed as part of the reengineering effort so that an equivalent system of batch processes or a replacement system that runs in real-time can be created as part of the new solution.

Refactoring

Code refactoring occurs when consumers leverage most of the application code base and slightly modify the design of that code. Only parts of the application are reengineered, which involves basically restructuring the code without changing external APIs and interfaces. Refactoring typically does not impact other applications that depend on the refactored application. The business functionality is also largely unchanged. Refactoring an application's code base every couple of years enables the application developer to take advantage of new APIs or libraries that are available.

Sometimes, new language features can be used for performance improvements or complexity reduction in the existing codebase. Code refactoring also allows for repeated logic occurring in multiple locations to be consolidated into one area and reused wherever necessary. Maintainability is improved when custom code written to implement certain functionality can be replaced by an API call that is made available in the core language libraries. This provides a better abstraction and replaces custom logic, possibly in many locations within multiple applications.

Rewrite

To rewrite an application, the implementation of logic from scratch to replace existing logic is necessary. Some poorly designed applications may need individual segments of the code to be rewritten. Sometimes, application code bases are entirely shelved, and the functionality is written completely from scratch. The ultimate decision to rewrite typically arises when an application has evolved over time, through a series of enhancements, and has reached a point where it has become extremely complex and difficult to maintain or enhance. The underlying architecture of the application may also be so inflexible that it may not be conducive to accept architectural improvements without some modification of the application. Sometimes, organizations may decide to abandon the entire technology stack or platform upon which the application was initially implemented, and they choose a wholly new direction for the portfolio. I know of several examples in the industry where COBOL or PERL applications were completely rewritten from scratch on the Java platform.

Legacy code bases are especially good targets for complete rewrites. In some cases, the source code may not even be comprehensively available because of missing documentation and the lack of developer knowledge of the existing application. Ultimately, this situation creates a business risk, because the existing legacy application will most likely result in error-prone and expensive modifications. Such situations warrant rewrites. To take advantage of new technologies that were not available when the original application was created, a reimplementation of the application functionality is also necessary. To steer legacy applications away from hierarchical databases and toward the adoption of relational databases or in-memory NoSQL databases, it may be essential to rewrite large parts of the application or even to implement the application from scratch using a different technology stack

Package Implementations

As enterprises modernize their existing application portfolios, it is important that they consider replacing ageing applications with newer ones. Package implementations involve purchasing a commercial off-the-shelf (COTS) product and customizing the package to meet an organization's requirements. Custom applications are typically built from scratch, maintained, and enhanced as per the needs of the organization. Whether an enterprise chooses to buy COTS software or build a custom application depends on several factors. The effort and cost to build and enhance a complex application for private use can sometimes be quite substantial. If a company wants to preserve a specific competitive advantage by building a custom application to protect underlying algorithms, that could provide a strong justification for the business case. There may also be specific business areas in vertical industries where there is no readily available software that meets the business requirements. In such cases, custom applications may need to be developed.

In other situations, however, off-the-shelf vendor products can suffice after some minimal configuration and customization. Sometimes, a custom application is built using commercial frameworks or libraries. This hybrid approach enables the application build to be agile, grounded in well-designed and tested commercial components. Another consideration is source code ownership. With custom applications, the company retains all use rights, whereas with a commercial product, the vendor would own the source code for the COTS software.

On many occasions, buying and customizing a vendor product will be the most cost-effective solution. Designing and building complex applications requires a deep understanding of both the business domain and the technology, as well as the ability to hire the right developers to create the custom applications. With this business requirement in mind, a vendor selling the COTS software might provide periodic version upgrades and feature enhancements, thereby keeping overall post-implementation operational costs contained. With home-grown custom applications, these resource and cost variables remain unknown. The question of whether to purchase COTS software versus building a custom application is one that each organization will need to answer for itself, based on its unique situation and specific business parameters. There is no one-size-fits-all answer. In either case, this decision-making process is key when evaluating modernization options.

Application Decommissioning

The process of application decommissioning identifies applications within a portfolio that should be phased out or altogether removed from the current list of IT systems supported by an enterprise. Applications are ready to be decommissioned when they become obsolete or when other applications with similar functionality are made available to the end users in the organization. Appropriate stakeholders must consent prior to applications being decommissioned.

Any application that has a large user base and is critical to business is nearly impossible to eliminate entirely from a portfolio, and application decommissioning does not usually target such critical applications. As part of the APM process, the discovery and analysis exercise may yield applications that are very low in business value to the organization and are of poor technical quality or obsolete technology. The application could also have a very small user base. Such applications are good candidates for a quick decommissioning.

If the application functionality exists within another application in the enterprise, the decommissioning process can be accelerated. Even if the functionality does not directly exist elsewhere in another application, the fact that there are limited users and low utility of the application to business objectives make the process of decommissioning occur quickly, often within a few months.

One prime target for application decommissioning occurs in the context of corporate mergers and acquisitions. In an M&A situation, each company has its own intellectual property and portfolio of applications and must find a way to combine various departments, processes, and systems into one functioning unit. If the merging companies are in the same line of business or same vertical industry segment, it is likely that each company will have similar application assets. In such cases, it would be extremely expensive and redundant to maintain two or more applications that provide similar functionality. An application decommissioning exercise would benefit the merged entity by reducing unnecessary operational costs.

Because of application decommissioning exercises, data migrations may be necessary. Hardware consolidation and data archival could also become imperative with respect to a decommissioned application. Application interfaces and data integration points need to be addressed before an application can be consolidated and decommissioned. An established governance mechanism will be necessary to oversee the decommissioning process along with key performance indicator (KPI) adherence to manage the progress and final outcome. End users may also need training for the replacement system.

In some cases, depending on the business logic contained within the decommissioned application, and the modular design or object-oriented design of the application, it may be possible to repurpose part of the business logic. Specifically, a set of classes could be exported into a library and reused in other applications based on the business or technical functionality encapsulated by the extracted portion of the code from the decommissioned application. This is not a typical situation, but it could happen, especially in the context of decommissioned Java applications.

Modernizing Java Applications

The previous section presented various modernization options for legacy applications; this section specifically addresses the migration and reengineering options for legacy applications on the Java platform, including Java applications running on older versions of the code base. An enterprise that has invested in building a custom Java application will not typically reengineer that application on a different technology platform. It is an incredibly rare occurrence that the Java technology application is rewritten in PHP, .NET, Python, or some other platform. In fact, there are probably more examples of applications written in PHP, Ruby on Rails, COBOL, and other such technologies that are rewritten in Java. The most common scenario that comes up is the migration of a Java application to a newer version of the Java platform. In this process, several open-source Java libraries and third-party or custom-built in-house Java libraries are migrated. Also, every few years, it is not uncommon for applications to be refactored, reengineered, or re-architected to take advantage of feature additions to the Java technology platform, new libraries becoming available, or added improvements to existing libraries.

The Java platform is here to stay. Enterprises have invested considerable time, money, and effort into writing billions of lines of code on the platform. Just as COBOL applications have not completely phased out, even after 40-plus years of existence, the Java platform, which has been in existence just over two decades at the time of this writing, will likely similarly live on. In 20 years, we will most likely see new enterprise application portfolios being built using Java technology in addition to other disruptive technologies alive at that time.

Migration

As Java applications age and become legacy applications, new releases of the platform arrive at regular intervals. At least going forward, Oracle has promised some regularity. In the past, Sun Microsystems did not have a regular release schedule for the next newest version of Java. Regardless, enterprises that run applications on JDK 1.4.2, 1.5, 1.6, or even 1.7 should strongly consider the proposition of migrating the applications to JDK 1.8 or 1.9. Apart from the JDK consideration, if open-source libraries or third-party Java libraries have been adopted, newer versions might be available that include added features or fixed defects. It is also worth mentioning that running an older public version of JDK 7 prevents an enterprise from benefitting from hundreds of security fixes currently available. This situation can be even worse for enterprises running on even older versions of the JDK.

NOTE
Major releases of the Java Platform, Standard Edition (Java SE), are identified as 5.0, 6, 7, 8, and 9. At the time of publishing this book, the Java technology end of public updates policy has been clarified to confirm public availability of Java SE major releases for at least:

- *Three years after the general availability date (GA) of a major release*

- *One year after the GA of a subsequent major release*

- *Six months after a subsequent major release has been established as the default*

Oracle will post an "end of public updates" notice for each major release well in advance, indicating that the release has entered its transition period. Once the release has completed its transition period, no new downloads of that release will be made publicly available on the public Oracle web sites, and will only be available through the My Oracle Support web site. Previously available older releases may continue to be available unsupported but are definitely not recommended for production use.

Another important point to consider is whether you have deployed your Java applications on an application server such as WebSphere, Tomcat, or JBoss. These application servers also release new versions on a regular basis with enhanced features, management, scalability, and security. These newer application server versions also upgrade to newer JDK or other open-source or vendor libraries.

I am aware of only a few organizations that have Java applications deployed on older JDK versions like JDK 1.3 and JDK 1.4.2. This means that most enterprises have had to migrate their Java applications and upgrade other libraries, applications, and infrastructure to integrate and interoperate with the migrated Java applications. Typically, most enterprises that I have interacted with have tackled these migrations by targeting just a few Java applications at a time, rather than approaching the project as a portfolio overhaul to adopt a new Java platform en masse. But this is not the best decision. This piecemeal approach results in heavy fragmentation of the Java application portfolio to be distributed across multiple JVM versions within an organization.

With the evolution of the Java platform from JDK 1.0 to 1.8, enterprises have migrated and upgraded their applications approximately four times. Essentially, each upgrade skips one version and jumps to the next one. In practice, this results in organizations with a portfolio of applications split between two to three major JDK versions at a minimum and infused with a mashup of older and newer features.

On average, at the time of this writing, organizations have heavily invested in JDK 1.6 or 1.7, with several additional applications lingering in JDK 1.5. Moreover, newer applications are being written in Java SE 8, since Java SE 7 reached the end of public updates in April 2015. It is difficult to change policies, SDLC processes, and the tools of an organization overnight. However, the trepidation of many enterprises to invest in a full platform overhaul to JDK 1.9 creates a situation in which organizations are forced to do the best that they can with Java applications bring written in JDK 1.8 or even the unsupported JDK 1.7. By the end of 2018, most organizations will have heavy investments in Java SE 8 in terms of the bulk of their Java applications. Some stragglers will still be around on JDK 1.6 and 1.7, and the newer applications will be written in Java SE 9. For those organizations still clinging to JDK 1.4.2 or earlier, I would like to hear about your experience.

Although not the suggested method, the most popular way of adopting a newer version of Java is to deploy the old JAR file to the new JVM and hope that it runs without incident. Some organizations will also try to recompile the source code with the new Java compiler without modifying any of the source code at all. Warnings and other messages are typically ignored or suppressed at the time of recompilation of the source code, and the newly compiled JAR file is deployed to run on the new JVM. Some organizations have compiled applications or libraries with a new JDK; however, older JVMs are used upon deployment of the application or JAR file. Although these two approaches may seem to present an easy upgrade pathway, they both have some major pitfalls. Unfortunately, most of these issues will not immediately come to light if the Java application seems to be functional and operational. But everything will come to a grinding halt when it is too late.

When an existing Java application is compiled using one version of the JDK and deployed to an entirely different JDK version, three categories of incompatibilities are possible:

- Binary incompatibility

- Source code incompatibility

- Behavioral incompatibility

These categories are analogous in name to the compatibilities typically discussed in the Java Language Specification (JLS). Although the nomenclature is similar, our definition and scope of the above three incompatibilities differs from the JLS discussion. JLS approaches this topic from a compatibility perspective between two JVMs. Our discussion on Java modernization is with respect to Java applications and the business functionality of those applications that need to be preserved. We approach this topic from that viewpoint and discuss the incompatibilities between two JVMs.

It is indeed an onerous task to identify all possible incompatibilities that might exist between two Java SE versions across all APIs. Additionally, if popular open-source libraries and other external libraries used by most business applications are included, the list of incompatibilities becomes even more daunting. Imagine a situation in which the application migration has skipped a version or two; the degree of difficulty and risk of introducing incompatibilities is magnified. Later chapters in the book introduce automation principles that enable an organization to tackle migration with a greater level of predictability and success.

Binary Incompatibility

Binary incompatibility occurs when Java applications that previously executed and linked at runtime to other binary libraries without issues abruptly become unable to link correctly. The simple compiling with depreciation warning signs of certain methods, however, does not rise to the level of binary incompatibility. The Java platform has evolved to ensure that the old deprecated methods still exist in the core platform. As a result, during migration, several warnings would appear if the original application was written using a particular version of the JVM and then run on an entirely newer version. In general, binary incompatibilities due to upgrades in JVM are rare. Poorly written third-party libraries could cause issues, however.

If new methods were added to an interface or class, the code would still compile and link correctly. And this also does not rise to the level of binary incompatibility. The generated Java class files typically have upward-compatibility with a newer JVM version. Every release of Java lists the binary incompatibilities that you would experience when building the source code against the previous version of the JVM and running that compiled code against the newer version. If versions are skipped, all the binary incompatibilities between the original version and the new version would have to be independently combined.

Some byte code obfuscators have also been known to produce class files that do not conform to the class file format. Such class files may have run on an older JVM, but there is no guarantee that the obfuscated code would continue to run on a newer JVM. In this situation, the class files may need to be recompiled again to run on the new JVM. In the past, the general policy of Sun Microsystems, and present-day Oracle, has been to help preserve binary compatibility as far as possible so that Java source code compiled against a previous version of the Java SE APIs can continue to run on the new Java version.

Source Code Incompatibility

Our definition of *source code incompatibility* and how we interpret source code compatibility from the Java modernization and portfolio management viewpoint varies a bit from the way source code compatibility is defined for the JVM and the JDK. The JLS views this purely from the perspective of maintaining and evolving the JDK. In portfolio modernization and management, however, the context is a business one. It monitors the technical and financial impact to business units as well as overall organizational health.

For that reason, we focus on the incompatibility of the source code in a way that differs from the JLS compatibility frame of reference.

For the purposes of Java modernization, we group various types of incompatibilities that affect the source code into the source code incompatibility category. Also, included within this category are the following:

■ Serialization identifier–related problems

■ Addition of generics (impacting both SDK libraries and client programs)

■ Addition of new language features or modifications to APIs

■ Provision of overloaded methods

The deprecation warnings generated against the source code upon compilation is one example of source code incompatibility. The addition of new methods to classes and interfaces is another example. Although the act of compiling and executing code may not produce source code incompatibilities that materially affect the execution of the application, in the future, these incompatibilities may ultimately fracture the application. For example, if a deprecated method is removed in a future release, the application will break, since the method will no longer be available in the core API when the application code tries to call that method.

When it comes to overloaded methods, hidden issues could be lurking in the code base that could produce different results. The OpenJDK web site has a great statement concerning overloaded methods: "Not all overloaded methods are behaviorally equivalent; some are just *compilation preserving*." The web site also provides a simple example to illustrate the point of overloaded methods and the introduction of source code incompatibilities. The next example is derived from the original example provided on the OpenJDK site.

Imagine a class defined as follows:

```
// Original source code
public final class Square {
 public double area(double side) {
 return side * side;
 }
}
```

If we added a new method, that method is distinct from any existing methods and hence it does not introduce binary incompatibilities or source code incompatibilities:

```
// Binary-preserving source compatible change
public final class Square {
 public double area(double side) {
 return side * side;
 }

 // Method with new name added
 public double perimeter(double side) {
 return 4 * side;
 }
}
```

Next, let's add an overloaded method to that same class:

```
// Binary-preserving source compatible change
public final class Square {
 public double area(double side) {
 return side * side;
 }

 // Method with new name added
 public double area(int side) {
 return side * side;
 }
}
```

In this class, we overloaded the area() method to accept an integer input. Previously, when an integer was provided as the method argument, the value would have been converted to a double, as defined in the JLS under the primitive widening convention. Previously, a call to compute the area would have simply called the same method for double, int, and long arguments. Now, the overloaded method for an integer argument is called. Still, since the integer argument is first converted to a double, there might be behavioral equivalence and nothing might be noticed amiss, although it is a different overloaded method that is called for integer arguments.

Now let's add another overloaded method for circumference that takes a long parameter as an argument. Only the relevant snippet of code is shown here and not the entire class:

```
// providing an overloaded method that takes a long argument
public final class Square {
// Original method
public double perimeter(double side) {
return 4 * side;
}
// Overloaded method
public double perimeter(long side) {
return (double) (4L * side;)
}
}
```

In the original version of the class, a long argument would simply call the only available method that takes a double argument and the value of long would have been converted into a double before calling the method. The converted double would have been multiplied by 4 and returned as a double. In the overloaded method now, a long argument is preserved as a long, multiplied by 4, and then finally converted to a double and returned. Since the sequence of operations is different now compared to the original class with just one method and the new class with the overloaded method, the results obtained can be different. In fact, for large long values, multiplying by 4 could cause an overflow to a negative value, and the resulting value returned could be a negative double. In the original case, a large positive double could have been returned. This kind of subtle change in overloading behavior occurred with the addition of a constructor to the BigDecimal class that took a long argument as part of JSR 13.

Behavioral Incompatibility

Behavioral incompatibility results when the same inputs produce a varied effect or result when executing the code against multiple versions of the Java platform or different versions of any API or library. Programs that use reflection, timers, multithreading and other features outside a reliable contract can be impacted by behavioral incompatibilities when moving from one version to another. Behavioral incompatibility is also inclusive of any functional differences in how a business application behaves. To ensure compatibility, there should be complete code coverage, unit tests, regression tests, and functional tests so that any deviations in terms of behavior can be appropriately identified and fixed.

NOTE
The JDK Enhancement Proposal (JEP) is a process drafted by Oracle Corporation to collect proposals for enhancements to the Java Development Kit and OpenJDK. According to Oracle, JEP is intended to serve as the long-term roadmap for JDK release projects and related efforts. The JEP process is not intended to replace the Java Community Process (JCP), which is still required to approve changes to the Java API or language. Rather, JEP enables OpenJDK committers to work more informally before the JEP becomes a formal Java Specification Request.

Some of the APIs in the sun.* packages change between releases. These APIs have always been intended for internal use only, and enterprises use such internal interfaces at their own risk. It is strongly recommended that you find alternatives to using these internal packages as soon as possible. If you are planning to move to Java 9, you should review the code for dependencies on internal APIs!

NOTE
The com.sun. packages are a mixture of internal and "exported" (publicly supported) APIs. Some APIs have the @jdk.Exported annotation, which helps distinguish them from internal APIs. They are part of Oracle's JDK but are not part of the core Java SE platform. JEP 260 specifies the critical internal APIs that remain accessible until a replacement API is available in a future release. Other internal APIs are inaccessible by default. A new command-line tool, jdeps, has been included in the Java platform since JDK 8. It is a static analysis tool that helps you understand the dependencies of applications and libraries. To help prepare for migration to JDK 9, run the jdeps utility to determine whether applications and libraries depend on any internal APIs of the JDK.*

Compatibility and Known Issues Guides for JDK 8

Oracle published a compatibility guide that documents potential incompatibilities relating to the release of JDK 8. This guide also shows the features that have been removed from JDK 8. This complete list can be found at www.oracle.com/technetwork/java/javase/8-compatibility-guide-2156366.html.

Oracle has also published a list of known issues for a particular JDK release. The current list of known issues for JDK 8 can be found at www.oracle.com/technetwork/java/javase/8-known-issues-2157115.html.

The Java class file format has been updated for the Java SE 8 release. The class file version for Java SE 8 is 52.0 as per the JVM Specification. Version 52.0 class files produced by a Java SE 8 compiler cannot be used in earlier releases of Java SE. A document has information on changes to the Java Language Specification (JLS) and the Java VM Specification (JVMS): "JSR 337 - Java SE 8 Release Contents."

Compatibility and Known Issues Guides for JDK 9

Every new Java SE release introduces some binary, source, and behavioral incompatibilities compared with previous releases. The modularization of the Java SE Platform in Java SE 9 brings many benefits but also several changes, many of which can affect your application as you migrate to JDK 9.

After you download and install the latest release of JDK 9, run your Java application without recompiling and see what happens. That is a good indicator of incompatibilities you may find. If it runs as-is, at least you know that you have used standard JDK libraries and have written backward-compatible code! You can now update third-party libraries if they are available compiled against JDK 9. You can also now recompile your application with JDK 9 and then run `jdeps` with the `-jdkinternals` option on your code. If you use internal APIs, `jdeps` suggests replacements to help you update your code. Since some VM options have been removed in JDK 9, look for warnings from the JVM about unrecognized VM options. You need to run all your regression tests and ensure that all tests run correctly. Oracle has reported instances of dates and currencies formatted differently. The compilation of the application itself could fail in JDK 9. Almost all of the JDK internal APIs are inaccessible by default. If your application is dependent on internal APIs, you may get compilation errors or IllegalAccessErrors at run time. You may also get deprecation warnings or deprecation with removal warnings. The later needs to be addressed to avoid future problems.

The layout of files in the installed JDK and JRE image has changed in JDK 9. There are still separate JDK and JRE downloads, but you get the same directory structure regardless of the image that you download. The JDK image contains the extra tools, such as javac, and libraries that have historically been found in the JDK. There are no more jdk/ versus jre/ wrapper directories. The previously deprecated methods from the packages java.util.logging .LogManager and java.util.jar.Pack200, have been removed in JDK 9.

JDK 9 provides a new simplified version-string format. Code that explicitly relies on the version-string format to distinguish major, minor, security, and patch update releases, has to be updated. The format of the new version-string is: $MAJOR.$MINOR.$SECURITY.$PATCH

While there is no change to the deprecated no-argument Thread.stop() method, Thread.stop(Throwable) is unsupported in JDK 9. Thread.stop(Throwable) forces the target thread to stop and throw a given Throwable as an exception. This has the potential to compromise security. Objects may be left in an inconsistent state or the exception may be something that the thread is not prepared to handle. You will get an UnsupportedOperationException if you attempt to use this method.

The default garbage collector on JDK 9 is the Garbage-First Garbage Collector (G1 GC) on both 32- and 64-bit server configurations. A low-pause collector such as G1 GC should provide a better overall experience for applications. The Parallel GC is the default garbage collector in JDK 8.

There are many other issues you should be aware of while migrating to JDK 9. Oracle has provided a migration guide for JDK 9 that can be accessed at the following url: https://docs.oracle.com/javase/9/migrate/toc.htm

Reengineering

Reengineering an existing Java application is a much more involved and complex process than migration to a newer JDK. Java applications that evolve over eight to ten years can be considered legacy applications. Over time, documentation underlying these applications can become sparse or nonexistent, and the developers who initially designed and implemented the original system may no longer work at the company. If the application is critical enough, some base maintenance and incremental enhancements will be allocated to appease the business stakeholders, but that will not be enough. The only recourse in such a situation will be to reengineer the application from the ground up. If existing system documentation, functional documentation, and the technical architecture details can be identified, that is a great start. It is important to ask how current those documents are. If the information is more than three or four years old, the documentation is out of date and has fallen behind the existing enhancements.

Conducting a top-down analysis, documenting the business processes supported by the application as well as the functional and the technical decomposition, will enable proper dissection of the application to reveal its functional blocks. It is also important to document the functional requirements and the business rules that underlie and support the application. Sometimes, it is possible to reuse parts of the application if it was well designed and well implemented from the outset. Even then, however, unless the Java code base is plain vanilla and able to be recompiled with minimal changes, it is probably not wise to reuse large parts of the original source code. In other cases, if the API design of the application is extremely sound, allowing for integrations with external applications, then some of the API calls exposed to the outside world via the application's interfaces are prime candidates for reuse. Essentially, the implementation changes but certain API signatures would be preserved as-is.

The reengineering effort for complex *n*-tiered Java applications will be substantial. Certain UI technologies such as older Java Server Pages code, Java Swing, older Enterprise Java Beans versions (especially entity beans), and poor use of threading or collections can cause the new architecture for the same application functionality to look much different. From Java 8 onward, Streams API and lambdas are available to parallelize tasks and take advantage of multicore processors.

This reengineering effort becomes a re-architecture endeavor followed by the actual engineering of the application to the new design. The application engineering is, for all practical purposes, a rip-and-replace exercise. Only a thorough analysis of the existing application will indicate the nature and size of the reengineering exercise. I have seen actual situations in enterprises where within five years an application has become antiquated, requiring re-architecture and reengineering to satisfy new business requirements. The new requirements could be either functional or nonfunctional in nature. At its inception, the application in question made assumptions with respect to its database design and integration needs with external applications. When that fell short, no other option remained other than a complete re-architecture of the application to avail of new technology components since the application first deployed.

For applications relying on external third-party or open-source libraries, their external libraries may have become defunct or no longer in active development. In such cases, an equivalent library may need to be discovered to allow for the expression of those functionalities in the newly reengineered application. If no suitable equivalent is available in a third-party library, the task of identifying and implementing a similar functionality will fall on the shoulders of the application implementation team. With that said, it is highly unlikely that new libraries would be unable to provide the functionality of a currently defunct library. This risk should occur only in rare situations with very specialized libraries that target specific domains or industries.

As part of reengineering an application, the application may need to be reverse-engineered to understand the inner workings and current design. An analysis of the existing application code base as well as reverse-engineering the available bytecode from the compiled libraries might occur. Both types of reverse-engineering analyses are basically static investigations of an application. Dynamic analysis involves an inquiry of the runtime characteristics of the application, including memory usage, object creation, heap analysis, performance analysis, multithreading, memory leaks, CPU usage, and other similar characteristics. Dynamic analysis might shed some light into the nonfunctional characteristics that need to be considered while re-architecting the application.

Ultimately, to leverage new technology trends, meet future performance needs, and introduce major functional enhancements, all existing applications need to experience a base level of re-architecture and reengineering. The ease or difficulty of that endeavor will depend on the processes in place within an organization, the maturity of the EA team, adoption of service-oriented architecture principles, reuse of application components and services, governance, and establishment of an APM discipline.

Summary

Most application portfolios contain older legacy applications written in established languages such as COBOL or modern languages such as Java and .NET. To manage business risk, enterprises continue to maintain and enhance legacy applications. Legacy portfolio modernization involves reengineering legacy applications with applications built on newer technologies, decommissioning some applications, migrating a legacy code base to run on Windows or Linux while keeping the legacy language such as COBOL intact, and replacing the legacy application functionality with a packaged off-the-shelf application.

For application portfolios containing Java applications, a few options are available when the portfolio becomes outdated and unmaintainable. Migration to the latest JDK version or completely reengineering the Java application can be explored. Migrations of Java applications involve a thorough understanding of the incompatibilities between the current version and the target version of the JDK. Additionally, any other third-party or open-source libraries used by the application must also be examined.

There are three types of potential incompatibilities relating to the adoption of a newer version of the Java platform. Source incompatibility arises when compiling Java source code into class files on the new JDK version. Binary incompatibility fractures preexisting binaries if they previously linked without error but are now not able to link correctly. Behavioral incompatibility includes code semantics executed at runtime that may be inconspicuous and not immediately obvious. Only through thorough testing will lurking behavioral incompatibilities be identified.

Re-architecting and reengineering an existing Java application may be the only option if the application is several versions behind, lacks appropriate documentation, was poorly architected, requires leveraging of new technologies, or needs to change dependence on third-party libraries.

CHAPTER
6

Java Modernization
Approach

The modernization of application portfolios requires an exhaustive analysis and diagnosis of each architectural layer for redundancy and adequacy of the individual components. The previous chapter delved into an assessment of heterogeneous application portfolios comprising legacy applications, including mainframe applications. We also looked at various modernization options such as migration, reengineering, refactoring, rewriting, and possible replacement by off-the-shelf packaged applications. For Java applications, considering that we still want to leverage the Java platform, we also saw migration and reengineering as options for modernization.

This chapter provides an overall methodology and approach to modernizing Java application portfolios by presenting the frameworks for its development and adoption. Although we have seen the assessment steps previously, they were contextualized to the APM discipline. Our discussion will now focus on the specific measures necessary to modernize Java application portfolios.

The key concepts of project portfolio management (PPM), and investment risk management (IRM), as explained in Chapter 3, are also germane to Java application portfolios. These two management methodologies play an essential role in the ongoing administration of the Java application portfolio since Java applications are built and enhanced under project charters with allocated budgets. Many concepts pertaining to legacy modernization, as discussed in Chapter 5, are also relevant to the discussion of Java modernization.

Java Modernization Explained

What do we mean when we refer to "Java modernization"? In this context, we focus on taking an existing portfolio of Java applications, applying a set of methodologies, and measuring them against established baselines to conclude whether they are able to provide the highest business value continually while aligning to the business objectives of an organization. These actions and operations collectively encompass Java modernization.

After a thorough evaluation, some applications may be removed completely from the portfolio, or the source code of other applications could be modified to adopt advances and new features in the Java language or the core libraries. Sometimes, for cost-saving reasons, applications are consolidated or moved to a cloud-based infrastructure. Changing the essential business processes that support and enhance application functionality may have the unintended result of transforming those applications completely from the top down. In this way, when the entire application portfolio is analyzed as a whole, several initiatives could be identified in a roadmap and executed over time, changing the very nature of the application portfolio and leaving very little in terms of its initial footprint. Such large-scale overhauls happen infrequently and typically indicate that the Java application portfolio has degraded in technical quality and business value, justifying the major investment and transformation. The Java applications in such a portfolio are ideal candidates to be transformed to conform to a service-oriented architecture composed of a set of services and technical components that run on a service platform and provide the application functionality to orchestrate business processes.

Once a portfolio is in a steady state, only a select set of applications are usually affected by modernization decisions. Java application portfolios that have been assessed, analyzed, and modernized previously require continuous management to ensure a long-term successful strategy.

Establish a Java Application Portfolio

Modernization in the context of a portfolio of Java applications is an exciting topic! Chapter 2 illustrated how to establish the creation of a portfolio for Java applications and how to manage the entire life cycle. This includes a three-step process:

1. Collect the various data points and attributes of applications in the enterprise.

2. Select the applications based on a set of criteria to establish the application portfolio.

3. Define the objectives, metrics, and processes to manage and govern this established Java application portfolio.

Once the portfolio has been established through the "collect, select, and define" methodology, the management and governance phase of the Java application portfolio begins. This is not a one-time discrete function; instead, it is an ongoing operation that provides the ability to generate reports on the portfolio, provide dashboards, and facilitate in decision-making regarding the very existence of the Java applications.

The portfolio management implications extend beyond just the technical aspects. Figure 6-1 shows a portfolio of Java applications represented by bubbles of various sizes. Four areas of relevance to the applications are identified. The applications themselves are not organized but have been identified and grouped into a portfolio. Applications should be managed and modernized according to four pillars of the Java application portfolio:

- Finance
- Operations
- Functionality
- Technology

Figure 6-2 shows the same application portfolio under the effective management of the four pillars. In this figure, the bubbles representing applications are arranged and arrows are drawn between the various applications. This structure identifies a well-understood portfolio, with its functional and technical architectural layers having undergone decomposition and complete documentation of all the applications. Relationships between the applications, integrations, and the information architecture have also been captured. The metamorphosis from what is shown in Figure 6-1 to what is in Figure 6-2 takes time and commitment from an organization. The core APM and EA teams must collaborate to bring

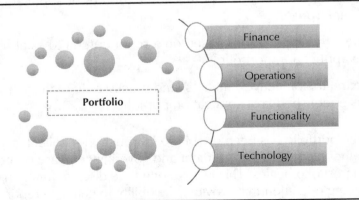

FIGURE 6-1. *Java application portfolio identified*

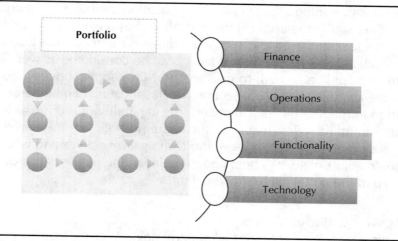

FIGURE 6-2.   *Java application portfolio brought under effective management*

the applications under effective management. It is not an easy task but yields great rewards if executed efficaciously.

The four pillars form the fundamental framework to help decision-makers understand the utility of the application portfolio and determine whether it meets the following criteria:

- Organizational business objectives

- End user needs

- Budgetary constraints

- Operational targets

- Support and maintenance criteria

- Performance and SLAs

- Technical architecture

- Best practices

- Solution to functional needs of the enterprise

- Realization of high business value and superior technical quality of applications

Chapter 3 presented a laundry list of application attributes to be collected as part of managing the application portfolio. These features should be tailored to specific objectives, and depending on the technology and functional characteristics, additional facets can be considered as well. Those attributes are applicable both to Java and non-Java applications alike. To simplify the analysis, the several sections of classification can be consolidated to conform to the four pillars. Ultimately, the capability of individual Java applications and the performance of the entire portfolio are measured by the success of meeting the business and technical objectives and whether appropriate adjustments can be made to optimize the performance of the portfolio and the cost of such modifications.

Financial Considerations

One of the cornerstone reasons for modernizing a Java application portfolio is the negative financial impact of an inefficient portfolio. Chapter 2 reviewed the complete life cycle of a Java application and considered the process of how new applications are vetted and built. As we all know, static IT budgets complicate the business case justification for new applications. If we apply "the squeaky wheel always gets the oil" analogy here, we can understand how limited IT resources are spent merely to keep the lights on rather than to improve and advance portfolio health. The labor costs for maintenance of existing applications in the portfolio drain a significant portion of the available budget. By reducing run-rate costs and determining where to invest the freed-up money, an organization can begin the strategic journey down the Java modification path.

Another significant step along this path would see the discontinuation of investments in noncritical applications and poorly architected applications sustained by financial life-support. The overall costing needs of the Java application portfolio must be contained and investments made in the right areas to maximize business value. To that effect, several application attributes need to be collected on a regular basis and analyzed so that the cost of operating the application portfolio, and the individual run-rate costs of applications and their spending trends, are understood. Once this occurs, inferences can then be drawn to project future spending commitments.

Operational Considerations

Operating the application within a portfolio depends on financial resources and labor skills. Technical teams toil to support the business and maintain appropriate SLAs for each application. It cannot be assumed that only business-critical applications consume more resources. Sometimes, applications of poor technical quality and incomplete functionality tend to deplete more resources to maintain and support the application. There can also be a mismatch in the skill sets vital to the operation of an application. If underskilled and inexperienced resources are assigned to certain applications, employee resources and cost of operations could be much higher than otherwise warranted. Maintainability of the applications, along with historical and projected spending forecasts, must be collected and analyzed; the cost of operating similar applications should also be considered.

Applications that are great candidates for consolidation or retirement should be identified based on a thorough financial and operational analysis. Similarly, applications that are outsourced for maintenance need to be optimized to show the derived value from the service provider. If these application attributes have not been collected or analyzed in the past five years, there could be significant room for cost savings. Operational risks, business risks, reliability, scalability, business criticality, and other such attributes can be measured to build an operational profile of the applications.

Functionality Considerations

The business functionality of Java applications, along with functional decomposition and business process drill-downs, should be thoroughly documented for all applications in a portfolio. The business and functional attributes for applications identified in Chapter 3 are all relevant for Java applications as well. Having a good understanding of functional decomposition and business process orchestration will help you successfully modernize a Java portfolio from a business process transformation and functional consolidation standpoint. The identification of shared services across department boundaries and components for reuse among applications can be achieved by collecting and analyzing their relevant attributes. The business value of an application can be computed by creating graphs of the functional and business attributes against its financial and operational attributes. The functional health of the application, the flexibility to reuse functional components to enhance application functionality, and the reliability of the application functionality for meeting end user demands can be measured with the aid of these attributes.

Technological Considerations

The key values for any Java application include excellent technical quality, adherence to best practices, and a flexible technical architecture. At the portfolio level, technical decomposition uncovers the nature of the technical components in the portfolio and exposes redundancies, thereby aligning Java applications to the technology principles established by the enterprise architecture team.

Several detailed attributes were discussed in Chapter 2. Collection of those attributes, scoring them, and combining them to form 2×2 views enables the portfolio to be measured in terms of technical quality, technical risks, performance, technology obsolescence, dependence on third-party or custom components, architecture flexibility, complexity, scalability, reliability, and overall technical health. Using automation tools, you can discover an extended set of attributes, including specific details of the API and third-party components being used, lines of code, cyclomatic complexity, and business rules embedded within the application. Application of a rules knowledge base can also pinpoint all the changes and improvements introduced into the core Java libraries as well as third-party libraries used by the application, and where exactly there has been an impact within the application code. Understanding and documenting the mod points within each application will provide a logical basis to estimate the effort and cost of reengineering, refactoring, rewriting, or migrating the Java applications. A mod point can be thought of as an atomic unit of modification that happens within a code base to modernize that code base.

Management of the Java Application Portfolio

Once a Java application portfolio has been identified and ascertained, the APM discipline and its processes are applied to govern and manage that portfolio effectively. The application attributes can be leveraged to form an understanding of the performance of the portfolio along the four pillars: finance, operations, functionality, and technology. Effective management of the Java application portfolio naturally leads to a transparent decision-making dialogue between the stakeholders, ultimately leading to the modernization of that portfolio. Modernization exercises extend far beyond just the technical migration and improvement of applications or the reengineering of those applications. In fact, those technical decisions are the direct result of effective management of the application portfolio.

The Java applications in a portfolio need to be assessed periodically and systematically to determine the business value each application delivers to an enterprise. The cost of building, enhancing, and maintaining an application needs to be well understood before addressing topics such as the total cost of ownership (TCO) or returns regarding ongoing investments made in an application. The technical quality of an application should also be evaluated before justifying any further enhancements or investments. Finally, the business uncertainty and technical implications should be assessed as part of the risks posed to the operation and support of these applications.

The four pillars of finance, operations, functionality, and technology ultimately translate into cost, risk, business value, and technical quality. Figure 6-3 illustrates how an effectively managed Java application portfolio can be modernized. This figure plots technical quality versus business value. One can similarly plot cost versus business value or attributes of any one pillar versus attributes of another to help make modernization decisions.

The standard quadrant model depicting application portfolio decisions that industry analysts have shared in the past apply equally to the Java application

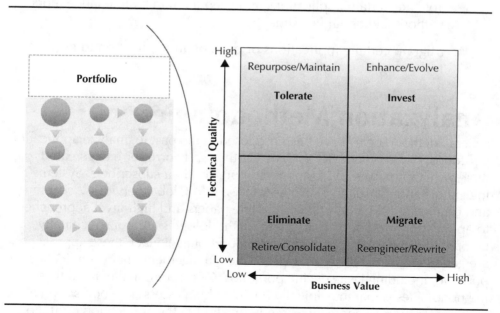

FIGURE 6-3. *Making modernization decisions on a Java application portfolio*

portfolio managed under the four pillars. The modernization decisions lend themselves to tolerate, invest, eliminate, and migrate an application or set of applications in a portfolio. A deeper view into the decision model illuminates some of the actual modernization decisions to be made:

- Upgrade Java technology platform version.

- Leverage new technology features through refactoring or rewriting.

- Address new business needs through functional enhancements.

- Improve business processes via reengineering.

- Improve governance model by capturing relevant application attributes and metadata.

- Shut down or eliminate applications.

- Determine consolidation strategies to eliminate functional or technical redundancies.

- Tolerate certain applications and keep them in maintenance mode without additional investments.

- Migrate certain applications or parts of an application to newer technology.

Analyzation Methodologies

Several methodologies have been proposed in the past to analyze application portfolios. Industry analysts such as Gartner and Forrester have created their own approaches and fashioned reports for their subscribers. Systems integrators and consultants such as Infosys, IBM Global Services, Accenture, and Cognizant have also published white papers and high-level approaches to application modernization. These methodologies are not specifically tailored to modernizing Java application portfolios. In fact, these approaches are generic in nature and can apply to the management of any application portfolio, including Java-specific portfolios. One commonality in all these methodologies is that they initially begin with an assessment or discovery exercise for the management or modernization of the application portfolio.

This typically involves identifying the applications in the portfolio and then conducting information-gathering sessions and interviews to fill standard templates with data collected about the applications.

For the past two decades, the evolution of IT has embraced modernization as an important aspect of application portfolio management. Whenever a promising new update or upgraded version of a technology component becomes available, there is a desire to adopt it immediately. However, this typically holds true for smaller companies with a more nimble acquisition process. Larger organizations tend to stay with what works until it breaks. In both cases, time, money, and resources are the most inhibiting factors. Lately, there is a noticeable directional shift in thinking regarding technology adoption. Previously, larger enterprises were slow to embrace new technologies, but with the rapid pace of innovation and availability of open-source components, some larger enterprises are also willing to move faster with respect to embracing new technology. Although there are challenges, people generally like technology and want to adopt the latest and greatest in the marketplace.

The modernization of an application may evaluate the entire application across its various architectural layers, or it could be isolated to a specific tier of an application, such as the file server. The scale of modernization could vary from modernizing a component of a particular application to the entire IT application landscape, including hundreds or even a few thousand applications.

Figure 6-4 depicts the modernization of Java application portfolios. The three phases of assess, evolve, and optimize rest at the heart of the methodology. Each phase is further divided into three steps to simplify its approach and execution. Since APM and EA are closely intertwined with modernization, they are also depicted in this picture. APM applies governance and program management to the modernization initiatives that arise from the modernization strategy, whereas EA is involved in all aspects of the modernization and interacts with the specific team that executes the initiatives identified on the modernization roadmap. The typical software development life cycle (SDLC) processes are used for all projects. DevOps also plays an important part in ensuring a successful interaction between the build and operations teams.

So how does an organization assess the cost, effort, risk, and time required for a planned modernization exercise? It all kicks off with an assessment. One of the most challenging tasks in any modernization exercise is the initial

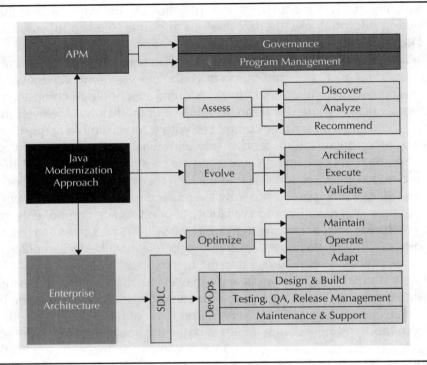

FIGURE 6-4. *Modernization methodology for Java application portfolios*

assessment of the portfolio and any influential factors that may determine the outcome. After that, the portfolio is reviewed and evaluated against a series of initiatives identified during the assessment stage. Finally, the portfolio is optimized, managed, and enhanced based on its new capacity. From a purely compliance point of view, a deep assessment may again be needed after a couple of years to bring the Java application portfolio back on track if it has reached a state of dissolution.

Assess the Java Application Portfolio

No modernization exercise should commence without a thorough assessment of the portfolio. Figure 6-5 characterizes the elements of modernization and how a modernization engagement starts with an assessment. There are four main elements to modernization upon which the design, activities, expectations, and outcome of the assessment are based:

- Importance
- Scale
- Challenges
- Impact

The importance of modernization to the enterprise is the first element. Modernization exercises should be conducted, at the very least, every five years; then the application portfolio can be evaluated for out-of-date applications. The importance of modernization for Java application portfolios that are not actively managed and maintained cannot be overstated. There will most likely be several inefficiencies inherent in such portfolios.

The element of scale is apropos to the number of applications in a particular portfolio. A portfolio with hundreds of Java applications will not have the same scale or approach to modernization as one with 10 or 20 applications. (An in-depth discussion of large-scale portfolio modernization approaches will be presented in Chapter 14.)

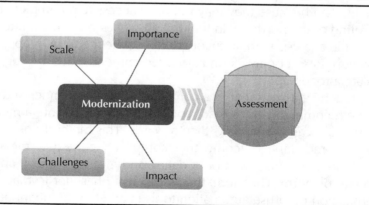

FIGURE 6-5. *Modernization exercises start with an assessment*

Modernization of Java application portfolios also comes with several challenges, either technical or operational in nature. Associated challenges could include issues with performance or inflexibility of the existing architecture. These challenges are discussed further later in this chapter in the section "Challenges."

The duration of these assessment exercises usually span eight to ten weeks, depending on the number of applications. This exercise may require three to five people to collect the data, interview the stakeholders, and analyze the information to generate recommendations in an assessment report. In this exclusively manual process, it is almost impossible to delve into the depths of every Java application in the portfolio. The manual assessment of Java portfolios begins with a distribution of a predefined template to all the application owners, with questions and application attributes in question. These individuals are then given a couple of weeks to fill out the questionnaire and return the completed template, which is often in Excel format. The assessment team then collates the information to analyze its contents.

I have successfully led these types of assessments, and there are some clear complications with this type of approach—namely, not all application owners comply with the information-gathering stage. As with all of our workdays, we have several competing daily requirements on our time. There are few additional hours in our schedules to prioritize and tackle a lengthy and complex assessment questionnaire. Other times, the current team that owns and maintains the applications may not be able to provide all the requested data because they may not have access to a complete historical background of the portfolio. In the end, the assessment team attempts to conduct the analysis with an incomplete knowledge base of application information. Based on this foundation, recommendations are suggested to formulate a roadmap.

Approaching assessment in a completely manual manner and then relying upon the recommendations made to formulate and execute a modernization strategy could carry more risks than rewards. This method does not result in a highly predictable outcome, thus complicating the determination of the exact scope of any migration or updating and moving the Java applications to a newer platform. Therefore, the assessment phase for Java application modernization must use automation tools in addition to the input collected through templates to yield a comprehensive analysis.

The last issue encountered is the impact to the team when dealing with 50 to several hundred Java applications. In that case, the time required to analyze each application can quickly add up. If a typical engagement spans approximately eight weeks, there would be insufficient time to collect information across all the applications and analyze the facts. One way to tackle this problem is to segment and categorize the applications quickly based on a few attributes. After that, a discussion with the application owners identifying about 15 to 20 percent of the applications from the entire population would significantly reduce the scope of the inquiry. Analyzing those applications under the assumption that decisions made from that inquiry would also hold true for that category of related applications could be concluded.

It is evidently clear that this is not a perfect approach; however, conducting a manual analysis on large Java application portfolios, bounded by finite time, leaves very few choices. An alternative would be to continue the haphazard maintenance of the Java applications in a portfolio, and when issues crop up, try to provide quick fixes at that time. This "fire-drill" approach is typically what occurs in most enterprises today, leading to expensive enhancements and excessive maintenance costs and posing a significant business risk of running applications on older JVMs. This practice is inflexible and does not take advantage of the evolved APIs and new components available on the Java platform.

One answer to these possible issues is an augmentation of the manual assessment exercise with automation tools. Figure 6-6 outlines an automated assessment with a three-step approach: discover, analyze, and recommend. The methodology for Java application portfolios is similar to the assessment methodology shared in Chapter 4, except that, in the case of a Java application portfolio, specific automation tools are additionally engaged as part of the assessment approach. Chapters 7 and 8 discuss existing tools that can be leveraged to automate some assessment tasks and also share approaches to building or customizing available tools for assessment of Java application portfolios.

The mechanics of the assessment approach are shown in Figure 6-7, which identifies the typical subject matter experts who interact with the automation tools or who conduct the information-gathering process. These automated assessments reduce the time to market significantly in terms of producing similar deliverables from comparable manual assessments.

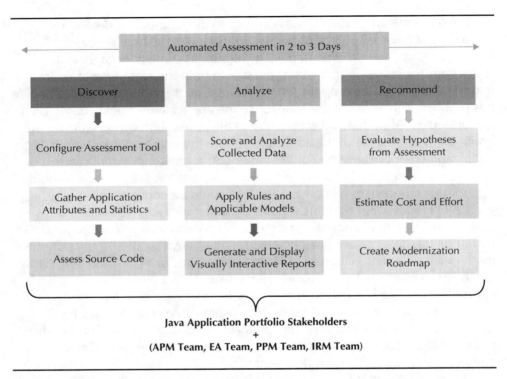

FIGURE 6-6. *Java application portfolio assessment methodology*

Discover

The discover phase of the assessment is a critical first step toward modernizing a Java application portfolio. In reality, it is never possible to make any portfolio assessment 100 percent automated. It is possible, however, to drive the assessment completely by automation tools. That is an important distinction. A wealth of information can be collected about an application by analyzing the source code, configuration files, meta-data, and the environment. The use of predefined templates to collect application information manually can complement and supplement the automated process of source code analysis. As a result, the automated information discovery process, along with interviews, documentation, and other information to create a knowledge base, can be analyzed using tools and manual processes; this combination offers the best of both worlds.

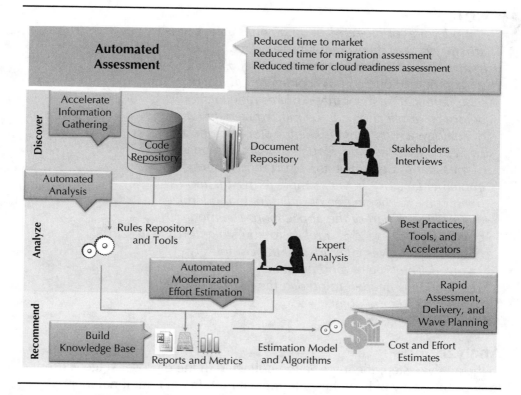

FIGURE 6-7. *Mechanics of the automated assessment approach*

The manual information collection can reveal financial- and cost-related information about an application, supported business processes, and other operational characteristics. The source code analysis will yield information about the APIs, code quality, the necessity of modification to the application, the complexity of the identified modernization points (or mod points), technical risks, and other pertinent technical information. As you can see in Figure 6-7, the discover step should result in a code repository as well as a document repository containing the automated source code, configuration files, overall environment analysis, stakeholder interview information, and other application attributes.

NOTE
A mod point, or modernization point, is an arbitrary unit of measurement related to an application and used to identify a particular section of the source code, configuration file, or other application asset that requires modification before an application can be modernized. In terms of analogy, a mod point is like the story point used by Scrum and Agile development teams—a unit of measure to determine the effort required to implement a story. In very simple terms, the mod point conveys the degree of difficulty to modernize that particular part of the application. The mod point does not exactly correlate to hours of effort or cost, but it gives a fair idea of the complexity involved. The type of mod point and other baseline information is needed to predict the level of effort related to the mod point.

Analyze

In the analyze step, the information collected in the discover stage is used to apply a variety of hypotheses to the data set. In the traditional manual approach, this analysis relies on the experience of the assessment team and their knowledge of the Java technology platform to evaluate similar application data and attributes to prepare a detailed analysis report. Once the report has been generated, stakeholders can rely on the conclusions to make appropriate recommendations. Although a highly experienced assessment team can conduct a fairly comprehensive analysis in this manner, it is important to remember that most enterprises have a variety of stakeholders, some of whom are professionally inexperienced or are new to the organization, which impedes their ability to collect the data and deliver a complete report exhaustive of any variables.

The decision to migrate an application to the latest Java platform, on premises or on the cloud, requires a probe into the level of resource effort, the associated cost, the available application attributes, and the conclusions drawn to reach a final decision. On the other hand, if such information was combined with a deep analysis of the application source code, the richness of the results would be remarkable. This profound inquiry would additionally scrutinize an understanding of the specific methods to be modified, the specific locations within the application source code requiring modification, the number of occurrences of such modifications, the complexity of the modifications, and other data regarding the technical environment. These factors will materially augment the manual analysis approach, collectively yielding an evaluation report that provides greater accuracy and insight into the application modernization decisions.

In the automated assessment approach, the analyze step leverages a rules repository that contains knowledge about the various Java APIs, commonly used third-party and open-source APIs, differences between the various versions, Java coding best practices, pitfalls, changes between various versions, and other related information. The Java application code that was parsed and stored as part of the discovery process into a code repository can be analyzed as an abstract syntax tree (AST) and the rules from the rules knowledge base can be applied to this AST tree to find patterns and matches. This will result in a very detailed analysis report with complete knowledge about the mod points that need to be addressed within a Java application. Figure 6-7 depicts the analyze step with a rules repository and the tools to apply the rules to parsed source code files. The manual analysis augments an expert's experience and background to the automated analysis. Chapter 8 addresses leveraging and customizing automation tools in detail.

Recommend

The recommend step is the critical third step in an assessment exercise. This step suggests the action items that should occur within the Java application portfolio. The report should include a roadmap with an overview of the recommended initiatives, including a high-level summary of the cost and effort associated with such initiatives. In the manual approach to assessments, this recommended roadmap would have heavily relied upon the results and documentation that were collected without a deep knowledge of the applications at a source-code level. In effect, the suggestions for budgetary cost and resource allocation would be quite inaccurate. Without basis in an automated approach, the roadmap developed from a purely manual assessment would be highly circumspect and organizationally risky to rely upon.

The numerous benefits of an automated approach include a knowledge base with estimation models, metrics, and estimation algorithms for the mod points and other data points identified in the automated analysis step. This advanced methodology will result in the calculation of costs and alignment of resources to be computed with a higher degree of confidence. Building such an encompassing estimation model takes considerable experience, a strong comprehension of data points, and the collection of data over a period of time across multiple projects through well-designed procedures. Moreover, the data points should take into account developer skill levels, technology maturity, application complexity, customer-specific influences, and a variety of metrics captured via software development processes pertaining to developing and maintaining Java applications. A roadmap constructed using an automated assessment approach will have an intrinsically better set of hypotheses generated and will align business objectives to project priorities more accurately, resulting in more predictability in the analysis outcomes.

When dealing with large Java application portfolios, it is necessary to group applications into waves based on certain criteria so that not all applications are addressed in a "big bang" approach to modernization. Especially for the migration or upgrade of applications to newer versions, applications are better tackled in smaller groups or waves.

Evolve the Java Application Portfolio

In the evolve stage, a governance and change management process is established. As the modernization team executes each project, as defined in the roadmap, each initiative involves the architecture of a solution to meet the business objectives. The most commonly executed projects involve migrating Java applications and retiring outdated applications. The modernization initiative itself will fit into a particular type of category including the following:

- Migrating application to new APIs and new JDK version

- Reengineering

- Refactoring

- Integration

- Rewriting

- Business process transformation

- Information architecture design

- Functional enhancements

- Introduction of new technology components and technical enhancement

- Reduction of functional or technical redundancies

- Retiring or decommissioning outdated applications

In contrast to the assessment stage, where a hypotheses-driven analysis culminates in prioritized initiatives, the evolve stage of modernizing a Java portfolio mostly centers around executing the vision behind the roadmap through defined programs. While the assessment stage employs estimation models and predicts the necessary resources and costs for identified initiatives, there is still a strong need to conduct a thorough business case analysis as part of the program charter before an initiative begins. The evolve stage can be broken down into three steps: architect, execute, and validate. It is essential to architect the modernization roadmap, execute the solution blueprint, and validate the solution to meet requirements, all before the official release.

Architect Phase

Architecting a modernization solution can be quite straightforward or very involved, depending on the scope of modernization. The particular architectural layer impacted will also vary based on the modernization need. In cases where the business process needs redesign or the information architecture requires an overhaul, all four architecture layers can be affected. While most people may consider the architect step to be a purely technical exercise, designing and executing a new technical solution, in reality that is only a subset of the possible ways in which the Java application portfolio could evolve.

When new business needs are identified and prioritized for a current portfolio, the scope and execution of those initiatives becomes the primary focus. The easier types of initiatives to architect include migration, upgrading, and refactoring type engagements. More involved projects involve consolidation of functionality, business process redesign, or information architecture redesign. Introducing new technical components and integration between existing components can be characterized as moderate complexity. This is also an opportunity to undertake business capability-driven transformation, functional decomposition, and technical decomposition of the portfolio to rebuild the business architecture, functional architecture, technical architecture, and infrastructure architecture to support the transformed business.

Execute Phase

The execute phase resembles the execution of any typical software development life cycle (SDLC). The application is enhanced, migrated, or refactored based on the scope of the initiative. Portfolio governance principles are not only important to application portfolio management, but they are also directly applicable to the Java portfolio modernization discipline. The metrics that were identified as part of the governance and change management process are similarly applied and tracked for the Java application portfolio.

Validate Phase

It is necessary to validate newly modernized applications so that they continue to meet their functional and nonfunctional requirements. This validation step should resemble the standard testing conducted as part of the SDLC process already in place at mature organizations. Automated testing as well as other classic testing approaches should be used during the modernization of any application.

Optimize the Java Application Portfolio

The optimize stage is extremely critical to the ongoing successful management of the Java application portfolio. While the assess and evolve stages ensure that the Java application portfolio has been successfully renovated and integrated, the bulk of the manage step falls within the optimize phase. In addition to setting up processes to maintain the Java portfolio, during the optimize stage, governance and change management processes are established with specific tailored metrics to measure the transformation of the portfolio. During this stage, the Java application portfolio shifts into a maintain, operate, and adapt mode.

The evolve stage ensures that the application and information architectures of the Java portfolio are reengineered to include emerging technologies, so that the reengineered applications take advantage of new technologies in the stack. In the optimize stage, the architectural layers and their individual components continue to be maintained, monitored, and managed.

Similarly, while the evolve stage executed engagements involving the consolidation of functionality or infrastructure to eliminate functional redundancies and infrastructure redundancies, the optimize stage incorporates maintenance and adjustments of the consolidated functionality and infrastructure.

Another key focus of the optimize stage is the operation of the Java application portfolio. This involves the introduction and stewardship of DevOps-related processes: identification, monitoring, ownership of metrics, and the governance process itself.

Occasionally, applications reach their end of life and exhaust their usefulness in an enterprise. Such applications are retired or phased out and existing users are migrated to other applications offering similar functionality. For legacy Java applications that have outlived their practicality, the business knowledge, functional knowledge, and data associated with those decommissioned legacy applications must be retained while they are replaced with newer applications or packaged COTS applications. Many portfolios contain these "non-value-added" applications that rampantly consume resources. Very few enterprises have the requisite governance and APM discipline in place to extract these applications gracefully without material impact.

Executing a Java Modernization Program

The success of any Java application modernization initiative depends on some key factors. Chapter 3 covered in great detail the relationship of APM to its peer disciplines of project portfolio management (PPM) and investment risk management (IRM). Chapter 4 covered the role of APM and EA and how they collaborate for the success of application portfolio management initiatives. The application portfolio management discipline spawned Java application modernization, with the core APM team driving the project. The aspects leading to the triumph of Java modernization programs mirror many of the characteristics that lead to the success of APM. In fact, it is necessary to have a flourishing APM program to maximize the benefits of modernizing Java applications. The seasoned APM program establishes necessary processes, industry best practices, governance, enterprise architecture involvement, identification of relevant stakeholders, and measurement of the progress of modernization initiatives. It cannot be said often enough that successful modernizations are not a standalone strategy. Rather, the modernization of Java application portfolios depends upon a deep and detailed understanding of the application portfolio itself—in other words, the successful operation of APM.

Why Modernize Java Applications?

There is a significant association between successful portfolio modernization and enterprise growth, which takes into account the financial and operational impacts to the organization. Notable risks exist for companies that choose to forgo modernizing their Java applications.

NOTE
As a bit of background information, Oracle ceased public updates for JDK 1.6 in February 2013, and public updates for JDK 1.7 ended in April 2015. Oracle had originally proposed that public updates to JDK 1.8 would be halted in September 2017! Given the massive delays for JDK 1.9, it is highly unlikely that JDK 1.8 would abandon public updates as early as September 2017. It would be in everyone's best interest for Oracle to wait a year or two after the release of JDK 1.9 before they discontinue public updates to JDK 1.8.

Chapter 1 illustrated several platform vulnerabilities and explained that upgrading to JDK 1.8 would provide a resolution for this susceptibility. Java SE 8 has introduced numerous security related enhancements, including the following:

- Client-side TLS 1.2 enabled by default

- Stronger algorithms for password-based encryption

- SSL/TLS Server Name Indication (SNI) extension support in Java Secure Socket Extension (JSSE) Server

- SunJSSE provider enhanced to support Authenticated Encryption with Associated Data (AEAD) mode–based cipher suites

- SHA-224 message digests

- Enhanced support for NSA Suite B Cryptography

- Better support for high entropy random number generation

Some performance improvements and key features have been added along the way. The new garbage collector, G1, was introduced in JDK 7u4. The G1 garbage collector provides the following:

- More maturity in terms of a garbage collector that supports large heaps, typically 6GB or larger

- More dependable pause times that are stable and predictable with latencies of less than 0.5 second

- No longer necessary to tune the permanent generation

- More consistent command-line flags

- Recommended for large enterprise applications that face undesirably long compaction pauses from current GC

Considerable reference literature exists for the following topics:

- Lambdas and streams that were introduced in Java SE 8 that increased the support for parallel programming, aggregate operations, collections, and reduced boilerplate code

- Performance improvements for HashMaps with key collisions

- Improved date and time APIs

- Improved diagnostics

A variety of new tools have also been introduced:

- jjs command-line tool to invoke the newly introduced Nashorn engine

- Java command to launch JavaFX applications

- Updated Java man page
- jdeps command-line tool for analyzing class files
- JMX remote access to diagnostic commands
- New option in jarsigner tool for requesting a signed time stamp from a Time Stamping Authority (TSA)

There are numerous reasons to modernize Java application portfolios. The exploitation of platform vulnerabilities is one serious consideration. The risk of exposure for out-of-date applications also creates a compelling interest for investment in application portfolio management, transforming the existing Java portfolio with an eye toward the future.

Leveraging APM with EA

In the context of Java portfolios, the APM discipline strives to align Java applications and the business functionality along with the business objectives of the departments that require these applications. Apart from reducing overall costs, APM also influences which applications can be replaced over time and determines where future investments should be made. EA, on the other hand, helps the core APM team conduct functional and technical decomposition of the Java application portfolio. This helps to identify opportunities for shared services and the reuse of such services across a variety of applications. In Chapters 10 and 11, we will address this topic in more detail and discuss how service platforms and services come together to provide application functionality.

When new JDK versions are announced or an updated API for third-party components is released, EA is an integral part of the decision-making process. Thus, APM and EA must be harmonious when applications migrate to a newer version. This synergy establishes a continuous mechanism to reduce business risk, optimize business value, and enhance the technical quality of a Java portfolio.

Leveraging the Stakeholders

The key stakeholders for Java application modernization include the application owners, technical architects, developers, business analysts, and project managers. This group owns and maintains the applications. Any decisions made regarding the application portfolio will impact this group; hence, it is vital to involve them early in the decision-making process. The end users of the applications are also stakeholders, but they will not feel any impact if the upgraded application fundamentally performs in the same way. These end users are also a part of the modernization process, but only at the time of user acceptance testing. It is important to keep them informed about the process and the expectations. Other stakeholders include operations, support personnel, and senior executive sponsors. They should also be kept informed throughout the execution of initiatives. These stakeholder groups are created in the context of a specific modernization program, and its members are transitory. On the other hand, the core APM team and constituent members of the EA group are permanent fixtures who are solely responsible for all modernization programs. As a refresher, Chapter 4 reviewed the process of identifying and forming stakeholder groups.

Sustaining Modernization Through the EA Discipline

Enterprises have executed APM projects in the past; however, the last five to seven years have seen organizations applying APM concepts to modernizing Java portfolios. Moreover, APM has typically been leveraged in one-time instances to assess a single application portfolio to improve its performance. Many of these assessments do not align with APM implementation processes that continuously monitor and manage their application portfolios, applying a clear set of objectives driven by the need to modernize. Very few organizations have established APM as a core discipline. Organizations that have established APM as a core discipline have reversed their traditional, and sometimes wasteful, budgetary spending percentages. After implementing modernization methodologies, these organizations, instead of spending 80 to 90 percent of their dollars on applications that keep the lights on, can reallocate priorities to enable more money to be apportioned to new development, thus decreasing that number to approximately 40 to 50 percent of the overall spending.

Organizations that embrace APM and leverage it for Java application portfolio modernization appreciate the amount of effort required. But EA must be intertwined with APM to create a sustainable adoption of the discipline. The modernization of application portfolios requires the involvement of highly skilled enterprise architects who recognize how architectural decisions impact the other applications or business processes that they manage. Many applications may be amenable to deployment in the cloud, whether private, public, or hybrid in nature. EA can influence those decisions during the assessment and analysis phase of the modernization effort. This is also a time when new technology components can be identified, introduced, and implemented into the portfolio. By integrating EA with APM processes, an organization can safeguard management methodologies and transform the application portfolio across all the architectural layers to optimize and maximize business value.

Benefits of Modernizing a Java Application Portfolio

The majority of Fortune 1000 companies have made significant investments in the Java platform to build their business applications. In fact, most of the Fortune 1000 companies have built a portfolio of custom Java applications over the past 15 years. In many such companies, these Java applications exist along with Microsoft .NET-based applications, mainframe applications, and applications increasingly being built with other emerging platforms. As discussed in Chapter 3, because of the budgetary constraints of building applications in enterprises today, these applications tend to be inflexible and poorly integrated as a result. Although Java, as a technology platform, is immensely flexible, developer friendly, and exceedingly scalable, the evolution of the applications over time has imposed constraints on its architectural development.

Many of these Java application portfolios are ill-equipped to take advantage of emerging technologies. Organizations with such portfolios find it extremely challenging to introduce NoSQL, cloud infrastructure, mobile technologies, and the like, into the applications in their portfolios. Many of these applications function in a legacy mode because of the nature of their architecture; hence, they are unable to take full advantage of the cloud-era technologies.

Modernizing these types of Java portfolios immediately unlocks enormous benefits in both a private or hybrid cloud infrastructure. The incorporation of a robust DevOps culture, coupled with the right processes, can positively impact Agile development approaches; building, testing, provisioning, deploying, monitoring, and managing the applications in a continuous fashion also becomes possible. Scaling these applications is another benefit of modernization, leading to ease of development, developer productivity, and improved operational efficiency. Ultimately, with APM practices in place, metrics can be measured to reveal significant long-term cost savings and abatement of business risk. Application enhancements and ability to meet changing business needs become easier to address, and the entire Java application portfolio is optimized for maximum business value.

Using automated tools and processes at the individual application level makes it practically effortless to upgrade and migrate to the latest Java platform. Collecting the right metrics, accurate cost estimations, and reengineering efforts to keep applications abreast with the new JDK becomes feasible. Chapter 7 discusses how to build these automation tools.

Governance of a Java Application Portfolio

The governance of a Java application portfolio is similar to the governance of any application portfolio being managed under the APM discipline. These high-level metrics were discussed in Chapter 3, and a more detailed discussion of the metrics and processes will be examined in Chapter 12. The core APM and EA teams jointly define the governance policies approved by a steering committee. Portfolio holders have ownership of the tools and processes as well as the data collected about a portfolio. This ensures that the entire organization has visibility into the stakeholders who have access to that data. These application owners are responsible for the execution of the specific projects and for providing application-specific attributes, in cooperation with portfolio owners and representatives from the PPM team. Key stakeholders ensure that the proper inputs are provided for operation of the APM process; the outputs are then shared with principal collaborators. The supporting roles and responsibilities for APM were outlined in Chapter 4. These criteria are applicable to Java application portfolios as well.

Challenges of Modernization

The challenges encountered in the modernization of Java application portfolios can be classified into business risks, operational process, and technical challenges. Following is a list of several challenges:

- *As applications are modernized, they should still be made available to end users.* Business-critical applications, especially, cannot afford any downtime; they must continuously meet their SLAs. There could be considerable challenges to developing a coexistence strategy and modernization schedule with minimal impact to the business.

- *Time-to-market for modernizing applications within the portfolio can vary depending on the specific scope of the modernization exercise.* It can be challenging to launch a modernization strategy given limited existing resources and budget allocations for primarily running existing applications.

- *Functionality of the applications may not be well documented, leading to a gap in the understanding of the applicable use cases that form the basis of the portfolio analysis.* If the application portfolio becomes a candidate for reengineering or consolidation with another application, there could be functional gaps in the modernized approach.

- *If applications are migrated from one application server to another or from one version of a third-party component to another version, these applications must be thoroughly tested.* If discontinuity is found in the test cases, either in unit tests or functional tests, there is a heightened risk of encountering issues in the deployed modernized applications.

- *Infrastructure consolidation or deployment to a cloud infrastructure would change the environment and configuration of the applications in the portfolio.* Challenges arise if this process is not addressed correctly.

- *The available source code may not align with the version of the application in production.* Such cases pose huge risks and challenges in identifying the baseline source code to evolve and modernize the application further.

- *The assessment of the Java applications in the portfolio might not be comprehensive.* An incomplete collection and documentation of certain attributes can lead to inconsistencies in the knowledge base and fragmented interactions with other applications.

- *The financial plan and operating model of an application portfolio can be difficult to quantify and record.* If the associated attributes are not captured correctly, attempts to build operational models for the portfolio and develop investment and risk profiles for the applications will become onerous.

- *To estimate the effort and cost associated with application modernization, metrics need to be established and collected over a period of time.* Lack of available historical data with respect to these metrics, or the absence of estimation models, will lead to incorrect predictions regarding total cost of ownership, return on investment, and timelines associated with completing modernization initiatives.

- *If source code, configuration files, and environment details are not analyzed thoroughly using automation tools, the modernization exercise will primarily rely on interviews and manual questionnaires completed by individual stakeholders.* This will lead to unpredictable and incomplete results for portfolio modernization.

- *Modernization depends on the availability of resources with sufficient knowledge for existing applications, the functionality of those applications, and a detailed technical design of the applications.* Availability of exhaustive documentation, test cases, environments, source code, and other related information is a must for a successful modernization program. There has always been a struggle to find the appropriate avenue to bridge the gaps intelligently between available data and necessary information; only then can there be a successful execution of portfolio modernization.

- *Complexities, interdependencies, and integration points between applications in the portfolio and on applications outside the portfolio can pose a substantial strain on one or more applications.* Applications may depend on a vendor-supported library not under the control of the modernization team; hence, there is a risk that a modernized application could fracture while trying to use the older version of the library.

Summary

The success of modernizing Java application portfolios depends on several factors. A core APM team along with participation from the EA team must drive modernization efforts. The key stakeholders and secondary collaborators in the application portfolio management must be involved from the beginning of the project. Modernization efforts start with an assessment. Automating the assessment phase will greatly reduce the effort, time, and risk, and it will greatly enhance predictability of the engagement. A rules knowledge base needs to be built, capturing all the differences between the various JDK versions and any third-party API library versions. These rules around best practices, code analysis, and other SDLC areas can be applied to the source code analysis to determine the exact mod points within the Java application source code. Other tools can be built for automating the modifications. If complete test cases are available and integrated into the process, a great deal of automation can be achieved for migrating and reengineering Java applications.

The next two chapters will address how automation tools can be built and geared toward the architects and developers of Java applications. These tools enable the process of modernization, driving the assessment, analysis, and estimation of the modernization efforts and help to formulate a roadmap. The evolve and optimize phases address the actual migration or reengineering of Java applications. These phases also employ automation tools where appropriate. Some of these tools may be homegrown, and others could be off-the-shelf; they will be used as long as they provide the functionality needed for modernization. The overall framework, the process of governance, and the portfolio management used are all meaningful to the overall evaluation.

CHAPTER
7

Automating
the Assessment:
Framework and Tools

Many enterprises have tried their hand at developing Java applications. Most organizations have embraced the Java platform by deploying Java applications into production. Even in companies where the dominant application platform consists of non-Java technologies, there will likely be a pocket of development in which a Java application has been prototyped. Today, many large and medium-sized enterprises have millions of lines of Java code in production. If the number of all third-party and open-source Java libraries used to build these applications were tallied, the number of lines of Java code deployed would be quite staggering.

Although these enterprises own the Java applications they developed, they often do not have an in-depth understanding about them. Such organizations would undoubtedly struggle to recount the total lines of Java code existing within the company's applications, provide a break-down by application, and state with confidence how many bugs or issues have been logged across the company spanning all applications. I am certain that there are exceptions to the rule, but I have yet to encounter a company that has complete knowledge of its Java applications in all respects and that has assembled a complete knowledge repository.

Chapter 6 delved into methodologies and approaches for modernizing a portfolio of Java applications. Figures 6-5 and 6-6 depicted the assessment process to discover the contents within a Java application portfolio. Most organizations today leverage Excel sheets and employ a team of consultants to conduct application group interviews and document information collected about the Java application portfolio. As an extension of that process, we looked at the benefits and mechanics of an automated assessment approach and briefly discussed the three-step assessment methodology—discover, analyze, and recommend. In this chapter, we will closely analyze the assessment step by identifying the benefits of using automation tools, rather than relying on purely traditional manual approaches. Automation enables organizations to bring efficiency, speed, and better insight into the assessment exercise.

Enterprises that leverage automation tools for conducting Java application assessments can build a comprehensive understanding of their total Java assets and application dependencies. The automation of metrics collection can add to the existing knowledge base to provide a better understanding of the cost and effort necessary to maintain the application portfolio. This automatic collection will allow for enhanced future design of migration and reengineering exercises. With these enhanced automation-derived metrics, the new robust knowledge base can then be mined for patterns and application traits that are not readily visible using traditional methods. In this chapter, we will review what features to consider in tools for the application analysis, effective visualizations that contribute to the overall design of application portfolio modernization roadmaps, and also aid in the recommendation stage as the Java application portfolio evolves. This chapter is a fairly technical chapter and requires that you understand many software engineering concepts and that you read up on tools and understand their inner workings.

Framework and Tools to Automate Java Portfolio Assessment

Any process is only as good as the tools that enable that process. So, where do we begin? How is the assessment process automated? What sorts of tools are useful? Are these recommended tools readily available? Are different tools necessary for each stage of the assessment process? These are the types of questions to consider before you launch into automation of the Java portfolio assessment stage.

Framework vs. Methodology

There is considerable debate about the definition of "methodology" and how it relates to an overall framework. There seem to be multiple definitions, variations, and interpretations of what constitutes a framework or methodology and whether the terms are interchangeable. Without a clear understanding of the fundamentals, these concepts can become confusing or mistakenly used. For the purpose of this book, we specifically distinguish between "methodology" and "framework."

A *methodology* is a set of principles, best practices, and prescriptive rules typically used to bring consistency and repeatability to a discipline. For example, earlier chapters provided a well-defined methodology and approach to the practice of the APM discipline.

A *framework*, on the other hand, is a fundamental conceptual structure that provides guidelines and processes for executing complex tasks or a set of activities. The specific details and the tools to execute the processes

(continued)

are left to the adopter of the framework. In our case, the automation of assessing the application portfolio is guided by a framework; however, the specific tools and how they are implemented to support those processes are left to the enterprises. So two enterprises can implement a completely different set of tools or leverage the same tools to derive different assessment automation outcomes.

Conceptual Architecture and Process of Automating Assessment

Let's assume for a moment that an assessment toolset can be built to automate the assessment of a portfolio of Java applications. A few question come to mind immediately:

- How will this solution function conceptually?

- What are the main steps and processes of using such a solution?

- What would be the output of this solution?

The main assets in a Java application portfolio are the Java applications themselves. The applications are essentially made up of the Java archive files such as WAR, EAR, and JAR files. These archive files are a bundle of Java class files that are compiled from the Java source code. Also, the source code was written for a specific target JDK and the class files were obtained by compiling the source code with a specific version of the compiler that supported a specific Java platform version. So, as part of the discover stage, our tools must be capable of analyzing the Java class files and source code and be able to identify within those files whether specific parts of the Java code can be modified to adopt the new features, syntax, or API of another, later JDK version. For example, consider a Java application that consists of Java class files that were compiled against JDK 1.6. The assessment tools would first have to discover the source code and class files of the application.

Then, as part of the analyze stage, an analysis could be conducted of the source files, class files, or both to determine what portions of the code must be modified to upgrade the code to JDK 1.8, JDK 1.9, or whatever is the latest Java version. The output from such an analysis could provide, among other things, a visual report of the Java packages, affected Java source code, categories of recommended modifications to upgrade to the latest JDK version, and specific locations with the source code where the modifications need to be made.

Further, as part of the recommend stage, a recommendation would be made regarding the priorities of the suggested modification, the complexity of the suggested modification, and whether the suggested modification could be automated or would involve manual intervention to change and recompile the code base against JDK 1.8, JDK 1.9, or the latest JDK at the time.

Where would we begin when conducting this type of analysis? We need to go beyond a simple parsing of the source code and ask the following questions:

- How could such a solution know about every API and every third-party library or open-source library used by a Java application?

- Could the application be selectively analyzed against certain Java source files or upgraded to specific APIs or libraries?

- What if a follow-up analysis of the Java application needed to be conducted again after a few weeks? Would that be possible without having to analyze the entire code base again?

In answering these very relevant questions, the analysis prompts us to consider a conceptual architecture solution that broadly meets the following criteria:

- The Java application should be analyzed and the results of that analysis stored in a canonical form for future retrieval so that the application will not need re-analysis at a later date to determine its contents.

- A set of rules could be applied to the application during the analysis, which could assist in the determination of specific features to look for and flag as potential modifications.

- The set of rules should be extensible to accommodate analysis scope changes at a later date and should be capable of including APIs used by the application.

- The results of the analysis must be made available visually to allow for easy interpretation of the analysis results.

- The final report should provide relative recommendations including the identification of high priority modifications. The knowledge base should track such priorities across JDK and third-party library versions to determine the level of complexity and effort involved in making the identified modifications.

The Java application portfolio is not composed only of Java source files and class files. Many other artifacts come under the purview of the portfolio and require discovery and analysis as well. We can apply the overarching framework of discover, analyze, and recommend, enabling the assessment process with a specific set of tools. This set of tools will meet the requirements of the solution stack and facilitate the process of modernizing the Java application portfolio. Figure 7-1 provides an assortment of recommended functionalities to expect from tools to assess and migrate a portfolio of Java applications. Several open-source and proprietary tools meet some of the suggested functionalities. Subsequent sections of this book examine some of these available tools in more detail, compare specific tool traits, and make suggestions about the important tools and their proper usage.

The Solution Stack Conceptual Enablement

To recap, Figure 6-7 in Chapter 6 illustrated the three-step assessment methodology and the mechanics of an automated assessment. This assessment methodology provided a conceptual explanation of the process. To implement such an approach, you would have to use the correct tools to carry out the envisioned tasks; however, no single tool can completely and accurately perform each step of the assessment methodology alone. The successful combination of tools, each with its own features and applicability, will collectively contribute to the final automated assessment results.

This section discusses the composition of a solution stack during an automated assessment and migration of a Java application portfolio. For this analysis, the solution stack is analyzed using available tools and dividing the tools into three distinct areas for comparison:

- Discovery and analysis

- Recommendation and visualization

- Database modernization

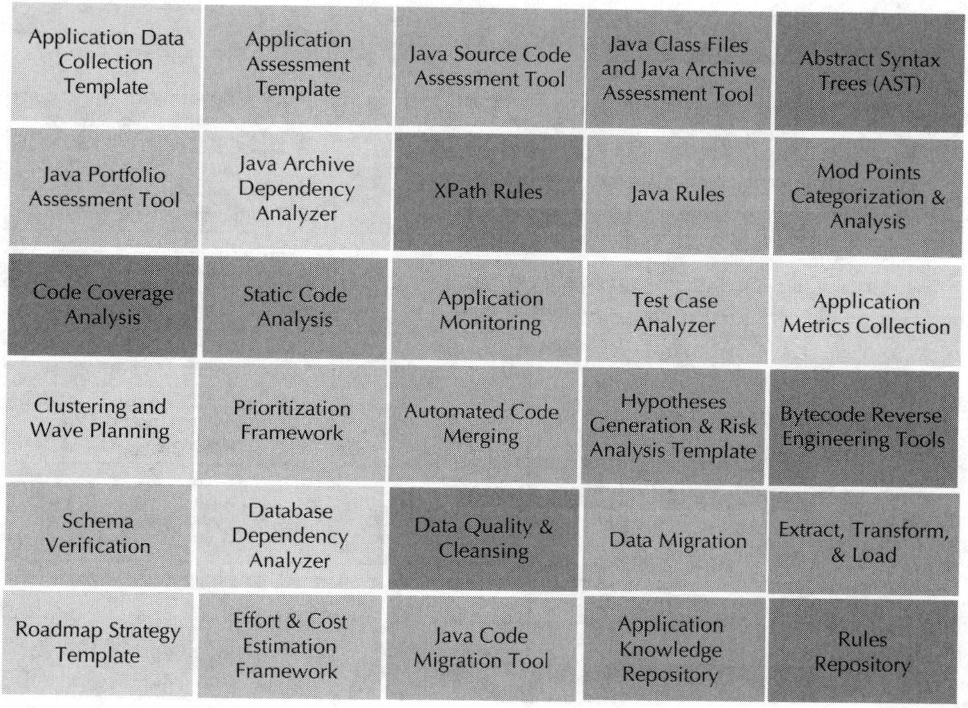

Application Data Collection Template	Application Assessment Template	Java Source Code Assessment Tool	Java Class Files and Java Archive Assessment Tool	Abstract Syntax Trees (AST)
Java Portfolio Assessment Tool	Java Archive Dependency Analyzer	XPath Rules	Java Rules	Mod Points Categorization & Analysis
Code Coverage Analysis	Static Code Analysis	Application Monitoring	Test Case Analyzer	Application Metrics Collection
Clustering and Wave Planning	Prioritization Framework	Automated Code Merging	Hypotheses Generation & Risk Analysis Template	Bytecode Reverse Engineering Tools
Schema Verification	Database Dependency Analyzer	Data Quality & Cleansing	Data Migration	Extract, Transform, & Load
Roadmap Strategy Template	Effort & Cost Estimation Framework	Java Code Migration Tool	Application Knowledge Repository	Rules Repository

FIGURE 7-1.   *An assortment of features expected from tools that support automating assessment and migration*

Although many tools have overlapping functionality, some of them have intrinsically unique features. It is also important to recognize the inherent gaps in available toolsets, especially when it comes to recommendation and visualization. At that stage, it may be necessary to implement missing features and functionality by building out additional tools or extending the applicability of existing ones. Figure 7-2 lists key features that must be available in the selected toolset and organizes the features of the tools by mapping them to the three stages of the assessment framework where they are more relevant.

Discovery and Analysis
To assess Java application portfolios properly and make calculated go-forward migration decisions, the first step requires discovery of the repository and the creation of a knowledge base of the portfolio. Java application portfolios

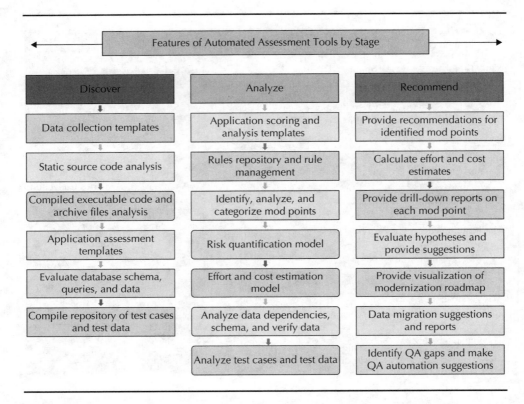

FIGURE 7-2. *Sets of features provided by automated Java application portfolio assessment tools by stage*

are more than just a compilation of Java application source code. The applications must be viewed in their entirety. Apart from the application code, there are multiple environments, build and QA processes, databases, user interfaces, and other artifacts.

Typical Java application portfolios consist of the following elements:

- Java source code
- Third-party libraries
- Open-source libraries
- Application server

- Configuration files
- UI artifacts, including HTML, CSS, JSP, and other files
- Database server
- Database scripts
- Test data
- Unit tests
- Build processes
- Test harness for test automation
- Deployment scripts
- Build, QA, and runtime environments
- Various archive formats, such as EAR, WAR, and JAR files
- Management and monitoring scripts

This list is just an illustrative sampling of the types of artifacts a specific portfolio can use. Most of this information can be discovered automatically using a collection of tools. In the process, these tools will run against a given portfolio, read its source code, process executable files and other artifacts, and finally build a knowledge base of information. This knowledge base can contain information such as the following:

- Number of Java class files
- Number of lines of source code
- Specific libraries used and their versions
- Dependencies
- Environment-related information
- Types and versions of APIs used by an application
- Number of specific types of components
- Java Message Service–related configurations
- Micro services and service interfaces

Some of the tools used as part of the discover and analyze steps can also conduct static code analysis and document violations of standard best practices. Another interesting use of a discovery tool is to parse the application source code, using automated analysis, to build abstract syntax trees (ASTs) as a representation of the source code.

Ideal Features of Discovery and Analysis Tools

An ideal discovery and analysis tool should be simple for an end user to install and use. The end user in this case would be someone on the Java application portfolio modernization team with a software developer or business analyst skill set. The tool must have a web-based UI. Although you could try making a convincing argument that the UI need not be web-based, you can imagine the effort to install and maintain yet another GUI application on several user's laptops and desktops. My experience has been that a web-based UI enables upgrades to the server and rollouts of new features to the toolset with minimal impact. The users must be able to use the provided UI and load several Java applications and determine the associated assets. Then these assets, which include Java source code and executable code, must be examined using proper toolsets that provide a detailed understanding of the application, and this information should be documented in a knowledge base. The tool should also enable users to collaborate and manually add application-related data to the existing collection of automatically derived application data. There must be a built-in mechanism to view the auto-generated data and manually collected data and import or export that data into a standardized format. The ideal discovery tool should provide a view of the constructed application portfolio knowledge base and a way to associate the several application attributes spanning technical details, financial information, application quality, and others key features.

Figure 7-2 provided a rubric of the expected toolset features that can be applied for all three steps of the assessment framework. While enabling this framework, an enterprise can use this illustrative rubric to define its expected toolset features and evaluate the selected tools that meet its needs. Later in this chapter, several tools are presented along with their descriptions and capabilities to kick-start and enable the assessment framework.

Additionally, the tool must be able to create and store rules in a rules repository that can be applied to the discovered source code, executable code, and other assets. These rules must allow the tool to find such places in the Java application where changes must be made to upgrade the application code.

While static code analysis merely applies rules for best practices and improving the code, these rules must go beyond such basics and actually determine places in the code base that are outdated or stale when compared to newer JDK version or newer versions of third-party libraries or open-source libraries.

Figure 7-3 highlights and describes the key activities of the five major steps of the rule generation and execution process:

- Identification

- Modeling

- Gap analysis

- Creation and verification

- Deployment and execution

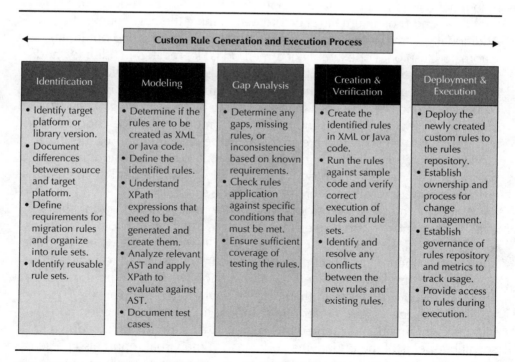

FIGURE 7-3. *Process of custom rule generation and execution*

The tool must also have an intermediate representation of the parsed applications so that the discovered application code base does not require reanalysis in the future when new rules are created.

Recommendation and Visualization

After discovering and analyzing all the assets associated with a portfolio of Java applications, the tools in the solution stack must also be capable of making appropriate recommendations regarding that analysis. These recommendations need to be in a visual form so that end users can easily understand and correctly interpret the results.

These recommendations are dependent on a specific set of relevant objectives and hypotheses in an organization, so they must be contextually interpreted and prioritized prior to execution. If, for example, a tool makes a recommendation to replace a particular method in a million lines of code with another method, the organization must first carefully evaluate the recommendation in the context of operational challenges, requisite effort, total cost, and project timelines before determining the best course of action. Additionally, some of these recommendations could be carried out in an automated fashion. For example, if a method is deprecated in a library, and the tool suggests a replacement of that method with an equivalent method in which only the method name has changed in the newer version of that library, there may be no repercussions in replacing the method name globally. This could be done automatically and the resulting modified source code compiled and tested. Not all scenarios are so trivial, however. When an organization modernizes a code base to a new JDK version, it matters how old the code base is. If the original code base is several JDK versions behind, then chances are that the modernization exercise will not be simple.

When an enterprise wants to apply a custom set of rules during the analysis step, those custom rules may also have associated recommendations for each rule. Thus, for a particular section of the code base where the rule applies, the documented recommendation can be displayed to indicate the level of the complexity involved. While a tedious report can be produced for every discovered point in the code base where a particular rule base applies, such reports are better understood with a visual depiction and high-level information presented in a manner that supports drilling down to specific aspects of the underlying code base. If the visual report also presents recommendations and associated priority and complexity levels as well as allowing previews of changes to the source code, then the overall decision-making process becomes more efficient.

Ideal Features of Recommendation and Visualization Tools

An ideal recommendation and visualization tool must present the discovery and analysis report in a manner that makes the results easy to understand. End users must be able to filter the analysis results and focus on particular areas of interest. One user may be interested in only a couple of specific applications and not the entire application portfolio. Another developer may be interested in the entire application portfolio but only regarding a specific API or library that the developer currently maintains. Those in other business roles, such as database administrators, may be interested only in environment-related information and associated configuration files.

If the visualization tools are flexible and provide the ability to generate custom visual reports, the value of the tool is greatly enhanced. There could additionally be standard out-of-the-box reports to save the user valuable time while figuring out analysis results. Such reports should also be highly visual and allow drill-downs and aggregations to enable users to traverse the analyzed application portfolio from top to bottom in a useful manner. If these visualizations are integrated into application portfolio management (APM) reports that provide an analysis of the various application attributes by providing 2×2 matrices comparing application health, technical quality, and business value, then consumers will be able to make thoughtful decisions about the overall application portfolio.

It is also possible for recommendations to be integrated with business objectives and hypotheses combining operational, financial, and technical data. Even if such integrations are not immediately possible or the tool does not support such a feature out of the box, at a minimum, the tool should support technical decision-making by providing recommendations regarding the complexity of the discovered source code violations. This is accomplished by applying custom rules and suggesting priorities to address the discovered violations.

Database Modernization

Most portfolio assessment exercises focus their efforts on the applications within the portfolio. There is very limited attention given to the application databases that store the data, conduct transactions, generate reports, and prepare analytics. These databases must be given importance as well. This section illustrates the typical tool features that focus on assessing and analyzing databases in this manner.

The most important tools in database modernization are the database discovery tools. These tools can be used to analyze databases, extract database details, and standardize data representation across the portfolio for easy analysis and retrieval. All relevant artifacts associated with the databases must be discovered and documented so that subsequent migration exercises ensure that certain databases are not inadvertently omitted.

Database dependency analysis tools can be leveraged to analyze dependencies of queries, stored procedures, triggers, database schema, and tables. The dependency matrix of database artifacts for the application portfolio is built in this way. It is crucial to analyze database versions for incompatibilities against application requirements as databases are upgraded. The knowledge base should also be updated with the repository of database information.

As applications are migrated or otherwise modernized, the underlying application data residing in the databases must be backed up and restored as necessary. As the databases themselves undergo modernization, data migration tools can be leveraged to bulk load data between database versions during the migration process.

The database schema might be modified under certain circumstances, especially if new business requirements are being implemented as part of the modernization efforts. In such situations, it is imperative that you undertake data comparison and verification of the new database schema to ensure that the previously stored application data appropriately fits in with the new schema.

As part of application portfolio modernization, several database-related tasks need to be planned and executed, including database upgrades, database testing, application code remediation and interaction with databases, database queries remediation, and report generation. The following database assessment tools are typically used during the migration and modernization of Java applications:

- **Discovery**   Analyze databases, extract database details, and standardize representation across the portfolio for easy analysis later.

- **Dependency analysis**   Analyze dependencies of queries, stored procedures, triggers, database schema, and tables to build a dependency matrix for the application portfolio. Analyze database versions for incompatibilities against the repository of database information.

- **Data migration**   Bulk load data between database versions during migration process.

- **Schema and data comparison and verification**   Compare source and target database schemas when there are changes, and verify schema and migrated data against a variety of test cases.

- **Database upgrade**   Test the database, remediate code, generate reports, and upgrade databases during application migration.

Some of the tools considered for database modernization and migration include Liquibase, Flyway, Scriptella, Phinx, Talend, and Pentaho. In addition to these main tools, several others exist, including comprehensive tools provided by database vendors.

Challenges Faced in Database Migration

Applications prove their utility by processing and presenting relevant data to requesting business units within an enterprise. Those applications that contain business logic without the data located in underlying databases are not very useful. As applications are modernized, so will these underlying databases. Database modernization exercises are fraught with difficulty and present a unique set of challenges. Enterprises typically underestimate the importance and effort associated with data analysis. This is typically because many stakeholders do not possess a thorough understanding of all the dependent data sources of an application portfolio. Enterprises can also have varied data sources spanning relational databases, spread sheets, NoSQL databases, hierarchical databases, and other related sources.

Data integrity and data quality are two foremost areas to keep in mind. According to industry analysts, more than 85 percent of data modernization and migration projects run into significant problems. The lack of project standardization, lack of collaboration among teams, poor system design, and inaccurate or incomplete data contributes to many of these issues. This section highlights typical challenges that enterprises face and provides guidance for creating an application modernization plan to avoid becoming part of the majority.

Schema Verification and Data Quality   Typical application portfolios have multiple databases that contain similar schemas and represent the same entities with overlapping attributes. The names used to represent the attributes also widely vary. This lack of canonical representation of database schemas is rampant in enterprises, as each application team and business unit decides to create its own schema and data dictionary. Such inconsistent and incompatible data schemas pose a challenge during data consolidation and transformation. It is equally important to identify and validate data schemas using a defined canonical data model. Data quality poses significant issues for an application. Therefore, validation rules should be created to check source data and ensure the timely flagging and rectification of data quality issues.

Data Mapping and Validation As part of application portfolio modernization, multiple source systems of data might be merged or rationalized. This will require the underlying databases also to undergo some elimination, consolidation, and modification. One of the outcomes of this exercise is that dissimilar data from multiple source systems may be mapped to a canonical model or a target database schema. As the data is extracted, transformed, mapped, and loaded from a source schema into the new target schema, it is essential to validate that data. To carry out this validation, certain tools can be leveraged, including specific extract, transform, and load (ETL) tools. It is critical to understand the mapping and merging of data profiles thoroughly. Some of this data mapping transformation could be complex, especially if there are referential integrities and normalization of data elements. Employing multiple stages to check, test, and validate the transformed data will aid in successful modernization results.

Data Redundancy The challenge of data redundancy is slightly different from the issue of similar schemas. With data redundancy, similar data could be present in multiple databases, and each application or set of applications could access its own database and modify entities. This poses significant concerns, because there are multiple systems of truth for these entities. The question becomes, which database possesses accurate and reliable data? For example, what if there are three databases, each storing and modifying customer data, but all three have slightly different values for a particular customer? If existing or new applications are consolidated with or integrated into other applications, then accessing necessary customer data can become an unreliable activity. These types of complex issues often surface in enterprises, especially when functionally redundant systems have evolved over a period of time.

Some approaches to address data redundancy issues involve reviews of data dictionaries, entity relationships, source code review, and data analysis to identify the single source of truth. It could also involve consolidating or accessing databases through specific micro services to read or write to the existing underlying database. The particular modernization strategy to be adopted depends on a thorough analysis in a given context. The consultation of subject matter experts and business stakeholders may be necessary to determine the significance of data elements and ownership of the entities along with their identified attributes.

The Solution Stack for Java Portfolio Assessment

Earlier in this chapter, we discussed the conceptual architecture and enablement of the solution stack for Java application assessments. Several tools are available to support these assessments, many of which have been created using open-source software. Because there is no single comprehensive tool that can address the needs of an entire solution stack, the best approach would be to mix and match the best-of-breed tools to assemble the solution stack. Before many of these tools became available, I built a solution stack from the ground up. However, with technological advancements over the years, it is not necessary to custom tool the entire stack. In fact, it is more economical and efficient to use existing resources first.

Although this section will also touch upon some of the proprietary tools available today, it is important to note that none of them provides a complete solution and, in many respects, none provides feature sets as complete as some open-source options. Regardless of the selected toolset, a significant time and budgetary investment is necessary to train available resources and familiarize the teams with the adopted solution stack. Additionally, enterprises must also account for the inevitable implementation of supplementary supporting tools to fill in the gaps and achieve complete solution stack automation.

The ideal solution stack will consist of tools that can do the following:

- Automatically discover all the assets contained in a Java application portfolio.

- Provide interfaces to add, delete, and update application related attributes manually and programmatically.

- Score various attributes and generate comparison graphs.

- Enable creation of rules that can be applied to the migration automation.

- Apply in-built and custom rules to analyze the portfolio.

- Recommend modernization and migration options.

- Automatically replace existing code with suggested options.

- Verify and validate modernized or migrated code with full test automation.

   The sections that follow delve deeper into the available tools and present the features and capabilities of these tools so that enterprises can make their own determination as to what tools they should adopt and further customize.

Open-Source Tools for Application Analysis and Testing

Application analysis tools are used to perform automated parsing and static analysis of the source code, class files, configuration files, and other application-related assets. Testing tools are used to analyze source code, generate unit tests, and automate the overall testing process. Some of the tools and techniques related to automated testing are addressed separately later in this chapter. Together, analysis tools and testing tools can form a powerful combination to bring in an unprecedented level of automation to the general problem of application modernization. Although the intended purpose is for automating Java application modernization, an unintended consequence could be to improve the application development process significantly, where the usefulness of the tools can range from aligning with best practices, to flagging deprecated methods, auto completion of code, generating and running unit tests, and debugging application programs during application development.

NOTE
In the case of programming languages such as Java, source code parsing is the process of analyzing Java source code to create an internal representation. This is accomplished by using a parser. The parser reads the Java source code, divides it into smaller components for easier analysis, gives a structural representation for the input, and checks for correct syntax in the process. ANTLR and JavaCC are two well-known parser development tools for the Java language.

The following sections discuss tools used for source code analysis for Java applications.

Checkstyle

Checkstyle is a static code analysis tool that can be used to check whether the Java application source code adheres to specified coding standards. It automates the process of checking Java code and is ideal for enforcing a set of coding best practices. Checkstyle is highly configurable and can be made to support almost any coding standard.

The programming style adopted by a software development project can help to meet specified standards that improve the code quality, readability, and reusability, and reduce the cost of development. Checkstyle can find problems associated with class and method design and check code layout and formatting issues.

Although this tool checks for standards and focuses on presentation, the correctness or completeness of the program is not analyzed. The violations that Checkstyle detects are classified into three severity levels: information, warning, and error. The applied rules can be categorized and an associated message can be displayed in a report. Checkstyle can be integrated in any build process or development environment.

FindBugs

FindBugs is a static code analysis tool that examines Java class or JAR files. FindBugs identifies potential problems by matching the byte code against a list of built-in bug patterns. You can analyze applications without actually running the program. FindBugs uses the visitor pattern and analyzes the form or structure of the class files to determine the application's intent.

FindBugs is a good choice for static code analysis of an application. Developers benefit greatly because FindBugs can help detect common issues and provide quick fixes for the code base resulting from the static code analysis. The new version of FindBugs is powerful and boasts several improvements. The only negative against FindBugs when comparing against a few other static code analysis tools is that the documentation is not as current and lacks sufficient examples.

PMD

PMD is a source code analyzer that finds common programming flaws such as unused variables, empty catch blocks, unnecessary object creation, and much more. It supports Java, JavaScript, XML, XSL, and other languages.

Additionally, it includes the copy-paste-detector (CPD), which allows PMD to find duplicated code in a variety of programming languages such as Java, C++, PHP, Groovy, JavaScript, and more. PMD scans source code in Java and other languages and looks for potential problems such as these:

- Possible bugs, such as empty try, catch, finally, and switch statements

- Dead code, such as unused local variables, parameters, and private methods

- Suboptimal code

- Overcomplicated expressions, such as unnecessary if statements and for loops that could be while loops

- Duplicate code

One impressive feature of PMD is its ability to define XPath Rules. Bundled with a Rule Designer, PMD allows for easy construct of new rules from code samples (similar to Regex and XPath GUI builders). It provides a detailed analysis with error and warning levels. PMD internally uses the JavaCC parser generator to parse the Java source code into an intermediate representation, the abstract syntax tree (AST). PMD currently supports parsing the Java language with grammars built on JavaCC. The generation of the AST structure from the Java source code is not a simple process. We will address PMD in greater detail in Chapter 8.

Figure 7-4 depicts the key steps in the process when PMD is used to analyze Java code. PMD loads Java code and applicable core rules and custom rules. A JavaCC-generated parser is used by PMD, which reads the Java code and returns a reference to an AST. PMD hands off the generated AST to the symbol table layer, which builds the scopes and finds declarations and usages. Rules that need data-flow analysis are addressed by handing the AST to a deterministic finite automaton (DFA) layer for building control flow graphs and data flow nodes. Each rule in the loaded rule set gets to traverse the AST and check for problem matches. Rules can also reference the symbol table and data flow nodes. PMD finally generates a report of the rule violations.

SonarQube and SonarLint

SonarQube is an open-source quality management platform that is applicable to an entire application portfolio. This platform can be used to analyze and measure technical quality continuously. Static analysis of the source code

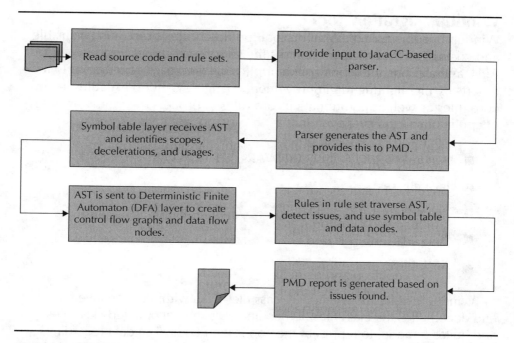

FIGURE 7-4.   *PMD process internals*

is supported for more than 20 languages at the time of this writing. For Java and a few other languages, static analysis of compiled code can also be performed. SonarQube provides an overview of the overall health of the Java application source code and highlights issues found within the code. It functions as a central server that processes and analyzes the application portfolio, triggered by the various SonarQube scanners. The process can be automated and run multiple times as part of continuous integration to give a 360-degree vision of the quality of the code base by analyzing all the source lines of a project on a regular basis.

SonarLint is installed only within an IDE such as Eclipse or IntelliJ. Its purpose is to give instantaneous feedback on new bugs or quality issues introduced into an application as lines of code are added or updated on-the-fly by a developer. It is a good tool to enforce code quality and best practices even as a developer is coding an application. SonarLint is also available as open source. SonarLint and SonarQube rely on the same static source code analyzers, written using SonarSource technology.

Windup Migration Tool

Windup is a rule-based migration tool for Java applications. It is extensible and customizable. This tool analyses the source directories, technologies, APIs, and artifacts used by the Java application and then generates HTML reports by highlighting the improvement changes. Windup executes its own core rules as well as additional custom rules to process the following types of application input artifacts:

- Archive files such as EARs, WARs, JARs

- Java classes

- JSP files

- Manifest files

- XML files

Windup extracts the compiled class files from within the archive files and decompiles the class files. It then analyzes the decompiled class files and builds a model to represent the application code. The data regarding application components and their relationships is then stored in a graph database. This graph database can be queried as necessary, and information is present in a visual form. The data is modified upon additional analysis of other components.

Windup provides a core set of built-in migration rules. It also supports the addition of custom migration rules. After the graph database is built, migration rules are executed against the data model. The rules themselves are independent and exist separately. The rules are applied and the Windup application tests the rule condition against the graph database. The results of the rule execution are then updated back into the graph database. Rules can interact with other rules, and complex rules can be created because of the inherent design of the graph database and how rules are applied.

Figure 7-5 depicts the key steps in the process when Windup is used to analyze Java code. Windup can be run against a Java application from the command line or from the Eclipse plug-in. Core rules as well as custom

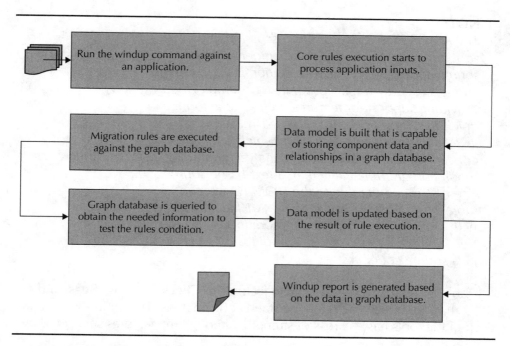

FIGURE 7-5.   *Windup process internals*

rules are loaded and executed against the specified application. Windup builds a data model from its analysis and stores the component data and relationships in a graph database. The migration rules that were loaded are executed against this graph database. Rule conditions are tested by querying the graph database and getting the component information against which the rules are applied. The results of the rule execution are updated back into the graph database. Windup finally generates reports based on the results in the graph database.

The HTML-generated Windup report consists of Application List, Report Index, Application Details report, Archive detail, Source report, Rule Provider Execution report, FreeMarker functions, and Directives report. We will review Windup in more detail in Chapter 8.

NOTE
The AST, in the context of this discussion, is a structured representation of the underlying Java source code. The AST representation is very useful, and it is used by the Eclipse IDE, for example, in providing support for features such as refactoring, quick fix, and quick assist. The AST maps plain Java source code in a tree form, which is a more convenient and reliable way to analyze and modify programmatically than a text-based source. The AST is comparable to the DOM (Document Object Model) tree model of an XML file. Just as with DOM, the AST allows for modification of the tree model and reflects these modifications in the Java source code.

Table 7-1 compares the available features of Checkstyle, FindBugs, and PMD that can be leveraged during static code analysis. The table shows that each of the tools has its areas of strength, although the features supported by

Types of Verifications	Description	Checkstyle	FindBugs	PMD
Naming conventions	Rules to be followed while naming variables, methods, and other entities in the source code.	Y	N	Y
Headers and imports	Imports are the APIs, packages, and classes included in the source code. Header is the place where we include the imports.	Y	N	Y
Formatting and white space	Source code typically has unwanted white spaces. Formatting and correct indentation helps to align the code.	Y	N	Y

TABLE 7-1.   *Comparison of Checkstyle, FindBugs, and PMD (Continued)*

Types of Verifications	Description	Checkstyle	FindBugs	PMD
Javadoc comments	Javadoc comments are in HTML format and are generated from the Java source code by the Javadoc tool based on the annotations provided in the source code.	Y	N	Y
Best practices and standard coding conventions	Standard coding conventions are the set of guidelines that need to be followed while writing code. Best practices ensure that developers adhere to the accepted and desired programming style.	Y	N	Y
Method parameters	Method parameters are the input given to a method while calling the method.	Y	N	Y
Cyclomatic complexity	A software engineering measurement used to indicate the complexity of a computer program.	Y	N	Y
Regular expression	Special sequence or an occurring pattern of characters that are used to search, edit, or manipulate data and text.	Y	N	Y
Possible bugs	Bugs that are present in the bug pattern that are frequently captured in the checks run against the code.	N	Y	Y
Dead code	A portion of code present in the source code that is executed, but the result is not used anywhere in the program.	N	N	Y

TABLE 7-1. *Comparison of Checkstyle, FindBugs, and PMD (Continued)*

Types of Verifications	Description	Checkstyle	FindBugs	PMD
Duplicated code	Instructions in the source code that are repeated more than once.	N	N	Y
Overcomplicated expressions	Sequence of code that complicates the execution of the program.	N	N	Y
Design flaws	Source code contains some unchangeable and inflexible program structures that consequently reduce software quality. Refactoring can also become tricky.	N	Y	N
Anti-patterns or bad programming practices	Portions of code or even entire classes are written in such a way that it could break during execution or affect maintenance. Such applications are difficult to evolve architecturally and many need major rewrites.	N	Y	N
Multithreaded correctness	Multithreading refers to two or more tasks executing in parallel within a single program. Improper code can result in race conditions or deadlocks.	N	Y	N
Code vulnerabilities	Vulnerabilities are parts of a source code that reduce or otherwise affect the security of the program.	N	Y	N
Custom rules	Customizable additions to existing functionality by adding XML, XPath, or Java code to extend the core functionality of the tool.	Y	N	Y

TABLE 7-1. *Comparison of Checkstyle, FindBugs, and PMD*

PMD are a bit more comprehensive than the other two. Certain features that are found in FindBugs but not in PMD can be easily implemented in PMD through custom rules or Java code. Given PMD's flexibility and extensibility, it is the go-to tool if budgets and resources limit the number of applicable toolsets. Although PMD is solid, a better option would be to automate the use of all three toolsets, resulting in a more comparative analysis.

Chapter 8 will address PMD and Windup in greater detail by comparing and contrasting those tools. Windup brings a different set of features to the mix and provides a crucial level of understanding about the Java application it analyzes to ensure that good decisions can be made regarding migration of the Java application. These aspects will be covered along with some example rules to show how PMD and Windup work in applying rules to analyze Java applications.

Commercial Tools for Source Code Analysis and Testing

Although the purpose of this chapter is to highlight open-source tools so that enterprises can automate discovery and analysis of their application portfolios, a few commercial tools deserve some mention as well. Although this chapter primarily discusses how to build an automated migration stack using open-source tools, this section highlights a few commercial tools so that enterprises can be aware of key features and differentiations between commercial and open-source solution stacks. Following is a truncated list of commercial source code analysis and testing tools for Java applications.

JTest

JTest is a comprehensive automated testing tool that integrates static analysis, metrics, code coverage, unit test generation, and coding policy enforcement into a single platform. The idea is to combine all of the latter technologies into a single tool so that they can all be run at once.

JTest can analyze Java code and automatically generate unit test cases with assertions. It generates these test cases based on the methods input and return value in the actual class. If required, developers can modify the test case methods generated and use those cases instead. This process generates a separate JTest project with same package structure used by the actual project. This helps to increase the readability of the test classes generated.

NOTE
Code coverage *is defined as the percentage
of code for which test cases are available and
covered by automated tests. Code coverage
measurement is a technique to determine which
statements within a segment of source code
have been tested and which statements have
not been subjected to a test run. The hallmarks
of a good code coverage measurement system
is the collection of application information, the
combination of that with source information,
and the generation of reports detailing the code
coverage of available tests.*

*Code coverage is an important part of
the feedback loop in application migration
automation. As application code is migrated to
newer platforms and libraries, additional tests need
to be developed. Code coverage can also highlight
areas of the code that do not receive adequate
testing. Each enterprise should decide its own level
of code coverage. This target can not only vary
in different organizations; it can also differ from
application to application.*

IntelliJ IDEA

IntelliJ IDEA performs code analysis by applying numerous code inspections
to the Java code. The inspections detect not only errors in compilation
but also different code inefficiencies. IntelliJ IDEA identifies problems of
unreachable code, unused code, nonlocalized strings, unresolved methods,
memory leaks, or even spelling issues. Using this tool, a solution is right
around the corner.

IntelliJ IDEA's code analysis is flexibly configurable. It can be easily enabled
or disabled for each code inspection and can change its severity, create profiles
with custom sets of inspections, apply inspections differently in different scopes,
suppress inspections in specific pieces of code, and more.

JArchitect

JArchitect simplifies managing a complex Java code base. Using this tool, architects and developers can analyze code structures, specify design rules, conduct effective code reviews, and understand how a particular application evolved by comparing different versions of code.

This tool supports a large number of code metrics and allows for visualization of dependencies using directed graphs and a dependency matrix. JArchitect also performs code base snapshot comparisons as well as validation of architectural and quality rules. User-defined rules can be written using LINQ queries.

Automated Test Generation

In software engineering, unit testing is a fundamental testing method that ensures that the code engineered by a developer is also tested immediately so that all basic execution paths are checked and expected results are computed based on control data provided as input to the developed code. What is considered a unit of code to be tested can vary. It could be a particular method of a class, an interface, an entire class, or even a fragment of code. Several test cases are created to verify these units of code. To test a unit, mock objects, mock methods or method stubs, and entire test harnesses can be used along with control data.

Many of the automation solutions can invoke these unit tests that have been automatically created. The unit tests can be sequenced and verified, and the generated report can be viewed and interpreted for correctness and coverage. Traditionally, unit testing has promoted healthy habits in software developers. Developers run tests often as an application evolves during its development, and an application can be effectively refactored multiple times during its evolution as a consequence of proper unit testing and code coverage. Problems are encountered early on, making it is easier to fix issues while the application is still evolving.

What we want to explore is not simply the automation of the testing process, but the creation of the test code and test cases in an automated fashion. That would take automation to a completely different level! Imagine that you modernize an application and modify some code using an automated approach. What if the corresponding test cases and scripts are also automatically generated and run, and then the modernized application is also automatically deployed? That would be completely insane, to put it mildly.

No interference from a developer or QA specialist? While such extreme automation seems to be out of grasp at the moment, it is actually quite possible to achieve near extreme levels.

The past decade has seen the emergence of new techniques and a paradigm shift in testing and verification. This is rooted in the original concepts of symbolic execution, which is a way to analyze programs to determine what inputs reach the logic of various parts of a program and cause each part of a computer program to execute. This is in contrast to traditional testing mechanisms, which can be called *concrete testing*. In concrete execution, specific input values are provided as defined in a test case, and the program logic evaluates the provided data and asserts the specific results that occurred. In this approach, several execution branches of a program may never be explored. It is also impossible to be able to envision and provide all possible sets of data to the unit test.

Symbolic testing has its drawbacks, too, and it may not scale well for large programs. The feasible execution paths in a program can grow exponentially large in large programs. You may have to resort to heuristics and pick certain paths. Code coverage may be affected.

Although symbolic execution itself is not new, a hybrid software verification technique has emerged called *concolic testing*. This approach performs symbolic execution but along a concrete execution path, thereby addressing the issues inherent in symbolic testing techniques. This is still an emerging area and holds a lot of promise for generating unit test cases and unit testing code automatically. A few tools are available, such as jCUTE, Jalangi, Microsoft Pex, and others. Open-source tools that support automated unit testing are also catching up in the area of automatic test generation as well. Some unit testing tools to be considered are JUnit-Tools, Randoop, Serenity, Concordion, jBehave, and many others. Any application modernization stack must at a minimum include the traditional unit testing tools to automate unit testing. Eventually, this solution stack can include tools for automatic test case and test script generation as well. Ideally, this automation should also give a high degree of code coverage.

Rule Management and Execution

The key to an automated assessment of a Java application portfolio is the ability of the solution to support the creation, management, and execution of rules. These rules control extensibility and scalability of the Java application portfolio analysis to future JDK versions and any future version of a third-party library or open-source library. The rule captures an existing feature or implementation in the application source version and provides the suggested improvement or recommendation available in a newer target version.

The knowledge base of rules or a rule base can be thought of as a database in which rules are stored. It typically provides a visual interface that is used to author rules, manage a collection of rules, and apply the rules during application analysis. One key objective of having a knowledge base of rules is that it enables you to reuse them as often as necessary. Tools such as PMD and Windup support the creation and management of custom rules in addition to the rules that come with the tool. It would be a great value addition to the Java platform if the community created and maintained rules in a public knowledge base. Developers could add newly created custom rules or modify existing rules that support modernized applications depending on a wide variety of third-party and open-source libraries. As newer versions of JDK are released, rules could be provided to upgrade existing applications to the new JDK.

Mod, or modernization, points are specific spots that are identified within a Java application that must be modified during the migration of a Java application from one version of the JDK or library to the upgraded version. These mod points represent possible replacement spots for APIs, methods, and classes that are used in the Java application but that are deprecated or otherwise improved in the later versions of Java or the libraries in which they are found. Applying the rules from the rule base to the Java application will help identify all the mod points covered by that set of rules.

PMD is one of the best static source code analyzers that can be selected for application analysis. Windup is a great migration tool that can be used to migrate a Java application from one version to another. PMD coupled with Windup makes for a great combination that covers several rules in their core. Both tools support extension and customization as well as adding custom rules. Custom rules can be authored in XML or Java.

Scope of Assessment Automation

The ultimate objective of the assessment automation is to generate visual reports and recommendations regarding the Java application portfolio. The reports would ideally identify all the mod points in the various applications contained within the portfolio, provide a comprehensive understanding of the complexity of the mod point, evaluate the effort involved in modernizing to a newer version of the JDK or library, identify dependencies to other code, and evaluate whether the mod point can be automatically rectified and modernized.

Beyond the assessment itself, a solution stack should support the automatic modernization of certain mod points depending on its complexity and readily available refactoring approaches that can be applied without impact. Sets of mod points that are too complex for automatic modernization may need to be manually explored and further researched before they can be modified. The migrated applications must also be completely tested via test automation to ensure adequate code coverage measurement. This code coverage measurement plays a key role in automated application portfolio assessment and migration success. It ensures that sufficient tests are available and determines the sufficiency of test cases by analyzing any gaps in the performance of those tests on the code base. As application code is migrated and modernized, test scope and test quality can suffer, and code coverage measurement will highlight these issues. A few open-source code coverage tools are Clover, Java Code Coverage (JaCoCo) Library, and Cobertura.

The modernization and migration roadmap can be generated based on this automated assessment analysis. This roadmap contains recommendations and includes a suggested sequence for carrying out the actual replacement of code by addressing the discovered mod points. This roadmap should not be confused with the roadmap discussed in Chapter 3 regarding APM—that roadmap was a result of an APM exercise and identified several prioritized initiatives, some of which may not even include the migration of Java applications at all.

The roadmap mentioned here deals with the actual migration and modernization of the Java applications contained within the portfolio. The initiatives identified as part of this roadmap will directly enable the applications within a portfolio to migrate to a newer version of the JDK and newer versions of other libraries used by the applications. The underlying databases can also be modernized. Certain other initiatives in this roadmap could refactor application code, move applications to the cloud, and adopt a modernized underlying infrastructure. Chapter 9 addresses this migration roadmap in greater detail.

The assessment automation focuses on bringing together a set of tools into a solution stack. The solution stack should be accessible through a modern UI and must provide a distributed architecture hosted on a cloud-based platform to tackle large-scale assessments of entire Java application portfolios.

The assessment should provide a report and a prescriptive approach to carry out the recommendations of the assessment. Not all enterprises will identically carry out all the recommendations presented on the roadmap.

Each organization should determine what is relevant to it based on organizational objectives, risks, available resources, budgetary cycles, and other factors.

Applying automation tools will enable enterprises to gain productivity, efficiency, repeatability, and predictability in the long run. It will take time to implement a solution stack and develop the necessary skill set to use these automation tools. Moreover, the solution stack requires customization for the particular needs of an enterprise. It is up to each organization to decide its way forward by narrowing the individual scope of the assessment.

This discussion would not be complete without the consideration of a few other items that establish the scope of the automated assessment and the identification of key stakeholders involved in ensuring that the automated assessment is a complete success. Oftentimes, a particular subject matter expert or an application owner in another area of the business that would be impacted by the modernized portfolio may inadvertently be missed in the assessment scope and subsequent modernization exercise. Training in-house resources and deciding whether to conduct the exercise solely inside the company, outsource the assessment exercise completely, or establish a hybrid team of employees and consultants is a key decision that can be influenced by factors such as timelines, budgets, and ability to build the skills in house. As always, it is important to understand business impact, return on investment, and overall total cost of ownership before embarking upon such an important program.

Summary

Automating the assessment of a Java application portfolio begins by defining a framework for conducting the assessment and identifying a set of tools that can provide the features and functionality expected from that framework. If such tools do not exist or if the feature set of existing tools are incomplete compared to the expectations of the framework, then an organization needs to fill the gap and extend existing tools. This expectation can be met by adopting available open-source tools that closely meet desired capabilities of the framework for automating assessments of Java applications.

This chapter discussed several open-source tools that can be successfully leveraged to build an automated assessment platform. The assessment takes place as a three-step process: discover, analyze, and recommend. The discussion in Chapter 6 reviewed the mechanics of the assessment process.

This chapter evaluated the tools necessary to implement the automation. Many of the tools contain features that span multiple steps of the assessment methodology and framework.

Several commercial tools were also presented to create a baseline comparison for enterprises to evaluate their open-source tools. The combination of open-source tools actually provides a more comprehensive feature set than just adopting one individual commercial tool. The open-source tools are also quite robust and stable, since they are actively being used by many enterprises for static code analysis.

Our approach is to leverage the core abilities of these tools and apply them beyond just static code analysis to create a continuous automated assessment platform for Java application portfolios. From this assessment, reports are generated and recommendations are made regarding the plan to migrate existing Java application portfolios to newer JDK and J2EE versions and newer versions of open-source and third-party libraries. The creation of a detailed knowledge base is also an outcome of implementing the automated assessment process. Ultimately, the automated assessment will yield an in-depth understanding of the application portfolio.

This knowledge base can be enhanced by a manual process that can be overlaid to collect additional application and portfolio attributes that may not be available to the assessment tools from the analysis of source code, compiled code, or configuration files. Eventually, some of the manual data collection around financial attributes, cost, and effort will be automated through the use of plug-ins to backend systems that house such data and appropriately mapped to the correct application portfolio knowledge base. The next chapter will explore the implementation of assessment tools into an automated assessment platform through the process of writing rules to extend the tools for migrating Java applications. The next chapter requires in-depth knowledge of programming and the ability to install and customize tools.

CHAPTER
8

Building the Java
Assessment Tool

In previous chapters of this book, the portfolio management frameworks and methodologies presented were primarily geared toward business analysts, group leaders, and other nontechnical roles. In this chapter, we will take the bull by its horns and delve into the specific tooling requirements for successful automation of these assessment exercises. This chapter is primarily intended for coders, developers, architects, and those holding other technical roles. Unlike the rest of the book, this chapter primarily consists of technical information and examines several computer science topics such as parsing source code, representation of source code in the form of an abstract syntax tree, creating XPath expressions to traverse the tree, and building rules to determine whether existing Java applications contain code that can be upgraded or migrated.

In this chapter, we will review several examples of these concepts and specifically evaluate two assessment tools—namely, PMD and Windup. At the time of this writing, PMD has been in existence for around 15 years, whereas Windup is a newer next-generation tool. These two tools incorporate many of the built-in features necessary to create a scalable automated assessment solution. More importantly, these tools are open source and quite amenable to modification and extension to suit a project's particular needs. The structure of this chapter includes a brief introduction to the PMD and Windup tools, a guide for installation, and information regarding how they operate. Although some IT departments use these tools, large sections of the Java community are unaware of how to benefit completely from their functionality.

At the heart of these two assessment tools is one similar concept: parsing either the source code or class files of the Java applications. Both these toolsets provide a mechanism to define rules that can be applied to the parsed Java applications to determine which specific locations within the Java applications meet the conditions imposed by the rules. This chapter spotlights some examples to demonstrate how these rules can be constructed and applied. There are differences in the rule formats and how the two tools function; however, conceptually they achieve the same result by identifying and locating specific lines of code in need of remediation.

Although other books and materials narrowly focus on the technicalities of tools such as PMD, probing into the source code of these assessment tools and making source code modifications to the core toolset is currently outside the scope of this book. That discussion would require several chapters to address the intricate topic adequately. Instead, this chapter will highlight how these tools can provide a solid foundation for building a customized, enterprise-wide automated assessment solution. I provide sufficient examples in this chapter that show how to extend the functionality of these tools via custom rules. This book is intended to be a unique reference guide that pulls together several distinctive aspects of modernization to create a holistic prescriptive solution for application portfolio management in general and Java modernization in particular. I would have greatly enjoyed writing an entire book focusing on technical discussions, modifying the core source code of PMD and Windup, providing detailed examples of source code modifications, and constructing hundreds of rulesets for migration to Java 8 and 9, but all that is not possible in one chapter. To bridge this gap, I plan to publish articles germane to these topics and augment the material of this book with additional examples.

NOTE
To completely understand the various concepts presented in this chapter, you'll need to have some knowledge of computer science, especially abstract syntax trees and how parsers work. You should also be comfortable programming in Java and creating XPath expressions. If you are not comfortable doing a lot of hands-on programming, I suggest that you skip ahead to Chapter 9.

Introduction to PMD

According to PMD's original creator, it was initially written to support a project at the Defense Advanced Research Projects Agency (DARPA). DARPA later agreed to open source PMD on SourceForge. Since then, PMD has been widely used, has undergone several iterations and improvements, has incorporated rule additions, and has integrated with many integrated development environments (IDEs) via plug-ins. PMD is a popular tool for static code analysis and engages an active developer and end user community.

How is PMD installed? First, you start with downloading PMD as a binary release or with all of the source code from the PMD GitHub web site. After you have downloaded the latest PMD binary release, unzip the archive to any directory so that you can immediately start using PMD from the command line and run PMD against the Java source files of a Java project. PMD comes preloaded with a few tools that you can launch to provide a visual interface for carrying out certain tasks.

There is no need for a separate IDE. You can run PMD from within many IDEs, including Eclipse, NetBeans, jEdit, Emacs, and IntelliJ IDEA. You can also run PMD using Ant or Maven. Because Eclipse is very popular, the following steps show you how to download and install the PMD for Eclipse Plugin.

NOTE
There is another plug-in named eclipse-pmd plug-in. We are not going to use that plug-in, however. Especially watch out for the file name of the plug-in that we want to install. It is named pmd-eclipse-plugin! The file names of the two plug-ins are so similar!

Installation and Setup

As of this writing, the latest version of PMD available is 5.7.0. You can download and install PMD from pmd.github.io/. You'll find adequate documentation available at pmd.github.io/pmd-5.7.0/ to get you started. Our discussion will complement and enhance the information already available, especially in areas that are not currently addressed by existing material.

Once you download and unpack the zipped archive, you can launch various scripts from within the bin folder available under the main installation directory of PMD.

This instruction presumes that Eclipse has already been installed in your environment. If not, you should do this before progressing through the following steps. The examples in this chapter have been created using the latest stable release of Neon downloaded from the Eclipse web site. Based on your comfort level, you can use PMD and its visual tools directly or you can install the PMD for Eclipse Plugin.

Here's how to find and install the PMD for Eclipse Plugin:

1. Open the installed Eclipse IDE and choose Help| Install New Software.

2. Click Add, and the Add Repository window will be displayed.

3. Enter the following, and then click OK:

   ■ Name: **PMD for Eclipse Update Site**

   ■ URL: **https://dl.bintray.com/pmd/pmd-eclipse-plugin/updates/**

4. Select the checkbox next to PMD for Eclipse4 – PMD-Plugin and then click Next.

5. Accept the license and confirm that you want to install a plug-in that is not digitally signed. Install the PMD for Eclipse Plugin.

6. Eclipse will prompt you for a restart. Restart Eclipse.

7. After Eclipse restarts, choose Eclipse | Preferences | PMD. You'll see four options. Make yourselves familiar with these options. Rule Configuration basically enables you to use the built-in rules globally; unchecking that option enables each project to apply its own set of rules. Use the options under Reports to export the PMD result into various formats. Figure 8-1 shows the PMD Preferences on a Mac installation. On a Mac installation, the Preferences are found under the Eclipse menu item.

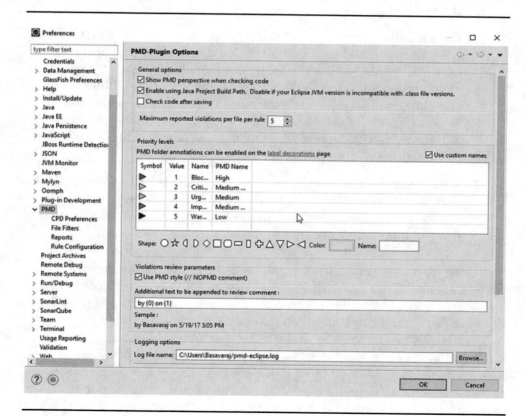

FIGURE 8-1. *PMD Preferences after installing the PMD for Eclipse Plugin*

8. You can either import a project into Eclipse or apply PMD to an existing project.

9. Switch to the PMD Perspective and go to the Eclipse project explorer window, right-click the project, and click PMD. Then click Check Code. The Review Code process executes.

10. After Review Code process executes, you'll see the following panes or views:

- Violations Outline
- Violations Overview
- CPD View
- Dataflow View
- XPath Designer

The Violations Overview window shows the various Java classes that were analyzed and arranged by their packages. You can also expand each source file to view the violations by category. You can also filter by the severity level of the violation. In the Violation Outline view, you can see number of violation rules with various color violation arrows revealing the line number of the Java code, the date created, and the rule that triggered that violation. When you click a row, the particular line within the source code is highlighted.

11. If these windows are not open, choose Windows | Show View | Other and then select PMD to show the five available views. Figure 8-2 depicts all the available views in the PMD perspective, which can be opened from the Windows menu.

Before we review a couple of examples using PMD, we should review the fundamental PMD rules. The intended use of PMD has been to analyze Java source code. PMD rules encapsulate the specific condition, situation, or violation that occurs in the analyzed Java code. It helps to identify incorrect code and flaws in source code, and it also enforces reliable coding practices. PMD offers a few hundred rules that flag specific patterns of occurrences in source code. At a minimum, using PMD will catch general coding violations and institute Java coding best practices, regardless of whether or not the overall plan is to automate the assessment and modernize the Java portfolio.

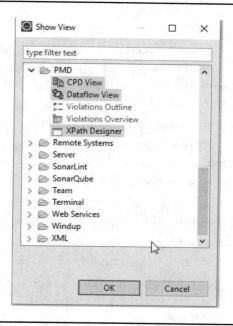

FIGURE 8-2. *PMD views available in Eclipse*

Table 8-1 references the PMD web page and provides a brief description of each category and its corresponding rules. Each category of rules is known as a ruleset.

Because you may not want to run all these rules on each project, you can enable or disable specific rules to customize the ruleset to run for a particular project. Although PMD includes this set of built-in rules to find general coding loopholes, PMD is an extremely flexible platform that can be extended to add rules for almost any scenario, including refactoring, migration, and reengineering of Java applications. PMD can be seamlessly extended by implementing custom rules to monitor usage patterns, enforce enterprise best practices, guard against anti-patterns, and detect poor programming practices. As newer Java versions become available, custom rules can catch deprecated methods and method calls that have newer replacements. This is also applicable to newer versions of other libraries used by the Java project.

Category	Rules
Android	These rules deal with the Android SDK and are mostly related to best practices. To yield better results, make sure that the `auxclasspath` is defined for type resolution to work.
Basic	This ruleset contains a collection of good practices that should be followed.
Braces	This ruleset contains rules regarding the use and placement of braces.
Clone Implementation	This ruleset contains a collection of rules that find questionable usages of the `clone()` method.
Code Size	This ruleset contains rules that find problems related to code size or complexity.
Comments	These rules are intended to catch errors related to code comments.
Controversial	This ruleset contains rules that, for whatever reason, are considered controversial. These rules are available for users to include within their custom rulesets.
Coupling	These rules find instances of high or inappropriate coupling between objects and packages.
Design	This ruleset contains rules that flag suboptimal code implementations and suggests alternate approaches.
Empty Code	This ruleset contains rules that find empty statements of any kind (empty method, empty block statement, empty try or catch block).
Finalizer	These rules deal with different problems that can occur with finalizers.
Import Statements	These rules deal with different problems that can occur with import statements.
Jakarta Commons Logging	This ruleset contains a collection of rules that find questionable usages of that framework.

TABLE 8-1. *Rulesets Available in PMD (Continued)*

Category	Rules
JavaBeans	This ruleset catches instances of bean rules not being followed.
Java Logging	This ruleset contains a collection of rules that find questionable usages of the logger.
JUnit	These rules deal with different problems that can occur with JUnit tests.
Migration	This ruleset contains rules about migrating from one JDK version to another. PMD advises developers not to use these rules directly, but to instead use a wrapper ruleset. PMD installation has a rulesets folder and subfolders with multiple files.
Naming	This ruleset contains rules regarding preferred usage of names and identifiers.
Optimization	These rules deal with different optimizations that generally apply to best practices.
Security Code Guidelines	These rules check whether the Java code follows the security guidelines and security best practices as originally published by Sun Microsystems.
Strict Exceptions	These rules provide some strict guidelines about throwing and catching exceptions.
String and StringBuffer	These rules deal with different issues that can arise with manipulation of the String, StringBuffer, or StringBuilder instances.
Type Resolution	These rules resolve Java class files for comparison, as opposed to a String.
Unnecessary	This ruleset contains a collection of rules for unnecessary code.
Unused Code	This ruleset contains rules that find unused or ineffective code.

TABLE 8-1. *Rulesets Available in PMD*

Custom rules can be written for PMD in two ways: via XML Path (XPath) language expressions or by Java code. Although this chapter will cursorily review the Java code approach for writing custom rules, we will examine rule writing via XPath expressions more in-depth as they are an easier, scalable, maintainable, and a quicker way to write and externalize the rules into a rule repository for later reuse across an enterprise.

Understanding XPath

Before writing custom PMD rules as XPath expressions, you need to understand the nature of XPath expressions and how they can be leveraged when writing rules. XPath uses path expressions to select nodes or node sets in an XML document. It is a major element in the XSLT standard. XPath can be used to navigate through elements and attributes in an XML document. XPath includes more than 200 built-in functions. There are functions for string values, numeric values, Booleans, date and time comparison, node manipulation, sequence manipulation, and much more. XPath expressions can also be used in languages other than Java such as JavaScript, PHP, and Python.

The following examples of XPath expressions have been adapted from the W3C web site. The W3C XPath tutorial has been adapted here for purposes of this discussion, since the web site explains XPath quite well, especially the way we plan to use these expressions, which is to locate certain nodes and values in the abstract syntax tree (AST) representation.

Here are some useful XPath expressions:

Expression	Description
Nodename	Selects all nodes with the name *"nodename"*
/	Selects from the root node
//	Selects nodes in the document from the current node that match the selection no matter where they are
.	Selects the current node
..	Selects the parent of the current node
@	Selects attributes

Consider the following XML code:

```
<?xml version="1.0" encoding="UTF-8"?>
<bookstore>
<book>
  <title lang="en">Good To Great</title>
  <price>15.99</price>
</book>
<book>
  <title lang="en">The Innovator's Dilemma</title>
  <price>19.99</price>
</book>
</bookstore>
```

The following table lists some path expressions and the result of the expressions based on the preceding XML:

Path Expression	Result
bookstore	Selects all nodes with the name "bookstore"
/bookstore	Selects the root element bookstore **Note:** If the path starts with a slash (/), it always represents an absolute path to an element.
bookstore/book	Selects all book elements that are children of bookstore
//book	Selects all book elements no matter where they are in the document
bookstore//book	Selects all book elements that are descendant of the bookstore element, no matter where they are under the bookstore element
//@lang	Selects all attributes that are named lang
/bookstore/book[last()-1]	Selects the last but one book element that is the child of the bookstore
/bookstore/book[price>14.95]	Selects all the book elements of the bookstore element that have a price element with a value greater than 35.00

Path Expression	Result
//title[@lang='en']	Selects all the title elements that have a lang attribute with a value of en
//book/title | //book/price	Selects all the title and price elements of all book elements
//title | //price	Selects all the title and price elements in the document
/bookstore/book/title | //price	Selects all the title elements of the book element of the bookstore element and all the price elements in the document

Developing a strong understanding of XPath expressions is very important before you can create custom PMD rules.

Creating Custom PMD Rule

PMD provides multiple pathways to create and deploy custom rules. The process of analyzing source code and dividing it into smaller pieces is known as *parsing*. A more formal definition for parsing in our context is the process of analyzing a string of symbols in a computer language, such as Java, XML, HTML, and so on, conforming to the rules of a formal grammar. It is a syntactic analysis of the source code into its component parts to facilitate the writing of compilers. At the core of PMD is the JavaCC parser generator. JavaCC refers to the necessary grammar or structure to generate the parser. There is another layer to the JavaCC known as the JJTree. The JJTree is the component that does all the heavy lifting by decorating the generated parser with the AST. The design of PMD enables it to be used for any language. In fact, PMD does support several languages in addition to Java, although PMD itself is written in Java.

Rules are the mechanism by which PMD can analyze the source code of a Java application to determine which parts of the source code are in violation of an expected standard. The rules capture the essence of how PMD inspects the source code. Rules also decouple what needs to be located, analyzed, and flagged within the Java code from how the Java code is ultimately analyzed. You can use XPath expressions or Java code to implement these rules. We will explore this in greater detail later in this chapter.

Understanding the Abstract Syntax Tree

You were introduced to a brief definition of AST in Chapter 7. This section will take that analysis further. Once the source code is parsed by the JavaCC-generated parser, it produces an AST. The AST represents the source code in a tree-like structure with nodes consisting of variables, constants, and operators. The AST representation is an enriched semantic layer on top of the tokens generated by the parsed Java source code. Therefore, instead of receiving a sequence of all the Java tokens found in the source code analysis, the JJTree creates a hierarchy of objects in a tree-like structure. AST representations are more voluminous and verbose than the original Java code base, so it is not prudent to analyze the AST for an entire Java class with hundreds of lines in its source code.

An example of an AST representation, with a hypothetical code snippet implemented as a Java class, is shown next:

```
public class ASTTest {
   public static void printAST() {
      int counter = 0;
      while (counter < 10) {
         System.out.println("Count: " + counter);
         counter ++;
      }
   }
}
```

Although this Java source code is just a few lines long, the resulting AST representation is much more extensive, as shown in the next snippet. This is why analyzing the AST of large Java classes can become quite unwieldy. For the purpose of authoring rules, you should typically isolate and implement just the Java code snippet for which the custom rule needs to be written.

```
CompilationUnit
   TypeDeclaration
      ClassOrInterfaceDeclaration
         ClassOrInterfaceBody
            ClassOrInterfaceBodyDeclaration
               MethodDeclaration
                  ResultType
                  MethodDeclarator
                     FormalParameters
                  Block
                     BlockStatement
                        LocalVariableDeclaration
                           Type
                              PrimitiveType
```

```
                     VariableDeclarator
                      VariableDeclaratorId
                      VariableInitializer
                       Expression
                        PrimaryExpression
                         PrimaryPrefix
                          Literal
            BlockStatement
              Statement
                WhileStatement
                  Expression
                    RelationalExpression
                      PrimaryExpression
                        PrimaryPrefix
                         Name
                      PrimaryExpression
                        PrimaryPrefix
                          Literal
                Statement
                  Block
                    BlockStatement
                      Statement
                        StatementExpression
                          PrimaryExpression
                            PrimaryPrefix
                              Name
                            PrimarySuffix
                              Arguments
                                ArgumentList
                                  Expression
                                    AdditiveExpression
                                      PrimaryExpression
                                        PrimaryPrefix
                                          Literal
                                      PrimaryExpression
                                        PrimaryPrefix
                                          Name
                    BlockStatement
                      Statement
                        StatementExpression
                          PostfixExpression
                            PrimaryExpression
                              PrimaryPrefix
                                Name
```

How can you interpret this AST to understand its intended purpose and utility? Using this example, you can see that the AST is in the form of hierarchical nodes. Source code is divided into small components known as *block* and *block statements*, which clearly represent the necessary details. Using an XPath expression, you can traverse the tree to check if particular conditions are met or if certain blocks and nodes contain values that you are interested in.

In the preceding code snippet, you can flag the use of the variable name `counter` and suggest that it is a violation. In this particular context, `counter` could be a reserved variable name that should be permitted only for very specific uses by an enterprise. In this hypothetical scenario, it is easy to create a custom PMD rule using an XPath expression to search and flag any use of the variable name `counter`. This functionality of allowing the user to navigate through the code base easily using custom PMD rules is truly a game-changer!

PMD comes with a few built-in tools to help you in this endeavor, including the AST Viewer and the PMD Rule Designer. I used the AST Viewer to produce the AST representation for our code snippet and copied the depicted tree to a file. I formatted the tree to appear indented, since the viewer does not intrinsically produce well-formatted AST representations that can be downloaded into a separate file. Figure 8-3 depicts the AST Viewer and shows the Java code snippet in the left pane and the AST representation in the right pane.

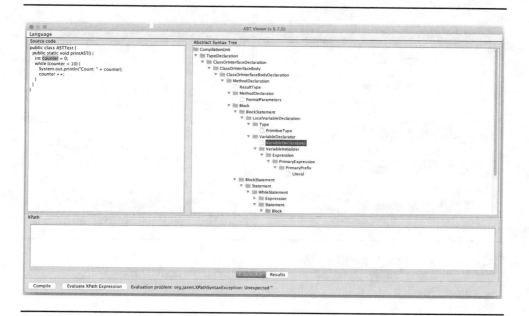

FIGURE 8-3. *AST Viewer*

The PMD Rule Designer enables viewing of not only the AST representation itself, but also select nodes in the tree. While formulating the XPath expression, the AST attributes and values are available to the XPath expression to validate and verify in a separate pane. Another pane allows for the creation and edits of the XPath expression as it checks against which nodes of the AST representation will be affected by that XPath expression. Once you are satisfied with the XPath expression, you can launch an XML rule editor from the Actions menu at the top left. The PMD Rule Designer actually offers two menu items in the menu bar at the top. The Language menu shows support for a variety of languages, including various versions of the JDK up to JDK 1.8, ECMAScript 3, PLSQL, XML, and JSP. From the Actions menu, you can create an XML rule or copy the XML to the clipboard. Figure 8-4 shows an illustration of the PMD Rule Designer.

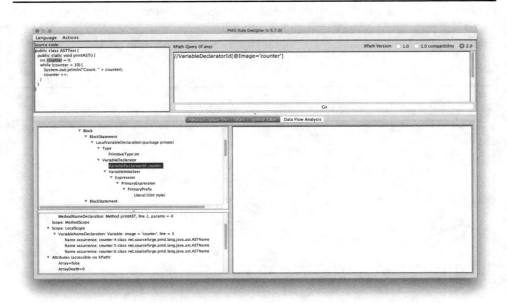

FIGURE 8-4. *PMD Rule Designer*

Creating a Custom XPath Rule

Now that we have reviewed how to create custom PMD rules, let's create and deploy a hypothetical custom XPath-based rule:

```
Ruleset
    Rulename:
    Message:
    Description:
    External info URL:
    XPath:
```

Figure 8-4 depicts several panes of the PMD Rule Designer. The top left pane is where you input the source code snippet. Again, remember that you should isolate and insert only a few lines of code when designing the rule to keep the size of the generated AST tree manageable to traverse. The pane below the top left pane depicts the AST representation. The AST represented here is a bit different from the one shown for the AST Viewer. In this view, the specific literals, names, and tokens are noticeable.

Here are three distinct examples of the PMD Rule Designer nodes:

- `ClassOrInterfaceDeclaration: ASTTest (public) (class)`

- `MethodDeclarator: printAST`

- `VariableDeclaratorId: counter`

When you select one of these nodes, you will see the details of the AST representation for that node in the pane below it. Figure 8-4 depicts the details of the `VariableDeclaratorId: counter`. When you select this node in the AST pane, the pane below the AST representation will highlight details about `counter` to assist in the construction of the desired XPath expression. I have highlighted counter in the code snippet and `VariableDeclaratorId: counter` in the AST window below the code snippet window.

Figure 8-5 depicts the PMD Rule Designer with the XPath expression and the particular node and corresponding `Image` attribute highlighted in the AST view. I have highlighted the line `Image=counter` to indicate our interest in that XPath attribute of the node `VariableDeclaratorId`. The actual XPath

FIGURE 8-5. *XPath expression for identifying any variable that uses the name* `counter`

expression that achieves this objective is `//VariableDeclaratorId[@Image='counter']`. This XPath expression is shown in the top right pane. Click the Go button, and the pane just below it depicts `ASTVariableDeclaratorId` at line 3 column 9. The @ sign is used to denote the `has` property. You can use these properties to get information about specific instances of elements. For example, the `Image` property stores the value of the element. So, the `//VariableDeclaratorId[@Image='counter']` XPath expression will match if it encounters any variable declared where the variable name is `counter`, since the `Image` property will now have a similar value that matches our XPath expression.

Next, choose Action | Create XML Rule. You'll be asked to provide a Rule Name, Rule Msg, and Rule Desc, exactly with those labels. Now you are finally ready to create the XML rule. Once you provide the information and

click the Create ruleXML button, the empty pane is filled with the XML rule.
Figure 8-6 shows the Create XML Rule pane with the rule pasted in it.

```
<rule  name="NoCounterVariable"
    message="Creating a variable called counter is not allowed"
    class="net.sourceforge.pmd.lang.rule.XPathRule">
    <description>
    The name counter is reserved in our applications for special
variables that are created by our internal frameworks.
    We do not want Java classes using this name for variables.
    </description>
    <properties>
      <property name="xpath">
        <value>
<![CDATA[
//VariableDeclaratorId[@Image='counter']
]]>
        </value>
      </property>
    </properties>
    <priority>3</priority>
    <example>
<![CDATA[
public class ASTTest {
  public static void printAST() {
    int counter = 0;
    while (counter < 10) {
        System.out.println("Count: " + counter);
        counter ++;
    }
  }
}
]]>
    </example>
</rule>
```

You can copy and paste this rule into a file for later use. Now let's explore
how to use and deploy this rule snippet.

Deploying Custom XPath Rules

If you want to deploy the custom-created XPath rule to a project, you should
ensure that you are in PMD Perspective and you have the project explorer
view available. Ensure that you have selected your project in project explorer.
From the top level Eclipse menu, under Preferences, select PMD and then
the Rule Configuration item. Uncheck the Use Global Rule Management
checkbox. Then, under the specific project properties in the Eclipse menu,

Create XML Rule

Rule name : NoCounterVariable

Rule msg : Creating a variable called counter is not allowed

Rule desc : The name counter is reserved in our applications for spe cial variables that are created by our internal frameworks . We do not want Java classes using this name for variabl es.

Create rule XML

```
<rule  name="NoCounterVariable"
 message="Creating a variable called counter is not allowed"
 class="net.sourceforge.pmd.lang.rule.XPathRule">
 <description>
 The name counter is reserved in our applications for special variables that are created by our internal frameworks.
 We do not want Java classes using this name for variables.
 </description>
 <properties>
  <property name="xpath">
  <value>
<![CDATA[
//VariableDeclaratorId[@Image='counter']
]]>
  </value>
  </property>
 </properties>
 <priority>3</priority>
 <example>
<![CDATA[
public class ASTTest {
 public static void printAST() {
  int counter = 0;
  while (counter < 10) {
    System.out.println("Count: " + counter);
    counter ++;
  }
 }
}
]]>
 </example>
</rule>
```

FIGURE 8-6. *Create XML Rule pane populated with our custom rule.*

select the PMD option. In the window that pops up, select the Enable PMD
checkbox and select the Use The .Ruleset Configured In A Project File. When
you select Apply, a .ruleset file is created for the specific project. Open that
file in an editor to view several additional rules that are included along with
PMD. Next, we will add our rule snippet. Figure 8-7 shows my MacBook with
our rule added in between other rules in the Brackets editor. Save this .ruleset
file and build your project.

Now, right-click the project and choose the PMD option. Select Check
Code to apply the custom rule that we added to identify any rule violations
in the code. Assuming that you have code that uses the variable named

```
345    <rule ref="rulesets/apex/performance.xml/AvoidDmlStatementsInLoops"/>
346    <rule ref="rulesets/apex/performance.xml/AvoidSoqlInLoops"/>
347    <rule ref="rulesets/plsql/dates.xml/TO_DATEWithoutDateFormat"/>
348    <rule ref="rulesets/plsql/dates.xml/TO_DATE_TO_CHAR"/>
349    <rule ref="rulesets/plsql/dates.xml/TO_TIMESTAMPWithoutDateFormat"/>
350    <rule  name="NoCounterVariable"
351    message="Creating a variable called counter is not allowed"
352    language="java"
353    class="net.sourceforge.pmd.lang.rule.XPathRule">
354    <description>
355    The name counter is reserved in our applications for special variables that are created by our internal frameworks.
356    We do not want Java classes using this name for variables.
357    </description>
358    <properties>
359    <property name="xpath">
360    <value>
361 <![CDATA[
362 //VariableDeclaratorId[@Image='counter']
363 ]]>
364    </value>
365    </property>
366    </properties>
367    <priority>3</priority>
368    <example>
369 <![CDATA[
370 public class ASTTest {
371    public static void printAST() {
372        int counter = 0;
373        while (counter < 10) {
374            System.out.println("Count: " + counter);
375            counter ++;
376        }
377    }
378 }
379 ]]>
380    </example>
381 </rule>
382    <rule ref="rulesets/apex/security.xml/ApexBadCrypto"/>
383    <rule ref="rulesets/apex/security.xml/ApexCRUDViolation"/>
384    <rule ref="rulesets/apex/security.xml/ApexCSRF"/>
385    <rule ref="rulesets/apex/security.xml/ApexDangerousMethods"/>
386    <rule ref="rulesets/apex/security.xml/ApexInsecureEndpoint"/>
387    <rule ref="rulesets/apex/security.xml/ApexOpenRedirect"/>
388    <rule ref="rulesets/apex/security.xml/ApexSharingViolations"/>
389    <rule ref="rulesets/apex/security.xml/ApexSOQLInjection"/>
390    <rule ref="rulesets/apex/security.xml/ApexSuggestUsingNamedCred"/>
391    <rule ref="rulesets/apex/security.xml/ApexXSSFromEscapeFalse"/>
392    <rule ref="rulesets/apex/security.xml/ApexXSSFromURLParam"/>
393    <rule ref="rulesets/java/sunsecure.xml/ArrayIsStoredDirectly"/>
394    <rule ref="rulesets/java/sunsecure.xml/MethodReturnsInternalArray"/>
395    <rule ref="rulesets/java/strictexception.xml/AvoidCatchingGenericException"/>
396    <rule ref="rulesets/java/strictexception.xml/AvoidCatchingNPE"/>
```

FIGURE 8-7. *Including custom rule in the project-specific .ruleset file*

counter, our custom rule should have flagged this code. Figure 8-8 illustrates a Java source file containing the variable named counter. The Violation Overview window indicates that the rule triggered and flagged line 17 of the source code file named PMDTest.java under the project named PMDCustomRules. In the Violations Outline window, a few other metrics, such as #Violations, #Violations/KLOC, and #Violations/Method, are also displayed.

NOTE
The steps of this hypothetical example are the same ones that you would follow to create your own custom rules. If I applied PMD rules to one of my real projects, I would not be able to capture screen shots to show the hundreds of violations and other generated issues for illustrative purposes.

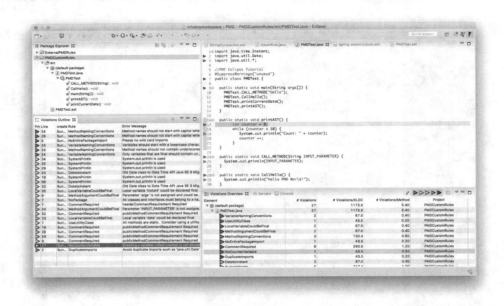

FIGURE 8-8. *Deployed custom rule*

The PMD rule can be retroactively applied to existing code. Consider a hypothetical scenario where several applications are in use before an IT policy prohibiting the use of counter as a variable name goes into effect. By slightly modifying our simple custom code, making it a bit more useful, and leveraging automation, we can easily flag such retroactively defined violations. You can also automatically rename the variable from counter to granite and also accomplish the following:

- Flag all subsequent places where counter is used.

- Run other custom rules for the project from the PMD command line.

- Recompile the code base.

- Run all your code coverage and regression tests.

- Deploy it into production once the code passes.

Behold the power of automation when applied to application modernization!

Severity Levels of Rules Violations in PMD

The priority of the rules and triggered severity levels are project- and content-specific. In this regard, PMD provides some useful guidelines:

- **Change absolutely required**   Behavior is critically broken/buggy.

- **Change highly recommended**   Behavior is quite likely to be broken/buggy.

- **Change recommended**   Behavior is confusing, perhaps buggy, and/or against standards/best practices.

- **Change optional**   Behavior is not likely to be buggy, but just flies in the face of standards/style/good taste.

- **Change highly optional**   Behavior is nice to have, such as a consistent naming policy for package/class/fields.

In the PMD for Eclipse Plugin, you can configure the names, descriptions, color, and shape of the symbol to depict these five severity levels. Figure 8-9 shows the configuration screen used to configure custom severity levels. The preconfigured severity levels are Blocker, Critical, Urgent, Important, and Warning.

NOTE
You may encounter a few issues while using the PMD for Eclipse Plugin. There are installation issues, depending on the particular version of Eclipse and Java used. At the time of this writing, the PMD for Eclipse Plugin did not integrate with JDK 1.9 early access releases. If custom rules encounter errors, the PMD hangs. At that point, you can either entirely delete the project and re-create it with rules rolled back or uninstall and reinstall the PMD for Eclipse Plugin. If the Global Rules checkbox available under Preferences is unchecked in the plug-in, reports will not generate for that project and a dialog box with an error message will instead be shown.

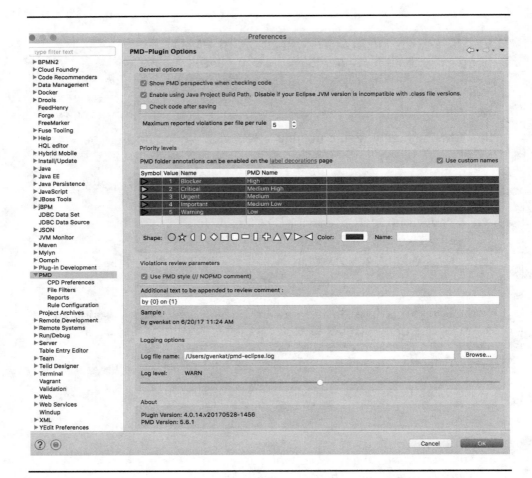

FIGURE 8-9. *Severity levels preconfigured in PMD for Eclipse Plugin*

Alternate Process to Create an XPath Rule

Instead of using the tools available from PMD, you can also use the PMD for Eclipse Plugin and the views available in the PMD perspective to author custom XPath PMD rules. To demonstrate this process, we'll create a custom rule to catch generic import statements of entire packages using a wildcard depicted as an asterisk (*)—for example, `import java.util.*`.

Before attempting the following exercise, create a simple Java program and use the import statement `java.util.*` or any other wildcard package import into your sample program.

Follow these steps to create the custom XPath rules using the PMD for Eclipse Plugin:

1. Right-click the Java file for which you want to create a custom rule and go to the PMD menu. Then click Generate Abstract Syntax Tree.

2. Double-click the generated Abstract Syntax Tree file in the folder structure.

3. By observing the Abstract Syntax Tree XML file, you can get an idea of the elements and how to formulate the XPath expression that can then be used to create the custom rules.

    You can also open the XPath Designer View, double-click the Java program of interest, and the AST representation will open in the XPath Designer. It is a lot easier to understand the AST representation here rather than looking directly at the XML file. You also have a tab you can select to test any XPath expressions that you formulate.

    Figure 8-10 shows the XPath Designer view at the bottom right side of the Eclipse IDE with the AST loaded for the sample code.

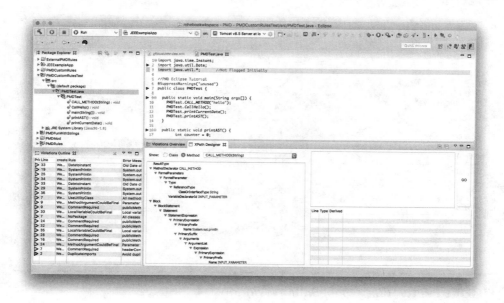

FIGURE 8-10. *XPath Designer*

4. Choose Preferences | PMD. Click Rule Configuration, and the Rule Configuration window will open.

5. Click the + (Add Rule) button to open the New Rule window.

   Figure 8-11 depicts the panel that is shown when the Rule Configuration option is selected under the PMD Preferences menu.

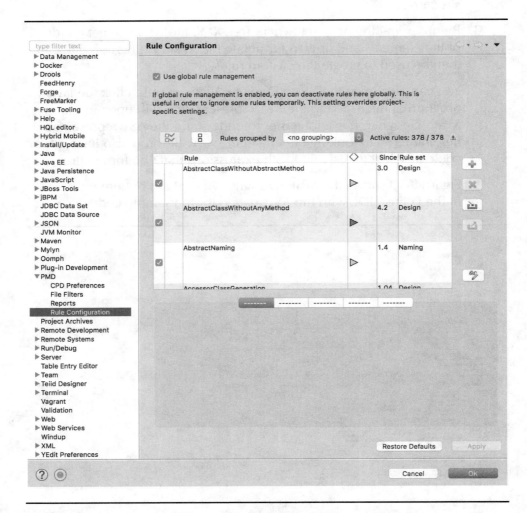

FIGURE 8-11. *Rule Configuration Window*

6. Enter the Rule Name and select the RuleSet. For Implemented By, select XPath script or Java class, provide the Implementation Class (if it is a Java rule), and provide the Target Language and the Priority. Click Next to continue the process.

7. Provide a Description, Message, and an External Info URL, if available.

   Figure 8-12 and Figure 8-13 show the values filled in for our rule to detect the complete package imports.

8. Enter the XPath expression for the rule, as shown in Figure 8-14, and click Next.

9. Enter the examples and click the Finish button, as shown in Figure 8-15.

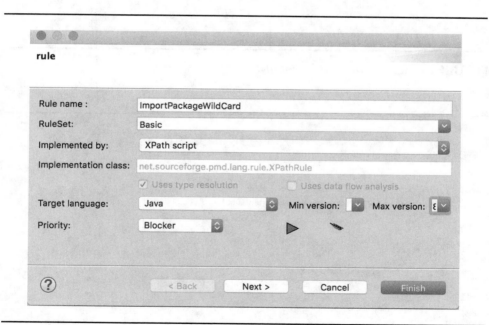

FIGURE 8-12. *Rule design in PMD for Eclipse Plugin*

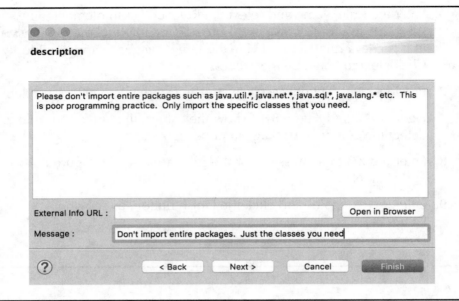

FIGURE 8-13. *Filling in rule details*

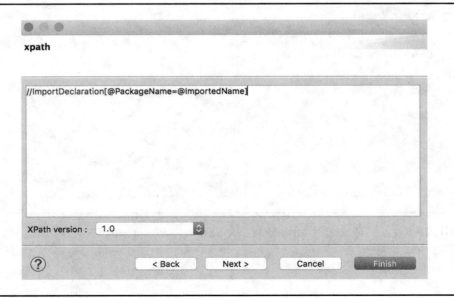

FIGURE 8-14. *XPath expression during rule design*

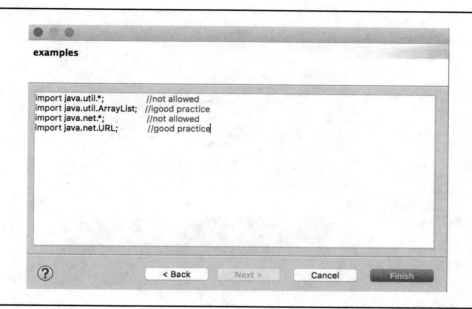

FIGURE 8-15. *Including an example of affected Java code within the plug-in*

10. Search for the newly created custom rule in the rule configuration table: You'll see Summary, Rule, Properties, Exclusions, and XPath for the newly created rule. Figure 8-16 shows the newly created rule under the list of rules accessible via the global rule management.

11. Click the OK button to complete. Click the Yes button to run the build.

12. Right-click the project name and go to the PMD menu item. Then click Check Code. Figure 8-17 shoes the code that we want to catch as a violation. I highlighted the package import `java.util.*` but have not yet applied the rule that we created.

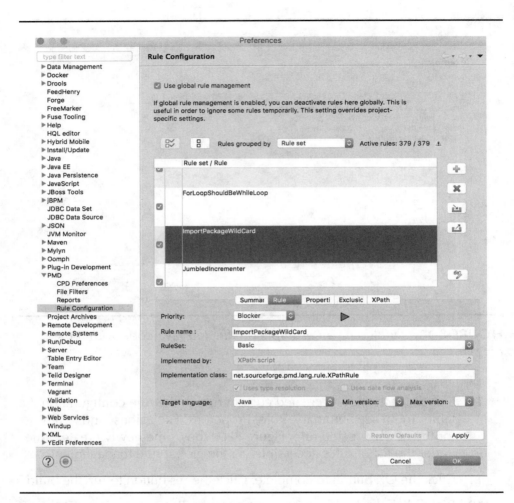

FIGURE 8-16. *Newly created custom rule*

13. The newly created custom rule flags the misuse of package imports. Figure 8-18 now shows the Eclipse perspective after the Check Code option was run against the Java class. After the rule has been applied, a red flag is displayed on the side confirming a severity level of 1 specified for this rule. Since the red flag is not too obvious in this figure, I have highlighted the particular line of source code in the source code listing that is in violation of the rule. I have also highlighted the red flag in the Violations Outline window in the bottom left corner of the figure.

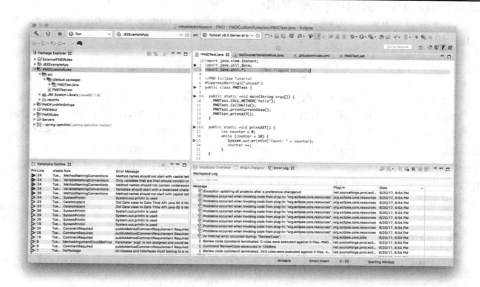

FIGURE 8-17. *Before applying custom rule*

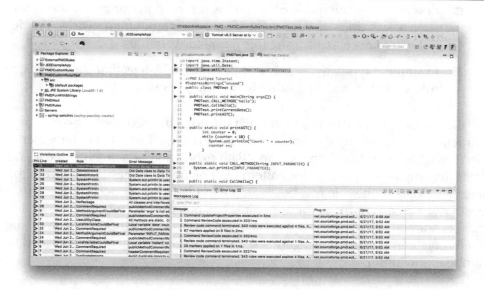

FIGURE 8-18. *After applying custom rule*

Creating a Custom Java Rule

You can also write a Java-based PMD rule by creating a new Java class that extends the class:

```
net.sourceforge.pmd.lang.java.rule.AbstractJavaRule
```

Once the Java class is written, the PMD runtime must be informed about the custom rule. The rule should be added to a ruleset XML file similar to the PMD core ruleset XML files. Refer to pmd-java/src/main/resources/rulesets/java/basic.xml. This file has the category of PMD rules grouped under the basic ruleset. You can create your own ruleset named pmdcustomrules.xml and add your custom rule definitions there. The rule definition must have all elements and attributes filled in correctly based on the following descriptors:

- **name**   NoCounterVariable.

- **message**   Creating a variable named counter is not allowed.

- **class**   The Java class where you will code the rule. This does not have to exist under the net.sourceforge.pmd package. The class location can be in any package you choose including or at com.gtl .pmd.rules.

- **description**   The name counter is reserved in our applications for special variables that are created by our internal frameworks. We do not want Java classes using this name for variables.

- **example**   Typically a code snippet in CDATA tags that shows the rule violation and a possible fix in some cases.

Generally, a PMD rule is a visitor that traverses the AST looking for a particular pattern of objects that indicates a problem. The rule implementer decides whether to match this via an XPath expression or actually write a Java class that implements the visitor pattern by looking for nodes of interest in the tree. This logic of the rule can be as simple as checking for occurrences of a variable named counter or as complex as determining whether or not a class is correctly overriding both equals and hashcode methods, or something even more complex such as figuring out existing logic that can be replaced by lambda functions.

The Java code for the custom rule is shown here:

```java
package com.gtl.pmd.rules;

import net.sourceforge.pmd.lang.java.rule.AbstractJavaRule;
import net.sourceforge.pmd.lang.symboltable.NameOccurrence;
import net.sourceforge.pmd.lang.java.ast.ASTVariableDeclaratorId;

import java.util.Iterator;

public class NoCounterVariableRule extends AbstractJavaRule {

    public Object visit(ASTVariableDeclaratorId node, Object data) {
        if (!node.getNameDeclaration().getImage().equals("counter")) {
            return data;
        }
        System.out.println("Variable counter is of type '" + node.
getNameDeclaration().getTypeImage() + "'");
        for (Iterator<NameOccurrence> i = node.getUsages().iterator();
i.hasNext();) {
            NameOccurrence occurrence = (NameOccurrence) i.next();
            System.out.println("The variable counter is used at line " +
occurrence.getLocation().getBeginLine());
        }
        return data;
    }
}
```

Here's a snippet included in the custom ruleset file:

```xml
<?xml version="1.0"?>
<ruleset name="GTL Custom Rules">
  <description>
This ruleset contains all the custom rules for the GTL enterprise
  </description>
  <rule name="NoCounterVariableRule"
        message="Creating a variable called counter is not allowed"
        language="java"
        class="com.gtl.pmd.rules.NoCounterVariableRule">
    <description>
The name counter is reserved in our applications for special variables that are
created by our internal frameworks.
We do not want Java classes using this name for variables.
    </description>
    <example>
<![CDATA[
public class ASTTest {
  public static void printAST() {
    int counter = 0;
    while (counter < 10) {
      System.out.println("Count: " + counter);
      counter ++;
    }
  }
}
]]>
    </example>
  </rule>
</ruleset>
```

After completing the PMD rules creation, you can put this ruleset on your CLASSPATH or refer to it directly via the command line from within a shell:

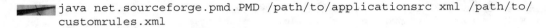

```
java net.sourceforge.pmd.PMD /path/to/applicationsrc xml /path/to/
customrules.xml
```

Advantages of Using PMD

PMD runs at the source code level and detects problems such as violations of naming conventions, lack of curly braces, misplaced null checks, long parameter lists, unnecessary constructors, and missing breaks in a switch. PMD also exposes the cyclomatic complexity of the code, which can be very helpful. The following list identifies and describes some of these advantages in greater detail:

- **Flexible analysis**   PMD analyzes the generated AST from the Java source code, and it is not required that the source code is compiled. Advanced, complex checks can be implemented. Rules can be added at a later time, and the source code can be analyzed without having access to the source code as long as the AST is available.

- **Great breadth and depth of verifications**   The types of verification that can be implemented using PMD has no limitation. PMD already has a rich set of categorized pre-built rules, as we have seen in this chapter. Detecting vulnerabilities in code, code complexity, flawed designs, and possible bugs can all help code quality.

- **Extending PMD**   PMD can be extended via custom rules. PMD is open source and written in Java. Since PMD exposes an API, the core functionality can be easily extended and integrated into a larger solution platform.

Introduction to Windup

The JBoss Windup tool (simply referred to as Windup) will be rebranded as the Red Hat Application Migration Toolkit (RHAMT). Windup is a flexible, customizable, rule-based platform that can be used to migrate portfolios of Java applications. Windup can analyze several types of assets associated with an application, including archive files, JAR files, source code, configuration files, and XML. Windup comes preset with core rules, mostly aimed at upgrading various application servers to the JBoss Enterprise Application Platform (EAP) or the community edition called JBoss AS (Application Server). Rules are also included to upgrade from one version of JBoss AS or Jboss EAP to the next available version.

After analyzing an application, Windup provides a comprehensive report. The core rules of Windup can be extended by creating your own custom rules. Because Windup is open source, you can also easily add new features, although that would be a complex and involved task, requiring a certain level of commitment and expertise. The next section of this chapter complements the Windup discussion by highlighting key points of the available Windup documentation.

Installation and Setup

At the time of this writing, the latest available stable version is Windup 3.0. You can download and install Windup from windup.jboss.org/download.html. After downloading the tool, unpack the zipped archive and launch the main windup script available in the bin folder.

The installation of Eclipse is a prerequisite to Windup Eclipse Plugin installation. The examples in this chapter have been created using the latest stable release of Neon downloaded from the Eclipse web site. Based on your comfort level, you can use the Windup Eclipse Plugin or Windup directly from the command line. The next section discusses how to find and install the Windup Eclipse Plugin. Note that the Windup Eclipse Plugin has dependencies on several JBoss tools. Be prepared to spend some time downloading and installing these dependencies.

Note that the Windup Eclipse Plugin works only with Eclipse Neon. To install the Windup Eclipse Plugin, follow these installation steps:

1. Launch Eclipse Neon.

2. From the menu bar, select Help | Install New Software.

3. Add the Windup update site.

4. Next to the Work With field, click Add.

5. In the Name field, enter **Windup**.

6. In the Location field, enter **http://download.jboss.org/jbosstools/ neon/stable/updates/windup/composite/**

7. Select all of the checkboxes under JBoss Tools - Windup and click Next.

8. Review the installation details and click Next.

9. Accept the terms of the license agreement and click Finish to install the plug-in.

10. Restart Eclipse for the changes to take effect.

Once the plug-in is installed, the Windup Eclipse tools are available in the Windup Perspective. To open the Windup Perspective, navigate to Window | Perspective | Open Perspective |Other. Select Windup and click OK. The Windup Perspective has four components available to analyze Java projects when using the Windup Eclipse Plugin:

■ **Issue Explorer**   Explore the Windup issues for projects that have been analyzed.

■ **Windup Server**   Execute the Windup server as a separate process, perform the Windup analysis on the project selected, flag the migration issues, and generate relevant reports. You can also start, stop, and view the status of the Windup server from the Issue Explorer.

■ **Issue Details**   Show detailed information about the selected Windup issue including the hint, severity, and any additional resources associated with that issue.

■ **Windup Report**   Show the HTML reports that are generated when Windup is executed.

From the Report landing page, you can navigate the detailed reports for Migration Issues, Application Details, and Dependencies. You must select the Generate Report option in the Windup run configuration before these Windup reports can be generated. If any of the preceding views are not visible in the Windup Perspective, you can open it by choosing Window | Show View and selecting the particular view.

Issues Observed During Windup and Windup Plugin Installation

The `WINDUP_HOME` environment variable should to be set to the Installation Directory of Windup so that Windup can be requested from the command line. The installation of Windup and the Windup plug-in was straightforward except for a few issues encountered in a Windows platform environment. I consulted with the Windup engineering team at Red Hat, and they confirmed that some Windows-related issues still exist. To generate examples for this book, I used a MacBook for my Windup installation and did not experience any of these issues.

Some exceptions related to the installation of the Windup Eclipse Plugin on the Windows OS include the following:

Exception:1

Message: An internal error occurred during: "Generating Windup Report for Run_configuration (1)."

Exception stack trace:

```
java.lang.RuntimeException: java.lang.NullPointerException at org.jboss
.tools.windup.core.services.WindupService.generateGraph(WindupService
.java:189) at org.jboss.tools.windup.ui.internal.launch
.WindupLaunchDelegate$2.run(WindupLaunchDelegate.java:99) at org.eclipse
.core.internal.jobs.Worker.run(Worker.java:55)
Caused by: java.lang.NullPointerException at org.jboss.tools.windup.core
.services.WindupService.generateGraph(WindupService.java:135)
   ... 2 more
```

Session data:

```
eclipse.buildId=4.6.3.M20170301-0400
java.version=1.8.0_121
java.vendor=Oracle Corporation
BootLoader constants: OS=win32, ARCH=x86_64, WS=win32, NL=en_US
Framework arguments:  -product org.eclipse.epp.package.jee.product
Command-line arguments:  -os win32 -ws win32 -arch x86_64 -product org.
eclipse.epp.package.jee.product
```

Exception:2

Message: No message

Exception stack trace:

```
java.lang.NullPointerException
    at org.jboss.tools.windup.core.services.WindupService
.generateGraph(WindupService.java:135)
    at org.jboss.tools.windup.ui.internal.launch.WindupLaunchDelegate$2
.run(WindupLaunchDelegate.java:99)
    at org.eclipse.core.internal.jobs.Worker.run(Worker.java:55)
```

Session data:

```
eclipse.buildId=4.6.3.M20170301-0400
java.version=1.8.0_121
java.vendor=Oracle Corporation
BootLoader constants: OS=win32, ARCH=x86_64, WS=win32, NL=en_US
Framework arguments:  -product org.eclipse.epp.package.jee.product
Command-line arguments:  -os win32 -ws win32 -arch x86_64 -product org
.eclipse.epp.package.jee.product
```

Exception:3

Message: URI is not hierarchical

Exception stack trace:

```
java.lang.IllegalArgumentException: URI is not hierarchical
    at java.io.File.<init>(File.java:418)
    at org.jboss.tools.windup.model.domain.WorkspaceResourceUtils.computePat
h(WorkspaceResourceUtils.java:86)
    at org.jboss.tools.windup.core.services.WindupService
.generateGraph(WindupService.java:130)
    at org.jboss.tools.windup.ui.internal.launch.WindupLaunchDelegate$2
.run(WindupLaunchDelegate.java:99)
    at org.eclipse.core.internal.jobs.Worker.run(Worker.java:55)
```

Session data:

```
eclipse.buildId=4.6.3.M20170301-0400
java.version=1.8.0_121
java.vendor=Oracle Corporation
BootLoader constants: OS=win32, ARCH=x86_64, WS=win32, NL=en_US
Framework arguments:  -product org.eclipse.epp.package.jee.product
Command-line arguments:  -os win32 -ws win32 -arch x86_64 -product org
.eclipse.epp.package.jee.product
```

One way to navigate around these issues is to use a Linux OS such as Ubuntu or a Mac and follow the installation steps previously outlined.

Windup Features

Windup provides several desired capabilities to assist with the overall assessment automation, including the planning and execution of fundamental migration steps. Windup goes beyond mere application of rules to catch violations in Java applications.

Here are some of the key features of Windup:

- **Identification of migration issues with suggested solution** The core rules of Windup identify migration issues and highlight specific impacted sections of the code. At the heart of the tool, Windup suggests code modifications and provides additional supporting information to assist developers resolve problems. Windup also contains several built-in rules to identify issues that typically arise when following a migration path from one application server to another. Some common migration issues encountered include hard-coded IP addresses and Java Naming and Directory Interface (JNDI) lookups. These Windup rules additionally recognize the use of proprietary functionality from other application servers, from deprecated subsystems, and from previous versions of JBoss EAP.

- **Rule extensibility and customization** Windup provides the ability to create complex rules. Developers can expand upon the core set of Windup rules and create custom rules to identify additional issues that are important to their individual organization. You can also override these core rules and create custom rule categories. In this respect, it is similar to the capabilities of PMD.

- **Ability to analyze source code or application archives** Windup can simultaneously evaluate application archives and the source code of multiple applications. To use the Windup features effectively, you can specify the particular package for evaluation, whether it is an entire application portfolio or smaller bundles of applications grouped together for assessment and migration. Another valuable attribute of Windup locates archives that are shared across multiple applications, which in turn support a higher degree of accuracy for derived estimations.

- **Planning and work estimation**   Windup assists migration teams and application owners by detailing the type of work and level of effort necessary to complete the identified migration tasks. Level of effort is represented in Windup reports as Story Points. Though this estimation is not rooted in detailed metrics such as an APM framework, this Windup functionality can be modified and integrated with an external estimation system that provides a better estimation model and a higher degree of accuracy. Windup offers API hooks so that the planning and work estimation functionality can be enhanced. If you would rather use the Windup tool without any modifications, your Windup estimates will be based only on the skills and the classification of the migration work required as per the identified category of issue.

- **Detailed reporting**   When it comes to report generation, the available out-of-the-box functionality of Windup is quite impressive. Windup can produce several reports that provide users with both high-level and drill-down views of the migration effort and the details of specific migration tasks. These detailed reports allow you to view the following:

  - migration issues across all applications

  - charts and summary information about issues within an application

  - a breakdown of issues by module within the application

  - reports of technologies used

  - dependencies on other applications and services

  - source files to examine the lines of code where the issue occurs

Using Windup from the Command Line

Table 8-2 lists all the available Windup command line arguments with a brief description of each. This table was created by referencing the detailed Windup documentation and reference materials available on the Red Hat web site.

Argument	Description
`--additionalClassPath`	A space-delimited list of additional JAR files or directories to add to the class path so that they are available for decompilation or other analysis.
`--addonDir`	Add the specified directory as a custom add-on repository.
`--batchMode`	Flag to specify that Windup should be run in a noninteractive mode without prompting for confirmation. This mode takes the default values for any parameters not passed in to the command line.
`--debug`	Flag to run Windup in debug mode.
`--discoverPackages`	Flag to list all available packages in the input binary application.
`--enableClassNotFoundAnalysis`	Flag to enable analysis of Java files that are not available on the class path. This should not be used if some classes will be unavailable at analysis time.
`--enableCompatibleFilesReport`	Flag to enable generation of the Compatible Files report. Due to processing all files without found issues, this report may take a long time for large applications.
`--enableTattletale`	Flag to enable generation of a Tattletale report for each application.
`--excludePackages`	A space-delimited list of packages to exclude from evaluation. For example, entering **com.mycompany .commonutilities** would exclude all classes whose package name begins with "com.mycompany .commonutilities".

TABLE 8-2.   *Windup Command Line Arguments with Detailed Descriptions (Continued)*

Argument	Description
`--excludeTags`	A space-delimited list of tags to exclude. When specified, rules with these tags will not be processed. To see the full list of tags, use the `--listTags` argument.
`--explodedApp`	Flag to indicate that the provided input directory contains source files for a single application.
`--exportCSV`	Flag to export the report data to a CSV file on your local file system. Windup creates the file in the directory specified by the `--output` argument. The CSV file can be imported into a spreadsheet program for data manipulation and analysis.
`--help`	Display the Windup help message.
`--immutableAddonDir`	Add the specified directory as a custom read-only add-on repository.
`--includeTags`	A space-delimited list of tags to use. When specified, only rules with these tags will be processed. To see the full list of tags, use the `--listTags` argument.
`--input`	A space-delimited list of the path to the file or directory containing one or more applications to be analyzed. This argument is required.
`--install`	Specify add-ons to install. The syntax is *GROUP_ID:ARTIFACT_ID[:VERSION]*. For example, `--install core-addon-x` or `--install org.example.addon:example:1.0.0`.

TABLE 8-2. *Windup Command Line Arguments with Detailed Descriptions (Continued)*

Argument	Description
`--keepWorkDirs`	Flag to instruct Windup not to delete temporary working files, such as the graph database and unzipped archives. This is useful for debugging purposes.
`--list`	Flag to list installed add-ons.
`--listSourceTechnologies`	Flag to list all available source technologies.
`--listTags`	Flag to list all available tags.
`--listTargetTechnologies`	Flag to list all available target technologies.
`--mavenize`	Flag to create a Maven project directory structure based on the structure and content of the application. This creates pom.xml files using the appropriate Java EE API and the correct dependencies between project modules. See also the `--mavenizeGroupId` option.
`--mavenizeGroupId`	When used with the `--mavenize` option, all generated pom.xml files will use the provided value for their `<groupId>`. If this argument is omitted, Windup will attempt to determine an appropriate `<groupId>` based on the application or will default to com.mycompany.mavenized.
`--online`	Flag to allow network access for features that require it. Currently only validating XML schemas against external resources relies on Internet access. Note that this comes with a performance penalty.

TABLE 8-2.   *Windup Command Line Arguments with Detailed Descriptions (Continued)*

Argument	Description
`--output`	Specify the path to the directory to output the report information generated by Windup.
`--overwrite`	Flag to force delete the existing output directory specified by `--output`. If you do not specify this argument and the `--output` directory exists, you are prompted to choose whether to overwrite the contents. Previous reports can get overwritten. Use this argument with care.
`--packages`	A space-delimited list of the packages to be evaluated by Windup. It is highly recommended to use this argument.
`--remove`	Remove the specified add-ons. The syntax is *GROUP_ID:ARTIFACT_ID[:VERSION]*. For example, `--remove core-addon-x` or `--remove org.example.addon:example:1.0.0`.
`--skipReports`	Flag to indicate that HTML reports should not be generated. A common use of this argument is when exporting report data to a CSV file using `--exportCSV`.
`--source`	A space-delimited list of one or more source technologies, servers, platforms, or frameworks to migrate from. This argument, in conjunction with the `--target` argument, helps to determine which rulesets are used. Use the `--listSourceTechnologies` argument to list all available sources.

TABLE 8-2. *Windup Command Line Arguments with Detailed Descriptions (Continued)*

Argument	Description
`--sourceMode`	Flag to indicate that the application to be evaluated contains source files rather than compiled binaries.
`--target`	A space-delimited list of one or more target technologies, servers, platforms, or frameworks to migrate to. This argument, in conjunction with the `--source` argument, helps to determine which rulesets are used. Use the `--listTargetTechnologies` argument to list all available targets.
`--userIgnorePath`	Specify a location, in addition to ${user.home}/.windup/ignore/, for Windup to identify files that should be ignored.
`--userRulesDirectory`	Specify a location, in addition to WINDUP_HOME/rules/and ${user.home}/.windup/rules/, for Windup to look for custom Windup rules. The value can be a directory containing ruleset files or a single ruleset file. The ruleset files must end in .windup.xml.
`--version`	Display the Windup version.

TABLE 8-2. *Windup Command Line Arguments with Detailed Descriptions*

Custom Windup Rule Creation Process

Enterprise application portfolios (EAPs) have evolved over the years to incorporate open-source libraries, custom components, third-party software, varied architectures, and APIs. As a rules-based, open-source tool, Windup makes a set of standard application migration rules available upon installation. The application analysis process using Windup involves the following:

- Extracting files from archives
- Scanning and classifying file types
- Decompiling class files
- Analyzing application code
- Analyzing XML and other file content, including configuration files
- Building the reports

Windup internally uses built-in rules to execute the analysis process and build a data model based on these rule execution results. Windup stores component data and relationships in a graph database, which can then be queried and updated as needed by the migration rules for reporting purposes.

Any modernization endeavor would be hard-pressed to rely solely on out-of-the-box rules to migrate, upgrade, and modernize either a few applications or an entire enterprise-wide portfolio. Although there are several cost- and time-saving advantages to using standard out-of-the-box rules, they can never be comprehensive enough to address all the complexities of a migration exercise. Windup has taken this into consideration by enabling you to write your own custom rules for seamless assimilation into the migration process. Similar to our discussion of PMD rules creation, the process of writing custom Windup rules will be explained in greater detail later in this chapter.

Custom Rule Formats

Before you can write custom rules and deploy them to an enterprise production, you need to author these specific rules and test them against possible code snippets to ensure that the customizations satisfactorily meet the intended scenarios not covered by standard built-in Windup rules. The best option for creating custom rules is to adopt XML-based rules. The following rule pattern is provided for illustrative purposes.

Windup XML-based rules use the following rule pattern:

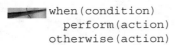

```
when(condition)
   perform(action)
otherwise(action)
```

By definition, a *ruleset* is a group of one or more rules, typically targeting a specific area of migration. All XML rules are defined as elements within rulesets. All rulesets and all rules must have unique IDs within the Windup execution environment. Otherwise, Windup will report a conflict. According to Windup documentation on custom rules, all rules must follow this basic structure:

<ruleset id="UNIQUE_RULESET_ID">   A unique ruleset ID.

- **<metadata>**   The metadata about the ruleset.

    - **<description>**   The description of the ruleset.

    - **<dependencies/>**   The rule add-ons required by this ruleset.

    - **<sourceTechnology/>**   The source technology.

    - **<targetTechnology/>**   The target technology.

    - **<overrideRules/>**   Setting to true indicates that rules in this ruleset override rules with the same ID from the core ruleset distributed with Windup. Both the ruleset ID and the rule ID must match a rule within the core ruleset or the rule will be ignored. This is false by default.

- **<rules>**   A set of individual rules.

    - **<rule id="UNIQUE_RULE_ID">**   Defines the rule and gives it a unique ID. It is recommended to include the ruleset ID as part of the rule ID, for example, `UNIQUE_RULESET_ID_UNIQUE_RULE_ID`. This allows for easier tracking and categorization of rules and the association of similar rules together in one group. One or more rules can be defined in a ruleset.

        - **<when>**   The conditions to match on.

        - **<perform>**   The action to be performed when the rule condition is matched.

        - **<otherwise>**   The action to be performed when the rule condition is not matched.

        - **<where>**   A string pattern defined as a parameter, which can be used elsewhere in the rule definition.

- **<file-mapping/>** Maps an extension to a graph type.

- **<package-mapping/>** Maps from a package pattern (regular expression) to an organization name.

For greater detail about these XML elements, consult the Windup rule creation documentation on the Red Hat web site. Following is a template that you can use to create your own custom Windup rules. This template illustrates the use of the preceding XML elements:

```
<ruleset id="UNIQUE_RULESET_ID"
     xmlns="http://windup.jboss.org/schema/jboss-ruleset"
     xmlns:xsi="http://www.w3.org/2001/XMLSchema-instance"
     xsi:schemaLocation="http://windup.jboss.org/schema/jboss-ruleset
http://windup.jboss.org/schema/jboss-ruleset/windup-jboss-ruleset.xsd">
     <metadata>
         <description>
             <!-- Ruleset Description -->
         </description>
         <dependencies>
             <!-- Ruleset Dependencies -->
         </dependencies>
         <sourceTechnology id="SOURCE_ID" versionRange="SOURCE_VERSION_RANGE"/>
         <targetTechnology id="TARGET_ID" versionRange="TARGET_VERSION_RANGE"/>
         <tag>Reviewed-2015-05-01</tag>
     </metadata>
     <rules>
         <rule id="UNIQUE_RULE_ID">
             <when>
                 <!-- Test for a condition here -->
             </when>
             <perform>
                 <!-- Perform an action -->
             </perform>
         </rule>
     </rules>
</ruleset>
```

Using the template, I created a custom rule. This custom rule can be applied to applications so that the usage of `java.util.Date` can be flagged. Applications that are modernized to Java SE 8 or Java SE 9 can migrate their existing code base to the new `java.time.Instant`. This rule has been saved to a named file gtlcustomruleset.windup.xml. Note that all custom rules must be saved with the file extension .windup.xml. Otherwise, the rules will be ignored by Windup and not loaded into the file.

The following rule uses an element named `<javaclass>`. Use this element to find imports, methods, variable declarations, annotations, class implementations, and other items related to Java classes.

```xml
<?xml version="1.0"?>
<ruleset xmlns="http://windup.jboss.org/schema/jboss-ruleset" id="custom"
xmlns:xsi="http://www.w3.org/2001/XMLSchema-instance"
    xsi:schemaLocation="http://windup.jboss.org/schema/jboss-ruleset http://windup.
jboss.org/schema/jboss-ruleset/windup-jboss-ruleset.xsd">

    <metadata>
        <description>
            This ruleset provides custom rules from gtl
        </description>
        <dependencies>
            <addon id="org.jboss.windup.rules,windup-rules-javaee,2.0.1.Final" />
            <addon id="org.jboss.windup.rules,windup-rules-java,2.0.0.Final" />
        </dependencies>
        <sourceTechnology id="java" />
        <targetTechnology id="java" versionRange="[8,)" />
        <tag>reviewed-2017-06-19</tag>
        <tag>custom</tag>
    </metadata>
    <rules>
        <rule id="custom-01000">
            <when>
                <javaclass references="java.util.Date" />
            </when>
            <perform>
                <hint title="Java Instant usage" effort="1" category-id="mandatory">
                    <message>Replace with the `Instant` class from Java SE 8.</message>
                    <link href="https://docs.oracle.com/javase/8/docs/api/java/time/
Instant.html" title="Java SE 8 Instant" />
                    <tag>custom</tag>
                </hint>
            </perform>
        </rule>
    </rules>
</ruleset>
```

Creating custom rules for enterprise-wide modernizations can be a very powerful and necessary vehicle with limitless possibilities. This section merely scratches the surface of using Windup to write custom rules. Refer to the extensive Red Hat documentation and materials better to understand all the available elements and their utility.

Applying the Rules

Before applying your custom Windup rules, they must first be installed. This can be accomplished by copying the file containing the rules and rulesets to the appropriate Windup folder. Windup scans for these rules, which are files that end with the .windup.xml extension. These files can be located in the following way:

- The directory specified by the --userRulesDirectory argument on the Windup command line.

- The WINDUP_HOME/rules/ directory. WINDUP_HOME is the directory where you have installed the windup platform. This is not the recommended option since these custom rules could be lost if you install a new version of Windup distribution and don't remember to move these custom rules.

- The ${user.home}/.windup/rules/ directory. On Windows machines, this location is at \Documents and Settings\USER_NAME\.windup\rules\ or \Users\USER_NAME\.windup\rules\. This directory is created by Windup the first time it is executed and contains rules, add-ons, and the Windup log.

You can also override or disable existing rules and create custom rule categories. Windup uses the concept of Story Points to estimate the level of effort to migrate the affected code flagged by the rule.

NOTE
Windup Story Points are modeled after Agile Story Points and are intended to be an abstract for estimating the level of effort needed to implement a feature or design change. It is by no means an accurate measure, because it is highly dependent on how an enterprise wants to use this metric, if at all. Earlier chapters of this book described other sophisticated techniques to measure cost and effort as viable measurement metrics. Windup uses Story Points to express the level of effort needed to migrate particular application constructs and the application as a whole. Windup Story Points attempt to bring some uniformity to the analysis and interpretation relating to magnitude of effort.

Estimating the level of effort for Windup Story Points as a rule can be tricky. The following synopsis lists some general Windup guidelines used to estimate the level of effort required for a rule. The following table has been adapted from existing Windup documentation and materials available on the Red Hat web site:

Level of Effort	Story Points	Description
Information	0	An informational warning with very low or no priority for migration.
Trivial	1	The migration is a trivial change or a simple library swap with no or minimal API changes.
Complex	3	The changes required for the migration task are complex but have a documented solution.
Redesign	5	The migration task requires a redesign or a complete library change, with significant API changes.
Re-architecture	7	The migration requires a complete rearchitecture of the component or subsystem.
Unknown	13	The migration solution is not known and may need a complete rewrite.

Once the custom rules have been applied, they can then be included in your analysis either from the command line, using the Windup Eclipse Plugin, or using the newly introduced Red Hat Application Migration Toolkit Web Console.

NOTE
*The Red Hat Application Migration Toolkit
(RHAMT) is an assembly of open-source tools
that enable large-scale application migrations
and modernizations. RHAMT is essentially the
rebranded Windup migration tool with some key
additions and repositioning of the Java migration
strategy. The tooling consists of multiple individual
components that provide support for each phase
of a migration process. RHAMT includes command
line tools, a web console to access and run
migrations, and tools for Eclipse. The command
line interface provides an advanced interface for
performing batch analysis of many applications in
an automated manner. The Web Console provides
a simplified interface for managing large volumes
of applications for assessment and analysis.
The RHAMT Eclipse Plugin provides interactive
implementation time assistance for developers.
At the time of this writing, Windup version 3.0 and
RHAMT version 4.0Beta2 are generally available.
The steps and processes surrounding the Windup
installation discussion are also applicable if you
download and install the migration tool under the
RHAMT moniker.*

RHAMT Web Console

Windup and RHAMT are fairly identical in their availability of tools and
features except for the fact that one major component has been enhanced
in RHAMT. Certain features of the Web Console are available only under
RHAMT. With that said, the trend suggests that Windup 3.0 will be the
final stable version released under the Windup brand. There may be minor
versions to patch Windup issues; however, going forward, the name and
versioning will officially change to RHAMT and will include many other
tools in addition to the existing migration tools and the RHAMT Eclipse
Plugin. I find it interesting to note that the first iteration of RHAMT will
start at version 4.0!

Since the RHAMT Web Console has some additional features over Windup, this section addresses how to analyze the existing application archive and generate reports using the RHAMT Web Console. It will also discuss how to apply our new custom rules using the RHAMT Web Console so that reports can be generated and accessed for analysis.

RHAMT comes bundled with a sample enterprise application archive file named jee-example-app-1.0.0.ear. We will use the RHAMT Web Console to run an analysis on this file. You can start the RHAMT Web Console by going to the bin directory located under the RHAMT installation folder and running the scripts, either `run _ rhamt.bat` or `run _ rhamt.sh`, as appropriate for your operating system. This in turn will run the `standalone.sh` or the `standalone.bat` script. Other scripts in the bin directory will also be appropriately invoked.

To begin, an instance of JBoss will start and load the RHAMT Web Console. Ensure that there are no other servers such as Apache or Tomcat occupying port 8080. You will also need to ensure that the RHAMT_HOME environment variable is set correctly to point to the installation folder of RHAMT. Once you start RHAMT, you can then go to your web browser and type in **http://localhost:8080/rhamt-web/**.

This command will initialize the RHAMT Web Console and automatically take you to the project list page. I have not provided any admin configurations or passwords to restrict access, although that is always an option. Additional details on how to enable secured access to the RHAMT Web Console are available in the documentation available at the Red Hat web site. After an automatic redirection, your browser will load the following URL: http://localhost:8080/rhamt-web/project-list.

When you access the RHAMT Web Console for the very first time without any password restrictions, you will see a Welcome page. Figure 8-19 highlights the Welcome Page when you first set up the Web Console on your server.

The project list will be empty if you have not added any projects to the RHAMT for analysis. On the Welcome page, you will see a New Project button. Click this button and assign a name for your project. On the next page, you can add an application for analysis for this newly created project. Figure 8-20 illustrates an example of how I added the file jee-example-app-1.0.0.ear from the Samples folder to this project.

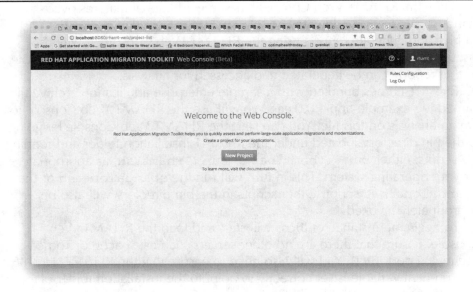

FIGURE 8-19. *RHAMT Web Console Welcome page*

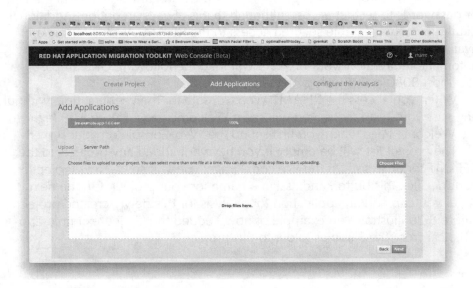

FIGURE 8-20. *Screen depicting the option to add multiple applications to a project*

Once you add the applications to your project, click the Next button to advance to a screen where you can configure the project to be analyzed. Figure 8-21 shows the configuration screen for our SampleJEEProject.

One new option in RHAMT is the Cloud Readiness Analysis Feature. This feature enables you to load custom rules, exclude packages from the analysis, set other advanced options, run the analysis, and save the project. Figure 8-22 shows that the SampleJEEProject has been analyzed and the results are now available for review. The analysis took approximately 15 seconds, as shown in the figure. You can click the Report icon to view the actual analysis report.

If you created and analyzed multiple projects, when you access the URL http://localhost:8080/rhamt-web/, RHAMT will redirect as before to http://localhost:8080/rhamt-web/project-list so that you can see the list of projects available. Figure 8-23 indicates that I created two projects during my installation of RHAMT.

Clicking SampleJEEProject will take you to the page shown in Figure 8-23. Selecting the Reporting icon directs you to the Application List page shown in Figure 8-24. You can see at a glance the high-level details of the analysis for each application. In our example, there are 86 Story Points that translated into 103 incidents. Fifty of the Story Points were classified as mandatory and nine

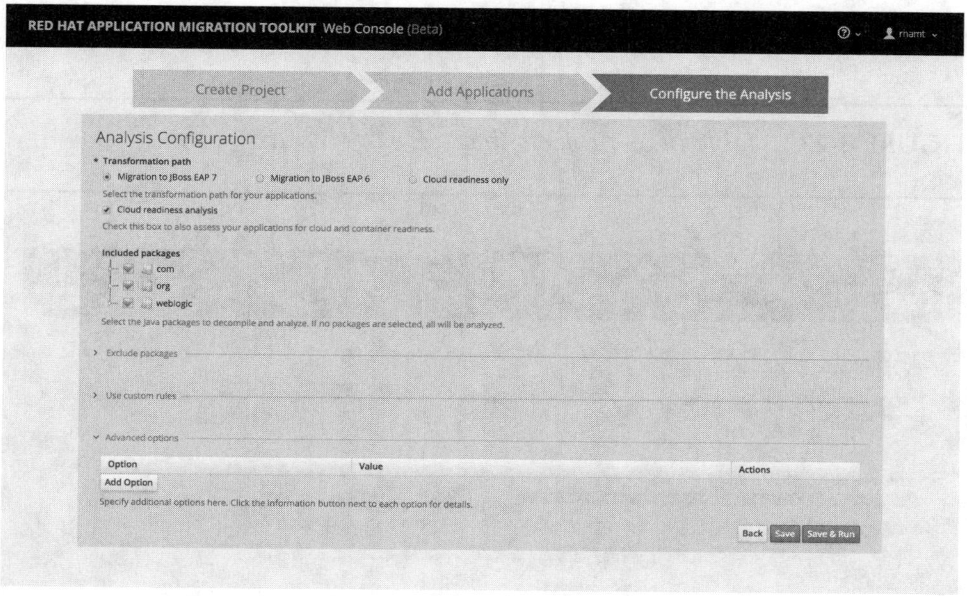

FIGURE 8-21. *Analysis configuration screen before analyzing a project*

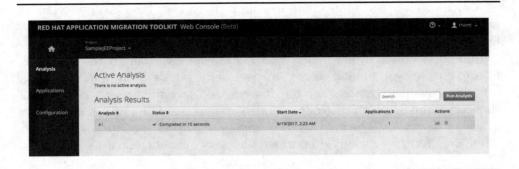

FIGURE 8-22. *Screen showing that analysis is complete and available for SampleJEEProject*

FIGURE 8-23. *Table of all projects that were analyzed*

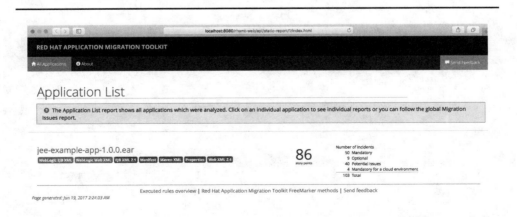

FIGURE 8-24. *List of applications analyzed under a particular project*

as optional. There were 40 potential issues identified along with 4 mandatory incidents related to Cloud Readiness.

Click the application to see Report Index page. This page has a lot of information to scroll through before showing the generated graphs and pie charts. There are four bar charts and one pie chart that depict the incidents and Story Points. These include the following:

- Incidents by Category

- Incidents and Story Points

- Mandatory Incidents by category

- Mandatory Incidents and Story Points

- Java Incidents by Package

Another section, Additional Reports, contains links to various additional details. Figures 8-25 and 8-26 show these bar charts, pie chart, and the additional reports section.

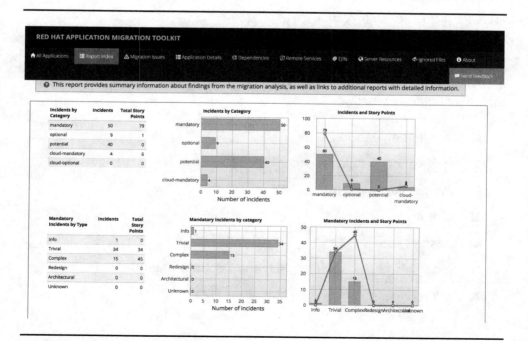

FIGURE 8-25.   *Results of analysis 1*

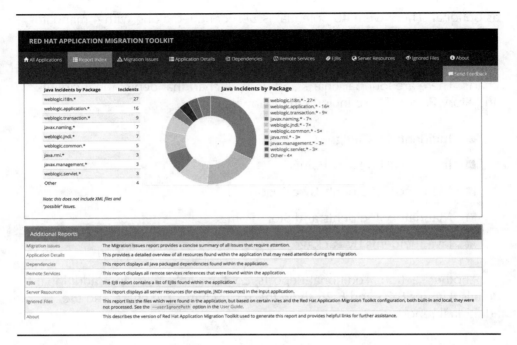

FIGURE 8-26. *Results of analysis 2*

Along the top of Figure 8-26 are menu options that enable you to drill down and view several interesting details about the analysis of your application, including the following:

- Detailed migration issues

- Application details on decompiled Java classes

- Java package dependencies

- Remote services

- EJBs

- Server resources, such as JNDI and JMS information

- Ignored files

From the Migration Issues list, you will be able to drill down all the way to the specific place in the source code where the incompatibility was found.

To apply the custom rule that I created in the previous section, I wrote a sample Java program. The following listing displays the program stored in a file named PMDTest.java. This Java program was also used to apply and test the PMD custom rules in the previous section.

```java
import java.time.Instant;
import java.util.Date;
import java.util.*;

//PMD Eclipse Tutorial
@SuppressWarnings("unused")
public class PMDTest {

    public static void main(String args[]) {
        PMDTest.CALL_METHOD("hello");
        PMDTest.CallHello();
        PMDTest.printCurrentDate();
        PMDTest.printAST();
    }

    public static void printAST() {
            int counter = 0;
            while (counter < 10) {
                System.out.println("Count: " + counter);
                counter ++;
            }
    }

    public static void CALL_METHOD(String INPUT_PARAMETER) {
        System.out.println(INPUT_PARAMETER);
    }

    public static void CallHello() {
        System.out.println("Hello PMD World!");
    }

    public static void printCurrentDate() {
        Date date = new Date();
        System.out.println("Date: " + date.toString());
        Instant instant = date.toInstant();
        System.out.println("instant : " + instant); //Zone : UTC+0

    }

}
```

Follow the steps outlined earlier to create a new project. Export the PMDTest.class and PMDTest.java files into a JAR file. From the Add Applications screen on the RHAMT Web Console, you can now add this JAR file. We still need to configure this application to include our custom rule. Figure 8-27 depicts the configuration screen for the PMDMod project. You can see that pmdmod.jar has been included in the application list. The Use Custom Rules option has been expanded to show that we have included a custom rules file named gtlcustomruleset.windup.xml. This contains the custom rule to catch violations in source code relating to the usage of the `java.util.Date` class.

Click the Save And Run button to generate the analysis report. If you run a report multiple times on one project, each instance is saved under a separate Report ID. You can delete older reports or keep them for comparison or archival purposes. Figure 8-28 shows the high-level results of the analysis on the pmdmod.jar application archive. There are two Story Points and two mandatory incidents.

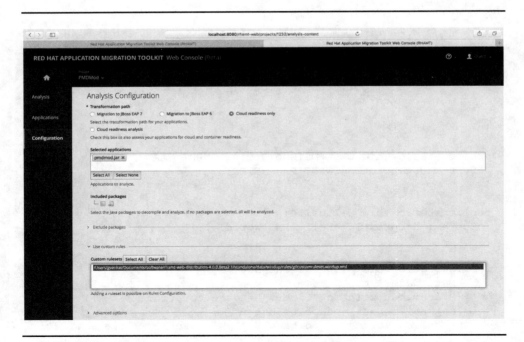

FIGURE 8-27. *Configuration screen for PMDMod project*

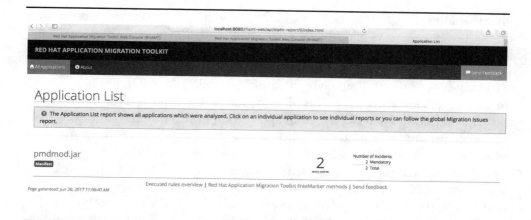

FIGURE 8-28. *High-level analysis of pmdmod.jar application archive*

Clicking the Migration Issues menu item directs you into the details of the migration, including a line item that shows Java Instant usage. This line also displays a message that states "Trivial change or 1-1 library swap" under the column Level Of Effort. Figure 8-29 characterizes the Migration Issues page.

By clicking Java Instant Usage, the analyzed Java class will be revealed along with some additional information. You can also view the actual rule that was applied. Selecting PMDTest will take you to the decompiled class file

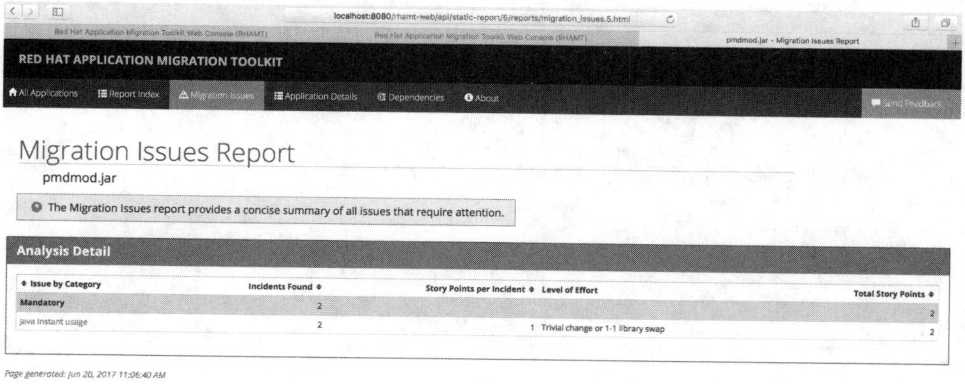

FIGURE 8-29. *Migration issues detail*

that identifies the specific locations in the file where the violations occurred. In our program, this would be line numbers 2 and 28. Figure 8-30 shows the decompiled class file with line 28 highlighted by the RHAMT.

This section demonstrated how to analyze several applications, generate assessment reports, and highlight the areas of applications in need of migration quickly and easily. This all depends on the available rules that can be applied during analysis. For large application portfolios with hundreds of applications and several hundred thousand lines of code, this is not a trivial exercise. To accomplish this, enterprises should invest considerable effort to assess an application portfolio, identify requirements, create custom rules, comprehensively test those rules, and finally review the generated analysis report. The migration of an application portfolio is not merely a technical issue that can be solved by the tools and examples shared in Chapter 7 or this chapter. The holistic treatment of modernization methodologies and the APM discipline, as a whole, compliment these technical solutions and capture the big picture issues so that enterprises can be aware of the colossal undertaking of such migration or modernization programs.

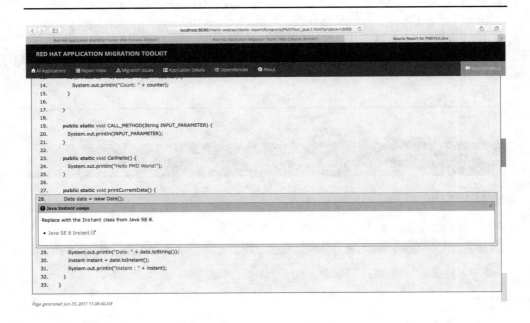

FIGURE 8-30. *Violation in source code highlighted for migration*

Advantages of Using the Windup Migration Tool

The migration of Java applications has always been a custom endeavor without a lot of other options to choose from. Most of these options involved a manual approach and a team of experts, including consultants, engineers, and application developers, who maintain and migrate these enterprise-wide Java applications. Although there are custom and proprietary rules available from third-party IT vendors, those rules are typically procured after engaging the vendor for a specific migration project. Windup has definitely taken strides in the direction of providing a viable open-source option for the Java community.

It is important to note that Windup is not just a technical tool. It also aligns with business goals to provide analytical reports for organizations to estimate, document, and migrate their enterprise applications. The Windup tool generally migrates toward the JBoss EAP. However, since it is open source, anyone can extend and add additional functionality. The following table highlights certain features that recognize Windup as a good migration tool option:

Feature	Description
Shared data model	Windup creates a shared data model graph that provides the following benefits: ■ Complex interaction among rules is possible, allowing rules to pass findings to other rules. ■ Even third-party plug-ins have an option to interact with other plug-ins, rules, and reports. ■ During rule execution, the findings in data graph model can be searched, queried, and used for reporting purposes.
Extensibility	Windup can be extended by developers, users, and third-party software: ■ POJO (Plain Old Java Object) plug-ins can be created to interact with the underlying data graph. ■ Other applications can be integrated into Windup using its API.

	■ Windup minimizes the effort to re-create everything by allowing users with domain knowledge to implement their own rules.
Work estimation	Based on the skills required and the classification of migration work needed, the estimation for the level of effort is calculated and is represented as Story Points in the Windup reports.
Better rules	Windup provides more powerful and complex rules: ■ XML-based rules are easy to implement and simple to write. ■ Java-based rule add-ons are rooted in an open-source component named Rewrite to provide greater flexibility. ■ In some complex situations, rules are nested using the AND / OR statements. This means you can nest simple statements rather than using complex XPath or Regex expressions.
Automation	Windup can automate some of the migration processes: ■ Rules can create Forge inputs and add them into the data graph. ■ Windup is integrated with Forge 2, which enhances it to generate projects, libraries, and configuration files. ■ The data graph inputs can be processed to generate a new project during the automation phase.
Better reporting	Windup reports are now targeted for specific audiences: ■ IT management: Applications are ranked by cost of migration. ■ Project management: Estimation of effort and type of work to complete the tasks. ■ Developers: An Eclipse Plugin provides hints and suggested code changes within the IDE.

PMD Rules vs. Windup Rules

PMD and Windup are both tools that can be leveraged to analyze Java applications. PMD is more mature and has been around for several years compared to Windup. Both tools really shine when it comes to customizing and extending their core functionalities. Both tools provide a set of rules that can be applied out-of-the-box to analyze Java applications. Custom rules can be written as XML rules or Java rules. The list below provides additional details comparing PMD and Windup:

- Traditionally, PMD has been used as a static source code analysis tool, whereas Windup has been positioned, from the beginning, as a rule-based Java application migration tool.

- PMD is primarily engaged to find programming flaws, unused variables, empty catch blocks, unnecessary object creation, and other best practices violations. The Windup tool analyzes the application archives, source directories, technologies, APIs, and artifacts used by the application before generating detailed analysis reports. Windup also provides level of effort and Story Points for the improvements.

- The best feature of PMD is its support for defining XPath expressions to build and deploy custom rules. The Rule Designer enables you to construct new rules easily by applying them against code samples. Both PMD and Windup support building rules in Java, but Windup can additionally generate XML-based rules.

- PMD performs verifications identifying possible bugs, dead code, duplicate code, cyclomatic complexity, and overcomplicated expressions. Windup provides a high-level view into relevant technologies within the application and a consumable report for organizations to estimate, document, and migrate enterprise applications to Java EE and JBoss EAP.

- The HTML-generated Windup reports consists of Application List, Report Index, Application Details Report, Archive Detail, Source Report, Rule Provider Execution Report, FreeMarker functions, and Directives Report. You can generate PMD reports in various formats including text, HTML, CSV, and XML. In the generated HTML report, you can view the file and line number for each captured issue.

Migration to Java 9

The techniques and tools shared in this chapter can be applied to migrate from any source JDK version to any other target JDK version. In fact, you can use these techniques for any programming language, not just Java. As long as you invest the time to write the rules, these rules can be used many times over. This section shares approaches to migrate existing Java code to JDK 9. To illustrate this, consider two features that are a part of the Java SE 9 platform:

- **Process API improvements** Java SE 9 provides enhancements to the Process API. Earlier, you had to resort to various workarounds to get the native Process Identifier (PID) from the underlying operating system. Java 9 adds new methods to the abstract Process class that let you obtain this Process's PID and return a snapshot of information about this Process.

- **_ character is a reserved key word in Java** The _ character is a reserved keyword in Java, and Java SE 8 flagged the use of a single _ as a variable name and threw a warning. Java SE 9 flags such usage as an error at compile time. So if your classes currently use _ as a variable name, you will have to modify all such instances with better names for your variables.

I will show you how to address these two scenarios by writing custom rules to target existing Java code for migration to Java 9. For the Process API migration, I will use a custom PMD rule using an XPath expression, and for migrating the _ variable, I will use a custom Windup rule. This will further reinforce the techniques and demonstrate how powerful custom rules are for migrating an existing code base to future versions of the Java platform in an automated manner.

Custom Java 9 Rule in PMD

Consider the following Java program for retrieving its PID:

```java
import java.lang.management.ManagementFactory;

public class ProcessInfo {
    public static void main(String[] args) {
        long pid = ProcessInfo.getPID();
        System.out.println("PID: " + pid);
    }

    public static long getPID() {
        String pName = ManagementFactory.getRuntimeMXBean().getName();
        return Integer.parseInt(pName.split("@")[0]);
    }
}
```

A custom method called `getPID()` was implemented using some fancy technique with a runtime MBean from the Java Management Extensions (JMX) API, and then parsing the returned result and assuming that the first String in the array split by a @ character is the PID! There are other fun ways to get the PID, and some of them may not work on all underlying operating systems. Now consider the elegant way of doing the same thing in Java SE 9:

```java
import java.lang.ProcessHandle;
public class ProcessInfoJDK9 {

    public static void main(String[] args) {

    System.out.println("***********************************");
        System.out.println("Current Process Id: = " +
ProcessHandle.current().pid() + "\n");

    System.out.println("***********************************");
    }
}
```

You only need to use a simple method call to the `ProcessHandle` interface, get the current `ProcessHandle` instance, and call the `pid()` method on it.

You can use the PMD Rule Designer and AST Viewer to design a custom XPath rule similar to how custom rules in PMD were created before. Following is a listing of a custom PMD rule that will flag all instances of the custom code used earlier to retrieve the PID:

```xml
<rule   class="net.sourceforge.pmd.lang.rule.XPathRule"
deprecated="false" dfa="false"
        externalInfoUrl=""
        language="java"
        message="Please replace custom code for getting PID
information"
        name="ProcessAPI"
        typeResolution="true">
  <description>
  This rule will flag typical custom code usage pattern for getting
Process Identifier (PID).  Java 9 has a Process API that can be used.
  </description>
  <priority>1</priority>
  <properties>
    <property name="xpath">
    <value>
```

```
<![CDATA[
//Name[@Image="ManagementFactory.getRuntimeMXBean"] | //
Literal[contains(@Image, '@')]
]]>
    </value>
    </property>
  </properties>
  <priority>3</priority>
  <example>
<![CDATA[
import java.lang.management.ManagementFactory;
public class ProcessInfo {
    public static void main(String[] args) {
        long pid = ProcessInfo.getPID();
        System.out.println("PID: " + pid);
    }

    public static long getPID() {
        String pName = ManagementFactory.getRuntimeMXBean().getName();
        return Integer.parseInt(pName.split("@")[0]);
    }
}
]]>
  </example>
</rule>
```

Figure 8-31 shows the source code with the newly created JDK 9 rule applied. Lines 11 and 12 have been flagged by the custom rule named Process API, on the bottom left pane, Violations Outline. The corresponding source code has also been highlighted in the image. Using this rule, you can migrate your existing custom code to the new Process API enhancements in Java 9 fairly easily.

Custom Java 9 Rule in Windup

Consider the following Java program that uses a single _ character for a variable:

```
public class UnderscoreVariableTest {
    public static void main(String[] args) {
        String _ = "Underscore Not Allowed in Java 9";
        System.out.println("The use of underscore _ as a variable
name will throw an error in Java 9");
        System.out.println("Java 8 throws a warning.  _ is a reserved
keyword!");
    }
}
```

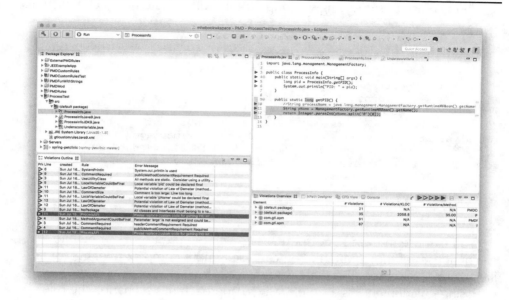

FIGURE 8-31. *Application of Process API PMD rule*

Upon trying to compile the program in Java 9, an error was thrown. Figure 8-32 shows this error. If your company had a practice of using single _ characters as variable names in specific situations and there were thousands or even hundreds of thousands of lines of code, how would you sift through your code base and flag this usage for remediation?

```
src — -bash — 124×31
...are/pmd-bin-5.7.0/bin — Java - run.sh designer   ...lop/mhebookwkspace/ProcessTest/src — -bash   ...lop/mhebookwkspace/ProcessTest/src — -bash   ~/.m/ndup/rules -- -bash   +
[BeemBook : src] gvenkat 3.2$ /Library/Java/JavaVirtualMachines/jdk-9.jdk/Contents/Home/bin/javac UnderscoreVariable.java
UnderscoreVariable.java:6: error: as of release 9, '_' is a keyword, and may not be used as an identifier
          long _ = 123456789;
               ^
UnderscoreVariable.java:7: error: as of release 9, '_' is a keyword, and may not be used as an identifier
          System.out.println("long number _: " + _);
                                                  ^
2 errors
[BeemBook : src] gvenkat 3.2$
```

FIGURE 8-32. *Compilation of Java code with _ variable using Java 9 compiler*

You can use the following Windup custom rule to catch all such violations:

```
<rule id="custom-01001">
        <when>
            <filecontent pattern="_" />
        </when>
        <perform>
            <hint title="Underscore _ use for a variable"
effort="1" category-id="mandatory">
                <message>Since Java 9, underscore _ cannot be used
for a variable since it is a reserved keyword</message>
                <link href="http://download.java.net/java/jdk9/
docs/api/overview-summary.html" title="Java SE 9 reserved keyword" />
                <tag>custom</tag>
            </hint>
        </perform>
    </rule>
```

You can use the <filecontent> tag with the pattern attribute to catch all uses of the _ pattern. You can use a more complex rule, but for an illustration, I have kept the use case simple.

Using <filecontent> is a simple way to approach this scenario. The rule enables one to search all the files just like a text search. There could be more occurrences that are caught than we could imagine since all occurrences of _ would be flagged.

One can improve this rule immediately by using pattern="^_$"

This modification to the pattern would atleast seek out _ only where it occurred by itself and not any _ anywhere in the file.

The same goal of tracking down variables represented by a single _ can be achieved in another way.

You could use the <javaclass> tag and catch all uses of the _ pattern.

Just replace the <filecontent pattern "_" /> with the following snippet between the <when> and </when? tags.

```
<javaclass matchesSource=^_$>
    <location>VARIABLE_DECLARATION</location>
<javaclass>
```

Figure 8-33 depicts the migration issues report. Upon loading the application containing the violation from RHAMT console and applying our custom Windup rule for analysis, the specific line of code was flagged.

This will only look at variable declarations within the Java class and see which of these variable declarations matches the regex pattern ^_$, which is basically the single _.

Figure 8-34 shows the application details and the actual location within the source code where the violation occurred.

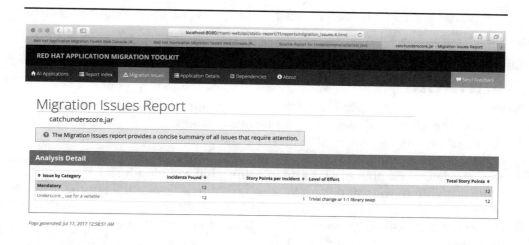

FIGURE 8-33. *Migration issues report showing violations of _ use for a variable name*

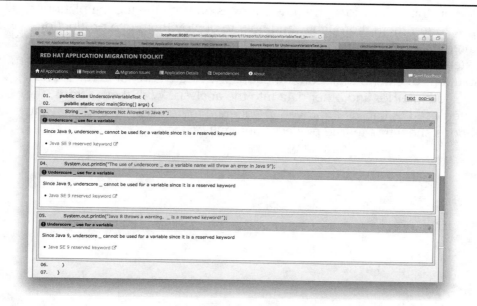

FIGURE 8-34. *Application details and source code location with rule violations*

You can see that it is not technically an onerous task to undertake migrations to Java 9!

Summary

Processes can be effective only if they are enabled with the right set of tools. This chapter discussed two distinct tools: PMD and Windup. The features of both toolsets were showcased to illustrate the automation and enablement of application portfolio assessments and migrations. Though tools are used in a standalone manner, such as in an Eclipse IDE via plug-ins, that method is not scalable beyond a few applications. That type of manual approach relies on individuals to use the tools, load the applications, and operate the process sequentially each time. Both PMD and Windup go beyond manual execution. Both are complete platforms that provide scripts and command line interfaces to build automation processes and automatically implement these tools.

Although PMD and Windup contain several prebuilt rules, they do not completely meet all the needs of an enterprise. As such, both tools enable developers to write rules to customize their projects. This chapter demonstrated how to author custom rules on both the tooling platforms, how to test them thoroughly, and how to deploy them into production. Enterprises can expand the range and functionality of these tools by externalizing the rule application for analysis and building comprehensive solutions to extend their core functionality, create additional rules, and integrate metrics and other data into the analysis. With these efforts, the enterprise UIs can be improved to generate more accurate and relevant reports showing the true power of automation.

CHAPTER
9

Java Application
Migration

I f a Java application has continued to survive for a few years, it likely has been modernized to some extent by the enterprise. At the very least, the first released application version and its associated code base will have evolved after a few years. Even within a few months of the release of an application to end users, new features were likely added. Additionally, if the application was not a standalone function, it would have integrated and communicated with other applications and databases within the organization. In the process of adding features to the application, the source code or attributes are refactored and some reengineering was probably involved.

Typically, an application undergoes changes to its design, code base, business logic, functionality, and user interface in the span of a few months. This is true especially early on in a new application's life cycle. Imagine how many modifications an application would endure after a few years! If updated JDK versions were released, the application may have also migrated to the newer release. This act of migrating a Java application to newer JDK versions should occur every few years. However, in reality, the adoption of new JDKs lags behind quite substantially. For those organizations that have large application portfolios, this migration activity ideally should be a repeatable process for resource sharing and scalability across migration activities. Because that can be a daunting and time-consuming process, organizations simply choose to adopt the status quo. Companies should, at a minimum, however, upgrade or migrate to the latest security release as soon as they are available, usually four times per year.

The content presented in Chapters 7 and 8 focused on the automation tools used to build and enable the Java modernization approach covered in Chapter 6. We considered the theory of abstract syntax trees, building rules, metrics, and a knowledge base to help automate the migration of Java applications. We focused on automated analyses resulting in the identification of mod points. This culminated in an understanding of the portfolio code base as well as the overall Java modernization methodology and APM, both of which are necessary to build and manage an application portfolio properly. These activities drive the very existence of portfolio management and support the macro-decisions made by an organization. Chapter 6 dealt with a high-level approach for modernization in general; this chapter focuses specifically on the migration of an application portfolio to a newer JDK and newer APIs. You will learn how automation tools can be implemented to leverage and execute the migration exercise effectively and successfully.

This chapter will elucidate the framework that enables you to understand what was discovered by the automation tools, how to estimate the complexity of what was discovered, how to determine the impact of an actual migration, how to build a migration roadmap, how to carry out the actual migration, and, finally, how to ensure accuracy of the effort and cost estimation. Building a metrics-based model will help in improving accuracy. It is neither optimal nor prudent to migrate applications in a piecemeal fashion. My own experiences over the last couple of decades indicate that there are efficiencies to be gained by combining a group of applications and migrating them together. We will first review grouping and migrating related applications and building migration roadmaps. Chapter 14 will take this notion to the next level as it discusses large-scale migrations of entire portfolios.

The Migration Methodology

The migration methodology is essentially a scoped-down approach of the modernization methodology depicted in Figure 6-4 of Chapter 6. This section delves deeper into the three phases—assess, evolve, and optimize—as they pertain to the migration of a Java application portfolio. APM-related processes are very much intertwined with migration. Enterprise architecture (EA) has a part to play as well, especially when migrated applications have dependencies and integration points to other application or services.

Assessment Framework

An assessment framework was recommended in Chapter 6 as part of the methodology applicable to Java modernization. The framework assessment is a three-step process—discover, analyze, and recommend—that is applied to an existing Java application portfolio. Subsequent chapters looked at building automation tools to help in the discovery and analysis of the Java code base to extract recommendations.

Here, we'll further discuss the importance of migration assessment in the specific context of application migration. This assessment framework is essentially the same assessment framework covered as part of the Java modernization approach; however, our current perspective specifically analyses Java application portfolio migration to a newer version of the JDK.

The assessment framework identifies the deficiencies that were discovered during the assessment and analysis phase of the application portfolio review and provides organizations with the necessary knowledge to make sub-macro decisions at the application level for groups of applications that require migration to newer JDK versions. This activity does not result in a major overhaul of the application portfolio from an APM perspective and does not impact business processes and application functionality. In fact, it is quite the opposite. The APM strategy and exercise must first be executed at the organizational level. Based on that, the decision to migrate a set of Java applications will be identified as a go-forward action item. As part of a long-term strategy, keeping applications migrated and up to date on JDK versions prevents the proliferation of several major and minor versions of the JDK.

Although the automated assessment exercise enables an organization to build the understanding and knowledge repository from a technical perspective, the scope of the assessment should also consider whether the modernization strategy is to migrate or reengineer an application beyond the technical needs. To validate the strategy properly, the framework should propose the estimated complexity, resource needs, and dependencies, and build a migration plan to carry out the actual migration in an organized fashion.

Similarly, the three steps of the assess phase—discover, analyze, and recommend—can also be applied to this analysis. However, in this section, we will delve deeper into the complementary details beyond the mere employment of automation tools. Figure 9-1 depicts the Java application migration assessment framework. This framework is a more detailed version of the assessment framework discussed in Chapter 6.

Discover Step

The discover step in the assessment of a portfolio of Java applications for migration to a newer JDK version is practically the same as the assessment framework discussed in Chapter 6. The aim is to automate the manual elements of the discovery process as much as possible. A prior APM exercise would have resulted in a centralized application repository. If not, one should be built. If such a repository exists, completeness of the attributes must be reviewed to confirm whether the application portfolio attributes collected previously are sufficient to make the recommendation to migrate the applications.

The automated tools are used to analyze the source code, archive files, and configuration files of the Java applications to build a knowledge base for the migration analysis. Chapters 7 and 8 discussed in detail how to build these automation tools, resulting in the identification of the specific mod points. For migration purposes, the specific type of incompatibility at the discovered mod point is important as well.

Depending on the specific type of incompatibility, a variety of efforts could be necessary to migrate, test, and release that code base. Note that

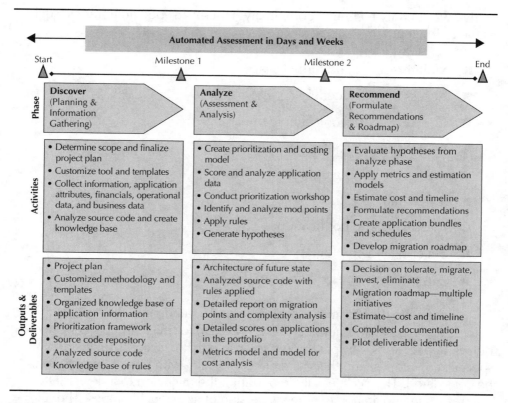

FIGURE 9-1. *Java application migration assessment framework*

not all incompatibilities can be automatically converted and migrated. Some of the mod points might need manual intervention because test cases could be missing, the target API for migration could be complex to implement, or the code logic at the identified mod point might need to be rewritten. It is essential to discover all the relevant information, including identifying any missing information, pertaining to an application to enable a seamless and successful migration. Most of the time, any missing information will be related to testing, third-party libraries or components, and dependencies of other applications on the application being migrated.

Analyze Step

The information discovered in the discover step requires a detailed analysis. In the analyze step, additional information is typically considered in a Java application migration context. Tools can be leveraged for further automated analysis to identify technical complexity patterns in specific libraries, such as the following:

- Multithreading and thread usage
- Access to native code
- Concurrency beyond simple threading
- Use of new I/O (NIO) class libraries
- Swing and other graphics
- Java database calls
- Messaging and notification
- Security and cryptography
- Any open-source or third-party libraries

In a traditional APM analysis, such an understanding of the technical complexity and detail is not necessary; however, for migration or reengineering of Java applications, it is paramount to ensure that usage of specific and specialized libraries, and their inherent complexity with regard to migration, be considered. This is especially important if the migration to a newer JDK also results in a migration to a newer version of additional libraries. The rules knowledge base should be populated with the necessary rules that enable automated analysis of the older and newer versions of these libraries, some of which may not be in the core JDK. In that case, the automated analysis of the source code would identify the mod point associated with the incompatibility. In some cases, a manual analysis of a particular API or library upgrade may be necessary to determine the modification to the source code and the impact of such a change.

In the analyze step of a migration exercise, the effort and cost estimations associated with the migration must also be scrutinized. This can be accomplished by leveraging a knowledge base that contemplates general cost guidelines for simple, medium, and complex mod points. Industry averages, as well as past experiences within the organization, if any, are also captured so that effort and cost calculations can be performed. Mod points are scored based on the type of incompatibility and complexity involved.

Application characteristics are examined and scored to derive a prioritization index for every application. These application characteristics could either be business, technical, operational, or quality related. Business criticality, technical complexity, application dependency, application bundling, and migration scheduling should be analyzed and ratified to provide the appropriate recommendations for a migration. The estimation of overall complexity of the migration considers several factors.

Recommend Step

The recommend step advocates the action items to be executed with respect to the migration of Java portfolio applications. Migration of a Java application portfolio is not just a technical exercise. There are several constraints and dependencies inherent within a portfolio, as well as several business aspects that need to be considered, including the availability of resources and their ability to manage the project, execute, test, and release the migrated portfolio. Applications should in a sequential fashion and not in isolation of one another. In legacy applications, there are typically tight dependencies between application components and external applications. For applications that are already architected using micro-services, it is conceivable that one could isolate and migrate specific micro-services to a different technology or a different library version. Such modifications are not characterized under a true modernization, but rather support feature enhancements or limited technology upgrades to take advantage of specific features.

Bundling related applications, scheduling when the migration can be performed, analyzing risks, and building a detailed migration plan are all equally important. The recommend step results in a migration roadmap factoring in all these details.

Application Characteristics

Application characteristics, in the context of application portfolio migration, span the following areas:

- Business

- Technical

- Operational

- Validation (QA)

These application characteristics are codified into a scoring framework to estimate the impact of the application characteristics on a contemplated migration. The applications are scored and prioritized for migration based on their characteristics in the four areas. There are specific attributes associated with the application characteristics, related to an application, that impact the migration decisions surrounding that application and related applications.

Business Characteristics

The following sample set of key business characteristics must be understood for an application:

- Application critical to the day-to-day business operations
- Application exposed internally or externally to other applications as Representational State Transfer (REST) service
- Financial impact of the application
- Application used by several users who will be impacted
- Only minimal downtime allowed

Technical Characteristics

The following sample set of key technical characteristics must be understood for an application:

- Dependency on third-party libraries and components
- Size of the application in terms of lines of code, number of classes, number of Enterprise JavaBeans (EJBs), and so on
- Usage of deprecated APIs
- Usage of coding patterns that are not acceptable or not advisable
- Several points of integration to the application

Validation Characteristics

The following sample set of key validation characteristics must be understood for an application:

- Availability of test plans and test cases

- Availability of test data

- Number of test cases, use case scenarios, and coverage

- Availability of automated or manual test scripts

- Automation of test data generation and test data setup

- Extent of unit testing that need to be created and performed on the to-be-migrated code

- Availability of testing environment

Operational Characteristics

The following sample set of key validation characteristics must be understood for an application:

- Blackout dates or windows during which an application cannot be migrated

- Preferred dates or windows during which an application must be migrated

- Code sharing among applications

- Deployment dependency

- Applications running in a shared JVM

- Dependency of other applications on a particular application

Estimating Complexity

Before you carry out the actual migration of a Java application portfolio, the nature of the applications must be determined from a complexity perspective. This enables an organization to understand how easy or difficult it will be to migrate the application portfolio. This complexity depends on a variety of factors. This section highlights typical complexity estimation. Different organizations can modify and derive their own frameworks suitable for their own needs.

Integration Readiness

Most modern applications are not standalone entities. They communicate with other applications, expose their own functionality through REST services or APIs, or leverage message-oriented middleware. Here are examples of various kinds of integrations:

- Some of the applications may integrate with legacy systems within their organization, and most applications communicate with relational databases.

- Some applications written in the past five years leverage NoSQL and in-memory databases and avoid relational databases for the type of functionality they encapsulate.

- Applications routinely use third-party libraries and open-source libraries to integrate those libraries into the application itself.

- In some cases, applications integrate with third-party APIs over their private networks or through the Internet.

- A small subset of applications could use public APIs and social medial APIs.

These various types of integration scenarios must be clearly understood before the integrations can properly function after application migration. In the case of tight dependencies among applications, the act of migrating one application in a set of dependent applications could break that interdependency and cause some applications to fail. This is one important reason why the practice of application architecture has evolved toward loosely coupled application components and applications designed as distributed services on a micro-service platform architecture. This approach to modernization is discussed in detail in Chapter 10.

Organizational Resource Needs

The management and execution of any undertaking in an enterprise, let alone an application migration project, requires the alignment of several resources. Depending on organizational structure and culture, there can be variations in program setup and administration. In an ideal enterprise implementation, business units and the IT department should have a collaborative relationship with respect to application portfolio management and ownership. Other stakeholders from business and IT may also be involved, especially if there are application dependencies.

Certain end users who use an application can influence the future requirements. IT functions such as security, infrastructure, DevOps, QA, support, and maintenance are all involved stakeholders in the development, testing, release, and production support of an application. Complex applications require strong organizational resource contributions by multiple stakeholders. This process must be clearly understood by an organization before it can adequately designate and execute the successful migration of an application and its dependent application bundle.

Prioritization

The prioritization framework is used to score applications within a portfolio. In Chapters 3 and 4, we reviewed a prioritization framework; however, that was in the context of prioritizing business capabilities for implementation as part of an APM roadmap. In contrast, the prioritization framework discussed in this section is specifically geared toward analyzing the Java application portfolio to determine the best way to formulate a migration path.

The application characteristics discussed earlier in the chapter are used to help prioritize the migration of portfolio applications. The prioritization framework basically defines a set of parameters and associates weights to those parameters. These parameters, also called prioritization indices, are derived from the application characteristics. A subset of these indices are grouped together to calculate a business index and a technical index. The framework provides guidelines on how these parameters can be used for prioritization and scheduling applications for migration. The calculated and weighted scores for the various applications are displayed in a quadrant for analysis.

An organization could typically use the prioritization indices to do the following:

- Calculate constraint quadrants for the applications in a portfolio.

- Schedule applications for migration from these quadrants.

- Identify specific application(s) for a pilot.

- Bundle applications so that the portfolio can be migrated in a few waves and not as a "single-shot, big-bang" migration.

- Further reschedule or break up an application bundle after bundling if required.

The business, technical, operational, and validation characteristics contribute to the technical and business indices. It is up to an organization to decide the depth and breadth of the characteristics it wants to leverage to compute the business and technical indices. Organizations could also provide a weight to such characteristics in the computation of those indices.

Technical Index

Table 9-1 shows a sample technical index and sample weights attributed to the characteristics that make up the technical index. The scale for the

Index	Description	Score	Weight
Third-party library complexity	Complexity involved in migrating third-party libraries used by a Java application	0–4	25
Number of available test cases	Number of documented test cases available to test upon migration of a Java application	0–4	20
Application size	The size of an application, including lines of code and number of classes	0–4	10
Test coverage	The types of tests that need to be conducted for this application and availability of test scripts and test data	0–4	15
Code modifications	Deprecated APIs modified and actual places in the code where modifications need to be made, either automated or manual, due to changes in the API versions	0–4	10
Integration points	Number of integration points to other applications via API calls or REST services	0–4	10
Information architecture complexity	Messaging, databases, message format changes, schema changes, and transformations	0–4	10

TABLE 9-1. *A Sample Technical Index Calculation with Weights*

contribution of a particular index to the overall complexity of the technical index complexity score is suggested to be 0 to 4:

- 0 = index has no effect
- 1 = low
- 2 = medium
- 3 = high
- 4 = very high

Figure 9-2 depicts an illustrative scoring framework for the technical index of an application. This sample technical index and scoring guidelines can be used as a starting point when customizing the exercise to meet an enterprise's

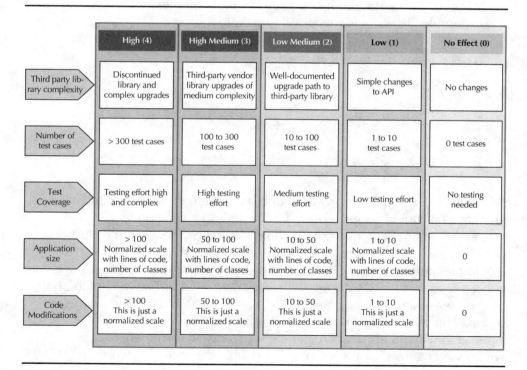

	High (4)	High Medium (3)	Low Medium (2)	Low (1)	No Effect (0)
Third party library complexity	Discontinued library and complex upgrades	Third-party vendor library upgrades of medium complexity	Well-documented upgrade path to third-party library	Simple changes to API	No changes
Number of test cases	> 300 test cases	100 to 300 test cases	10 to 100 test cases	1 to 10 test cases	0 test cases
Test Coverage	Testing effort high and complex	High testing effort	Medium testing effort	Low testing effort	No testing needed
Application size	> 100 Normalized scale with lines of code, number of classes	50 to 100 Normalized scale with lines of code, number of classes	10 to 50 Normalized scale with lines of code, number of classes	1 to 10 Normalized scale with lines of code, number of classes	0
Code Modifications	> 100 This is just a normalized scale	50 to 100 This is just a normalized scale	10 to 50 This is just a normalized scale	1 to 10 This is just a normalized scale	0

FIGURE 9-2. *Example scoring framework for the technical index computation*

individual organizational needs. This figure takes into account five of the index points from Table 9-1 and provides an explanation of how to score an application based on using a scale of 0 to 4 for each index point.

NOTE
This is just an illustration and must not be taken as the exact scoring framework for all application portfolios, since organizational goals and application portfolio goals vary. A scoring framework must be customized and weighted to meet an individual organization's objectives.

Business Index

Table 9-2 shows a sample business index and sample weights attributed to the characteristics that make up the description. The scale for the contribution of a particular index to the overall complexity of the business index complexity score is suggested to be 0 to 4:

- 0 = index has no effect
- 1 = low
- 2 = medium
- 3 = high
- 4 = very high

Tables 9-1 and 9-2 are provided only as a reference. Each individual organization should adopt and modify the index calculation to suit its specific situation. With that said, I would like to provide a sample illustration of "Blocked Windows" and "Allowed Windows" and how those indices would be interpreted using the preceding methodology. For example, what constitutes a score of 2? We know that the data is important to capture, but how do we assign it a value and grade it between 0 and 4? One possible scoring technique would be to score a 0 if there are no such windows associated with an application and a 4 if there is an extremely narrow window recognized by the team as impossible to meet. The scores in

Index	Description	Score	Weightage
Application end users	Number of users of this particular application across the enterprise who will be impacted by the application migration	0–4	25
Impact to business	Business units impacted, financial impact, business risks, external facing application, and so on	0–4	25
Blocked windows	Specific periods during which application cannot be migrated, including specific dates when application must to be available	0–4	20
Allowed windows	Specific allowed downtime of an application during migration, including factors such as specific dates, elapsed calendar time, and so on	0–4	15
Application knowledge	Business, functional, and technical knowledge about the application is well-documented, and in-house resources who are knowledgeable about this application are available to help with migration	0–4	15

TABLE 9-2. *A Sample Business Index Calculation with Weights*

between are relative and offer an idea of how to navigate the exercise after assessing how narrow or difficult the window will be.

Figure 9-3 depicts an illustrative scoring framework for the business index of an application. This sample business index and scoring guidelines can be used as a starting point when customizing the exercise to meet an enterprise's individual organizational needs. This figure takes into account the five index points from Table 9-2 and provides an explanation of how to score an application based on a scale of 0 to 4 for each point. (Again, this is just an illustration and must not be taken as the exact scoring framework for all application portfolios; organizational goals and application portfolio goals

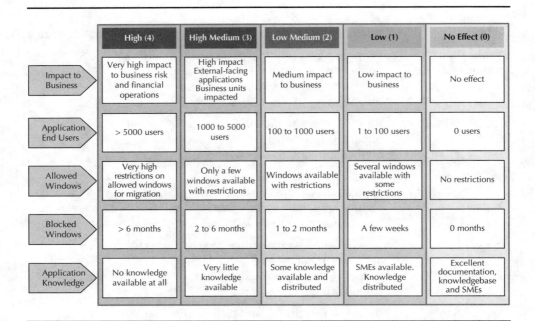

	High (4)	High Medium (3)	Low Medium (2)	Low (1)	No Effect (0)
Impact to Business	Very high impact to business risk and financial operations	High impact External-facing applications Business units impacted	Medium impact to business	Low impact to business	No effect
Application End Users	> 5000 users	1000 to 5000 users	100 to 1000 users	1 to 100 users	0 users
Allowed Windows	Very high restrictions on allowed windows for migration	Only a few windows available with restrictions	Windows available with restrictions	Several windows available with some restrictions	No restrictions
Blocked Windows	> 6 months	2 to 6 months	1 to 2 months	A few weeks	0 months
Application Knowledge	No knowledge available at all	Very little knowledge available	Some knowledge available and distributed	SMEs available. Knowledge distributed	Excellent documentation, knowledgebase and SMEs

FIGURE 9-3. *Illustrative scoring framework for the technical index computation*

vary and a scoring framework must be customized and weighted to meet the individual organization's objectives.)

Illustrative In-Depth Analysis of Third-Party Libraries

The suggested characteristics for computing the overall business complexity index and technical complexity index must be thoroughly evaluated to determine their impact on the index contribution and weightage.

This book will not discuss the specific details of how to analyze the availability of test cases or the sufficiency and coverage of test data, neither will it provide a more comprehensive in-depth examination of the financial impact to a business. However, to illustrate the fact that an enterprise should prioritize and understand these characteristics with a greater level of detail, the example in Table 9-3 shows an in-depth analysis for the use of third-party libraries by an application requiring migration and the potential impact of that exercise.

Category	Description	Migration Effort	Rationale
Library distributed with the application server	Library is distributed as part of the application server installation	Low	Library should come bundled with the application server; typically no deployment issues
External open-source library packaged at deployment	Open-source library	Low	Documentation should usually be available, but may need some testing to ensure migration went well
JDBC driver	JDBC drivers compatible with the application server	Low	JDBC drivers are well documented for compatibilities with an application server
External vendor library packaged at deployment	Commercial third-party vendor library used by an application running on an application server; this library is usually loaded at runtime	Medium	May require migration to a newer version that supports the new JDK; plus possible code changes may need interaction with external vendor
Discontinued, replaced, or obsolete library	Library no longer supported and must be replaced by alternative library	High	Requires research, evaluation for alternatives, POCs, extensive testing, and compliance to functionality and performance
Internal enterprise home-grown framework or library	Any library maintained by the enterprise internally but outside the application; these internal libraries are usually used by multiple applications and will have to upgraded by the enterprise	High If built as a shared library, multiple applications may use it	Requires a migration by the enterprise to be compliant with the new JDK, and must undergo rigorous testing

TABLE 9-3.   *Example Analysis on the Impact of Third-Party Libraries to an Application Migration*

Effort and Cost Estimation

It is widely accepted that organizations spend approximately 80 percent of their IT budgets it "keeping the lights on"—merely supporting and maintaining existing applications. There is always contention among project budgets and between the need to enhance existing applications versus the desire to build new ones. In both cases, enterprises typically do not maintain a detailed breakdown of expenses by individual application. Additionally, several resources are usually shared among applications, including developers, infrastructure, and management contributions. Those applications in a portfolio that remain inconspicuous and monopolize limited resources often catapult the cost of the application portfolio, which can quickly spiral out of control. As a result, the combination of constrained budgets and inadequate resource management prevents the application portfolio from becoming modernized, migrated to new technology, or reengineered altogether.

When organizations finally decide to migrate the application portfolio to a newer JDK version and newer APIs, many enterprises do not know how to estimate and devise the migration. This is where the migration approach based on automation and identification of mod points becomes relevant. Accurate estimations are necessary based on solid metrics and analysis. An estimation model based on metrics, identification of mod points, calculation and application of complexity-related factors, and a quantitative score helps the organization compile a complete understanding of the portfolio migration to allocate necessary resources and budget appropriately. Figure 9-4 shows the various steps involved in the estimation of cost and effort for an application portfolio migration exercise. Steps 1a, 1b, and 1c all focus on identifying the application portfolio–based input into the estimation process. It comprises the actual mod points identified, configuration changes, database changes, and infrastructural related changes including software and hardware. Step 2 applies a complexity factor to the estimation process. Step 3 applies a metrics-related adjustment factor. Step 4 generates a score on each application in the application portfolio to be migrated. Step 5 computes the effort and cost based on the estimation model and the result of the above four steps.

Gaps in knowledge of an application portfolio can introduce operational risks and contribute to deviations from a planned and estimated budget allocation. Following the APM principles laid out in the beginning chapters of this book will help the organization create a knowledge base that mitigates such risks and includes a wealth of information about each application in the portfolio. As discussed, the knowledge base should include financial,

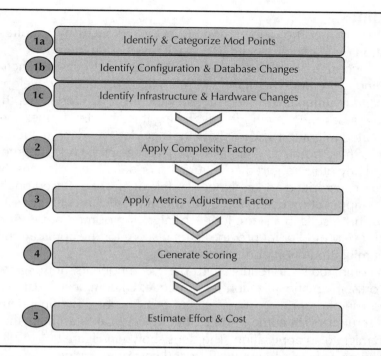

FIGURE 9-4.   *Steps to the estimation of cost and effort*

operational, business, and technical information. Estimation models should take into account specific organization-related constraints and complexity factors. Baseline measurements of process capability and cost should be conducted for past projects, if available, to help determine the efficacy of the portfolio migration plan. In addition to organization-specific data, industry average data and specific cost and effort data for particular applications should be collected to contribute to the accuracy of the estimation model.

The use of past metrics and data points to guide estimations for modernizing individual applications in a portfolio becomes more complicated if companies have engaged in the lax practice of consolidating maintenance and support costs together as a single budgetary line item. By following an APM approach, several companies in industries such as finance, insurance, telecommunications, manufacturing, retail, and government relations have been able to develop sound knowledge base and metrics-driven estimation models to migrate application portfolios while adhering to managed budgets and fixed timelines.

Guidelines

At the heart of a portfolio migration project is the necessity of collecting application details such as source code, lines of code, number of classes, test cases, configuration files, environment details, use cases, function points, and any other type of metrics related to application development, testing, and maintenance. These factors were all addressed in depth as part of the assessment methodology. Taking this one step further, the use of automated migration and analysis tools guides the identification and location of mod points and finds incompatible source code, deprecated APIs, and any other required configuration or database variations. Such mod points are categorized and assigned complexity factors. Based on the metrics related to application detail and other metrics, adjustment factors are also applied. This results in a score for each migration or mod point. Adding the score for every mod point provides a total score for the application itself in terms of migration effort and related cost.

This combined score reflects third-party components, home-grown frameworks, internationalization-related code, UI complexity, database-related changes, use of proprietary libraries, and other factors. The final derived score is scrutinized in comparison to the project plan to estimate the required effort to migrate an application. The steps shown in Figure 9-4 result from the estimation process to derive the effort and cost of migrating an application.

Total Cost Computation

Typical application-related costs include architecture, requirements analysis, design, development, testing, support, and maintenance. There could also be costs associated with frameworks and technical components, software licensing, implementation, and application integration. These direct, indirect, and infrastructure-related costs require strict scrutiny to discern any deviations after an application is migrated. Several interesting questions can be posed and answered in the context of computing costs associated with the migration of an application portfolio:

- Could support costs increase or decrease?

- Would the license fees for a third-party component increase or decrease?

- How many resources would be needed for maintaining the upgraded application?

- Could another application be sunsetted and eliminated from the portfolio?

- Would an external IT vendor reduce resources if it maintained the portfolio?

Even if clear metrics are unavailable for the application data, if the applications can be categorized as simple, medium, complex, and very complex based on available data points, then that information could instead be leveraged for the analysis. Take, for example, a sample set of applications from the entire portfolio that include a complete set of metrics, including cost baselines, and then compute the estimation of effort and cost. Next, contingent upon the categorization of the applications in this portfolio, a model based on the number of mod points discovered in the other applications can be extrapolated. Although this method does not provide cost estimation with a high degree of accuracy, a certain level of confidence can be correlated with the generated cost numbers. These numbers will definitely be more reliable than rough order of magnitude (ROM) models and can meet budgetary estimate levels in most organizations.

Migration Roadmap

A migration roadmap provides the blueprint for the migration of a Java application portfolio. The roadmap must contemplate all the necessary migration activities and provide a detailed plan for the migration. The design of the migration roadmap takes into account several factors, including the following:

- Overall effort required to complete the migration

- Underlying cost of the program

- Analysis of the development, QA, and production environments

- Deployment details of an application

- Skills available in-house

- Resource availability

- Sequence or staggered manner in which an application or bundles of applications must be migrated

- Dependencies between applications
- Blackout windows and other constraints
- End user needs during migration
- Perceived risks and mitigation
- Knowledge transfer, training, and change management

The project plan in particular must encompass the following:

- Project timelines for migration
- All resource requirements and when they are required
- Costs and budget analysis
- Risks factors to project execution

Application Scheduling and Bundling

The applications pending migration should be to be arranged into multiple groups based on a certain strategy. These applications are migrated as a batch rather than in a sequential fashion. Additionally, dependencies among applications and external factors must be taken into account when creating the groups of certain applications. Only after this step can these application bundles be scheduled for migration in a staggered sequence. This process will provide the most optimal experience for a strategic application portfolio migration:

- The scheduling strategy provides guidelines for scheduling applications. Scheduling leverages the indices calculated using the prioritization and bundling framework.

- The bundling strategy groups applications into migration bundles that can possibly be migrated simultaneously or staggered in some fashion. Bundling uses the indices calculated using the prioritization framework.

Application Scheduling and Bundling Guidelines

Guidelines must be followed to ensure the proper creation of a migration roadmap, and applications scheduled for migration must be subject to this protocol. There are several guidelines to consider, and the priority of each may vary among organizations. In no particular order of priority, here are some application scheduling guidelines for migration:

- Analyze the applications that are scored and projected on the quadrants identified in the prioritization framework.

- Ensure that blackout dates, fire-fighting windows, and preferred migration windows are considered in the application scheduling.

- Applications within a bundle that have conflicting blackout dates may have to be split into different bundles.

- Applications that share the same application server could be bundled and scheduled together.

- Applications sharing the same JVM could and probably should be scheduled together.

- Schedule applications with a high technical complexity index earlier, if they do not have a dependency on another application, given their constraints.

- Too many high-risk or highly complex applications should not be bundled together.

- Several applications that all require intensive performance testing should not be scheduled for migration at the same time.

- At any point in time, a staggered migration plan should not have a large number of applications being migrated. Although this number is flexible, experience has shown that no more than 10 to 15 applications should be simultaneously bundled and/or migrated.

- All applications with code dependencies must be bundled together.

- Applications that are related to the same functionality can be bundled together.

- If a preferred migration window cannot be accommodated within bundles, then established bundling and scheduling guidelines may have to be violated to split up the applications into different bundles.

- When in doubt, reschedule the migration.

Pilot Selection

In an enterprise, if a Java application portfolio consists of more than 15 applications, the migration of that portfolio can involve bundling groups of 8 to 10 applications. One suggested way to mitigate risks during the process is to develop an understanding of the migration path of that portfolio. This can be accomplished by first conducting a pilot migration exercise, carried out on a single application or a group of 3 to 5 applications. The results from the pilot exercise can be availed to ensure that potential risks are known and to automate the migration of the remaining application bundles.

Follow these guidelines for the selection of applications in a pilot:

- Select a few applications that provide good coverage from major functional areas. This will ensure that availability of test cases become known across various functional areas.

- Select applications that do not need major enhancements or code changes.

- Do not select applications that are of very poor technical quality. This will make the pilot too complex and provide a skewed understanding of migration complexity.

- Applications that have a low technical complexity index (not overly complex applications) and applications that have a low business complexity index (not overly business critical and risk prone) are good candidates for a pilot.

- Applications that are typically open in terms of migration dates and blackout periods are possible pilot applications.

Application Migration

The successful migration of a Java application portfolio depends on many factors. These factors are all addressed by specific work streams or tracks.

Work Streams and Program Management

The application migration program involves several important tracks that need to work together seamlessly:

- **Program management** Risk management, resource identification and allocation, ownership of the migration plan, communication among various stakeholders, tracking the success metrics of the program to completion.

- **Governance** Defines the success metrics, tracks compliance and best practices, and ensures that the program stays on track.

- **Technical migration** The actual execution of the project, migration of the various applications, changes to the code base, modification of the configurations to the new environment, changes to the database, message formats, and other technical changes to complete the migration.

- **Infrastructure and environment** Establishes that all environments (development, testing, production, and required infrastructure) are upgraded to support the migrated application portfolio.

- **Quality assurance** A validation track that is equally as important as the migration track. For the technical track to be successful, the QA track must ensure that adequate test cases and test data are available. Various types of testing may be necessary depending on the complexity of the application portfolio and the nature of the applications being migrated. The appropriate testing strategy should be created and executed in conjunction with the technical migration of applications.

- **Change management** Ensures that end users are aware of any modification to the process or functionality culminating from the migration. Additionally, other areas of the enterprise could be affected. The migration exercise itself could encounter risks necessitating changes to the program execution.

- **Knowledge management** Responsible for collecting and building a knowledge repository of all artifacts associated with the application portfolio. This track is also accountable for ensuring that the migration exercise results in knowledge capture about the application portfolio to facilitate governance, application portfolio management, and future migration and reengineering exercises.

Pilot Migration

The migration of a Java application portfolio requires thoughtful planning. The precise computation of business and technical indices to score applications that ultimately bundle applications into multiple groups is necessary before bundles can be migrated. The first bundle to be migrated is the *pilot bundle*. The key objective with pilot migration is to use the experience and findings from the pilot to enhance the productivity of subsequent application bundle migrations.

Applications requiring migration are typically evaluated on the complexity of the migration. However, for the pilot wave, application bundles consist mostly of less complex or simple applications and are selected with the consensus of other key stakeholders. Not all application owners or business units will be represented in the pilot migration, yet each business unit and application team can greatly benefit from the results. This collective knowledge share gathers valuable information to be applied to subsequent application bundle migrations, directly benefiting a particular stakeholder with a set of applications.

Evolve Stage

The evolve stage executes the specific roadmap and migration plan as defined in the discover stage. As part of the evolve stage, the existing governance and change management processes are established or tweaked to ensure coverage for migration engagements. The effort and cost associated with the migration would have already been calculated and incorporated during the analysis phase of the discover stage. Further validation of these metrics will occur during the initial phase of the evolve stage.

The experience and information gathered from the pilot migration should be leveraged to enhance the productivity and efficiency of migrations in subsequent waves. The approach to migration is continually evolving as each bundle of applications experiences migration. These collective learnings should be captured in a centralized knowledge base to enhance the migration "cookbook."

Architect Phase

The architect phase is the initial phase of the evolve stage. Typically, Java migration projects do not involve a complicated architecture phase. The focus of most migration exercises is to upgrade the JDK version, versions of third-party libraries, configuration files, application server versions, database versions, and in some cases other products or components that are part of the solution. Other modernization projects including reengineering exercises conducted upon a portfolio might need a more detailed and involved architect phase.

The architect phase secures the design and functionality of the target infrastructure platform on which the applications will be migrated. The migration environment to support the migrated application portfolio must also be recognized and designed correctly. Lastly, database upgrades, OS upgrades, and any impact to integration points should be studied to make appropriate architectural decisions to ensure a smooth and successful Java application migration.

Execute Phase

The execute phase, where the bulk of the migration exercise occurs, is critical to the evolve stage. The Java applications scheduled for migration in an application bundle will begin their migration exercise journey. Based on the library version and identified mod points, if the code needs enhancement at any specific point, then the SDLC process should be followed. This code can be modified either automatically or manually depending on the complexity and nature of the migration point.

It is necessary for the development team conducting the migration exercise to build unit test cases and unit test scripts for any code that is injected or modified at the identified migration point. This is critical to ensure that no new bugs or features are added to the code during upgrades to the Java application. Since this is just a migration exercise, there will be no functional enhancements or code reengineering. In some cases, the API of the new version of a library being upgraded could require code refactoring to interoperate with the new API. In many cases, the actual code modification during migration is not an overly complicated process. Situations where migration becomes complex occur sometimes when the mod points are complex or the identified mod point needs a major fix due to a new language feature that is adopted or a new API that needs to be implemented.

Validate Phase

The validate phase of the application portfolio migration is as important as the execute phase. The validate phase also follows the typical software development life cycle (SDLC) process of QA and testing. Even though the migration of a set of Java applications will involve minimal or controlled code changes at the identified mod points, it is imperative that functionality has not been altered. Performance of an application cannot be impacted.

The application must continue to meet its other nonfunctional requirements and SLAs. Additionally, any communications with external applications, third-party components, REST services, databases, and mobile applications must be maintained. These integration points should be tested to ensure compliance to the previously supported message and data formats.

The effort and cost of the validate phase depends to a large extent on the availability of a full-fledged test harness and completeness of test cases and test data. The QA team should be initially involved during the discover stage to determine the extent of testing necessary and the availability of existing tests that can be leveraged.

If test cases and test scripts are not available for certain applications, there is a potential risk that these applications may deviate from their expected functionality requirements and may not perform to SLA obligations. In the absence of functional test cases, one strategy would be the requirement of end users to engage with the existing premigrated application and document the steps, processes, inputs, and outputs during their use, including logging the clicks and data retrieval during their interaction with the application. Then, after migration, this entire scenario can be replayed to determine whether the application meets the expected functionality. Although this is not an ideal way to test an application, the lack of any available functional testing leaves no choice but to attempt to replicate the behavior that an end user sees, after the migration of an application. Because this process is limited by the extent of usage by an end user, this leaves open the possibility that some edge cases may fail but never come to light until an issue arises.

 NOTE
Here is an example of an edge case. At the time of this writing, when someone registers with Facebook, the first and last name fields do not allow users with single letter first names to join. The minimum first name requirement mandates two letters. The edge case of people with a single letter first name, such as myself, was not properly tested and vetted. As a result, I am known as "GG" on my Facebook page.

Testing should become an automated process to compress the time to migrate an application. This will safeguard the speed and accuracy of future migrations, modernizations, and reengineering efforts. Applications following

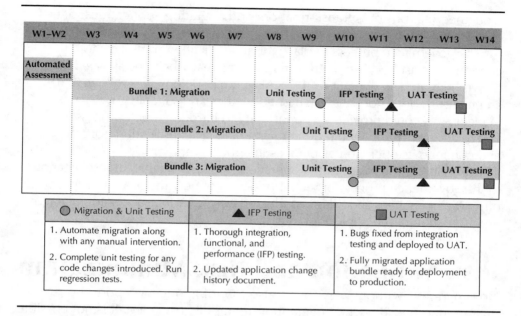

FIGURE 9-5. *Sample plan for migrating and testing application bundles*

this process can be effectively migrated and validated to meet necessary requirements.

Figure 9-5 depicts a sample plan for migrating and testing identified application bundles. In this figure, three bundles are shown. The actual migration of the application bundles is not sequential. Instead, it is staggered so that the total elapsed time for the migration of all applications in that portfolio is not a cumulative addition of the time taken to migrate each bundle. Bundles 2 and 3 have a dependency on Bundle 1, so they commence a couple of weeks later in the migration schedule. Each bundle is thoroughly tested and validated before being sent for user acceptance. Only after user acceptance testing (UAT), when the application meets all functional and performance criteria and SLAs, will the application be deployed to production.

Optimize Stage

The optimize stage is less important to a pure migration exercise because not much is expected to change in the maintenance, operation, and support of the Java application portfolio. Other modernization projects such as reengineering, business transformation, and migrating applications to the cloud would significantly impact the optimize phase.

The governance process in place for an application portfolio should continue to exist because metrics must have already been established for the visibility into its operations if the APM methodology was followed. If an enterprise does not have established metrics and suitable governance in place, this could provide an opportunity to introduce such processes. The recommendation would be to migrate the Java application portfolio and continue its operation as per existing policies and processes. Minor adjustments can be made to the operations, but any significant modification to the governance process or the introduction of new metrics, DevOps, or other major changes should be conducted only after the successful migration and validation of the application portfolio.

Risk Mitigation and Risk Minimization

No program is without risk. This is also true of application portfolio migration, especially when migrations are rapidly executed. It is not possible to alleviate all risks completely. In many cases, enterprises tackle risks with the time, resources, and budgets they have to devote. Even if it were possible to mitigate certain risks completely, oftentimes it would be too cost prohibitive and time consuming to do so. Following are some typical risks that are encountered in a Java application portfolio migration engagement and how to mitigate or minimize such risks with appropriate minimization or mitigation techniques:

- **Risk**   Unit test cases are not available for most of the applications to carry out the unit testing of the application.
  Risk minimization   Perform unit testing for only the code that is modified resulting from migration. Entire unit testing will not be carried out. This assumes that the application was otherwise performing correctly, even though there was a lack of unit tests. This approach ensures that newly introduced code is unit tested to ensure that the application does not break.

- **Risk**   Systems integration testing (SIT) and user acceptance testing (UAT) test cases are not available and users perform random testing during the UAT phase.

Risk minimization   Perform integration testing only for code that has been changed via migration if that code has any integration points. Entire system and integration testing need not be carried out since it is assumed that application was performing satisfactorily for users.

- **Risk**   Subject matter experts (SMEs) for the various applications are not available.
Risk minimization   Enterprises should identify SMEs and application owners for each application, if not already identified. An effort must be made to construct a knowledge base for each application, including a functional understanding of the application, requirements documents, traceability matrix, test cases, test data, technical documentation, and anything else that will be valuable to the understanding of the application.

- **Risk**   Many enterprise-specific home-grown libraries used in the application and their compatibility with target JDK and environment are unknown.
Risk mitigation   The enterprise must first port the home-grown libraries to the new JDK and test them before deploying it in an application build. Any impact to application migration should be identified.

- **Risk**   Issues exist after integration with mobile applications and other external applications.
Risk mitigation   Analyze compatibility of the new JDK with the mobile applications and external applications. Determine whether API calls can be converted to REST calls and decouple the application to be migrated from external applications so that integration is loosely coupled.

Summary

A key part of the Java application portfolio modernization journey is upgrading the application portfolio to the newest JDK version, as well as other open-source and third-party libraries. For applications running on an application server, the version of the application server also needs to be upgraded. Depending on the Java application portfolio, other components such as messaging middleware, third-party applications and components, databases, REST services, and infrastructure may also need upgrades.

In most enterprises, the assessment of the application portfolio is not always automated. In fact, it is probably the opposite. The previous two chapters discussed the importance of automation and how to build the necessary tools. Automating the assessment phase greatly reduces the effort, time, and risks and enhances predictability of the engagement. When the exact mod points are discovered in an application migration, the complexity of the exercise can be quickly ascertained. This allows for an accurate total calculation of the effort and cost associated with the migration.

Applications are not migrated simultaneously in a "big-bang" approach. Instead, applications are bundled and scheduled in staggered intervals, taking into account business and technical factors. The actual migration and testing follow SDLC practices but can be automated depending on the complexity of the identified mod point. If complete test harness and test cases are available, it further reduces the risk of deviating from expected functionality, ensuring that new bugs are not introduced.

The book continues to address the topic of modernization, and the next chapter is devoted to reengineering some or all of the applications in the Java application portfolio. We will discuss service platforms, micro-service architectures, and how Java applications can be modernized by exposing functionality as services that can be discovered and consumed. We will also review how a set of Java applications can be reengineered and, over time, be made available as REST services.

CHAPTER
10

Java Application
Reengineering

A s enterprises routinely upgrade and migrate their Java application portfolios, applications that have added new functionality or enhanced existing functionality will not be evident. As a result, application bloating, or application inflation, steadily increases over time. The phenomenon of bloated applications considers application size, application complexity, the amount of integration with other applications, and cost of application maintenance. At the same time, applications similarly undergo deflation, where factors such as the number of knowledgeable application developers, the amount of current or relevant documentation, and the tracking of various application metrics all decrease over time.

In the process of adding new functionality, legacy applications in a portfolio typically undergo reengineering to justify its relevance. Although it is difficult to anticipate the future needs of applications, reengineering an application should follow a logical course to align with and meet new business requirements. Such projects, especially for large applications, are expensive and take several months or even a few years to build, test, and deploy. The cost, effort, and complexity are compounded over time, and traditional reengineering projects pose a high risk, especially when dealing with large and complex Java applications.

To minimize business risk, a well-constructed reengineering project should result in a quick, easy, and contained cost-effective result. Organizations that undertake the reengineering of large application portfolios need to establish a repeatable process to scale across the application portfolio and share resources across the various activities.

Chapter 9 focused on the migration of Java applications to newer versions of the JDK while leveraging updated automation tools and frameworks. This chapter provides a fresh perspective on reengineering by introducing the concept of micro services and service platforms. This discussion will also examine how an enterprise architect can transform traditional Java applications into services by on-boarding them as part of the new services platform. The analysis will also expound on fundamental *core platform services*, which are infrastructural and foundational in nature and leveraged by other services. The future of Java applications depends on the services platform. Reengineering existing application portfolios to services will enable Java applications to flourish and naturally evolve as you leverage advances in the Java platform and incorporate new features with ease.

Services Platform Concept

The approach to service-oriented architecture (SOA) has evolved since the mid-1990s when the term was first introduced. Starting in early 2000, multiple vendors jumped into the fray to support the hype surrounding SOA. These service providers offered SOA platforms, tools, and services. SOA soon became synonymous with "web services," although SOA was more of a concept, strategy, and architecture realization. SOA existed long before the mainstream adoption of XML and web services.

One of the main purposes of SOA is to define services with macro granularity so that they can be accessed and used by other business services. This concept promotes reuse of certain basic services, thereby enabling that functionality to be used by multiple applications. Before SOA started gaining traction, an application was viewed solely as a set of cooperating services that orchestrated together and executed a business process or a set of processes. The concept of functionality reuse was not contemplated back then.

In 2002, the Java platform introduced the Java Web Services Developer Pack (Java WSDP). Java WSDP subsequently went through several iterations. Most Java application servers evolved to support emerging standards such as Simple Object Access Protocol (SOAP) and XML. Services could be created and deployed on application servers, exposing service endpoints for other applications or services to access them. Representational State Transfer (REST) was another way to expose and access web services over HTTP. REST started gaining popularity starting in mid-2000 because of its simplicity when compared to SOAP. SOAP necessitated the use of XML, while REST could work with XML or JavaScript Object Notation (JSON) data formats.

The services platform approach introduced in this chapter does not mandate either SOAP or REST. This book addresses the fundamental concepts of a service platform, and this chapter specifically examines how to reengineer monolithic Java applications into services to create and deploy technical and business services and expose the services for consumption. The first step to reengineering Java applications into services involves the identification of a services portfolio representing the business functionality encapsulated by the existing Java applications.

Figure 10-1 depicts the various layers in a stratified services platform model. In this reference design, the top-down view provides a consumer-oriented perspective with client platforms and channels. The services functionality is delivered via these client channels and accessed by the end users of those applications, who are ultimately the consumers. Consumers could also include other services, including those that are either internal to the organization or belonging to an external third party. The next layer identifies where the business processes orchestrate to provide the workflows and business functionality. This business process layer contains multiple business processes, each of which is executed by a cooperative set of services and micro services. (See the section "Core Services" for more about micro services.) Typically, an event-driven orchestrator of the business process manages and routes the calling of various services based on the occurrence of certain events. These fine-grained processes comprise macro business processes. The orchestration of the business processes is mirrored in the actual services layer directly below. Atomic services aggregate to form composite or macro services. When business processes execute without a central orchestrator, either directly through services or by systems interacting with each other via messaging, the process is said to be "choreographed." This interaction is especially true when the business process spans organizational boundaries.

The bottom-up approach to Figure 10-1 provides the service-provider perspective. Infrastructure services form the fundamental building blocks of

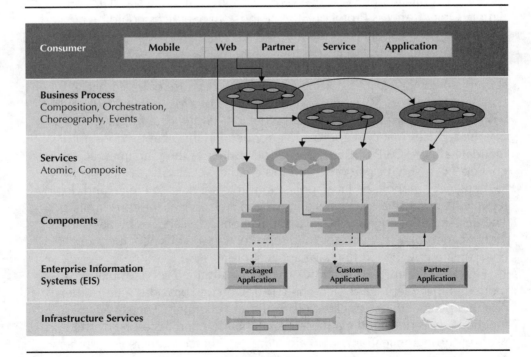

FIGURE 10-1. *Reference services platform-layered model*

the infrastructural layer, including message brokers, enterprise service bus, rule engines, and other technical components. Packaged applications, as well as custom applications, are built leveraging infrastructural components. Various applications are integrated, enabling them to communicate with one another. In the services platform model, to access the packaged or custom applications, such information services layers are abstracted via components exposing an information fabric to interface with Enterprise Information Systems (EIS) services. In turn, these components access the packaged or custom applications using supported APIs and data formats. This representation embodies a general layered services platform model.

Service Portfolio Identification

Java application portfolios can be reengineered into a portfolio of services only after the underlying elementary services have been identified and established. One definition of a *service* includes a block of code representing a logical grouping of operations that execute inside a container. For example, imagine a service called Customer Account that is used to create and manage customer account information. This service would have dependencies on other associated operations for its functionality. The associated operations for that service could include verification of customers, creation of customer accounts, creation of customer profiles, retrieval of lost passwords, retrieval of customer information, updates of customer information, and saving customer data to a database. Some of these operations could be services in their own right. This action of retrieving and leveraging customer information for potential reuse by other applications can vary in the granularity of the services; some may be fine-grained, while others are more composite in nature.

The types of services and their corresponding services layers are depicted in Figure 10-2, which also captures a high-level view of the service-orientation language. This figure represents the business process layer, technical layer, and the EIS layer in detail. Conceivably, there could be a higher level service orchestrating the business process based on the occurrence of specific business events. These business events act like triggers for the business process to continue on its path to completion. The execution of business processes is based on the successful operation of underlying business and information services. These services, in turn, encapsulate relevant business functionality and logic; they could also rely upon the technical services layer to provide services. These technical services could serve as wrappers to access technical components such as content management systems (CMSs),

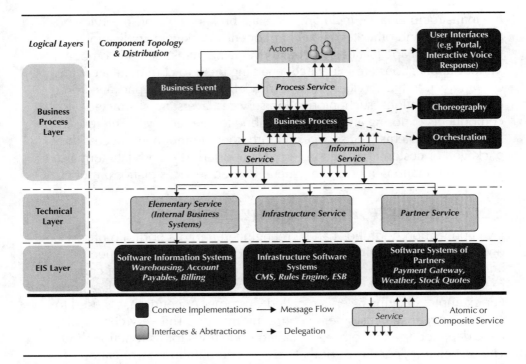

FIGURE 10-2. *The terminology and layers of service orientation*

databases, payment systems, warehouse management systems, and other EISs. Each service layer builds upon the previous layer to provide a level of abstraction.

Figure 10-3 illustrates a high-level methodology for the identification of services in an organization. The services can be either business or technical in nature. Business services have a functional focus and exist to implement the business functionality. As we reviewed in Chapter 4, these business capabilities typically define the services to be built by an organization. Technical services, on the other hand, have an architectural or technical focus and exist to support the implemented business functionality. Technical services are almost always fundamental services that are reused in several applications; they have a wider applicability to several business units. These technical services can be conceived independently of business services or application functionality. These services arise out of a desire for technical capabilities to be built by the IT organization to satisfy pressing business requirements.

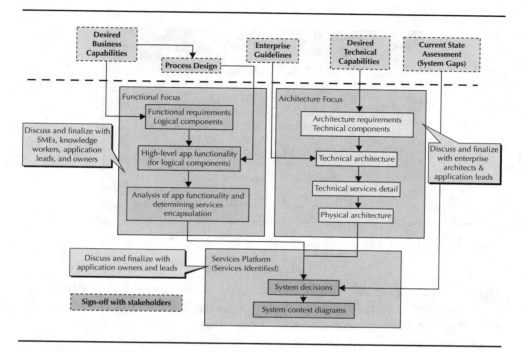

FIGURE 10-3. *Service identification process*

Desired business capabilities serve as inputs into business process design as well as functional requirements that need to be understood before building a service or component. Process design drives the understanding of high-level application functionality. From a technical perspective, desired technical capabilities drive the identification of the technical components. Enterprise guidelines and best practices serve to guide the technical architecture. An assessment of the current state of systems, compared to the desired future state, leads to an awareness of their inconsistency. Thus, potential services are identified to address functional and technical gaps in the existing systems.

To create a portfolio of services, an enterprise must first identify and understand the constituent parts. It is important that the enterprise recognize the natural information flow of business processes and how that information is consumed, aggregated, modified, and used in its various business domains. The information is also physically stored and manipulated by systems. Information held by an enterprise must be managed and governed carefully. Figure 10-4 shows one view of the enterprise information fabric model.

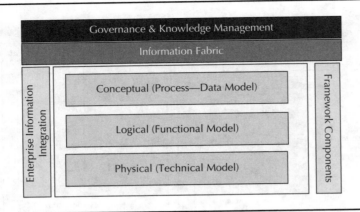

FIGURE 10-4. *Information fabric and information model*

Data retention, audit, archival, and management are central components to the business continuity of an enterprise. The overall information fabric is further divided into three main layers: conceptual, logical, and physical.

At the bottom, the physical layer represents the technical model of enterprise information, where technical systems manipulate information and store it in databases and other heterogeneous data stores.

In the middle, the logical layer represents a functional model where data from the physical systems is represented in terms of entities and objects, presented in a format relevant to its functional application to the business unit.

At the top, a conceptual layer exists where data used by functional systems is mapped to specific processes and tasks. A business process by itself cannot accomplish anything; it must act upon data, manipulate it, and make decisions based on that processed data. Business processes exchange messages, call various business services, pass through relevant information, and enable interaction with other enterprise information systems.

The ability to support a unified view of data and information across an entire organization is called *Enterprise Information Integration (EII)*. EII enables loose-coupling between services and systems that consume data and the actual heterogeneous data stores. Thus, the information fabric view, modeling enterprise information across the physical, logical, and conceptual layers, enables identification of micro services needing to consume the data.

Figure 10-4 represents a high-level portrayal. Ultimately, a successful services portfolio must be created by combining a top-down approach, a bottom-up approach, and a middle-out approach, taking into account both business processes and information architecture.

Top-Down Approach

In the top-down service identification approach, illustrated by Figure 10-5, the process model and data model need to be discerned along with mapping of the layers that represent these models. The process hierarchy starts at the highest level of the enterprise with its set of associated business processes. Business process models can exist at the level of a business unit or at the macro level of the enterprise itself. The functionality of the business process is implemented within an application container. This application, in turn, is constituted by a set of business components that have application logic

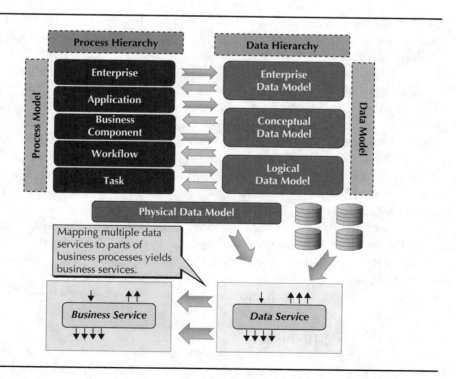

FIGURE 10-5. *Top-down service identification process*

programmed into them. At the business component level, business processes are contextualized for a particular business unit, representing its relevant activities. The business components are orchestrated together to form a workflow. The business process associated with a particular workflow may use multiple business components for its orchestration and support the business functionality for multiple business units. The workflow can be broken down further and represented by a set of tasks. Task flow level is where the business process is understood at the micro and submicro perspectives of a specific task. A set of tasks make up a workflow.

The data hierarchy, on the other hand, mirrors the enterprise information fabric discussed earlier. The enterprise model or fabric is at the top of the hierarchy. The tasks and workflow act upon the physical data. The application functionality and business component logic act upon logical data elements while providing a specific functionality. Underlying all of this is the physical data model.

From a services platform point of view, the business components consist of cooperating business services that rely upon data services. These services access and manipulate data from the physical data stores. Thus mapping multiple data services to various parts of a business process yields the business services.

This top-down representation can also be referred to as the *business activity model*. This representation essentially decomposes the business processes of an enterprise down into its subprocesses, workflows, and tasks. The tasks are basically mapped to portions of functionality provided by the applications. Consider a diagram with multiple swim lanes to illustrate the business processes mapping to IT system boundaries. Interactions across the swim lane boundaries are candidates for services. The services can be further separated into data services; accessing the data stores and mapping the data service operations representing create, read, update, and delete (CRUD) functions to entities in the logical data model. The business services encapsulating the business process logic, as grouped by related business operations, are mapped to micro services and APIs. In the end, services are depicted as business, information, or infrastructure services.

Bottom-Up Approach

Figure 10-6 highlights the bottom-up methodology for identifying services. In this approach, IT applications are scrutinized as opposed to business processes. The application analysis leads to an understanding of the following:

- Application functionality

- Interfaces exposed by the application

- Input/output of data and information

- Application logic encapsulated in methods

- Data and information models

Also included in this evaluation are data models, schemas, application tables, stored procedures, business rules, and business events associated with an application. In addition to the application analysis, some amount of reverse-engineering of the application could also take place. The bottom-up approach results in a similar type of understanding with respect to data services. The programming logic acts as a necessary wrapper for the underlying data models, forming the basis of the data services. Mapping these data services to logical blocks of functionality, within the business context of an application, provides a greater view of the business services.

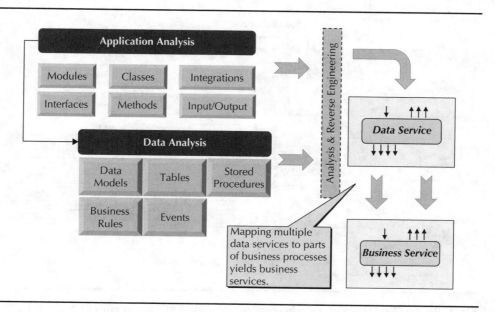

FIGURE 10-6.   *Bottom-up service identification process*

Integrated Middle-Out Approach

Figure 10-7 portrays the integrated middle-out methodology for identifying services. This approach undertakes both a top-down and bottom-up pathway to service identification. In addition to the application analysis, maps of business processes to service and available applications for identified services are also created. The obtained list of services is rationalized to ensure completeness of the service portfolio without any redundancies. Both methods ultimately have one commonality: identifying a core understanding of the data services from both process and application points of view.

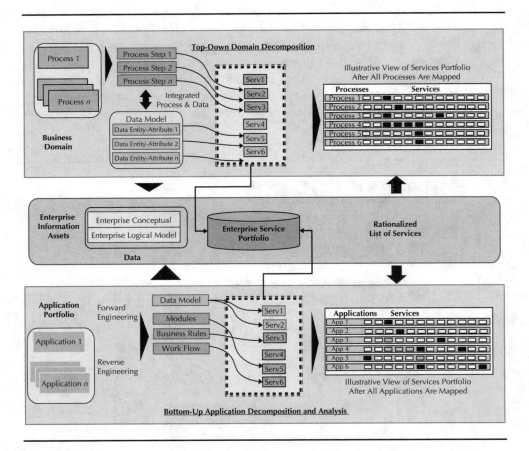

FIGURE 10-7. *Hybrid middle-out service identification process*

Figure 10-8 provides a visual explanation of how a business process is mapped to services. This figure illustrates a common functionality—for example, this could include an application for a store rewards points card. The highest level of the business process is shown as the L0 process, represented in our example by physically applying for the purchase rewards point card. This can be further broken down into L1 processes: Activate Account and Validate Account. The L2 level breakdown of the business process is represented by the following tasks: Retrieve History, Request Credit Report, Compute Score, and Determine Applicant Eligibility.

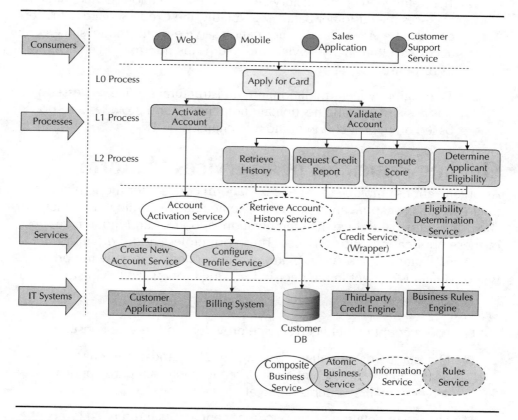

FIGURE 10-8. *Sample business-process-to-service mapping*

The services layer contains a composite service called the account activation service. This service relies on create new account and configure profile services. The four tasks of Retrieve History, Request Credit Report, Compute Score, and Determine Applicant Eligibility are ultimately mapped to three underlying services—namely, Credit Service (wrapper), Retrieve Account History Service, and Eligibility Determination Service:

■ The Credit Service, a wrapper service, calls a third-party service endpoint and supports two tasks.

■ The Retrieve Account History Service, an information service, directly accesses the customer database. Notably, the Credit Service (wrapper) can also be viewed as an information service in this model since it accesses a third-party service and returns the information received as its response.

■ The Eligibility Determination, an infrastructural service, accesses a business rule engine (technical components) and provides a response based on the execution of the rule engine.

Guiding Principles of a Services Platform

As organizations embrace the services platform concept for modernizing their existing Java application portfolios, some relative guiding principles should prioritize and drive the identification, adoption, and modernization of these applications into services. These principles should drive the conceptualization of a services platform and become especially important when conflict is present in the decision-making process. Following are some of these guiding principles:

■ Loose coupling between service providers and service consumers

■ J2EE standards compliant, leveraging J2EE standards to enable development and deployment of services into standard application server containers such as Tomcat

■ Service orientation of every component across the service layers

- Highly configurable runtime parameters
- Reusable set of services
- Highly scalable and extensible services platform

Loose coupling provides that a change in one service does not impact another service; each service evolves independently. It is essential that modifications to the internal logic of a service provider do not impact a consumer of that service. This can be achieved by ensuring that the contract (interface) of the service provider does not change.

Depending on the service layer, a component could provide capabilities such as these:

- Core technical capability, such as security, caching, or messaging
- Core infrastructural capability, such as registry, versioning, or push notification
- Core business capability, such as subscriber management or call routing

Providing a service orientation of every component across the service layers indicates that, regardless of the nature of the components, all components are architected and exposed as services.

Highly configurable runtime parameters can be realized if there is proper service monitoring and service management built into the services platform. The platform should be capable of administration at a fine-grained level so that each service can be controlled and configured as necessary.

The services platform should also provide services that promote reuse at various levels of granularity. Ideally, reuse must be possible at framework and subframework levels so that either coarse-grained services or fine-grained services can be reused.

A highly scalable and extensible services platform must be capable of providing services in a distributed manner so that services can be horizontally scaled. Services can also be pooled so that they are always available. Extensibility comes from the abstraction of functionality and exposure of APIs and SDKs so that the implementation can be configurable and functionality can be extended by pluggable providers.

Core Services

Although an organization may have a portfolio of services that meets business and technical capabilities, several business processes can also identify and leverage some common services in an organization. Such services are called *core services*.

The past few years have seen the emergence of *micro services*, the self-contained, fine-grained services that can exist separately, deploy separately within a container, and change and modify independently. Micro services can communicate with other micro services, thereby satisfying business functionality. Multiple micro services can be deployed together or distributed across process boundaries. Micro services must be capable of communication via REST or SOAP calls or some other network-based communication metaphor through a well-defined API. Micro services within the same virtual machine can also communicate directly with each other via exposed interfaces.

There are benefits and drawbacks to hosting multiple micro services within the same Java Virtual Machine (JVM). Deployment of the services occurs quickly because it essentially copies the JAR or WAR file to the application server running within that JVM, allowing for efficient use of resources. The downside is that the services are not isolated from each other. Because the services all share the same JVM heap, if one service misbehaves, it can take down other services as well. The alternative is to deploy each service within its own VM or within its own container. The open-source Docker and Kubernetes cluster tools have emerged at the forefront of container-based deployment of services.

Services Platform Stack and Frameworks

A typical services platform can be thought of as a distributed set of components that provide core services, enable an enterprise to define its own services, and deploy such services onto the platform. The deployed services must conform to a particular specification to be a part of the services platform.

The key layers or components of a services platform stack are shown in Figure 10-9.

The various layers and components are discussed in detail next in this chapter and also in Chapter 11.

High-level descriptions of key layers or components are detailed in Table 10-1.

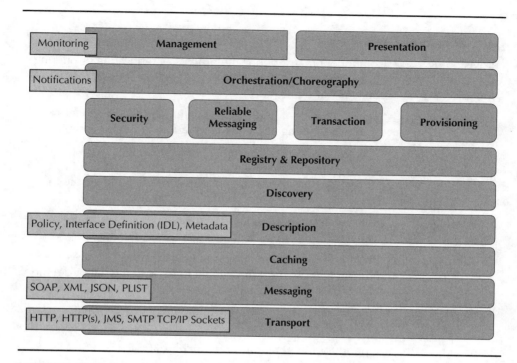

FIGURE 10-9. *Service platform stack conceptual reference architecture*

Layer/Component	Description
Registry	Serves as a "yellow pages" or lookup where service producers advertise their availability and service consumers find and use available services
Repository	Stores service endpoints and metadata about services
Discovery Framework	Framework for registering service consumers and allowing discovery of registered services
Service Description	Service metadata and the interface definition of a service using standards such as Web Application Description Language (WADL) and Web Services Description Language (WSDL)
Policy	Policy regarding a service covering its usage

TABLE 10-1. *Description of Conceptual Service Platform Stack (Continued)*

Layer/Component	Description
Provisioning	Component that supports the process of requesting or offering access to a service through a negotiated contract between consumer and producer
Security	Security model for addressing different aspects of services security, including authentication, authorization, encryption of data, or communication between services
Management	Service management defined by the implementation of a management interface that enables services to be visible to a management layer and displayed in dashboards
Monitoring	Monitoring services and seeing various service attributes displayed in dashboards
Caching	Ability to store data in an intermediate location for low-latency retrieval without the call needing to retrieve the data from the main data store
Message Format	Support for different message and data delivery formats such as SOAP, XML, JSON, PLIST
Transport Protocols	Support for different transports such as HTTP, HTTPS, JMS, TCP/IP sockets
Orchestration/ Choreography	Developing enterprise systems by loosely coupling interoperable services via business process management and asynchronous event triggers
Reliable Messaging and Notification	Reliable delivery of messages and notifications between distributed services and applications
Transaction	Handling of distributed transactions across applications and databases

TABLE 10-1. *Description of Conceptual Service Platform Stack*

Services Platform Features

The services platform conceptual reference architecture portrayed in Figure 10-9 can be further divided into a list of key features. This feature set is represented by Figure 10-10, which describes some of the main components identified in Figure 10-9.

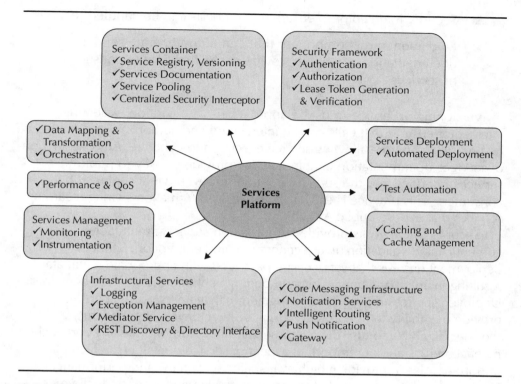

FIGURE 10-10. *Service platform features*

The services container that hosts the micro services provides basic functionality such as the following:

- Services registry for registering the services

- Versioning the services since not all consumers will upgrade to the latest service available

- Service pooling to make the service instance available at web scale

- Security interceptor to ensure that requests can be handled securely

- Documentation component that can auto-generate services documentation as well as provide contextual help to consumers of services

Versioning of services must be approached with caution. A security interceptor ensures that calls can be intercepted and authorization checks can be undertaken before allowing service execution to continue. Auto-generation of services documentation enables service providers easily to publish a services interface and the services contract for eventual acceptance by consumers. This practice is especially useful for information sharing regarding services that expose public APIs.

Security frameworks provide authorization services, multifactor authentication, validation, token generation, and encryption. Services deployment ensures that services are packaged with appropriate metadata, resulting in automatic unpacking and deployment into the services container. Deployed services require monitoring and management. Containers also provide the ability to operate services at different levels of granularity, with the specific ability to turn the instrumentation on and off. Caching and cache management is another important aspect of service containers, which play important roles in providing high availability, scalability, and performance. Containers must also provide test automation allowing for easy deployment, comprehensive testing, and continuous transition into production.

Some core infrastructural services provided by the services container include the following:

- Logging

- Exception management

- Mediator service

- REST discovery and directory interface

The messaging framework in a services container must support features such as these:

- Core messaging infrastructure

- Notification services

- Intelligent routing

- Push notification

- Gateway

Data mapping, data transformation, and service orchestration are all essential features of a services container. Some services containers may not provide these features directly but may allow the use of a business process management component in conjunction with the messaging framework. Other services containers allow leveraging an enterprise service bus or message-oriented middleware as well. Performance and quality of service (QoS) of a services container determines the type of mission-critical services that can be deployed on to that container.

On-boarding Java Applications as Services

Monolithic Java applications can be modernized and reengineered into a set of services that can be deployed in a distributed fashion. To break up Java applications into services, the applications must undergo decomposition. This application decomposition in many ways mirrors the architecture decomposition that we saw in Chapter 4. In fact, application decomposition goes beyond architecture decomposition that dissects an application across the architectural layers. Architecture decomposition employs a top-down view of the business domain, identifying various components across business, functional, technical, and infrastructure architectures. Some of the components identified in the business and functional layers could be further broken down into smaller units. If a self-contained boundary can be created around a component, it can become a service. In the case of business and functional layers, the identified services include business services, process services, and information services. The components identified in the technical and infrastructural layers are either wrapper services for other EISs or technical/infrastructural services.

Java applications can be deconstructed into a set of services. Within the Java application code, functional boundaries must be identified determining which Java classes will map to functional blocks in the architecture. Two approaches can be adopted in the modernization of a Java application into services:

■ **Direct reengineering** In this approach, the Java application is modernized into one or more services by brute-force reengineering. A set of classes that form a functional boundary are separated out and modified so that the functionality of these classes becomes exposed through a well-defined interface. If the Java application is complex or needs to be decompiled into several micro services, then this time-consuming task could pose a business risk. The direct reengineering approach is easy to implement for less complex applications, requiring only a few micro services.

■ **Service wrapper** In this approach, the Java application is initially kept as is; however, a set of services are introduced to act as a pass-through layer for the underlying Java application. These services exist only to ensure that consumers are able to request and access certain functionality by calling the exposed services API. In the interim, this leads to additional maintenance efforts since some services need to be created and deployed in addition to the existing Java application. Over time, portions of the Java application logic that map to a particular service are transported into the service itself. Eventually, as the Java application logic is dismantled and absorbed into each service wrapper, the Java application becomes a shell containing little to no logic. At this point, the application can be sunsetted because of to its low value and utility to an organization.

These services wrappers act as placeholders and eventually become micro services when the Java applications ultimately disintegrate. Figures 10-11 through 10-14 show two examples of the services wrapper reengineering approach, slowly migrating away from legacy Java and non-Java code to service-orientated Java code.

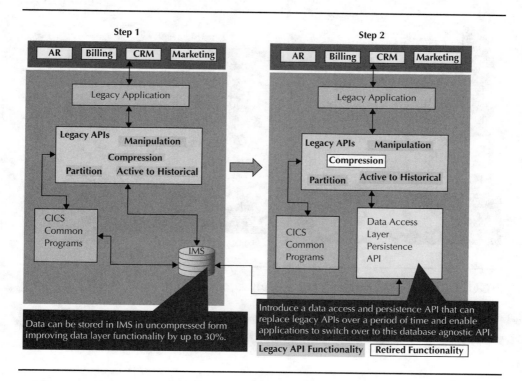

FIGURE 10-11.   *Remediation of a legacy Java database application*

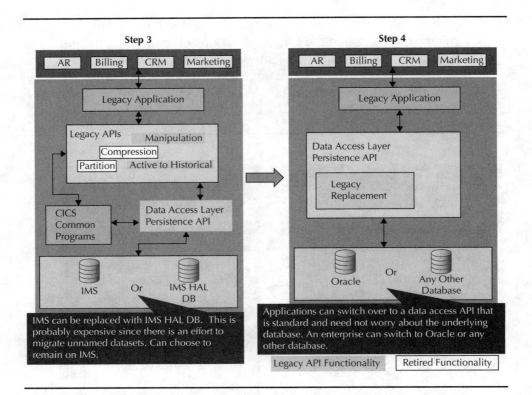

FIGURE 10-12. *Move to Oracle or any another database*

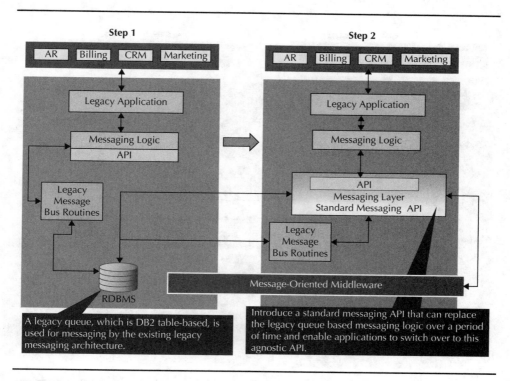

FIGURE 10-13. *Remediation of a legacy Java messaging application*

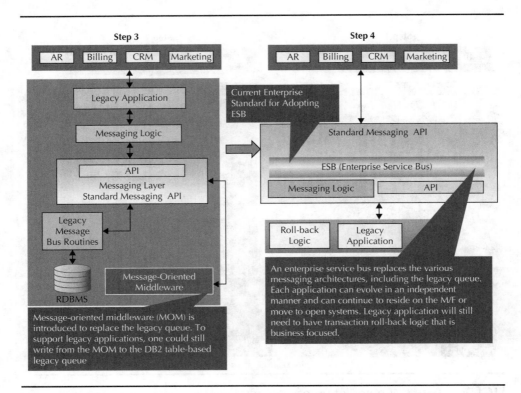

FIGURE 10-14. *Move to ESB and/or stay with new messaging API*

Summary

An important step to reengineering an existing Java application portfolio requires identification and creation of a set of services representing the business processes supported by the application functionality of that portfolio. During the execution and orchestration of business processes, the data and information that flows through the processes are modified, aggregated, transformed, and finally stored or shared with other internal or external business processes. Thus, we see that business process execution is tightly coupled with the actual information flow that occurs within the enterprise. This information can be modeled into entities as well as conceptual, logical, and physical data models. Data is retrieved, manipulated, and stored via data services that are used to access the underlying physical data models. The data services themselves exist at the conceptual and logical levels of the information architecture. Mapping data services to business processes that consume and operate the data yields the requirements to implement the business services that encapsulate the business logic.

A service portfolio must be deployed and executed within a services container. This chapter presented one implementation of the reference services container, discussed the various components of a services container stack, and identified the features that must be supported by a services container.

Legacy Java applications can be reengineered into services. If this reengineering exercise is not planned in well-formed stages, it will disrupt existing consumers and end users. A step-by-step approach must be followed. Transitional wrappers for legacy application functionality enable existing applications to continue while portions of the service are reengineered. Pieces of the legacy application are progressively replaced via loosely coupled interfaces, eventually becoming reengineered into services. The next chapter will address the details and components of a services container and the overall life cycle of a service.

CHAPTER
11

The Service Life Cycle

The mainstream adoption of service-oriented architecture (SOA) is no longer a new phenomenon. The reengineering of legacy Java applications into SOA models can be an arduous task, especially when efforts are not aligned with the architectural vision. Many organizations recompile and redeploy their legacy Java code base to newer versions of application server platforms, mistakenly concluding that their applications have achieved service orientation just because the new application server versions support SOA. For anyone who has reengineered Java applications into SOA, it is clearly evident that the architectural vision has not been realized in such a case.

SOA platforms and APIs provide support only for some standards and theoretical ideas. The newer services paradigm goes beyond merely writing applications that communicate using SOAP or expose a REST API. Today, we define services using a new meaning. The conception of SOA, automated service discovery, reuse of services, and loosely coupled architectures began materializing with the advent of *micro services* deployed on a *micro-services container.*

The previous chapter introduced the concepts of micro services and service platforms, approaches to transforming traditional Java applications into services, and the process of on-boarding them into a services platform. That chapter also covered fundamental infrastructural and foundational services, known as core platform services that can be leveraged by other services.

This chapter takes that discussion further by reviewing the stages of a services life cycle. The discovery and consumption of deployed services by other services is an important milestone when declaring the success of a services platform reengineering strategy. Lastly, this chapter discusses the governance and management of those new services. Although there are some similarities with the life cycle, governance, and management phases of an application, there are also some significant differences between the characterizations of services for SOA applications.

Understanding the Service Life Cycle

As organizations advance and execute their vision around SOA, the scope and expectations for a services platform become defined as a consequence of this SOA adoption. The enterprise vision is finally realized upon the creation of a services platform that exists to deploy, host, support, and run services. These services do not appear randomly on the platform. A fair amount of background work goes into the identification and definition of a service, and the actual service creation is the result of careful planning and execution of the services. Once the service has been deployed on the platform, continuous management is required.

Basically, services are software assets owned and operated by an organization. Services are conceptualized, created, provide a specific functionality, and eventually become replaced or shut down due to lack of utility. From an organizational or financial perspective, enterprises can effectively and efficiently manage this process if the life cycle of a service is clearly understood. Even the technical development and maintenance of a service is heavily influenced by the life cycle of a service. A service is useful only if it is in demand and consumed by end users. Thus, a sound understanding of the services life cycle advances the overall strategy and day-to-day tactical operations of those services. This understating will also help to automate the steps of the service life cycle so that the primary manual touch points can be eliminated.

In a loosely coupled SOA, an application is composed of multiple cooperating services. This enables an application to be easily maintained and enhanced. This approach also promotes reuse of services across the organization, because a service could be a part of more than one application.

Figure 11-1 provides a high-level view of the service life cycle. From the developer's standpoint, the service life cycle is similar to the life cycle of

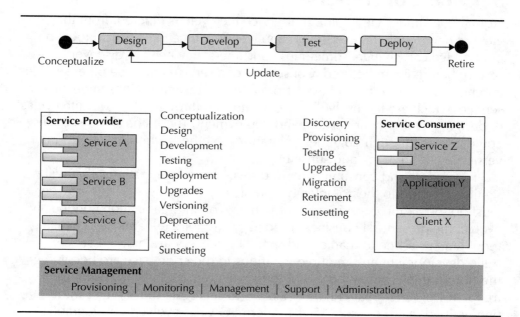

FIGURE 11-1.   *A high-level view of the service life cycle*

any other application or software. The service first has to be conceptualized. Then it is designed, developed, tested, and deployed. Periodically, the service could be enhanced and updated. At some point, the service could be retired.

As you delve deeper into the process beyond the simplistic developer viewpoint and the application-centric software development, the service life cycle becomes a bit more complicated. Although applications are created by a team of developers and consumed by end users in a particular line of business, services are notably different.

Service Providers

Services are conceptualized and created by the provider of that service. Apart from the similarities to the traditional application development life cycle, the deployment of services varies from the deployment of an application. When services are deployed onto a services platform, they are housed within a micro container. Services could be deployed in multiple versions with different consumers in mind. Certain parts of a service could deprecate over time, becoming unavailable to consumers eventually. Thus, the life cycle of a service is much more complex than that of a traditional application.

Service Consumers

From a consumer's viewpoint, the service life cycle is different from the view of traditional end users of an application. Since the physical location of a service can change, sometimes consumers may need to discover the service before it can be used. Consumers of a service could be other services and not necessarily the end users from a line of business. Consumers of a service, which are themselves services, must go through their own life cycles of design, development, testing, and deployment. These consumer services could also go through upgrades, migrations to other technology platforms, versioning, retirement, and sunsetting.

If providers and consumers require several service iterations, that will significantly add to the complexity of a life cycle. Changes to the provider must not break the consumers. As the needs of an organization continually evolve, the present-day business models will require dynamically changing requirements. Time to market and speed of delivery are of the essence. Agile development and multiple iterations to the code base are becoming the norm in enterprises today. The best way to meet this increased frequency of functional enhancements is to segregate the services into fine-grained micro services. This modern SOA has evolved considerably from the original definition of service orientation. Finely tuned service management ensures that deployments of all services are

- Provisioned correctly
- Monitored and managed for their performance
- Discoverable and available to the consumer
- In compliance with SLAs and other nonfunctional requirements of the system
- Supported and administered to meet consumer services needs

Service Registry

In simple terms, the service registry is a catalog of available services that can be accessed and invoked by a consumer. In reality, a service registry encompasses much more than that. A service registry facilitates the registration, discovery, use, and governance of services. One of the earliest implementations of the service registry concept was the Universal Description, Discovery, and Integration (UDDI) registry, which was originally proposed as a core web services standard. UDDI implementations enabled the registration of web services in a directory along with a Web Services Description Language (WSDL) document that described the protocol bindings and message formats required to interact with the registered web service. SOAP was used by a requesting application to interact and exchange messages with the web service. UDDI did not gain wide acceptance and quietly slipped into oblivion.

As REST services gained popularity, the need for a service registry started to surface again. With the transformation to the micro-services architecture, a need for a service registry has gained significant traction. The micro-services architecture results in several fine-grained services built and deployed by an organization. These services undergo rapid metamorphosis with new services constantly added. Multiple versions of the same service also co-exist. Proliferation of services in an organization without proper tracking and governance leads to maintenance issues. Duplication of services across various business units of an organization is also another challenge. The service registry functions as a directory of sorts; a single repository owning the responsibility for housing all the available services, and its multiple versions, belonging to an organization.

This chapter introduces the concept of a registry for REST services, called REST Description Discovery and Integration (RDDI). You may never have heard that term used before because RDDI is neither a standard nor reference implementation available publicly. I invented the concept of RDDI; implementing several variations of the registry during consulting engagements for specific enterprises. So what exactly is RDDI? It is a registry geared specifically for current REST services that does the following:

- Serves as a registrar, repository and discovery mechanism for all services provided by the services platform

- Contains programmatic descriptions of businesses and the services that they support

- Provides programmatic description of the REST services themselves

- Uses XML, JSON over HTTP and other data formats while providing a programming model and schema that is platform agnostic

- Maintains a contract (Like WADL) which consists of URIs, resources, the structure and content of service representations, their formats, and HTTP methods for each resource

Before a business unit embarks on building a new service, the team can reference the catalog of services available in the service registry repository. The service registry contains meta-data and descriptions about each service available for use. If such a service already exists, then it could be a candidate for reuse.

A service registry, like the proposed RDDI, has both a design-time contract and a run-time contract. Figure 11-2 shows one such example of an RDDI service registry. This registry standardizes WADL to represent the services contract. The REST services developer creates the REST service and registers the service with RDDI. The developer publishes both the service interface and implementation to RDDI. The client service developer or consumer develops a client service and registers that service with RDDI. The services are accessed via the published WADL contract interface. Thus, at design time, the client service must develop and test against the published WADL contract in order to be in alignment with that interface.

A sound implementation of a service registry should contain more than just a database or repository of the services. It should incorporate information

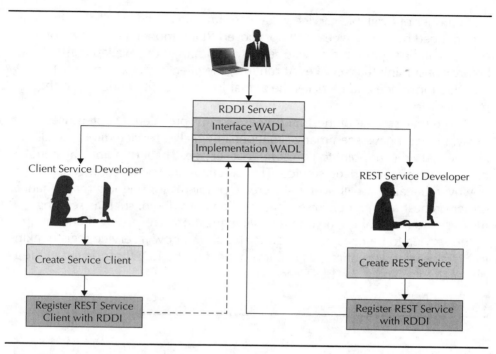

FIGURE 11-2. *The design-time contract of a service registry like RDDI*

from all available instances of a service, their locations, registered clients, meta-data, usage characteristics, analytics, and other pertinent data. As new services or new instances of existing services deploy, such information is also registered with the service registry. Services that go offline must also be tracked. All performance and usage metrics of the services are traced and made available through the service registry. Many major enterprises, especially those that adopt and implement cutting-edge technologies, have their own internal adaptation and implementation of a services platform and Services Registry. Since there are no open standards available around the concept of a service registry, the internals of the implementation in use at various organizations are not widely apparent. The only open standard was the UDDI, which never completely fulfilled the needs at that time, and it quickly went out of favor.

Although each instance of a service exposes the same API, the location of each service instance can dynamically vary. For the purposes of this discussion, a service and service instance may be used interchangeably.

The number of available service instances can also change based on the load experienced by the service. In the proposed RDDI model, consumers of a service will first query the service registry to discover the available instances before consuming that service. At runtime, the client service connects to the RDDI instance and receives the actual location of the endpoint to the provider service.

There may several orchestration mechanisms prevalent at enterprises today. In fact, I have seen many situations in which a service directly calls another service endpoint to consume that service. That endpoint was hard coded into the consuming service. This practice must be discouraged, however, because it will eventually create problems for ongoing maintenance. Other orchestration mechanisms can also be considered, such as sending messages to a global queue and receiving a response regarding the location of the service to be consumed. Figure 11-3 shows how a service registry akin to RDDI is used at runtime, as clients connect to the RDDI server to get the physical endpoint of the REST service.

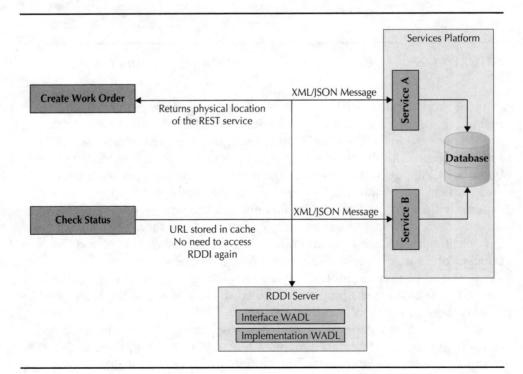

FIGURE 11-3. *The runtime contract of a service registry like RDDI*

In Figure 11-3, the client service contacts the RDDI server and receives the physical endpoint of the provider service that the client in interested in calling. The client service communicates via XML or JSON messaging and invokes a "Create Work Order" method that is fulfilled by Service A. It then calls Service B to "Check Status" on the order. For future checks on order status, the client service could directly call the endpoint, possibly by caching the service URL, if that endpoint does not change. In that case, for this particular illustration, the registry need not be contacted again. Later in this chapter, we will see that the registry implementation is not as simplistic as the illustration shown in Figure 11-3.

Given the importance of the service registry to the micro-services architecture, it must be highly available and cannot provide a single point of failure. If a service registry itself goes offline, consumers of services may not be able to locate available services. The location of the service registry must also be published to all consumers. Preferably, service registry instances must be configured to well-known static IP addresses. Service consumer configurations must be updated in the event that the location of service registry instances change. The multiple instances of a service registry must be kept in sync with the repository so that all service registry services contain the same information. Change to the underlying database of one service registry must propagate quickly to all service registry instances.

The internals of a registry can be simple or highly complicated, depending on the needs of the service platform. Figure 11-4 shows the internals of a service registry.

In Figure 11-4, a block named Registry API is shown. Service providers and consumers must access the registry only through this API exposed by the service registry. The API provides an abstraction of the registry functionality, such as the following:

- Life cycle management of the services registered with the registry

- Version control of services

- Policy management

- Compliance and validation

- Management of access to services by various mechanisms including tokens, leases, and multifactor authentications if necessary

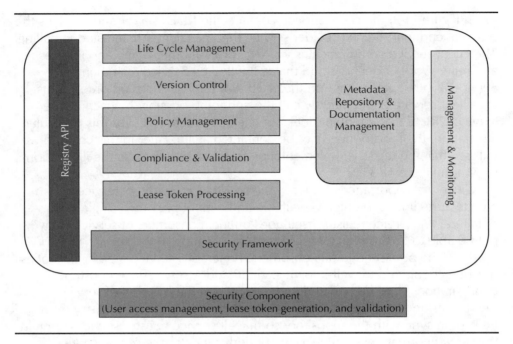

FIGURE 11-4. *The internals of a registry*

A security framework must abstract authentication, authorization, user access management, secure token generation and validation, as well as other security needs. The registry functionality supports a meta-data repository and document management for the registered services. The registry also provides management, instrumentation, and monitoring of all deployed services.

The repository function of the service registry stores various service-related artifacts, policy files, configuration information, and meta-data. Some of this information is advertised and discoverable upon accessing the registry so that consumers are able to search and find services of interest. Prior knowledge about the existence of a particular service can occur at the design time of the consuming service. If the service provider and service consumer interact at design time, relevant instances can be specifically built for that specific service. In some cases, consumers contact the service registry and discover services dynamically at runtime with no prior knowledge of the available services during design time. A central repository ensures that there is no duplication of a service across the organization. This ultimately promotes reuse, partnership, and ongoing dialog among various business units of an organization.

Service Deployment and Registration

Before a consumer can discover and use a service, that service must be deployed and registered with the service registry. In fact, a well-designed architecture would ensure that all instances of a particular service are registered. When a service instance shuts down for any reason, the service instance could also be deregistered from the service registry. "Service" in this context refers to all service instances. In a cloud environment, it is quite common for a system to spin up additional instances of a service automatically if needed for load-balancing purposes. When a service instance is deployed, it is responsible for registering itself with the service registry.

Figure 11-5 depicts an illustration of the deployment and registration process for a service.

Service registrations can happen in one of two ways:

- Service registrar
- Self-registration

Service Registrar

The service registrar provides maximum flexibility to the process of service registration. The service registrar allows registration of a service at design time. Even before deploying a service instance, it is possible that a service owner can use an associated UI service interface to provide the service description and other meta-data to register the service into the service registry. This registration process can also be automated by uploading the service archive containing the service and its description to the service registrar. The responsibility of unpacking the service archive, deploying the service to the correct location, and registering the service resides with the service registrar.

This approach keeps the core code base of the service very clean and centralizes the service registration logic inside the service registrar. This approach also provides flexibility regarding the exact moment when a service is registered. In many organizations, the business unit that produces a service may be different from the one that wants to consume it. At design time, the two groups may elect to communicate with each other to decide on APIs, data to be exchanged, and other key information. In such cases, well before consumers start to use a service, the service provider will register the service with the service registry.

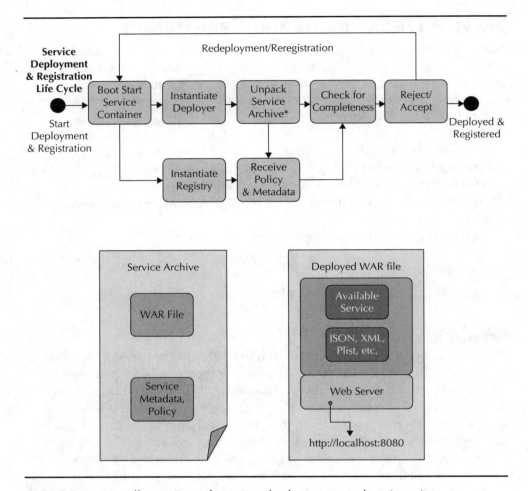

FIGURE 11-5. *Illustration of service deployment and registration*

Business units should refrain from producing and deploying services on an ad hoc basis without regard for the consumers of that service. In such cases, consumers would need to search for a specific functionality and hope that someone has deployed a service for that functionality in the service registry.

An optional feature of a service registrar is its ability to monitor the health or availability of a service or its instances. It may be advisable to create a separate service that periodically conducts this compliance review so that the service registrar is not tasked with additional responsibilities at first. It may also be wise to have all services implement a management interface that can be engaged to ping the service and receive a heartbeat, revealing the health and proper functioning of the service.

Self-Registration

The alternative to a central registrar is a self-registration process at the beginning of a service instance. The service instance contacts the service registry through an advertised interface and provides information including its location and other meta-data. This makes the service discoverable by an interested consumer that contacts the service registry looking for a service with that functionality

The service registry can periodically check on the health and availability of the service instance by calling its management interface. Alternatively, the service instance can periodically reregister itself with the service registry. In any case, if the service fails for any reason, the service registry must be able to determine that and accordingly update its information.

This approach tightly couples the service to the service registry, since one must implement the service registration logic in each service. This will eventually lead to a system that is difficult to maintain, since every service has registration logic. Any simple change regarding service registration will need all deployed services to upgrade their registration logic.

Service Discovery

In a micro-services architecture, service discovery is one recommended approach for the consumers of a service to discover the availability and location of that service through the service registry. This consumer could be an end application or another coarse-grained service that exposes a higher-level API to an end consumer. Most services run in virtualized environments and containers. The location of such service instances changes dynamically. The number of available instances of a particular service can also vary. Thus, the consumer is best served by first going to a service registry that is aware of all the information and context around a service. Proper governance of a service registry enables usage policies to be applied at the point of service discovery. Figure 11-6 illustrates the service discovery mechanism and registration of a consumer.

The client-side discovery or discovery by the consumer tightly intertwines that consumer with a service registry. Every consumer implements the same

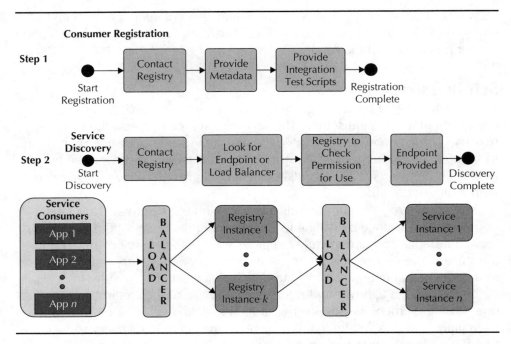

FIGURE 11-6. *Service discovery mechanism and registration of a consumer*

logic of discovering and using a service. One advantage of service discovery is that it minimizes network hops to enforce governance.

Another service discovery approach enables a consumer to request a load balancer that runs at a published location. This load balancer in turn serves as a proxy and contacts the service registry, locates the service instance, and then forwards the consumer request to the service. This approach is called *server-side service discovery*. The response from the service is forwarded to the consumer. The client-side code is now less complex since discovery is not performed by every client instance. It is possible to bundle the service registry into the load balancer, in which case, the service registry is the proxy and load balancer in addition to being the repository of service information. Figure 11-6 shows how a consumer registers itself first with the service registry and then subsequently discovers and uses a service through the mechanism of service discovery. This figure also portrays how a load balancer is placed between service registry instances as well as between service instances if the services are deployed on service containers running at different physical locations.

The concept of service virtualization enables the endpoint to change its location without affecting the lookup of the provider service. Consumers can look up services since there is built-in location transparency. Endpoints that change but that do not affect the lookup capability is a major benefit to an organization.

Service Consumption

While services are created to be consumed, service providers may additionally want to specify the conditions of how a service should be consumed. Especially for services that are publicly built and available for general public consumption, service consumption is a highly managed and monitored occurrence. Even in an enterprise setting where both service consumers and service providers are either from within the enterprise or the partner ecosystem, services advertise their availability and service-level agreements (SLAs) ahead of time to consumers of the service. This promotes service reuse with an enterprise and enables another department to consume this service rather than having to write and maintain their own service. The service consumer is also able to see which department has produced the service. It is actually quite common in enterprises where owners of a service and the intended consumers of a service meet and agree upon SLAs in advance.

Consumption requests might first be reviewed by a team and approved in advanced. Configurations may be loaded into the registry along with updates to policies that govern the permission and usage of a service by a particular consumer. These policies might decide the authentication and authorization contexts, allowable consumption levels, allowable versions of service, and other such factors.

At runtime, the consumer is provided with a specific service instance to communicate with to consume the service. The service registry has the option first to determine whether the consumer is allowed to consume the service it is requesting. Different consumers might be granted access only to certain parts of a service. Such access restrictions may surface in the case of a coarse-grained service requesting to be consumed. The coarse-grained service might be encapsulating other fine-grained services, and some of them may be restricted and not accessible to a particular consumer. What this means is that, based on role-based authorization, a consumer might not be allowed to make all the API calls exposed by a service. Consumers may also consume different versions of a service. Some consumers may be allowed consumption of a service only for a short period of time, whereas other consumers might be granted consumption only upon special authentication and authorization or via a special token.

Consumers of a service should be able to query the service registry for meta-data about the service. If the consumers have authorization, they might also be able to receive and process service provider meta-data. Service interface definitions and documentation could additionally be retrieved by service consumers from the service registry.

In many cases, consumers are interested in engaging with coarse-grained or high-level services that in turn may need to aggregate data and functionality from multiple services. In this case, one pattern that is widely used employs a service mediator that performs as a coarse-grained service.

Figure 11-7 depicts a consumer service communicating with a mediator service. The mediator service is actively registered and advertised through the service registry. This is a coarse-grained service, which in turn communicates with multiple fine-grained services. The fine-grained services can each provide parts of the data that need to be assembled and sent to the consumer. The mediator service aggregates the results of the requested fine-grained services and might also be able to manipulate the results before returning a

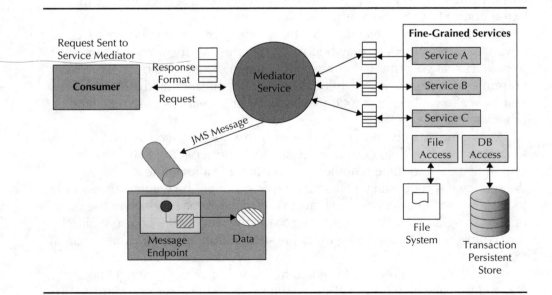

FIGURE 11-7. *Mediator service providing access to fine-grained services*

result set to the calling consumer service. This service mediator is actually a façade to the fine-grained services in this case.

By the same token, there could be more than one consumer for the mediator service. Each consumer could expect a slightly different data format or different data set. In that case, the mediator service could contain logic to recognize the identity of the calling consumer. The mediator service would use a transformer that maps and converts the aggregated data to the appropriate format for consumption by the calling consumer.

Service Governance and Management

The traditional SOA governance model called for a centralized governance function. In that model, the entire technology stack standardized the tools, programming language, best practices, test automation, continuous integration, and delivery of the application. With the advent of the micro-services architecture, virtualized environments, and APIs, centralized governance has given way to a decentralized governance model.

The evolution of the traditional SOA into a virtualized container-based micro-services architecture is a direct result of organizations maturing toward decentralized business capabilities belonging to multiple business units or groups. This evolution of the way business processes and business capabilities are handled, along with the difficulty of maintaining and scaling monolithic applications, resulted in the deconstruction of the application architecture that initially deployed applications to application servers.

The urgency and speed with which functionality needs to be ready for the marketplace and the dependency of business units on other internal groups resulted in developer groups building and launching services, and their APIs, to production with very little governance oversight. In many of these cases, the developers also ended up supporting and maintaining these services without proper mechanisms in place to capture modifications and enhancements to those services adequately.

The development and operations teams previously had clear demarcations for their roles in an enterprise. As more collaborative workplaces emerged, these functions evolved and consolidated into one unit. This progression led to the creation of the DevOps paradigm, which blurs the lines between development and operations. As a natural outcome, the sphere of governance and service management has evolved to address the challenges of multiple groups creating and maintaining services, and exposing APIs for consumption by other client services, either within the organization or outside.

Service governance encompasses the following:

- Policies and processes that ensure a standards-based adoption of SOA principles from conception to implementation and ongoing management

- Controls that are put in place to align business expectations in the adoption of SOA

- Enabling business units to make a conscious decision about services, acquisition of services and technology, and introduction of new solutions to meet pressing business needs

- Managing expectations of the service community, comprising providers, administrators, and consumers, across the service life cycle

In the absence of correct service governance, several problems arise, such as the following:

- Lack of visibility for businesses to understand services and for IT to discover and use services

- Poor alignment between service needs of business and IT implementation of services

- Lack of trust between consumers and providers of services

- Difficulty in defining and monitoring SLAs and other nonfunctional requirements

- Uncontrolled and unmanageable growth of services with little reuse

- Ultra-fine-grained micro services leading to nano-service anti-patterns; such services are not very useful by themselves and almost always used as part of a coarse-grained service

The Management Interface

The practice of service or application management, whether for a legacy application, a modern application, or even new micro services, is often an afterthought, a result of a departmental fire drill when a mission-critical issue arises. Because of its proliferation and swift adoption, Java has become the most popular language of choice within enterprises. However, insufficient thought was given to the governance and management of those applications. Java Management Extensions (JMX) was a core feature of the Java platform, yet most developers and architects unfortunately never used this API to help manage their Java applications. Eventually, application servers provided hooks to JMX so that deployed applications could be managed on the servers.

With micro services and deployment to micro-service containers, Java applications can greatly benefit from the loosely coupled services implementing a management interface. Even a simple interface providing the ability to probe the health of a deployed service becomes an indispensable management tool that enables a consumer to determine availability of a service by contacting a service registry before calling that service. Figure 11-8 depicts a service registry with a listener mechanism to detect the heartbeat of all deployed services on a periodic basis. The listener component communicates with service heartbeat and interceptor components of the registry. The overarching service monitoring and management platform ensures that all deployed services are available. Depending on the design and implementation of the service management interfaces, sophisticated instrumentation and management of services is possible.

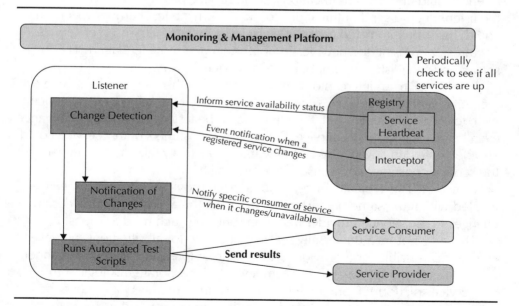

FIGURE 11-8. *Checking a service heartbeat*

Service Versioning

During the life cycle of a service, both the provider and consumer of the service undergo enhancements. The enhancements to the business logic of the consumer have no bearing on the service provider. Similarly, modifications to the inner workings of the service provider should not impact the service consumer, provided the advertised functionality of the service provider is itself not changed. It is important that the service consumer does not break when a service provider is enhanced. Most of the enhancements to a service provider will normally change only its internal implementation and not affect the service consumer. Sometimes, however, there could be API changes or functional changes to an existing service provider API that could affect consumers. To avoid this disruption, service providers may choose to make multiple versions of the same service available so that consumers can opt to stay with an older version or choose to enhance their implementation and upgrade to the new service version.

In some service registry implementations, a listener component is aware of services that change based on the service provider's accreditation with the registry. Upon detection of an alteration in a service provider, the listener contacts all the consumers of this service and notifies them of the change. The listener could also send notifications to the service provider. In some designs, the listener could send notifications to the underlying test harness system that could then run automated tests to determine whether the consumer service fractures upon using the new version of the service provider. Figure 11-9 shows one such listener component of a service registry.

In this design, an interceptor component notifies the listener whenever a registered service transforms. One might argue that if the provider of a service were to break the service API, then that should be tested and known in advance even before deploying the service. In that case, consumers of that service could also be notified in advance so that they may proactively take steps to enhance the service consumer code base for compatibility with the modified service provider API. This typically occurs with service providers and consumers located within the same organization who have the ability to discuss design changes to the service provider before introducing such modifications.

This may not be a universally realistic outcome for all situations, however. Even if it is possible for a provider and consumer to engage in such a manner, it is still a good practice, at the system level, to incorporate this logic into the services platform. From an automation standpoint, this will remove the contingency of reliance on human interactions to convey API changes to dependent consumers. In addition to human interactions of design-time

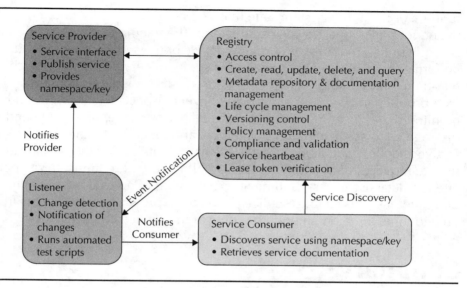

FIGURE 11-9.   *Listener component of a service registry*

API modifications, the approach outlined in this section also allows for failure detection to be captured automatically when API adjustments to services are made.

Service Registry Cleanup

The service registry should always be current and should never contain stale endpoints to services that no longer exist. As part of the governance process, service management must ensure that the service registry embodies the awareness of which new services are generated and which services have been halted or entirely shut down. Critical services might be monitored more closely in near real time, whereas other noncritical services might be monitored more infrequently. The availability of management interfaces on a service to probe its heartbeat makes it easy and convenient for a service registry to detect the service availability and keep that information current in the service registry.

Service Analytics, Log, and Trace

All active services generate instrumentation data, logs, and traces and can be subject to analytics. Service execution can also lead to exceptions being generated in the execution stack; sometimes these errors could stop the runtime or result in a system state that was not envisioned. Other times, the performance of a service can degrade. The tracing component should be equipped to monitor and provide details of the service operation, its performance, and its impact on the consumer or service provider. Such real-time traces and logs can be useful to rectify an issue or address and fix a problem in a subsequent release. Several aspects of a service can be monitored and instrumented, including its performance, messaging and message payloads, execution stack trace, and functional logic. Service analytics collect data about a service regarding its availability, response time to requests, concurrent requests, total number of requests, throughput, latency, database access, uptime SLA, utilization of network bandwidth, and other metrics. This enables service providers to provide improvements from time to time based on an understanding of the service characteristics.

Summary

A service goes through a life cycle that is much more complex than an application life cycle. There are providers and consumers of a service. Consumers find and use a service through a service registry, where a service has previously registered itself. The contract between a consumer and provider can be established at design time, or, in some cases, consumers dynamically discover and use a service from the service registry at runtime. Especially for publicly available services, where consumers cannot be anticipated in advance, dynamic discovery of services is an essential feature. In enterprises where business units collaborate in advance, design-time discussions are possible.

The service registry provides several functions, including acting as the repository of services, storing meta-data, and providing of governance policies for a service. The service registry tracks service instances, monitors the health and availability of services, informs listeners of changes to a service, and maintains the physical endpoints of services to determine whether a consumer should be given access credentials to a service and for what duration.

Services have to be monitored and managed throughout their life cycles. This ensures that services can be versioned and provided without material impact to consumers resulting from adaptations and modifications to APIs. Service analytics help ensure that performance SLAs can be supported with oversight.

The advent of service containers and micro-services platforms has transformed the advancement of software builds. This is primarily accomplished by services that support the rapid evolution of a business without the burden of supporting monolithic applications with long development cycles. The software engineering methodologies, automation, approach to service design, discovery, and consumption are all areas undergoing innovation. It will be interesting to watch the metamorphosis of micro-services architectures and platforms and see how some of the larger technology companies will tackle large-scale service consumption. Perhaps that is a relevant topic for a future book!

CHAPTER
12

Java Portfolio
Management

The creation of a well-managed and well-governed Java application portfolio is by no means an easy undertaking. This book has explored several topics, including the life cycle of a Java application, the concept of an application as a set of cooperating services, and various approaches to establishing an application portfolio successfully. Understanding and implementing the suggestions will contribute to and strengthen an effective modernization strategy. Management, modernization, and governance of a Java application portfolio are ongoing processes, not a single, one-time task.

To ensure that an application portfolio remains refreshed and renovated every few years, it is essential to inaugurate a comprehensive and continuous Java portfolio management strategy. And a necessary and critical part of Java application portfolio management is the establishment of portfolio governance, including introducing organizational processes, collecting and measuring relevant metrics, tracking key performance indicators (KPIs) for the portfolio, and making informed decisions on the application portfolio. The objectives of each organization are different, driven by their specific business model and the performance goals of an enterprise. This is typically reflected in the KPIs that are tracked by an organization.

The level of maturity attained by an organization can be tracked and improved upon as the organization embraces the concept of Java application portfolio management. The maturity model considers governance procedures and an organization's adherence to the processes and tools that have been implemented. By following this practice, an organization can eventually institute a measurement model to gauge the value derived from the portfolio and its return on investment (ROI) into the application portfolio.

Application Portfolio Governance

The central objective of Java portfolio management is the governance of the application portfolio. The concept of governance itself, as it relates to an enterprise, has many types, including the following:

- Corporate and financial governance

- IT governance

- Architecture governance

- Application portfolio governance

Figure 12-1 shows the four broad types of governance that an organization must institute as part of its overall organizational governance structure. These four broad types are highlighted here because each type involves different stakeholders and requires slightly different skill sets to manage the associated governance process. Some of the types are technical in nature, while other types require knowledge of financial controls or business operations.

The corporate and financial governance discussion is beyond the scope of this book. From a very high-level perspective, however, corporate and financial governance ensures the following:

- Direction and management of the company
- Oversight of management by the board of directors
- Accountability to the shareholders of the company
- Transparency and disclosure
- Compliance with regulatory requirements and other laws

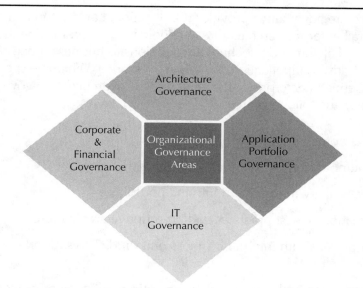

FIGURE 12-1. *Overall organizational governance areas*

- Establishment and guidance of corporate and financial metrics

- Monitoring and management of company performance based on the set of metrics

Although a complete analysis is beyond the scope of this book, IT governance defines the processes and structural framework for managing enterprise IT resources and assets that support the business objectives of an enterprise. IT governance institutionalizes best practices around enterprise IT execution and performance. There are significant business risks if IT declines in its primary function, especially during cyber-attacks, natural disasters, nefarious social engineering, fraudulent transactions, undetected virus attacks, or an overall failure of IT systems to perform. IT governance also encompasses security-related controls, practices, and management to ensure reliability and safety of enterprise IT to deliver business needs. The COBIT (Control Objectives for Information and Related Technology) framework is a well-regarded IT governance framework. The IT Governance Institute has addressed and incorporated maturity models, critical success factors (CFSs), key goal indicators (KGIs), and key performance indicators (KPIs) as part of the COBIT framework.

Architecture governance provides the direction, control and management of the overall enterprise architecture, technology decision-making, best practices, and alignment of technology decisions to business processes. It is a close relative of application portfolio governance. While the specifics may vary between enterprises, the central focus of architecture governance encompasses the following areas:

- Technology management

- Technology selection and adoption

- Technology introduction into the portfolio

- Creation of best practices and prescriptive architectures

- Partnering with internal business units and IT to support application life cycle

- Participate in the application portfolio management processes and function

We draw a distinction between architecture governance and technology management by depicting technology management as one of the areas of architecture governance. This is true because the scope of technology management, as defined in this context, exists to ensure the management of areas such as technology strategy, policy, technology roadmaps, and technical project management.

Application portfolio governance, on the other hand, comprises several key focus areas, including the following:

- Establish a framework to measure and manage the application portfolio.

- Work with various stakeholders to identify and establish metrics of relevance to meet business objectives.

- Measure application portfolio performance.

- Maximize ROI from the application portfolio.

- Measure and derive the greatest business value from the set of applications in the portfolio.

- Help architecture and IT governance functions modernize the application portfolio.

Architecture governance and application portfolio governance overlap and collaborate to manage the application portfolio. The scope of the discussion in this chapter is geared toward application portfolio governance. In Chapter 3, where we discussed APM (application portfolio management) in detail, we touched upon the performance of an application portfolio and defined four broad classes of metrics applicable to an application portfolio. Figure 12-2 shows the categories of metrics that were covered previously:

- Application metrics

- Application portfolio metrics

- APM process metrics

- APM effectiveness metrics

The governance of an application portfolio must consider these four broad categories of metrics. Although these categories are mainly applicable to the field of APM, this chapter deals specifically with Java portfolio management.

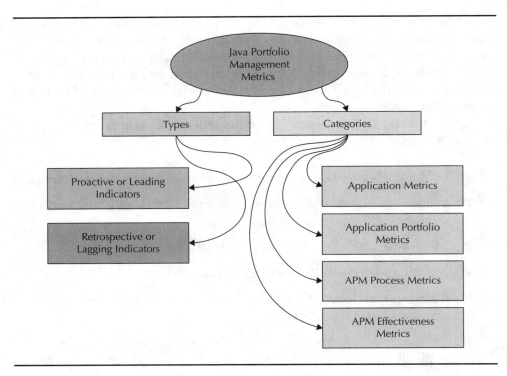

FIGURE 12-2. *Categories of Java portfolio management metrics*

In this context, we will delve deeper into these categories and examine specific metrics that are directly applicable and relevant to this discussion. Some of the metrics will be proactive or leading indicators, whereas other metrics will be retrospective or lagging indicators. In addition to the identification and definition of metrics, to be truly successful the governance of a Java application portfolio must incorporate a holistic approach to governance through a properly instituted governance framework.

Java Portfolio Governance Framework

The key to a successful governance framework is a sound architecture discipline underlying Java portfolio management. This practice is possible at the organizational level by leveraging a governance framework that applies certain dimensions to the portfolio and then connects, measures, and

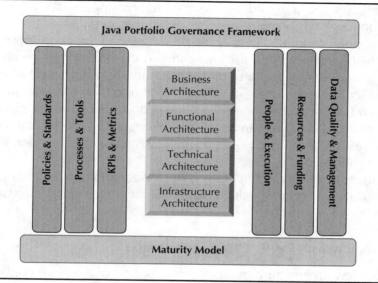

FIGURE 12-3. *The six dimensions of the Java portfolio governance framework*

manages those dimensions. Figure 12-3 illustrates the governance framework and shows the six dimensions that must be addressed by the framework:

- Policies and standards
- Processes and tools
- KPIs and metrics
- Data quality and management
- Resources and funding
- People and execution

Policies and Standards

We cannot govern a Java application portfolio without establishing some tenets and guidelines that need to be followed. Organizations must identify a specific set of criteria or tasks that are critical to the decision-making process relevant to their Java application portfolio. These criteria then shape a set of policies and standards, some of which are applied at the individual application level, while others are relevant at the portfolio level.

For example, certain policies could be established for the purpose of pushing the organization and the application portfolio toward a higher maturity level over the course of the next 18 months. Another set of policies could be incorporated to help shepherd the organization toward transforming and modernizing their existing service-oriented architecture to a micro-services–oriented container architecture. Policies and standards should always have a present focus to guide and influence the future vision for the application portfolio.

In conjunction with architecture governance, an illustrative set of tasks associated with influencing a subset of the policies and standards are listed here:

- Comply with OAuth 2 for authentication.

- Review architecture quarterly for adoption of a service container.

- Partner with an application group and help analyze conformance to core entities, data schema, and data quality.

- Review service-hosting environment and tools to ensure adherence with best practices.

- Help establish and review user-interface guidelines for new initiatives.

- Identify, select, and adopt development and testing tools for the organization.

- Promote widespread dialog within the enterprise among business units, enterprise architects, and IT managers.

From a standards perspective, the portfolio governance team should collaborate with enterprise architects to influence and enforce the following policies and standards for all new applications, as well as the modernization of prioritized existing applications:

- Identify and build reusable micro services.

- Register new services and make them discoverable.

- Provide extensive documentation and service contract specification.

- Provide a versioning strategy for micro services.

- Provide coarse-grained interfaces and gateways to access a set of cooperating micro services.

These are just illustrative examples of establishing policies and standards. It is important that the actual polices and standards not be established in a silo by a select group of people. As we have all experienced, those types of narrow-focused requirements are incredibly difficult to adopt and comply with. Instead, there must be widespread engagement of key stakeholders who socialize the process and deliverables. This will ensure that not only are practical policies and standards created for the success of an organization, but that there is consistent adherence and adoption across the organization.

Processes and Tools

To carry out the governance of Java application portfolios, a set of processes must implemented. These processes must then be enabled by a set of tools. If the policies and standards address the "what" question, then the processes and tools question the "how" of application portfolio governance. Typically, processes and tools are engaged for the following:

- Collect and monitor various metrics to benchmark against a baseline.

- Define Java application life cycle, including the design, development, deployment, and ongoing management.

- Define services life cycle, including design, development, deployment, and ongoing management.

- Establish a program management office (PMO) to manage the application portfolio.

- Establish processes and practices for communication and assessment of the portfolio for compliance against established criteria and best practices.

- Select tools, reporting formats, and reporting process.

KPIs and Metrics

Metrics and KPIs are the actual and relevant observations that are identified and then measured to provide insight on the application portfolio. Metrics cover various areas, including the overall performance of the portfolio, cost effectiveness and return on investment, operational risks and business value, and a variety of other application-specific and portfolio-level measurements.

A metric can be loosely defined as a system or standard of measurement. It is mostly a numerical assessment, and, in the context of portfolio management, it measures one or more dimensions applicable to application-centric attributes, financial data, operational data, technical attributes, business attributes, and the like.

The KPI is a special measure. It provides a way to quantify the success or progress toward a business objective. All KPIs are metrics, but all metrics are not KPIs. In the next major section, we will discuss metrics and KPIs in greater detail.

In general, organizations should understand the reasons behind the metrics they collect. The application of the SMART rule to identifying and collecting metrics is necessary in this regard. SMART stands for specific, measurable, actionable, relevant, and timely:

- **Specific**   The metric is clearly understood without ambiguity of what is being measured. Usually a specific owner or accountability is associated with the performance of the metric.

- **Measurable**   Challenges could exist around accuracy, timeliness, conformance, or even how to measure a metric. Unless a metric is easily measurable, it will not be useful.

- **Actionable**   The result of measuring a metric must result in some action that positively impacts an outcome. Merely measuring something without purpose will have no business value.

- **Relevant**   Focus should be on metrics that address the objectives and have a strategic purpose.

- **Timely**   The metric should be measured and made available within a timeframe that makes for an effective decision with the right impact. The metric should also measure current data and not old input.

The SMART rule has typically been applied as criteria for setting project management objectives or goals for personal development and employee performance; however, with certain tweaks, SMART can also be applied to the area of portfolio life cycle metrics identification and management. Often, organizations track metrics but do not use the information purposefully. Sometimes, the tracked metrics are not directly useful or relevant. Applying SMART to metrics identification and definition can help to weed out unnecessary metrics from a portfolio governance perspective. In some cases, metrics may play a part in providing insight for other functions not related to governance, thereby adding value to other processes. From a portfolio governance perspective, metrics can be used to track the maturity of the organization itself with respect to the Java application portfolio management processes and their execution.

Effectiveness of best practices, service life cycle, application life cycle, and other success factors can also be tracked with the establishment of the correct set of metrics. Metrics can also be used in the decision-making process to decide how a Java application portfolio should evolve in the future, including which applications need to be sunsetted and which applications need to be enhanced and modernized.

Here are some examples of metrics relevant to portfolio governance:

- Return on investment (ROI)

- Opportunity costs (of not modernizing a portfolio)

- Blended cost of resources

- Execution risk for in-flight projects

- Impact on bottom line (cost reduction)

- Capital expenditure

- Percentage of spending in running the business versus creating new applications

- FTE resource use

- Portfolio consolidation

- On-time and on-budget adherence

- Percentage variance in cost and effort

- Amounts committed but not spent

■   Spending by month (to determine whether all the budgeted money is spent quickly before the end of the year or gradually throughout the course of the year)

Data Quality and Management

Analysis, decision-making, and management of a Java application portfolio are dependent on the detailed inventory and availability of data regarding the applications in the portfolio. It is not a trivial undertaking to ensure the highest levels of data quality for collected input, especially in an ongoing manner. To ensure consistency and quality of data collection, the governance process must have appropriate data quality methods in place along with the right tools to leverage data collection, quality, and management.

Most organizations collect Java application portfolio data in Excel sheets. Some stakeholders may even graduate to a knowledge repository with web-based access to the data. Regardless of the collection method, the depth and breadth of information that needs to be collected on each application in the portfolio makes it necessary to involve multiple groups or business units, especially since ownership of the different pieces of the data for an application is likely split among various departments in an enterprise. This makes it quite challenging to maintain consistency of relevant data on all applications in a portfolio. The data can quickly become stale, rendering the metrics and KPIs that depend on the collected data irrelevant as well.

To ensure truly successful management of Java portfolios, current application attributes must be collected so that metrics and KPIs can properly be applied to the decision-making process. RACI (responsible, accountable, consulted, informed) charts assign clear ownership for the various tasks and decisions to help eliminate confusion. Transparent workflows should also be adopted to indicate clear responsibilities for data capture, audits, and detection of conflicts in the data collection process. These rules for data quality validations must inherently become part of the data collection process.

Resources and Funding

Enterprises adopt a wide variety of funding models for their initiatives and projects. The task of identifying and deploying resources to these projects can be quite challenging. Sometimes, the type of project dictates the availability of resources and funding. For example, marketing and PR initiatives are measured against completely differently criteria compared to a document repository project that the legal department wants to implement; however, both projects could be sidelined by a traditional IT proposal that fulfills and meets business objectives for the supply chain organization. Although an enterprise can execute a successful Java application portfolio management strategy with varied approaches to resource deployment and funding, it is nevertheless important to ensure that it is a complete model that is managed and measured under the portfolio management program.

At the outset, the core team that owns and drives the portfolio management function within an enterprise must ensure that their funding models also incorporate a comprehensive governance framework. The IT executive, business, and finance teams must work collectively to align funding models. Successful teams identify joint business and IT owners for the portfolio governance process. Securing high-level business sponsorship and executive-level stakeholders for the steering committee ensures that resource and budget allocations are sustained throughout the portfolio governance process.

People and Execution

The implementation of a successful governance framework requires the right people in the right place at the right time. Identifying and defining the appropriate roles and responsibilities of individuals as well as the contributions of other business units is an integral step in the execution of a successful governance process. A simple checklist for this might include the following:

- People and stakeholders exhibit a willingness to participate in Java portfolio governance activities.

- People are empowered with the appropriate responsibilities to drive improvement and management of the portfolio.

- Program initiatives build competency levels in the portfolio management disciplines for the enterprise.

- New roles are identified and established as desired.

KPIs and Metrics Implementation Strategy

In the last section, we reviewed the six dimensions of a Java application portfolio governance framework. In this section, we will analyze the dimension of KPIs and metrics and how they are applied to this process. What we want to measure is tied to the objectives and the questions we want answered. KPIs are metrics that are specifically tied to a business objective and indicate the ability of an organization to reach a specific target. KPIs are almost always business metrics. A metric, on the other hand, is simply a measure or number. Some examples of metrics include the number of applications in a portfolio, the number of lines of code in an application, and the number of unresolved open issues in an application portfolio. It is important to discern that although all KPIs are metrics, none of the metrics mentioned above is a KPI.

Before we can measure the metrics, we first need to identify the pertinent questions that we want answered. KPIs can measure the budgetary allocation for new applications versus spending to "keep the lights on" and maintain existing applications. If accurate metrics can be captured, an analysis could reveal additional dollars available for reallocation to fund new applications, thereby meeting the objective of lowering the spending on application maintenance. Following are some suggested metrics that an organization can measure to track the performance of their Java application portfolio:

Application metrics

- Lines of code: number of lines of code contained in the application

- Integration points: how many other applications, services, and systems interface with the application

- Technology complexity: the amount of multiple tiers and distributed components in the application

- Business criticality: the criticality of the application to the business and the financial impact if it is not available

Application portfolio metrics

- Spend mix: percentage spent on maintaining existing applications versus spending on enhancing existing applications or building new applications

- Short-term spend: spending on short-term projects

- Long-term spend: spending on long-term projects

- Application usage: percentage of applications in high use and percentage of applications used rarely within the portfolio

- Age: average age of applications within the portfolio that includes when they were built and delivered for use

- SLA: percentage of applications with well-defined SLAs

- Business risk: percentage of applications marked as posing a business risk

- Technology risk: percentage of applications marked as posing a technology risk that could be due to obsolete technology, lack of vendor support, or other factors

APM process metrics

- Productivity: measure of productivity against a baseline established within the organization

- Resource management: deployed resources and their effectiveness, skillset match, and use within the portfolio

- Earn versus burn: projects in flight, budgets, and overall earn versus burn calculations on projects in flight

APM effectiveness metrics

- IRR: the internal rate of return, or the rate of return on investments in this portfolio

- On time: percentage of projects completed on time

- On budget: percentage of projects completed within budget

- Issues: number of open issues against the applications in the portfolio

- Critical issues: open issues that are prioritized and ordered based on severity levels

- Health: overall severity status and critical risk inherent in the portfolio

- SLA deviation: percentage of applications (that have a defined SLA) that deviate from their SLA

- Savings: amount saved from previous spend measurements by adhering to APM process

Several metrics listed here can be computed from the application attributes that were discussed in Chapter 3. Based on specific objectives, the attributes involved in evaluating and quantifying a metric can vary. For example, measuring and quantifying technology complexity, business criticality, technology risk, and business risk depends on the enterprise and the maturity of the organization with respect to its architecture discipline.

The interpretation and use of these metrics will be left to the enterprise to determine. Some enterprises use business and technology risk measurement as part of a business continuity and mitigation plan; the use of this metric when it crosses a specific threshold might be determinative of a go-forward plan in one enterprise, whereas another enterprise might use the same metric for decommissioning an application. Pursuing, quantifying, and acting upon these process metrics is not a direct activity. Productivity, effectiveness of resource management, and similar measures are directly tied to performance metrics. Organizational baselines depend on their available resources and skills. Each enterprise must establish its own baseline according to its level of maturity and make improvements in conformance with that established baseline.

Many effectiveness metrics have dependencies on financial systems, budgeting processes, and attributes associated with finance and operations that are tracked against IT spending on applications. If that data could be tracked against applications over a three-year span, an enterprise could be in the advantageous position of creating cost-savings opportunities for its application portfolios. Taking this one step further, an organization could also map this collected data to KPIs that can predict financial performance of the application portfolios more accurately.

Deployment of Metrics

Once metrics and KPIs have been defined and agreed upon, these metrics need to be gathered, analyzed, and acted upon. This act of collecting and acting upon these metrics is referred to as *deployment of metrics*. Some metrics are effortless to appraise; they are a direct measure of some quantity. Typically, metrics collected to monitor and measure mutually exclusive attributes are easy for an enterprise to identify. An example of this would be running a nightly build script on a certain application and tracking whether the build failed or succeeded. This straightforward measure clearly identifies the successful percentage of completed builds on this application at the end of each month. If the percentage drops below 95 percent, there could be a specific action such as moving an additional resource to help with the application or manually building the application to figure out the bottleneck or where the build failed.

For all metrics and KPIs, the deployment process consists of four steps:

1. Define

2. Implement

3. Measure

4. Improve

Although it is relatively simple to define a metric, it is not easy to deploy that metric and actively collect data for future decision-making. Making the metric effective means that based on the measure, it should be easy to act upon and take decisions. While some metrics may be collected with ease, other factors could dictate how to act upon the information. In our previous example, because the automated builds failed and the threshold dropped below 95 percent, the organization may not have sufficient funds or skilled resources to deploy and improve upon the build process. It is important to note that metrics must be measurable right from the initial period of collection. With that solid foundation in place, the governance framework will eventually improve the maturity model associated with the Java portfolio management processes.

Measuring Value and Returns

One significant outcome of implementing portfolio management processes and governance frameworks is the ability to measure the value of the Java application portfolio and the ROIs. The SMART metrics associated with measuring value relevant to an organization must be identified in the beginning. Most organizations that are just starting to implement portfolio management practices find the financial and operational metrics associated with a Java application portfolio quite challenging to gather. At a high level, many organizations know the amount of money being spent on application portfolio maintenance, application enhancement, or the creation of new applications. However, many organizations do not accurately track these numbers in real time. Instead, due to limited resources or inexperienced project managers, many organizations simply track the number of full-time equivalents (FTEs) that are assigned to a particular manager, leaving that manager to decide the allocation of necessary resources based on projects already in flight. This ill-defined practice primarily caters to maintenance projects without much left for new project initiatives.

NOTE
Chapter 13 will address costing and estimation associated with modernization. That chapter will also delve into more detail about the type of metrics that must be captured and aggregated to develop a good understanding of the application portfolio ROI.

The measurement model requires several inputs to function accurately, including management of project budgets, adherence to allocated budgets, financial trends associated with individual applications, and financial trends associated with the overall application portfolio. The credibility of available data is also a crucial factor. If an organization relies solely on random data provided as input by IT managers and weekly time sheets to estimate project costs, the accuracy of the findings could be affected by large variances in the data. Although the measurement of value and returns from a portfolio should be captured, at the same time, an estimation of the risk inherent in a portfolio to business goals must also be given equal weight. Measuring revenue leakage and misappropriated resources in a portfolio can also significantly impact and affect the overall ROI. This is especially relevant for organizations that have a novice level of maturity in the portfolio management function.

Based on these findings, organizations may make operational decisions such as the following:

- Reducing the cost of operating a portfolio

- Rationalizing the portfolio in terms of application functionality and technology stacks

- Consolidating the skills of available resources

- Training resources on new skills

- Investing in strategic areas of the portfolio to realize better ROI after a few years

Maturity Model

The traditional application portfolio governance model called for a centralized governance function. However, the traditional definition of an application has morphed to include applications composed of multiple micro services working in conjunction to provide the application functionality. The entire technology stack of the micro services architecture has been completely standardized and made prescriptive including the containers, service platforms, tools, best practices, test automation, continuous integration, and the delivery of these micro services themselves. With the advent of the micro-services architecture, virtualized environments, deployment to the cloud, and exposure of functionality through APIs, the traditional centralized governance model has given way to a more modern decentralized governance model.

Enterprises are at varying degrees of maturity when it comes to managing their Java application portfolios and instituting a governance framework that captures relevant metrics and KPIs to drive application portfolio decision-making. The key questions to address are, what does this maturity level look like and how can this maturity level be measured so that an organization can realize its current level of sophistication and readiness or lack thereof?

This book proposes a five-step maturity level model, as depicted in Figure 12-4:

1. Darkness

2. Awareness

3. Competence

4. Intelligence

5. Excellence

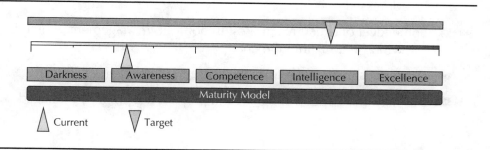

FIGURE 12-4. *Illustrative maturity model for a governance dimension*

Darkness

In this first step of the maturity model, all organizations are by default in darkness when it comes to applying metrics to measure a Java application portfolio so that appropriate decisions can me made based on those metrics and KPIs. Enterprises in this state of maturity have some similarities and exhibit the following characteristics:

■ Lack of Java application portfolio governance processes

■ No strategy in place even to define an application portfolio

■ Absence of recognition that portfolio management is a key driver and a governance framework is necessary for achieving business objectives

■ Senior management and application stakeholders do not evince interest

■ IT spending not well managed and typically not understood well enough by the organization

■ No alignment between business and IT, lack of business unit involvement

■ No PMO and poor project and program management of initiatives

■ Lack of policies, standards, and SLAs

Awareness

At the awareness level, an enterprise acknowledges that issues exist and that portfolio management is necessary to help the organization. An enterprise at this level of maturity exhibits the following characteristics:

■ Acknowledges and recognizes the lack of governance and its need to be addressed

■ Some level of executive interest in portfolio management, which is not widespread within the enterprise

■ IT spend is managed reactively to keep the lights on

■ Business and IT poorly aligned and projects not properly managed

- Resource availability inconsistent
- Limited involvement of stakeholders

Competence

An enterprise that has advanced beyond the awareness stage enters the level of competence maturity. In this stage of maturity, organizations have finally decided to pursue Java application portfolio management and governance whole-heartedly, although there are a lot of gaps in the implementation. The traits of an organization in this level of maturity are as follows:

- Enterprise architecture strategy and application portfolio management strategy in place but not fully aligned to business goals
- Basic metrics and KPIs identified with limited deployment
- Initial identification of business objectives but lack of complete alignment of KPIs to measure progress against objectives
- Measurement and tracking of performance indicators on a limited basis
- Planning and budgeting processes in place, accounting of annual budgets and management of spending against approved budgets
- Business users and stakeholders engaged in the portfolio management process

Intelligence

As the enterprise moves ahead from a state of competence to a state of intelligence, it positions itself to succeed in the Java portfolio management process. Organizations at the state of intelligence exhibit the following characteristics:

- Alignment of business to IT and articulation of business value driven by APM
- Enterprise architecture and portfolio management disciplines well defined with identified stakeholders participating in the success of the governance framework

- Budgets allocated and measured on a regular basis to monitor overall financial performance

- Metrics well defined and measured against previously established baselines

- Established internal processes to engage with application development teams and enable application development

Excellence

Enterprises that have reached excellence perform at a high level. They also have very well-managed Java application portfolios. These portfolios have been modernized, transformed, and governed by a framework employing relevant metrics and KPIs to assist the organization to track its progress and meet its business objectives. Some of the characteristics of an organization operating at an excellence level of maturity are as follows:

- Financial metrics and IT spend very well managed, ROI into the application portfolio tracked regularly; future decisions based on past performance data

- Business risks well understood and tracked with the right set of metrics

- Continuous governance processes and measurement tools in place with transparent visibility into the entire organization, incorporating dashboard reports for executive management

- Best practices and prescriptive architectures in place; architecture governance and portfolio governance synergistically work together

- Business-to-IT alignment an integral part of application portfolio management and planning

- Effective decisions-making and rationalization of application portfolios every few years provides the best results for meeting business objectives

Summary

As organizations seek to manage their portfolios of Java applications, they will need to implement resilient governance frameworks based on the six dimensions of application portfolio governance. As part of the metrics and KPIs dimension, organizations must identify specific metrics of interest following the SMART paradigm to identify the key performance indicators that enable organizations to measure their success against their business objectives.

Categories of metrics and examples of metrics in each category were discussed. Not all metrics are actionable, and they may have different uses depending on the stakeholder interested in that metric. Each of the governance dimensions can and will evolve over time. The maturity model enables organizations to understand the maturation levels of their portfolio management and governance processes.

Ultimately, organizations invest in Java applications to derive business value with an expectation of a certain ROI. This high-level consideration will be expanded in more detail in the next chapter, as we review the costs, estimations, and ROI for Java application portfolios.

CHAPTER
13

Modernization
Costing and Estimation

M odernizing an application portfolio is an intensive exercise. By analogy, as with any major overhaul in a home remodel, the task of modernizing a kitchen or bathroom, or building an entirely new floor or room in an older home, requires dependencies on many different factors. For anyone who has undertaken such massive projects or has heard the horror stories from those brave enough to gut their home, one thing is clear: A thoughtful and deliberate modernization exercise is not based on arbitrary decisions. Rather, a careful understanding of the costs, timelines, and exigent contingencies involved is crucial to completing the project successfully with minimal pain points. The same is true for an application portfolio, which is a critical asset to any enterprise. The survival of an enterprise depends on the functioning of its applications, business processes, and IT infrastructure. Before acting upon hypotheses to reengineer applications, sunset features or entire applications, or introduce new technologies or functionality, it is prudent that you first estimate the effort and cost of such modernization exercises.

Even smaller modernization projects that impact only a few applications have hidden costs, effort, and dependencies that must be exposed and understood before jumping headfirst into the endeavor. This chapter explores creating a costing and effort estimation model, instituting processes that identify relevant data points from within and outside the organization, collecting metrics for projecting and measuring effort and cost, and building a holistic decision-making framework for these estimations. This chapter specifically addresses the cost and effort estimations from both top-down and bottom-up perspectives and shares insights into identifying business risks that arise during such an exercise. Finally, this chapter highlights some assumptions that factor into making cost and effort calculations and lists some strategies for enterprises to gain a strategic advantage.

The Costing and Estimation Meta Model (CEMM)

Every organization needs a strong financial foundation to operate, scale, and achieve its objectives. Whether an organization is private, public, nonprofit, or otherwise structured, without proper cash-flow management the organization cannot survive. An enterprise is always in continuous competition with other organizations for talent, customers, revenue, and market share. It is a constant mission to find alternative avenues to leapfrog ahead of the competition.

Many enterprises have successfully leveraged technology to gain advantageous positioning ahead of their competitors. Technology is a powerful tool that rapidly advances itself to improve on its own utility. Successful enterprises embrace new technology and leverage its applicability into key business processes to maintain their leadership in their industries. We have seen the rise of "unicorns," private companies valued at $1 billion or more, and their ability to oust old stalwarts that did not take advantage of technological advances. Enterprises that future-proof their products and services invest in consistent modernization of their application portfolios, learn from the successes and failures of the exercise, and enjoy their well-earned return on investment (ROI). However, such returns are not always apparent at the level of technology or application functionality. Such favorable returns can be directly measured and seen in terms of top-line and bottom-line growth, new product launch, and new market entry.

Profitable organizations commission strong fiscal management strategies at the helm of an enterprise. The scope of this chapter is to take a closer look into the financial inputs that impact an application portfolio. Adopting a comprehensive estimation model and strong foundational framework is necessary before any investment can be made in the management and maintenance of an application portfolio.

Based on more than 20 years of experience in information technology across various roles, industries, and projects, I have developed a comprehensive meta model for computing the cost and effort for various types of IT projects. The Costing and Estimation Meta Model (CEMM) presented in this chapter is relevant at the portfolio level and is equally important from the perspective of a program tasked with the development or enhancement of an application. Costs and effort must be tracked at the level of an application as well as at the portfolio level. While CEMM tracks cost estimations of an application portfolio, the model can also be applied to individual projects and applications. The model should embody the activities and phases of the software engineering and application development life cycle. For example, the scope and development of an application includes effort estimates for various phases, such as architecture, design, development, QA and testing, project management, data modeling, performance engineering, and infrastructure management. The model presented here is totally agile and highly customizable for the unique needs of an entire enterprise application portfolio or the specific needs of an individual project or application.

The meta model does not occur by happenstance. The implementation of CEMM requires careful consideration to conceive the appropriate model. Figure 13-1 provides guidelines for enterprises to build their own costing and effort estimation meta model by following CEMM protocols. This parametric model is built and enhanced over a period of time. It is constantly updated to reflect the dynamics, skills, resources, and abilities of an organization to execute IT projects successfully. The parametric model must be able to provide assessments for various tasks such as data modeling, architecture, design, and other phases based on the complexity of projects under consideration.

Five key areas must be addressed by the meta model when building the enterprise-specific cost and effort estimation model:

- Application and functional components

- Technical component framework

- Infrastructure

- Legacy componentization

- Support and maintenance

All cost-related efforts can be categorized among the five categories, which exist to logically group cost components. Any cost-related item that you come up with should be associated with the category that closely matches the item. For example, if you consider business processes or information architecture, then it could be lumped into the first category of application and functional components. If micro services are being designed and developed, business services can be included in the first category and technical services into the second category of the technical component framework. The base projections from the parametric model are customized and applied to specific projects to derive the overall estimate for that specific initiative. In some situations, accurate valuations may not be possible. In such cases, rough order of magnitude (ROM) estimates are a convenient proxy to support budgetary decision-making based on a high-level understanding of the spending associated with an initiative. Over time, the reliability of these models improves and the variances for such ROM estimates tend to decrease.

An organization gathers data to create baseline financial estimates by taking into account past project duration, initial budgetary estimates, and final costs of the initiative. These data points can also be supported by standard industry averages. Additionally, enterprises can collect metrics from the vendors that develop and manage their applications to track the

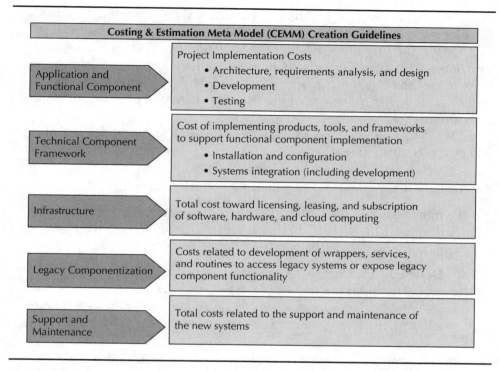

FIGURE 13-1.   *Guidelines to building the Costing and Estimation Meta Model (CEMM)*

various cost differentiators. Several factors influence the generation of these data points, including a combination of past initiatives, market and industry baselines, specific project and application data, and vendor-specific metrics. This baseline becomes rather complicated if projects are executed in a distributed fashion, with teams residing in corporate offices as well as at offshore or offsite development centers. In such cases, a clear understanding of application development baselines across the different locations is necessary when customizing and adapting the CEMM for the needs of an enterprise, since location of resources can impact projections.

Introduction to COCOMO II, the Constructive Cost Model

The constructive cost model, popularly known as COCOMO, was developed in the 1970s as a standard for estimating the effort, cost, and time schedule for software projects in the aerospace industry. Its origin stems from more than 60 initiatives varying in size, complexity, and programming languages. Developed in the mid-1990s, COCOMO II became the successor to COCOMO. The primary reason for this upgrade was to keep pace with software development and information technology and its evolution from mainframes and batch processing to server-side development, client–server technologies, code reusability, and the advent of prebuilt software components and packages.

COCOMO is designed as a hierarchy of three increasingly detailed effort and cost computation strategies:

- **Basic COCOMO**   Determines rough orders of magnitude.

- **Intermediate COCOMO**   Computes the application and software development as a function of program size and cost drivers; some of these drivers are subjective.

- **Detailed COCOMO**   Incorporates several additional components and determines the impact of cost drivers on various stages of the software engineering process; the detailed model also uses different effort multipliers for each cost driver attribute.

Our meta model, CEMM, partially derives from COCOMO II with a specific adaptation for modernization programs, application portfolio management, cloud-based applications, service-oriented architectures, REST-based services, and mobile and emerging technologies, and is flexible enough to extend to meet the changing needs of enterprises that adopt modern technology into their application portfolios.

Drivers for Modernization Costing

Modernization impacts all layers of the organization, from business to IT, making it susceptible to greater operational risk in an enterprise. Fundamentally transforming the information technology aspects of a company is a complex, multiyear, organization-wide venture. In addition to addressing the technical variables, modernization must also be segmented and analyzed from the context of business, financial, and operational processes of an enterprise including project duration, timelines, the number of initiatives associated with modernization, and available resources. The stakeholders today extend beyond middle management to the C-suite, including the CIO, COO, CFO, and even the CEO. These stakeholders all contribute in some function or capacity to the modernization of a portfolio of applications.

The key drivers in any modernization exercise are business risks, investment decisions, and benefits. These major drivers must be quantified and clearly understood to execute large-scale modernization programs. Investment decisions and the measurement of benefits must go hand-in-hand.

Figure 13-2 depicts the various types of costs considered as input in the decision-making process. Investment decisions are evaluated against a risk-versus-benefit result for the organization. Some of these benefits include business benefits, productivity improvements, and faster time to market. Conversely, innovation and transaction effectiveness are harder to quantify. Without getting into a technical financial analysis, which is beyond the scope of this book, the next section will identify risks and discuss measuring and quantifying business benefits using different approaches.

Risk Identification

Business risks associated with information technology projects can be classified into three main areas: execution risks, investment risks, and technology risks.

Project execution risks arise in many forms—most notably, how a project is structured, leadership of the project team, key stakeholder commitments, and dependence of the project on multiple business and operational units.

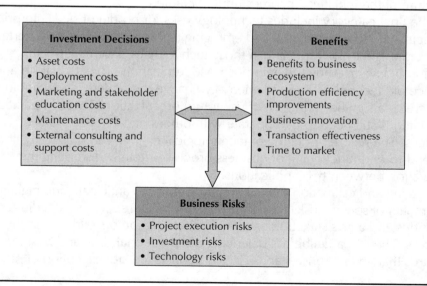

FIGURE 13-2. *Analysis of costs, benefits, and risks*

The staffing of resources requires matching appropriate skill sets and a base familiarity with proposed technologies. Without clear alignment of these factors, the overall execution of the project, budget, and timelines will be severely and negatively impacted. Moreover, the proper inclusion of end users, those who use the applications to carry out their day-to-day tasks, make decisions, generate necessary reports, and ultimately benefit from the project outcome, must be a priority. If end users are not engaged and do not participate in continuous discussions, the risk of delivering a final project that has low utility value is highly probable.

Investment risks are purely financial in nature. The continued funding of a project is specifically tied to availability of budgetary dollars. Even though a project has been approved for migration and supported by a solid business case that outlines the necessary investment projections, oftentimes that is not enough. As we have all witnessed firsthand, the business climate changes quickly and creates an adverse impact on certain initiatives that lose project funding. Depending on the size of the company, the issue could be a cash flow problem or a significant change to the cost of capital, both of which can create drastic revisions to departmental budgets. This is especially true of projects that are not viewed as critical within a company. Similarly, when there is uncertainty around the overall cost of a project, evidenced by several scope change requests made after a project takes flight, then the entire cost structure of the initiative becomes unpredictable.

The final category includes technology risks, or product risks. Enterprise projects that incorporate new and emerging technologies embody a certain level of inherent risk, especially if those technologies have never been previously leveraged by the enterprise. Modernization projects that rip and replace old technology or fundamentally change the underlying technology also create a significant degree of risk for an organization. These impacted applications still need to interoperate with other critical applications or services. The nature or degree of technological change can drastically affect the end-to-end functioning of business processes, totally disrupting the integration between two applications.

Costing and estimation models should attempt to anticipate and highlight the impact of specific risks that fall under the three areas. This risk adjustment identifies and alerts stakeholders of the mitigating factors early on in the process. There is a deliberate balancing of operational risks and business rewards that an enterprise stands to gain upon successful execution of projects.

Risk Management

The categorization of risks is not enough; there also needs to be clear management of that risk during the entire modernization project. The project management team and business leaders must be proactively engaged and involved in financial risk management throughout the entire process. Projects that overspend or run up a large variance on projected budgets tend to stall very quickly after launch. By collecting relevant data in advance, enterprises can use statistics and predictive modeling to quantify the financial impact of a project to ensure on-time delivery and on-budget execution of the initiative. The next section, "Calculating and Quantifying Business Benefits," discusses how data collection and metrics for building costing models can provide organizations with the necessary tools to provide clear visibility into their financial and operational risks.

Certain aspects of execution risk and technology risk can be managed through change management processes and organizational design to tackle modernization projects. Structuring the right team with the right resources and skills does not happen by chance. There must be active engagement by the leadership to make sound decisions surrounding project planning, staffing, and execution. Without a careful balancing of the necessary resources, modernization projects may be doomed to fail. In some cases, the lack of required skill sets may require hiring or training additional resources. This may require collaboration with partners or service providers to staff specific roles. In extreme cases, entire projects could also be outsourced. All of these scenarios have one commonality: the lack of a proper risk mitigation and risk management plan. In addition to being very costly, these categories of modernization projects fail because of their top-heavy structure. On-boarding several seasoned project leaders in hopes that their experience will result in a seamless project plan is a very risky gamble. Resource management is only one aspect of risk mitigation solution. Because of the highly technical nature of modernization projects, it is fundamentally important to formulate an optimal pyramid structure that balances the hands-on skilled resources, project management processes, and technical architecture in any modernization exercise.

Calculating and Quantifying Business Benefits

Many approaches and methodologies can be used for calculating and quantifying business benefits. Return on investment (ROI) and total cost of ownership (TCO) are well-known and accepted approaches. Forrester has developed its own approach, called Total Economic Impact (TEI) analysis.

Methodologies such as the balanced scorecard can help to quantify business benefits. Economic value added (EVA) is a true measure of the economic profit of an enterprise. The remainder of this section will further examine and define a few of these common methodologies.

Total Cost of Ownership (TCO)

TCO tools facilitate the collection and measurement of direct and indirect IT costs and service levels, enabling an organization to analyze and manage a wide range of cost- and risk-related issues within IT environments. The TCO approach can effectively measure the impact of IT decisions, while creating output that accurately communicates the real value of IT investments to the enterprise.

Balanced Scorecard Technique

The balanced scorecard model offers a way for a company to gain wider perspective on its strategic decision-making. This approach collectively considers the impact to finances, customers, internal processes, and employees. The analysis takes into account financial and nonfinancial measures, internal improvements, past outcomes, and ongoing requirements as indications of future performance. IT departments typically apply the balanced scorecard model to projects that span e-commerce, supply-chain management, and other business-focused projects to ensure that the progress of these initiatives can be adequately tracked.

Economic Value Added (EVA)

EVA is the ultimate financial performance measure for capturing the true economic profit of an enterprise. EVA is a performance indicator that is most directly linked to the creation of shareholder value and overall profitability of a company. Adopting an EVA-based financial management and incentive compensation system provides project managers with access to essential data to make necessary decisions that impact the financial health of any company, whether publicly owned or privately held.

Total Economic Impact (TEI)

TEI is a methodology developed by Forrester that enables technology vendors and IT organizations to demonstrate the value of technology investments and to communicate that value in business terms. TEI's analytical technique expands traditional cost analysis to include benefits and flexibility, filtering all factors through risk analysis.

Return on Investment (ROI)

ROI is a generic term referring to the financial benefits of a business, such as the production of income in relation to the capital deployed. It is a measure of the percentage return for a fixed investment over a defined period of time, usually expressed in a range of years (for example, three to five years). ROI is used as a forecasting tool by enterprises, often for cost justification when making investments. ROI can also be defined as a closed loop process that demonstrates actual business performance improvement, against the bottom-line (company profit and loss), from selective investment in enhancing a capability or adding a new capability.

Overview of ROI Analysis   ROI is often used as a collective term to refer to ROI and the other traditional financial measures such as payback, internal rate of return (IRR), and net present value (NPV). ROI is expressed as a percentage over a period of time. ROI offers several advantages: It specifies a particular time period so that the target time frame is known. It also takes into account the time value of money calculation. ROI has one disadvantage: it does not address the magnitude of the project at hand.

Although it is a powerful indicator, ROI has its limitations. After an organization has achieved a high level of maturity with respect to instituting an APM discipline, and successfully modernized several application portfolios, ROI may not be the best indicator of benefits. Figure 13-3 shows three graphs that represent relationship of ROI to maturity: ROI versus availability of data

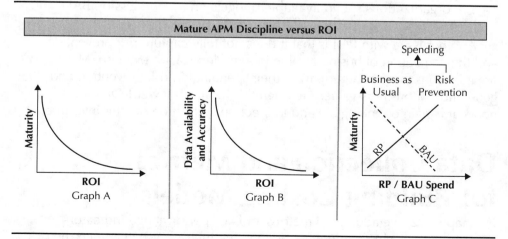

FIGURE 13-3. *Graphs showing behavior of ROI with respect to organizational maturity in implementing APM*

points and accuracy of the data, and maturity versus spending related to risk prevention and business as usual.

- In graph A, organizations low in maturity with respect to modernization and APM typically spend 80 percent or more of their annual budgets on "keeping the lights" on or "business as usual" expenses. With the primary budget almost fully spent on day-to-day operations, no funds remain to address risk. More mature organizations typically lower the ROI on APM investments, while organizations lower in maturity could save even 40 percent from APM. ROI does not fully capture risk prevention (RP) and business value (BV)

- In graph B, quantifiable benefits depend on the availability and accuracy of data and how amenable it is to compute and measure relevant metrics. ROI is an exercise in quantifying financial benefits. Because organizations have highly accurate portfolio data that is readily available, over a few years the ROI would be lower from APM investments into that portfolio since financial benefits would already have been extracted.

- Graph C shows the plot of maturity versus spend. This spend is represented as two components, namely business as usual (BAU) and risk prevention (RP). The solid line shows that organizations with lower maturity have increased spend focused on BAU activities and have less focus on RP, whereas the dashed line shows that mature organizations spend available budgets on RP and less on BAU.

Another issue with ROI is that it does not fully capture risk prevention and the generation of business value in a modernization exercise. Mature organizations focus a larger part of their spending on risk prevention and generation of business value. Although this results in lower ROI, they see a noticeable gain on intangible and indirect quantification of their investments.

Data Collection and Metrics for Building Costing Models

In Chapter 12, we addressed metrics and key performance indicators describing the SMART rule when identifying metrics. We classified metrics across four broad categories:

- Application metrics

- Application portfolio metrics

- APM process metrics

- APM effectiveness metrics

Some of the metrics identified under these four categories were related to financial measurement, including cost effectiveness and ROI. Measuring values and returns on an application portfolio are relevant only if the cost and investment parameters can be determined. There are also metrics that do not directly measure financial performance, yet they still have a significant impact on costing. These metrics are quantifiable measurements of proxy factors that indirectly influence and impact financial costing projections. The next sections will address data collection strategies, relevant metrics, and the building of costing models. With these tools in place, you'll find that it becomes easier to understand the risks and benefits of cost and effort for better decision-making in investments.

Data Collection

A model is only as good as the data that it represents. Continuous data collection is imperative for an organization to be able to determine in advance the projected costs for various modernization-related projects. The primary questions to consider are what data points must be captured? Where does this data come from? How can the data be easily collected, stored, and analyzed on a regular basis?

The data referenced here derives from various aspects of technology projects, application development, software engineering, and modernization projects that have been successfully executed. These data points reflect the attributes associated with applications, details on technology, productivity, operational, and financial attributes, among other factors.

An organization must collect data from its own project execution. That will serve to build a baseline and understanding of past execution capability. Estimations on past projects and variances over the original estimation are an invaluable source, no doubt. This should lead an organization down a path of gathering insight into why there were cost overruns or, in the unlikely scenario of coming under budget, why the execution was efficient. An enterprise must also draw a distinction between data points collected for new projects versus data points collected regarding support and maintenance costs for various systems previously built by the company. Many organizations emphasize costing and budgets for new applications but do not adequately model the overall TCO, which includes the necessary support and maintenance outlay. Modernization of existing applications involves either adding functionality or upgrading the technology powering the applications. The cost of such enhancement initiatives, the actual expenditure and variances over the estimations, must all be measured and collected to provide an accurate TCO over the entire life cycle of the application portfolio.

It is not sufficient if an organization merely collects data from its internal project execution to build a baseline, however. For an organization to improve its own quality of execution, it is also important to collect similar data points from service providers and vendors that the enterprise leverages for modernization projects, so that baselines can be compared against the benchmarks of other enterprises. A comparison of data points between different vendors will provide useful insight into whether certain vendors execute projects better than others and how those actions impact the overall cost, effort, and productivity of a project.

Lastly, data points collected from the industry at large should also be compared and analyzed against an organization's own internal baseline and the benchmark of its vendors. These data points should be collected per the specific industry vertical as well as marking general trends across industries. To summarize, the three fundamental sources of data points are these:

- Organization-wide data points
- Vendor or service provider data points
- Industry data points

By collectively engaging these three sets of data points, comparing the sources, and establishing a baseline, an organization can establish best practices to continuously improve the maximum amount of returns from its execution of modernization projects.

Data collection employs both manual and automation techniques. Most of that data should have been generated and collected in a knowledge base when the application portfolio was built. Of all the metrics surrounding a project, financial data associated with past projects is the most challenging to collect. Figure 13-4 shows a metrics and data collection framework identifying a set of sample data collection areas. The next section delves deeper into these various areas and identifies a set of comparative metrics for each.

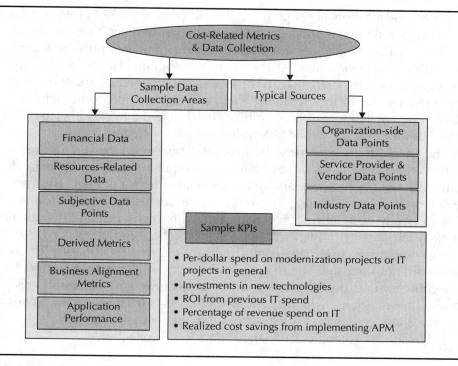

FIGURE 13-4. *Cost-related metrics and data collection framework*

Metrics Identification

The topic of metrics and data collection can be overwhelming for enterprises because most large organizations have an exorbitant amount of continuous data generation. The main question to consider is what data should be collected and from which sources? In earlier chapters, we discussed how to establish a knowledge base to conduct discovery exercises and collect data with an aim to implement APM processes. Executed properly, that exercise would have resulted in a central knowledge base and repository of information associated with an application portfolio under consideration for modernization.

Enterprise financial systems house corporate financial data. The collection of this financial data should be a continuous process for the various projects in flight within an organization. Once collected, this raw financial data must be transformed to compute necessary financial metrics tracking total expenditure costing models.

As an organizational best practice, the actual final project costs and the initial projected project budget must be compared to determine the degree of variance. These variances are then analyzed by the enterprise to determine the context and environment giving rise to the disparity. Factors such as plain oversight, aggressive budgeting, or mismanagement of funds are considered. These findings are further scrutinized and transformed into cost multipliers that can be applied to baseline attributes exhibiting the large variances. This inquiry is fundamental to our CEMM framework for costing.

The CEMM framework reviews the overall budget earmarked for the project and compares variances against the overall budget. Key financial data of interest must include the labor costs associated with a project. This can be determined by computing the number of resources deployed, computing average hourly cost per resource associated with the project and the duration for each resource associated with the initiative. These resources can be internal employees, externally contracted vendors, or a mix of both. These factors are not static and will require some degree of dynamic adjustment to account for unexpected changes as the project evolves. Mastery of this constant balancing act with a multitude of factors is what sets apart successful enterprise modernization exercises from the less successful ones.

Following are examples of financial data to be collected:

- Cost of labor

- Estimated budget

- Total development cost

- Percent budget variance

- Annual costs of operation

- Percent savings in labor costs through potential outsourcing (relevant if in-house skills do not exist for the technologies in question)

- Cost of consolidation / total cost (if projects are combined or managed together)

- Estimated TCO

- Average TCO after five years

- Percent variance in TCO

- Net present value (NPV)
- Return on investment (ROI)
- Internal rate of return (IRR)
- Payback period
- Risk-adjusted return on capital (RAROC)
- Adjustment factor for number of years since baseline financial data

Cost and effort estimation have a big dependency on the staffed resources who engage in modernization projects. The skills and experience levels of the resources will determine how long a team may take to execute a project. Inexperienced teams may initially struggle with project scope, make ill-informed decisions, or introduce defects requiring a significant amount of time and effort to detect and fix. The composition of the team, how quickly the group ramps up or down, and team size are all affected by the skills and experience level of the deployed resources. The CEMM framework allows for adjustment of these factors with multipliers that can project additional costs or reduced costs based on the particular team deployed for a project.

Here are some examples of resources data:

- Peak team size
- Average team size
- Team ramp-up velocity
- Team ramp-down velocity
- Skill set availability
- Average years of experience on similar technology
- Percent of resources with matching skill set

Although certain metrics are directly quantifiable, other measurements must be indirectly captured. These assessments affect the cost and estimation of engagements. For example, every organization needs to establish a measure of productivity when it comes to IT projects. Several questions should be asked: What is the quantum of work to be delivered? What is the expected productivity of the team? Is productivity measured by function points delivered, stories delivered in sprint sessions for agile development, number of lines of code written and delivered, or final deployed micro services?

However an organization chooses to measure baseline productivity, the productivity improvement above that baseline must be captured for every project. If this is determined to vary significantly, an organization must understand why that happened. Another important determination is the total elapsed time for project execution. For example, if the estimated time lapse includes 10 people working for 1000 hours, that does not mean that 100 people can deliver that project in only 100 hours. Project deadlines should not be arbitrarily established or influenced by external pressures, management decisions, and naïve estimations or underestimations by the leadership team. It is essential that organizations accurately predict project execution timelines and delivery dates. If this process is not successfully managed, then project delays could have several negative effects, transpiring in low team morale, end-user misperceptions, and lack of project team credibility.

These metrics are dependent on subjective data points:

- Baseline productivity (for example, velocity at which features are delivered)

- Percent productivity improvement

- Elapsed time for project execution (start date and delivery date)

- Support requirements

The inherent risk is crystal clear when a project is severely off schedule or over budget, or includes the upgrading of old, unsupported, or obsolete technology. In these cases, there will be significant impact to the effort and cost of the project. Conversely, some metrics are not directly measured but are derived from implied perceptions or a combination of inferred observations. Previous chapters in this book discussed how to compute technical capability and business criticality of applications. Such scores can be categorized as derived metrics.

Not all applications are created equal from a maintainability perspective. Some applications siphon off a significant amount of resources and effort for basic maintenance. These situations typically arise when poorly designed applications receive additional feature set requests. Because the initial application was faulty, all the subsequent modifications push the limits of its capability. This is why proper alignment of the technology choice to available skill sets must occur. Otherwise, it will be almost impossible to determine the application maintenance fingerprint. Without incorporating this information into estimation models, to account for future enhancements and interoperability, the costing multipliers cannot be adequately applied to determine the necessary level of effort to maintain, enhance, build from scratch, or integrate with other applications. This is why derived metrics are so crucial to initial project planning and risk assessment discussions.

Several metrics can be derived:

- Technology risk

- Obsolescence

- Technical capability composite score

- Business criticality composite score

- Application maintainability

- Application complexity

In today's business climate, project decisions are made at a rapid pace and often in siloes. Metrics that are typically aligned to business goals are seldom considered by IT, in the context of IT projects and modernization exercises. One key metric that impacts the costing model is recovery time objective (RTO). RTO is the targeted duration of time, per the agreed upon service-level (SLA), within which an organization must respond to the distress calls of disrupted business processes and restore the impacted application or service. Depending on the criticality of the application or service, the associated consequences to business continuity could range anywhere from minor inconvenience to complete company shutdown, or somewhere in between. It is important to incorporate that disaster recovery impact analysis while planning a project. If it is determined that a project cannot afford any break in business continuity, then it will be deemed to have a higher RTO cost. Unfortunately, many enterprises do not give special importance to projects requiring heightened RTO. They probably find it easier to determine the number of business processes supported by the application based upon how many business segments or units are impacted. This discussion of business criticality can also be applied in the context of business alignment.

These metrics are related to business alignment:

■ Number of critical business processes supported

■ Number of business segments impacted

■ Recovery time objective (RTO)

■ Business criticality

Another category collects metrics relating to the required performance level of an application and whether that application is able to meet the expected performance goals. These metrics include technology and functional performance, continuous availability of an application and coverage without disruption or downtime, and approximate recovery time from any expected SLA deviations. Overall, SLA deviations should be measured from a support perspective.

These metrics are related to application performance:

■ Performance SLA deviation

■ Availability SLA deviation

■ Current recovery capability

■ SLA deviation

The identified categories of metrics are for illustration purposes. An organization should use these factors as guidelines to determine their own CEMM framework to collect data and apply the findings toward future projects. Let's be clear: building and maintaining a proper framework takes time. It is not an overnight endeavor. At first, an enterprise can start by collecting a few basic metrics for its estimation models. Then it can gradually build up the competency to engage more accurate techniques over time. Although it may seem daunting to establish a metrics-based application performance framework, ignoring the matter will only lead to more projects that run over time and over budget.

Metrics and KPI Measurement

If an enterprise already collects data and compiles metrics, it is ready for the next phase of the analysis. The next step ensures that the data findings are incorporated into an established framework, such as CEMM, and adjusted so that the multipliers can determine cost and effort of a modernization project. By employing these techniques, an organization can effectively determine the business benefits and business value of its core initiatives.

There are several ways to translate this valuable information into quantifiable terms and KPIs that measure the ROI:

- Per-dollar spend on modernization projects or IT projects in general

- Investments in new technologies

- Previous IT spend

- Percentage of revenue spend on IT

- Realized cost savings from APM implementation

These KPIs can be used broadly to justify an organization's IT strategy. They can also be engaged to guide the direction of project investment to secure stakeholder buy-in. This structured cost and estimation model will keep project risks low by identifying inherent problematic issues up front in the project life cycle. These KPIs will empower organizational leaders to gauge the value of existing IT investments and the value of future IT investments in new technologies to further derive business value.

Building and Executing an Estimation Model

At this point in our approach, we have established a cost and effort estimation for modernization exercises. Those estimations have evolved into the creation of a meta model derived from COCOMO II. That model has been tailored to the individual criteria required by the project. With the new estimation model in place, metrics and data can be collected, and adjustments can be made to the multipliers, resulting in an overall customized framework for that particular organization. The next section will discuss how to leverage the collected data and populate the framework with estimations of cost and effort to execute a project successfully.

Top-Down vs. Bottom-Up

Organizations have typically applied a high-level top-down approach or a standard bottom-up approach to compute the cost and effort of pending projects.

The bottom-up approach is engaged by projects for which simple predictions can be made regarding the number of necessary resources and the basic requirements for building or enhancing applications. At this stage, enterprises might prepare and release a request for proposal (RFP) to compare vendor approaches, resources, and total project cost. Responses to RFPs include a proposed high-level approach to meet the requirements, a suggested project plan with staffing needs, and a subset of key resources who are integral to the project. Project cost can be calculated, in part, by multiplying the defined hourly rates of a resource (project manager, architect, developer, QA, and so on) by the overall estimated hours needed for project completion. A small contingency variable may be added to account for unknown factors. The final number computed for the overall design, build, and test effort is used by an organization as binding to the vendor if its proposed RFP is accepted. This is an example of a bottom-up approach.

The top-down approach hardly uses an established computation formula; it is more unstructured and ad hoc. Many enterprises allocate certain budgetary dollars to build or modernize an application. Instead of engaging in a cost-estimation analysis, they rely on an expert to determine the general amount of project spend. Once the initiative is complete, the project is then retrofitted and tagged under that budgetary line item placeholder. In some situations, a business case is built using an estimation analogy; the benefits of a project and the level of spend are primarily based on past projects and experiences to determine the cost of the contemplated project. Other times, RFP responses are culled and matched with what executives believe are project execution costs, catapulting those vendors that arrived at similar ballpark estimates onto the project shortlist for further rounds of discussion.

Based on these loose measures of estimation, it is no surprise that more than 70 percent of projects are over time, over budget, or a combination of both. In reality, although slightly flawed, the top-down and bottom-up approaches are actually good mechanisms. The problem is that these approaches are incorrectly applied. In many instances, a bottom-up method may even provide more accurate estimates than the top-down method but will require more data and a concise definition of tasks and estimation based on resources with appropriate skill sets.

By illustration, the CEMM framework provides a refined top-down apparatus with core ideologies and philosophies drawn from the legendary COCOMO II. The remainder of this section highlights how to employ a functioning bottom-up approach constituted from basic elements of a project. The combination of the CEMM framework with another framework targeting a bottom-up cost and effort estimation exercise results in a hybrid approach that can produce results with greater accuracy in cost estimations for modernization projects.

In general, it is important that enterprises make an effort to lay the groundwork for an estimation model and framework with at least the following points in mind, even if they have never formalized such a framework previously:

- Being directionally correct on cost, not the accuracy or precision itself, is important in the beginning.

- Institute a self-learning model on cost leveraging metrics and measurements.

- Eventually move toward better precision, not necessarily being accurate on prediction all the time.

- Over time, as the framework matures and there are sufficient data points and history, predictions will eventually have a fair degree of accuracy as well.

NOTE
Accuracy is considered as how close a measurement is to the actual value. Precision, on the other hand, reflects the consistency of a measurement when repeated multiple times. Estimating the cost of a project is a predictive process. We typically calculate a single point value as the estimated cost. In reality, this single point value, called the cost estimate, is a point on a probability distribution, which represents many possible outcomes for the cost estimate.

Bottom-Up Costing with the Scalable Costing Framework (SCF)

The SCF is a costing framework that was conceived by me a couple of decades ago to compute the cost of projects initiated for building new applications for the nascent world wide web of that time. Since then the framework has undergone iterations and I have applied it to many types of projects over the years and improved it as well. SCF is designed to provide a flexible mechanism to identify and cost the unit quantum of work in any project. It is a bottom-up approach that not only relies on resource planning, but also attempts to determine the constituent components of the underlying project. At the outset, this estimation mechanism compartmentalizes the project into key phases such as architecture, design, development, testing, and acceptance. Specifically, the build phase receives a ground-up estimation, while the other phases are computed as a percentage of that pre-established development phase. Then, the data that was collected to populate the CEMM model will be inputted to determine this percentage of contribution for the remaining phases. This percentage will vary based on the type of project. In the absence of any data, organizations may rely on two additional techniques: *expert advice*, an estimation by seasoned and experienced contributors, and *estimation by analogy*, an estimation based on past projects and the time spent on each phase.

The parametric model becomes established once concrete data has been collected to justify and determine the remaining percentage for the other phases. Parametric estimates are based on empirical observations of past project executions. Combining all three estimations—expert experience, estimation by analogy, and parametric models—will provide cross-checks and validation to ensure that all the phases of a project are correctly computed using the project build as a foundational baseline.

The question then arises, how is the build phase computed when other phases use this key estimation as their own baseline? Figure 13-5 represents one view of the SCF. The capability baseline is an avenue to capture expert advice, estimation by analogy, and empirical data points available in an organization. The parameterized model focuses on a completely bottom-up approach to estimating effort per unit of work. This will vary based on the work type and complexity. The parameterized model will be accurate only if it collects a large number of data points over a long period of time and across a wide variety of projects. In order to generate a budget for a modernization project with a fair degree of accuracy, it is not sufficient just to compute the

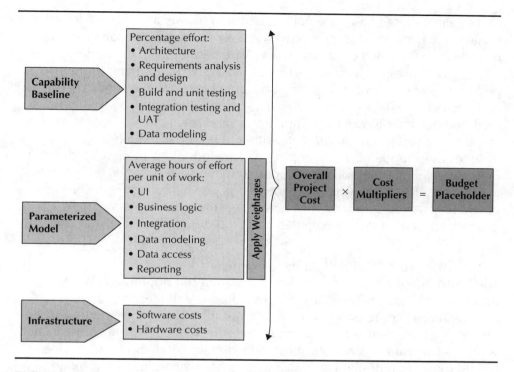

FIGURE 13-5.   *Parameterized bottom-up SCF built for deriving project costs*

project costs solely based on the basic parameterized model. Cost multipliers should also be applied to strengthen the calculation. These cost multipliers will be discussed in an upcoming section of this chapter.

Phases of Execution

Focusing further on the parametric model for costing, our approach breaks down the project into five phases:

- Architecture

- Requirements and design

- Build

- Testing and deployment support

- Infrastructure

Note that these phases are not sequential in nature, and this list does not suggest that they occur in a particular order or priority. This analysis does not advocate for a particular type of software development methodology either. The phases mentioned are merely illustrative of groupings from the perspective of cost and effort estimation. Enterprises should decide on using Agile, test-driven development, waterfall, or any other software development methodology after thoughtful consideration and research. Most companies employ SCF techniques in projects with a build phase, which typically includes most modernization projects. The methodology framework derives only the build phase effort and computes other phases as a percentage of that build phase. The framework does not incorporate infrastructure, technical components, or related costs as a percentage of the build phase. These amounts must be directly computed based on the specific project at hand.

Breaking Down the Phases

The build phase typically includes unit testing but not integration or performance testing. Those are addressed during the testing phase. The architecture-specific effort is separated out from the requirements and design phase since most new technology or reengineering efforts associated with modernization contain a substantial architectural component. Overall requirements and design can be viewed as both an architectural-related effort as well as a non-architecture-related effort. Application maintenance and support projects require much smaller architectural effort (maybe as low as 5 percent of the total); whereas modernization projects in general could have architectural related efforts ranging anywhere between 5 to 25 percent. The suggested standard guideline of total effort for a project averages at 12 percent.

Some experts suggest that architecture-related efforts should be called out separately from the requirements and design phase as a line item; on average the sum of architecture, requirements, and design efforts could collectively constitute around 30 percent of total effort for a modernization project. While general factors are useful for discussion purposes, it is important to reiterate that this total effort analysis should be tailored to the individual project type and scope.

Additionally, taking this equation one step further, the overall costing model must also include infrastructure-related expenses. These outlays include regular infrastructure, virtualized or cloud-based infrastructure, and software use licenses that are shared across projects. Depending on the size of the organization, the type of project, and the application, these amounts could be quite substantial.

The bottom-up approach to computing the build phase effort takes into account all the components that make up the build phase. Components that require build phase engagement include the following:

- User interface screens (web-based, mobile, and so on)

- Business logic developed as services, components, classes, and so on

- Number of integration points (between conceptual components)

- Data model and data access

- Reporting and analytics

- Messaging and data formats

Each identified component area should be analyzed, and a level of complexity for such components (simple, medium, complex, and so on) must be assigned. Using the ground-up method can only partially compute the level of necessary effort based upon historical data for the development of those components.

Cost Multipliers

A sample set of cost drivers include application attributes, system attributes, project attributes, and resource attributes. There could also be other constraints or inputs that factor into the cost multipliers. Ideally, these attributes should contribute a multiplier of 1, meaning that they do not greatly impact the overall effort or cost of the project either positively or negatively. Additionally, a mechanism could also be engaged where attributes contribute their weightage based on a scale from 0 to 100 percent. The collected metrics and the multipliers from various attributes can be rolled up to the level of a higher category and applied to this bottom-up effort computation.

Assumptions on Cost and Effort Estimation

Several assumptions factor into the actual estimation of cost and effort for a project. Organizations desire that their estimations be calculated with the confidence that variances will be quite small. Any modernization project should address the following basic assumptions:

■ The estimate of effort must include every step, including technical architecture, design, development, testing, project management, integration, data modeling, user acceptance, and documentation.

■ Developing estimates for various tasks such as build or data modeling should be based on a parametric model. The base estimates will be applied to each step of an initiative to compute an overall project estimate. The parametric model accounts for the use of specific technology in the development phase.

■ Ultimately, in the absence of data points, best-guess estimates are relied upon. High-level projections have a higher variance. Organizations that adopt this approach for the first time, without any significant available data points, most likely will experience higher variances. To lessen the impact, such organizations may look to data points from the industry or service providers to offset or recalibrate estimates. Over time, an organization can leverage its own data and metrics to develop its own baseline model.

■ Ideally, data points will be a combination of multiple sources such as market research, industry baselines, past executed projects, and vendor data.

■ If projects are completely or partially outsourced to a vendor, a determination of the unit costs charged by the vendor and the unit costs for an enterprise-led execution must be analyzed and compared. Typically, enterprise projects are blended with resources from both the enterprise and a vendor partner.

■ If the project execution extends across geographical boundaries, especially outside the United States, then the architecture and design phases would receive more stateside attention, whereas the development and testing phases could become more offshore intensive. These geographical decisions can impact project costs quite substantially.

Issues Encountered in Measuring Returns

When measuring ROI, some interesting issues can arise. Intangible assets are difficult to account for when computing financial returns. If a modernization project creates significant Intellectual Property, for example, should that value be quantified and included in the ROI? Many times, there is no easy answer for such questions. The implementation of an ROI methodology needs adequate time for its own maturation and adoption within a company. When multiple scenarios are presented, sometimes it is easier to compare them using a TCO approach. More importantly, there is some risk when an enterprise depends solely on ROI, TCO, or another methodology to make modernization determinations. The need for a holistic portfolio modernization approach that compares various events and provides comprehensive solutions should be driven by financial, technical, and other operational measures.

Strategies for Strategic Advantage

During the modernization of an application portfolio, the enterprise must aim to create a strategic advantage for itself. Although an enterprise may have previously built a set of applications and may currently run and maintain those projects, there is no inherent justification for the continuation of that strategy on a go-forward basis. Following are a set of suggestions to be considered by an enterprise while determining adequate effort and reliable cost for modernization activities. In this context, the total ongoing cost of ownership versus the benefits to an enterprise must be reviewed. Some potential approaches and strategies for acquiring new applications or enhancing existing applications are depicted in Figure 13-6.

Build vs. Buy   Consider buying packaged software or leasing hardware and infrastructure to address business needs for providing a cost-effective solution rather than internally developing the application. Figure 13-6 illustrates considerations for evaluating whether an application should be custom built to the organization or whether an off-the-shelf package or product should be bought, customized, and generally implemented. The selection process in an enterprise can be quite lengthy. This suggested framework and structure could aid the selection process by highlighting necessary checkpoints to drive the decision-making process forward.

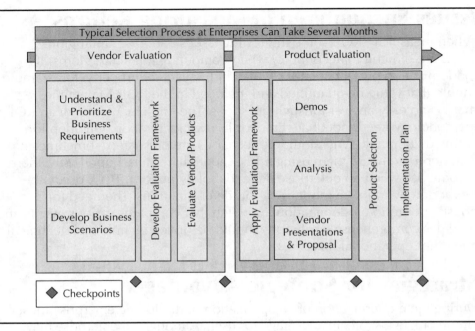

FIGURE 13-6. *Product and package evaluation methodology*

Share or Reuse Services Applications can comprise micro services and be designed from the ground-up for potential reuse across multiple lines of business. Development environments, QA environments, and infrastructure must also be reused to a great extent.

Determine the Right Quality of Service Not all applications are created equal. Some applications are business-critical, while others are a mere convenience. It is important to determine the necessary QoS to ensure that an application will meet or exceed the performance, scalability, availability, reliability, and security requirements established by the business. Considerable costs are associated with extremely high QoS, so it is important to understand the specific requirements of each application.

Keep Solutions Simple Architect only for need and do not over-engineer applications. Keep solutions simple so that estimation models and risk recommendations are easy to make. The application should be easy to maintain, enhance, and support over time.

Reduce Life Cycle Cost and TCO   Look at the overall life cycle cost of a solution and not just the development effort.

Adhere to Best Practices and a Specific Technology Stack   The design and development of applications must be based upon the use of industry standard tools, technologies, and techniques. Enterprises that establish their own best practices and technology stack will be better able to estimate effort because they have only one specific stack to master.

Summary

This chapter addressed estimation efforts and costing variables of modernization engagements. The primary focus of the discussion centered on the development of estimation models and metrics. Several factors determine the costs incurred for executing a modernization project or other IT initiative within an enterprise. For the modernization of an entire portfolio of applications, shared costs among similar projects should be identified.

The CEMM meta model was introduced and provided an avenue for the enterprise to customize and develop a top-down framework best suited to compute costs and efforts according to its own individual needs. In order for the framework to be useful and provide accurate estimations with low variances between estimates and actuals, it is important to populate the model with the best possible data points. These inputs can be obtained from within the organization, from past projects, partners and vendors, industry standards, and market research. SCF, a bottom-up costing framework was also introduced to help compute the effort for a quantum of work. As an enterprise builds and refines its baseline to derive costing estimates, it can slowly eliminate the guesswork from its analysis. Relevant and established metrics will continue to provide insight into the performance of enterprise projects and indicate the cost multipliers and weights that must be assigned to the calculation.

The costing and effort estimation is as much art as it is science. Adopting a combination of expert advice and experience, analogies and comparisons to past projects, and a data-driven set of algorithms based on a parametric model will ensure that organizations will be highly successful in anticipating and future-proofing their enterprise projects.

CHAPTER
14

Approaches for Large-Scale Modernizations

This book has canvassed the various aspects of modernization in general and Java modernization in particular. Although the discussion may seem exhaustive, there is one last topic to cover: the logistics of large-scale modernizations. We have already reviewed how to modernize and migrate Java applications within an enterprise. We have not analyzed how an enterprise or company with lines of Java code in the tens or hundreds of millions can ensure reliable, accurate, and cost-effective migration of that code base to the latest Java platform or other versions of various open-source libraries.

What is the approach or game plan for this type of mega-modernization? Can large-scale modernizations still maintain consistency and rapid agility? Can these projects be conducted on a regular basis as newer versions, interim releases, and updates to the Java platform and other libraries become available? We know that the coordination required to migrate just one large application portfolio containing a few hundred applications requires scaled efforts and the mobilization of resources for a significant duration of time. Without a great amount of planning and foresight, an enterprise could not undertake such an endeavor. Now picture a modernization exercise canvassing thousands of applications spanning many application portfolios across a global organization. Visualize a company with many products and versions of products that incorporate many millions of lines of Java code. Where do you begin? How can you keep track of it all? These are the questions that we will address in this chapter.

This chapter draws upon my experiences of designing and executing several large-scale application portfolio modernization exercises at global enterprises. Over the years, I pioneered targeted approaches and refined these methodologies to simplify this undertaking. The successful completion of a mega-modernization project requires consistency, organization, research, and accountability of the project team. During the course of this chapter, we will discuss solution stacks and necessary processes for large-scale modernizations to all but guarantee the success of such modernization programs. This final chapter builds upon all the information presented in the previous chapters and ties together the major concepts of this book.

The Java Modernization Solution Platform

The impetus for enterprises to modernize large Java application portfolios typically stems from rising dissatisfaction with the current status quo. These rumblings eventually make it to corporate executives, who then prioritize budgetary dollars and resources for this must-do program. However, not all organizations are equipped to handle these types of massive projects. Most companies tend to follow a less risky path by identifying specific applications or a group of applications to modernize. If reengineering is required, enterprises are even more selective about the applications they choose to tackle at any one time.

Very few organizations today have a mature APM process to carry out regular assessments and modernizations of their application portfolios. So what factors typically influence the departure from incremental upgrades and reengineering toward the adoption of large-scale modernization initiatives? The primary factors are the sheer cost and inability to manage haywire applications that create unnecessary havoc and frustration for business and IT stakeholders. Leaders then recognize that the business could be severely impacted without a planned intervention. Until that point, many organizations rationalize the problem by throwing maintenance dollars at the misbehaving applications to keep them up and running. Although that approach may be sufficient to address a few applications needing to be enhanced or sunsetted, it is not practical for large-scale portfolio decision-making.

The typical drivers that lead to large-scale modernizations include cost, redundancy and duplication, integration and process issues, and aging portfolios. In the next sections, we will closely review and analyze these factors in depth.

Unmanageable Cost

Application portfolios are central to the core business of any modern enterprise. It is inevitable that organizations will spend a few percentage points of the company's top line on annual IT spending. Most enterprises tend to prioritize older applications that siphon off available IT budgetary funds because they are characterized as a necessary evil to the core functioning of the company. The technology and application landscape of such portfolios also tend to grow and diversify haphazardly through the decades. Over time, the budgets for existing application portfolios begin to spiral. Maintenance costs radically increase due to inefficiently enhanced legacy applications that attempt to address new business requirements. This unmanaged cost and the diversity of application portfolios lead to inflexible and expensive ownership scenarios. Eventually, senior management must make cost-shifting decisions and undertake large-scale modernization to rationalize their tightly intertwined application portfolios. The unintended result of this cycle curtails necessary funding toward new projects.

Redundancy and Duplication

Functional and technical redundancies often result from the unchecked growth and creation of IT applications. This is a large-scale problem. The lack of a central database and clear communication among business units often permit multiple stakeholders to license redundant technologies independently to support their applications, which can include off-the-shelf software packages, custom applications built with technical libraries or components providing similar functionality, middleware and messaging components, or even multiple open source libraries that provide basically the same functionality. Even the adoption and use of open-source libraries is not uniform among various units within the same enterprise. This inconsistency leads to the proliferation and duplication of similar technologies, resulting in increased support and maintenance costs, training, and hiring of multiple resource skill sets.

Business units frequently build similar application functionality or implement similar business processes without ever consulting other portfolio stakeholders. In enterprises that lack centralized IT governance and best practices, there is widespread functional duplication and redundancy among their portfolios. I have witnessed situations in which an organization has five or six separate customer databases, with each business unit claiming that its version is the single source of truth for customer data!

Enterprises that proactively view IT portfolio modernization as a shared-services approach are better equipped to control functional and technical proliferation. However, this is much easier said than done. Rationalizing applications between business units can be tricky. Each application needs to be rationalized in the context of the larger application portfolio as a whole as well in as its interconnectedness with the other applications with which it interoperates. Similarly, mergers and acquisitions activity invariably leads to additional scenarios of redundancy and duplication. Successful M&A deals often result in heterogeneous application landscapes, disparate software versions, and a variety of third-party libraries and frameworks that require immediate rationalization and modernization to prevent material interruption to the newly combined business. Multiple applications that provide similar functionality also need to be culled to operate as one. If the M&A activity involves two large organizations, the scale of the required combined modernization will be large as well.

Ineffective Integration and Process Inconsistency

The serious business risk posed by inadequately managed IT application portfolios is a key driver for large-scale modernization initiatives. With a constant turnover of IT managers, developers, and analysts, a significant loss of domain and application knowledge can result. This attrition, combined with a lack of adequate APM processes and knowledge management, force enterprises into a difficult scenario, which results in application portfolios becoming a "black box" and IT teams struggling to keep the business running. I have seen situations in which business units are entirely unsure of which version of an application or library has been compiled to run in production, making it almost impossible to integrate a new functionality or enhancement or test a newly added application.

Without proper test cases, this problem reaches far beyond the technical and functional levels. This issue also manifests at the process level, where a lack of knowledge exists about the design of application functionality to support business processes. When these business processes undergo reengineering, it becomes very difficult to modify the applications adequately to support changing business needs. Similarly, integrations between applications and external vendor systems can become largely ineffective.

When an enterprise is faced with such an impending crisis, it calls for a large-scale modernization effort to rectify the situation and regain control of application portfolios. To be clear, this does not entail taking a "big bang" approach, ripping and replacing every malfunctioning application. Rather, it calls for a thoughtful and thorough assessment of the application portfolios, a systematic knowledge assembly about each application and a methodical approach to universal modernization. Later in this chapter, we will discuss wave-based approaches to large-scale modernization as a way to mitigate and minimize business risk effectively.

Aging Java Application Portfolio

Another contributing factor to consider during large-scale modernizations is the age of applications. I have run into several situations in which the entire portfolio of applications was a few decades old and a mix of Java and non-Java applications. In the case of Java applications and modern technology in general, after about five years, most portfolios become dated and significantly "behind the eight ball"; after a decade, these portfolios are obsolete. To illustrate this, imagine an organization with large Java applications portfolios containing three or four versions of the JDK dating back almost 15 years! I am astonished to see how companies in this situation attempt to move their business forward. On the flip-side, other enterprises choose to manage their application portfolios proactively and revamp them on a large scale every 5 to 10 years. They understand the gravity of aging portfolios and are not intimidated by the disparate versions of Java, numerous third-party libraries, or the fact that they may unearth a highly risky situation through this exercise.

So how can an enterprise interested in deploying a large-scale modernization exercise conduct one at the organization level or at an individual application portfolio level? Successfully migrating hundreds, or even thousands, of applications is not a quick fix or a simple transformation. This endeavor requires careful planning and the initiation of a program that will monitor the portfolio for a couple of years until completion. It also requires developing a reusable solution stack, since not all applications are designed to be migrated in one fell swoop.

The Solution Stack

The *solution stack* is our term for the comprehensive, all-inclusive solution to address large-scale migration efforts for hundreds or thousands of applications with millions of lines of code. Rationalizing application portfolios and modernizing Java applications should not be thought of as a static exercise, especially at a large scale. Such a program should be constant, agile, and long running, eventually becoming a part of the enterprise DNA. As such, it must be integrated into the inner workings of both IT and business units in a cross-functional way.

It is crucial that senior management and individual stakeholders who own and operate application portfolios be aligned. They must collectively understand the overall processes necessary for planning the modernization exercise, decision-making criteria, execution, investment, and operation of the migrated portfolios. One way to bring uniformity to this activity is to standardize on a solution stack. When a single solution stack is adopted enterprise-wide, it serves as a rallying mechanism for the overall vision of the execution.

This solution stack is not just a technical stack. It is a solution stack that lays out the processes and provides templates and other assets so that every aspect of the modernization initiative is addressed. If the enterprise maintains a central governance authority or a core APM team, that entity would be responsible for revising and keeping the solution stack current by incorporating updates in a continuous manner.

Figure 14-1 shows the different components of a modernization solution stack (in particular, the OpenMod stack, which will be discussed in the next section). In the context of application portfolio modernization, such a solution stack will contain the following types of assets:

- **Process plans**   Large-scale modernization leverages APM-related processes, templates, and governance mechanisms to ensure that company-wide modernization programs are successful.

- **Reusable components**   APM and portfolio modernization are continuous functions that lend themselves to be specifically tailored to an organization. Numerous repeatable and reusable artifacts can be created to support future large-scale modernizations.

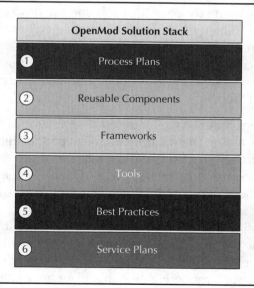

FIGURE 14-1.   *High level components of the OpenMod Java modernization solution stack*

■ **Frameworks**   Frameworks enable an organization to encapsulate functionality and effort so that future projects can leverage previous work already completed. The frameworks in a modernization solution stack provide conceptual building blocks and enable an organization to expand its initiatives quickly without having to research and build the analysis layer or algorithms needed to carry out management and modernization of the application portfolios.

■ **Tools**   All modernization and migration efforts involve assessing, analyzing, and decision-making about source code, application components, integration points, databases, configuration files, and many other tangible assets. Sometimes, application binaries require reverse-engineering, and performance characteristics need to be fully understood. Similarly, the migration of application code bases to the cloud or its deployment in a distributed architecture necessitates a set of tools to enable such efforts to be automated and executed to ensure maximum efficiency, productivity, and predictability.

■ **Best practices**   The creation and communication of processes, tools, and frameworks is somewhat easy. The challenge arises at the time of execution and compliance with the new guidelines. Unless there is uniformity in the usage of the tools and the processes to measure progress, it is difficult to improve upon defined best practices. Because of the inherent risk in the execution of large-scale (or even small-scale) application modernization initiatives, the establishment of best practices can capture the knowledge essential to achieving consistent success and the ability to measure and articulate that achievement.

■ **Support plans and SLAs**   Rarely do large enterprises own and execute IT programs alone. The majority establish partnerships with vendors to help build, test, support, and operate various IT applications. These partner resources could be integrated with the enterprise IT teams, or the applications could be completely outsourced. This decision will be different for each organization. It is important to define the roles and responsibilities of the vendor company: Does it have the right to "own" some of the applications? How will application knowledge be shared? Where will that knowledge reside? Enterprises must also keep in mind that such modernization initiatives are marathons, and not sprints. The segmented application portfolios are typically a subset or select group of applications identified to be modernized or migrated.

The Solution Stack Unpacked

This section lists the various assets under the main categories of asset types that were introduced in the previous section. This is a blueprint for an enterprise to create its own set of assets and customize them to support the solution stack in the context of the enterprise's modernization initiatives.

Process Plans

- Templates for a standard APM approach
- Migration and modernization methodology documents
- Governance process
- Costing and effort estimation process
- Segmentation and wave-planning approach
- Application attributes and data capture process

Reusable Components

- Knowledge base of rules to determine what gets migrated between two versions
- Costing and effort estimation templates
- Data collection and assessment templates
- Roadmap and project planning templates
- Business case building and ROI calculation templates
- Application portfolio assessment templates

Frameworks

- Rapid migration frameworks
- Application portfolio segmentation framework
- Application scoring
- Standard libraries useful for migration and modernization
- Effort and cost estimation framework
- Metrics collection

Tools

- Static source code analysis
- Analysis of jar, war, and other archive files
- Analysis of compiled class files
- Generation and analysis of AST
- XPath expression evaluators
- Migration point identification tools
- Integration points and API analysis
- Application log analysis
- Reverse-engineering Java applications
- Automatic code conversion and migration
- Database analysis tools
- Merging code bases
- Automated testing tools
- Performance analysis and workload estimation

Best Practices

- Modernization and migration best practices
- Java coding guidelines for easy maintenance and migration
- Best practices to use open-source libraries
- APM best practices
- Wave planning and program execution
- Best practices for outsourcing engagements
- Business case and ROI best practices
- Performance engineering

Support Plans and SLAs

- Modernization factory models for running large migration programs

- Outsourcing and partner relationships for APM

- Continuous support for maintaining and servicing application portfolios

To help enterprises easily establish an initial customized solution stack, it would be prudent to leverage a readily available meta-solution stack. The amount of time and effort required to create a modernization solution stack from scratch is extremely daunting. Teams that are not experienced with formulating such a modernization solution stack could follow the wrong path. To prevent this misguidance, a meta-solution stack could help teams leverage and deploy the correct plan.

One such solution stack that provides various assets is the *OpenMod solution stack* (OpenMod or OMSS, pronounced "Ohms"). I conceived and created this stack, along with the input and contributions from a few other industry veterans, who tapped into their collective experiences with several prior modernization exercises. It is our vision for OMSS to become the solution stack of choice for Java modernization initiatives across the globe. OMSS incorporates open-source components as part of the solution stack and also provides other assets, including Excel sheets and document templates to address areas such as processes, best practices, tools, and support. OMSS can be used for individual Java applications, portfolios of applications, or even very large-scale programs that encompass hundreds or thousands of applications. This solution stack uniquely benefits small, medium-size, and very large enterprises equally. Although we will review the salient features of OMSS, it is important to note that at the time of this writing, the OMSS has not yet been released to the public. When it does become available, it will be a rich resource that offers out-of-the-box ease of use.

The OMSS, depicted in Figure 14-2, provides a blueprint of the assets that make up the solution stack for large-scale Java migrations. These assets include detailed process plans, reusable components, frameworks, migration tools, service plans, best practice documents, and support services for an accelerated and smooth implementation of Java modernization initiatives. Whether it is an Excel sheet capturing portfolio assessment data or a sample costing template leveraging the COCOMO II derived Costing and Estimation Meta Model (CEMM) statistics, the universal solution stack brings consistency, quality, and acceleration to large-scale migration or modernization initiatives.

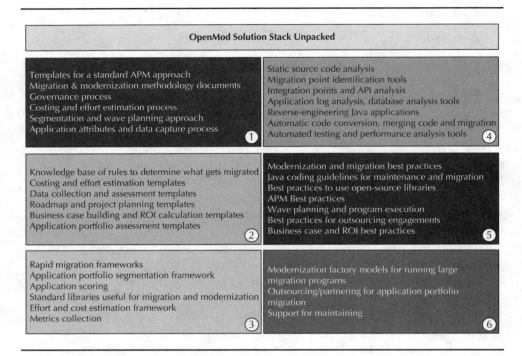

OpenMod Solution Stack Unpacked

Box 1:
Templates for a standard APM approach
Migration & modernization methodology documents
Governance process
Costing and effort estimation process
Segmentation and wave planning approach
Application attributes and data capture process

Box 4:
Static source code analysis
Migration point identification tools
Integration points and API analysis
Application log analysis, database analysis tools
Reverse-engineering Java applications
Automatic code conversion, merging code and migration
Automated testing and performance analysis tools

Box 2:
Knowledge base of rules to determine what gets migrated
Costing and effort estimation templates
Data collection and assessment templates
Roadmap and project planning templates
Business case building and ROI calculation templates
Application portfolio assessment templates

Box 5:
Modernization and migration best practices
Java coding guidelines for maintenance and migration
Best practices to use open-source libraries
APM Best practices
Wave planning and program execution
Best practices for outsourcing engagements
Business case and ROI best practices

Box 3:
Rapid migration frameworks
Application portfolio segmentation framework
Application scoring
Standard libraries useful for migration and modernization
Effort and cost estimation framework
Metrics collection

Box 6:
Modernization factory models for running large migration programs
Outsourcing/partnering for application portfolio migration
Support for maintaining

FIGURE 14-2. *OMSS schematic*

Once the assets are identified, whether a part of OMSS or another similar solution stack aimed at modernization and migration of Java application portfolios, these assets will need specific customization before the enterprise can leverage the stack. There are several reasons for the customization of assets in a modernization solution stack. Most importantly, application portfolios greatly differ among various enterprises. The organizations themselves may be small, medium-size, or large. The size of the application portfolio, defined either by the number of individual applications or the millions of lines of code, could vary as well. The specific technology components, versions of services, and libraries used will most likely be different among some or many of the applications.

Additionally, depending on the type of industry, enterprise applications will contain process and functional components that require deep domain knowledge before decomposition efforts can create a sound architectural understanding of the portfolio. Integration points can vary from simple to complex and come in many different flavors. The in-house skill set, application knowledge, ownership, budgetary processes, and support and maintenance for application portfolios will all influence the specific customization of a solution stack before it can be leveraged for modernization initiatives.

The first step toward adopting a solution stack is to identify a meta-solution stack that will meet enterprise needs. Before that solution stack can be customized and adopted, an accurate cost and effort estimation model to build and modernize the application portfolio is necessary. This estimation model is relative to each enterprise and its specific engineering processes, resources, and available skill sets. Each solution stack will come with assessment templates and an overall APM methodology, framework, and assets to roll out the initiative. When an organization undertakes APM for the first time, the enterprise is best served to take the initial steps to create a knowledge repository of its applications before leveraging the APM-related assets from the solution stack to build an understanding of its application portfolios. The assessment of related assets is not generic. This analysis should be a tailored customization to the distinct needs of an enterprise.

Ultimately, every organization is unique, and each customization must reflect the flexibility and adaptability of the particular enterprise. This also applies to the organization-specific decision-making necessary to evolve the governance, metrics, and reporting systems. To place itself in the best possible position, an enterprise must successfully customize its modernization solution stack, and this is especially true with large-scale modernizations.

Large-Scale Modernizations

For large enterprises with hundreds or even thousands of applications under management, the ownership of these applications can be fragmented with several business units and subunits operating them. Needless to say, each subunit or subgroup has its own idea about how to administer, maintain, and support the applications based on available budgets, business requirements, user-requested enhancements, availability of resources or skill sets, and many other related factors.

By taking a collective view of applications across multiple groups and business units, enterprises can enhance decision-making to allocate budgets and resources optimally to improve business goals. In this section, we will analyze the final piece of the APM puzzle: how to bring repeatability and scalability into the management and maintenance of multiple application portfolios.

Java Modernization Factory

The *Java Modernization Factory (JMF)* is a construct built for scalability to address enterprise application portfolios of all sizes. The JMF provides an opportunity for a high degree of optimization and automation of the modernization process across application portfolios over a long period of time. The JMF concept institutes a level of unprecedented standardization for processes, resources, and technology elements, enabling application development teams to greatly compress the time-to-market for delivery of modernization programs, reduce overall development costs, and improve predictability and productivity with minimal risk and cost.

The fundamental approach to this type of large-scale optimization is akin to a factory that produces thousands of widgets with the same quality and characteristics. These widgets are churned out based on this scalable approach, regardless of the specific shift or individual contributor. The JMF enables enterprises that own thousands of applications or product companies engineering millions of lines of code to automate the modernization of their Java application code base with consistent quality, predictability, and periodicity.

The concept of a software factory is not new. The idea existed decades ago when Japanese companies such as Hitachi, NEC, Toshiba, and Fujitsu adopted the term and applied it to their organizational approach to technology development, automation, and standardization. JMF-based application modernization addresses the problem of traditional migration where applications are individually transformed without taking advantage of the collective knowledge gained or the assets produced from previous upgrades of similar applications.

The JMF is enabled with a modernization solution stack platform with built-in tools and processes necessary to carry out the modernization of Java applications on a regular basis and in a consistent manner. Figure 14-3 illustrates one enterprise approach for establishing the necessary goals to institute a JMF: enterprise goals, JMF goals, and the goals for a blueprint to build and operate the factory.

The factory set up with requisite teams, resources, engineering processes, and engineering tools is contingent upon the widely varying application development tools and release management tools used by the teams. These modernization factory tools are separate and distinct from OMSS tools, processes, and other assets that are pertinent only to the Java modernization solution. This is akin to an automobile factory that has its own manufacturing

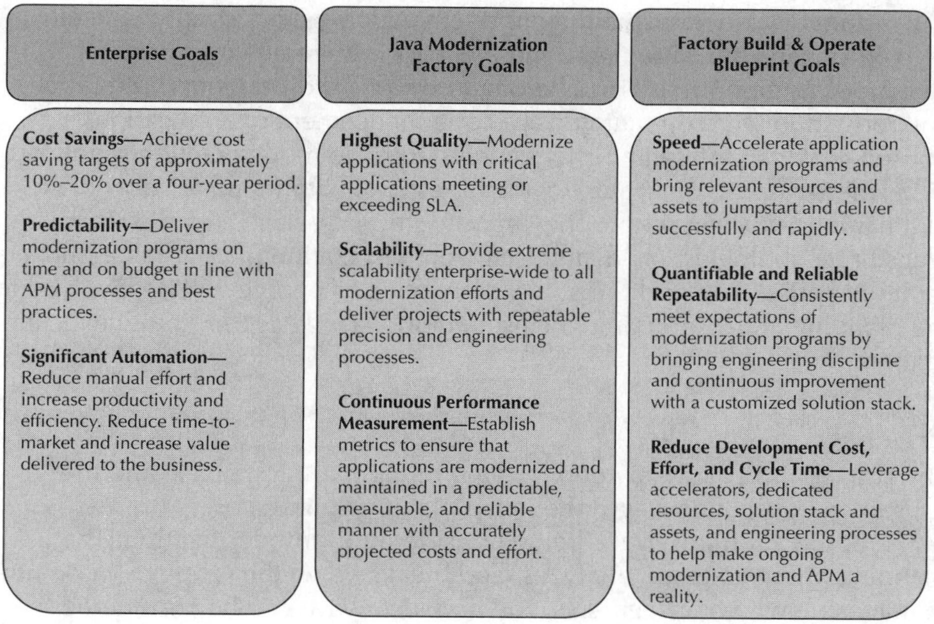

Enterprise Goals	Java Modernization Factory Goals	Factory Build & Operate Blueprint Goals
Cost Savings—Achieve cost saving targets of approximately 10%–20% over a four-year period.	**Highest Quality**—Modernize applications with critical applications meeting or exceeding SLA.	**Speed**—Accelerate application modernization programs and bring relevant resources and assets to jumpstart and deliver successfully and rapidly.
Predictability—Deliver modernization programs on time and on budget in line with APM processes and best practices.	**Scalability**—Provide extreme scalability enterprise-wide to all modernization efforts and deliver projects with repeatable precision and engineering processes.	**Quantifiable and Reliable Repeatability**—Consistently meet expectations of modernization programs by bringing engineering discipline and continuous improvement with a customized solution stack.
Significant Automation—Reduce manual effort and increase productivity and efficiency. Reduce time-to-market and increase value delivered to the business.	**Continuous Performance Measurement**—Establish metrics to ensure that applications are modernized and maintained in a predictable, measurable, and reliable manner with accurately projected costs and effort.	**Reduce Development Cost, Effort, and Cycle Time**—Leverage accelerators, dedicated resources, solution stack and assets, and engineering processes to help make ongoing modernization and APM a reality.

FIGURE 14-3. *Defining the goals for establishing a modernization factory*

processes and tools to fabricate vehicles; however, the tools, software, and processes needed for architecting future automobile designs are separate from the raw manufacture on the factory floor.

Although enterprises have typically followed traditional approaches to modernization, the documentation of resources and training programs is not enough to apply previously gained knowledge and insight consistently and effectively from prior application migrations. The JMF addresses such problems by capturing, codifying, and leveraging proven practices, processes, and tools to serve as a reusable blueprint for adoption by other enterprise teams with similar needs. The productivity improvements are enormous as migration becomes a repeatable exercise.

The age-old mantra of "people, process, technology" is applicable to the JMF as well. Although the ownership of the applications themselves is distributed across the organization, the modernization factory should be a centralized function that benefits the entire enterprise. So regardless of application portfolio ownership, the migration and modernization of Java applications can be carried out by leveraging this modernization factory.

People

The resources associated with the modernization factory should typically be well versed with APM, Java, and the tools and frameworks used for Java modernization. They may belong to various project teams within the enterprise and work on maintenance or enhancement of applications housed under a particular business unit. From the modernization point of view, these resources are subject matter experts with intimate knowledge of the applications in scope. They may additionally have expertise in niche areas or technologies. For a large-scale modernization program that impacts multiple application portfolios, this core group of people will be involved in the planning, effort, and timeline estimations as well as the overall execution of the program.

Process

The process is broadly divided into the initial planning phase and the subsequent execution stage. The initial planning phase covers the assessment of the application portfolios being considered for modernization. The planning phase assesses, analyzes, and breaks down the scope of work into manageable waves or segments. The first such wave can be considered the pilot wave, which typically identifies a few applications for migration. The pilot wave serves as an excellent time to iron out any kinks in the processes and mitigate any risks up front before attempting to migrate the various application portfolios en masse. The execution stage leverages the tools actually responsible for the overall migration. The execution stage identifies the required resources necessary to ramp up and ramp down operations. Finally, as with all processes and frameworks, the JMF must also establish a set of metrics to measure the modernization factory itself and its overall governance framework after successful execution.

Following is a suggested list of attributes that could be tracked and measured:

- Predictability (meeting delivery expectations)
- Predictability (dealing with risk mitigation)
- Agility
- Scalability
- Flexibility

- Adaptability

- Automation

- Cost reduction

- Efficiency (effort reduction)

- Optimization (repeatability)

- Standardization

- Churn management (plugging in new resources without drop-off)

- Resource management (ramp-up and ramp-down of resources)

Technology

The JMF must also assimilate the requisite technology for carrying out a repeatable modernization at scale. The adoption of an existing modernization solution stack will save time, effort, and cost by providing several key technology elements up front for the initiative. These software engineering tools and technologies must also be scrutinized to find any synergies or overlaps with the modernization solution stack. For example, using source code analyzers Sonar and PMD as part of regular software engineering efforts at an enterprise would be a good fit with the OMSS, because it leverages both PMD and Sonar. For reengineering and modernization to a micro-container services platform, several emerging container solutions such as Docker, Kubernetes, or Kontena can be leveraged. Messaging architectures, integration of mobile solution stacks, and other emerging technologies, including Internet of Things (IoT), all require these engineering and modernization tools. The OMSS provides the necessary blueprint to begin. This, coupled with best practices, solution architecture, and APM, will shape the software engineering technology strategy to customize the modernization solution stack. This process will yield the most comprehensive and thorough results for the enterprise in the long term.

Factory Design and Operating Model

Several prerequisites need to be identified and addressed before the factory can be planned, designed, and built for operation. The overall approach to building a successful factory relies on first implementing a process to establish these specific prerequisites for the enterprise. This general approach, a three-step process, is highlighted in Figure 14-4: analyze, plan, and design.

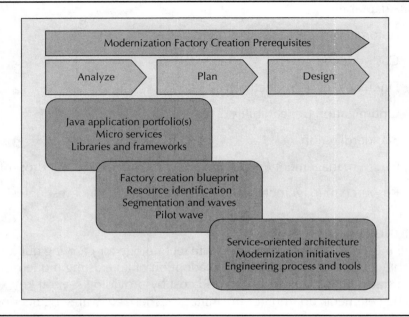

FIGURE 14-4. *Steps to build a JMF*

In the analyze step, the requirements for the factory are analyzed using the actual Java application portfolios in scope. If the project is an enterprise-wide effort, the analysis phase becomes more complex and could require more time or additional resources for the coordinated effort. The analysis must also take into account various homegrown or third-party libraries and frameworks that are used by the applications, including any open-source libraries or components. Coarse or fine-grained services, if any, must also be included in the analysis since the modernization of the portfolio can impact these services as well.

The plan step focuses on the creation of the factory blueprint. This stage answers the questions, what resources are needed and where will they come from? Segmenting and identifying the waves is also a prerequisite. Otherwise, the prioritization of the factory resources cannot be carried out efficiently. Depending on the scope of the pilot wave, the factory blueprint can be modified to build up and on-board necessary resources gradually.

The third and final step, design, involves the details of the factory blueprint. This blueprint highlights the engineering process and tools necessary for the factory to function alongside the modernization initiatives that are already in flight at that point in time. This is an opportunity for the factory resources to engage and provide expertise to current programs, thereby enhancing and expediting the business value to the enterprise. Factory resources can also engage in and contribute to micro-services architectures and SOA programs in flight, since those programs also involve modernization activities. This design step is carefully tailored to allow immediate factory involvement in the selected programs. The pilot wave is the model for this build-out of prioritized resources. Figure 14-5 depicts the overall factory operating model and highlights both the build and operate segments.

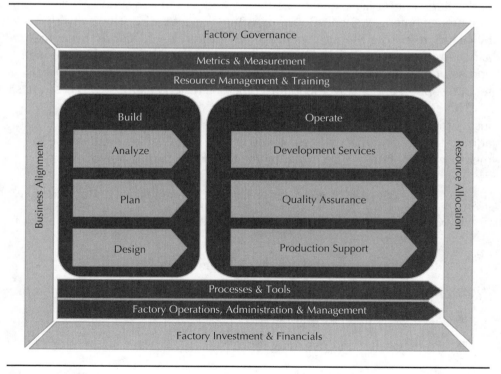

FIGURE 14-5. *Building and operating a JMF*

As Figure 14-5 illustrates, the Operate block captures the key operational items of primary concern to the factory:

- Allocation of modernization talent and alignment of skill sets from the available pool of resources for various projects

- Assisting with quality assurance and testing of the applications after successful migration or modernization

- Production support of migrated and modernized applications for a finite period until the application team takes management responsibility

The primary focus of factory operations is the successful management of development services, quality assurance, and production support of Java modernization engagements occurring within the enterprise. This is enabled by factory resources adequately engaged to support key functions. Resource allocation, governance of the factory, management of the financial investment, and assurance of business alignment are the key operational areas that also require support and involvement from other interested enterprise business units.

The consistent value-add of factory resources can be calculated to justify the additional cost to an organization. In fact, proper governance, administration, and management of the factory will enable an enterprise to measure all the benefits accorded by the factory, including the following:

- Reduced cost of modernization due to the efficiencies and productivity

- Optimizations achieved due to scalable and repeatable modernization processes

- Reduction in time and use of minimal resources

- Knowledge management and knowledge sharing across the enterprise

- Savings realized by automation

- Predictability and risk mitigation

The concept of shared services across an enterprise has been in existence for more than two decades. Specifically, several IT departments leverage virtualized infrastructure as shared services where business units are charged based on actual usage only. Although multiple mechanisms can fund the operation of enterprise programs, when it comes to the JMF, the best way to jumpstart the initiative begins with the centralized investment with an aim of enterprise-wide support for modernization programs.

Once the factory takes shape and becomes operational, the factory will be able to fund itself using charge-backs against the programs that leverage factory assets and resources. Because the cost of implementing modernization programs should be lowered by leveraging the factory, this will create a win–win situation for both the IT department and the business units. With this supplementary cost savings, enterprises can apply these additional funds toward new projects rather than the typical status quo maintenance and support of existing applications.

Figure 14-6 illustrates the first few years in the investment cycle for a JMF. As the factory evolves through its own metamorphosis of build, operate, expand, and sustain, the key milestones achieved help to transform the operations into a large cost-savings center for the entire enterprise.

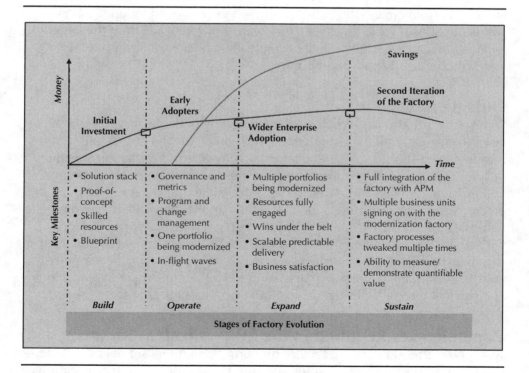

FIGURE 14-6. *The investment life cycle of a JMF*

Inside JMF

So how do these typical activities take place inside the JMF, and what is the JMF management scope for its day-to-day tasks and operations? The major focus of the factory and its resources are to meet the defined delivery expectations of the initiatives engaged in by factory resources. For example, it could be a wave of migration, a specific modernization project, or an APM engagement. The factory sets up the build, QA, integration, testing, and release of applications undergoing modernization. If modernization involves adoption of micro-services and the reengineering of applications into a micro-services architecture, then the scope of the factory's involvement will be to assist this process by creating and exposing available services.

Another important factory function includes the deployment and configuration of services prior to handing off the project to its original stakeholders. Although an enterprise IT department may have an in-house QA team for testing various applications, it is equally essential that the factory enlist and leverage skilled QA experts to perform necessary functional testing to ensure that the applications are modernized to function in the expected manner. Performance testing also becomes a critical need for applications with strict SLAs. Eventually, the factory team will disengage from the larger application team so that the application team can take over and run their newly modernized application portfolio.

Outside JMF

Some activities also occur outside the exclusivity of the factory, and these tasks are typically run by the larger application team. The coordination of business analysts and subject matter experts to determine whether specific business processes need enhancement or new business requirements need implementation takes place outside the JMF. Additionally, the involvement of enterprise architecture groups in SOA-related application transformations also transpires outside this scope. The identification of potential services, along with designing and defining those services, typically occurs outside the factory within a specific business unit and aligned IT group. Similarly, development of test cases, training, and ultimately supporting the modernized applications and services also falls outside the exclusive scope of the factory.

Competencies Required in the Modernization Factory

To execute a modernization factory blueprint, a minimal set of competencies must be gathered together during the build phase of the factory creation before it can become independently operational. This section enumerates some of those key competencies:

- **Best and highly qualified resources**   There is no substitute for ensuring that the pool of resources associated with the factory are very skilled and possess the expertise and talent to ensure the success of the factory. These resources will be relied upon to work on multiple engagements across the enterprise and will determine the success or failure of the modernization factory in both the short and long term.

- **Repeatable and scalable processes and tools**   The factory has two sets of processes and tools: the software-engineering processes and tools, and the modernization factory–related processes and tools. To be successful, both of these process areas must be well designed and implemented with consistency throughout the enterprise.

- **Comprehensive solution stack of assets**   The main goal of the factory is to deliver accurate projects on time and in a predictable manner. This can be accomplished by establishing standardization basics, best practices, tools, and other assets to be used across the various modernization engagements in an enterprise. The factory resources must also be well trained and knowledgeable in the solution stack to leverage that insight effectively and assist other application teams within the enterprise.

- **Quality, metrics, and performance measurement**   All resulting process improvements need to be measured against a baseline to justify its effectiveness clearly. The establishment of metrics is one key competency of the factory. This framework of measurement scrutinizes performance, allowing the quantification of benefits and business value for communication to the stakeholders in the enterprise.

- **Knowledge management, innovation, and COE (center of excellence)**   The modernization factory serves as the center of excellence for modernization across an enterprise. By establishing the COE, up-front investment and commitment of dedicated resources to the factory can be justified and rationalized among senior management. The factory resources must possess excellent leadership skills and produce innovative tools, improved processes, and the ability to encompass more business, technological, and functional areas for modernization over time as capabilities change within the industry and the enterprise.

Segmentation and Wave Planning

Anyone who has worked within the IT department of an enterprise, big or small, knows about unreasonable expectations: deliver high-quality, low-cost solutions before the expected due date! They know, however, that not all applications in an application portfolio are created equal, even if they are all based in Java. The nature of software development directs the functional requirements implemented by a particular application as it evolves. Each application has its own unique set of characteristics. The integration and interoperability with other applications is rooted in business process requirements, information architecture and data considerations, or technology needs such as API-level integration, messaging, or REST-based interactions. In some cases, the coupling between applications is so tight that any change to one application drastically impacts another either technologically, through its business processes, or with end-user influence. On a more benign level, although there may be no direct impact, a few applications may simply be related within an application portfolio because of some similarities: they were built using the same API or library version, built around the same time, built by the same team, or they support similar business processes and functionality.

Figure 14-7 provides a step-by-step view of how segmentation and wave planning should be approached. In this diagram, the applications and application groups are depicted as small circles and short cylindrical disks, respectively.

The process has been broken down into four distinct steps:

1. Application portfolio assessment

2. Grouping and clustering

3. Wave formation

4. Wave sequencing

As you analyze an application portfolio for modernization, rather than transforming the entire portfolio all at once, it is prudent to segment and group together related applications—business, functional, technical, infrastructural, or information architecture–based. This segmentation approach is as much an art as it is science. It derives from collective experience and specific knowledge of the application portfolio. By segmenting applications

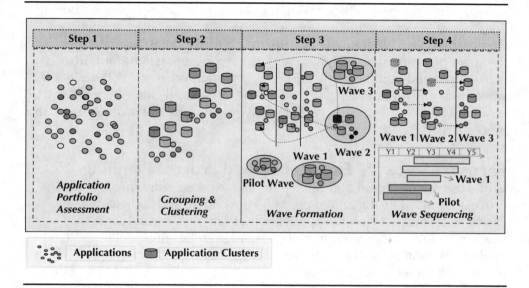

FIGURE 14-7.   *Steps in a segmentation and wave planning exercise*

based on logic and designing the modernization in waves rather than using a big-bang approach, you can eliminate some of the inherent project risk.

While modernizing the first group of applications, also known as the control or baseline, the enterprise teams will acquire considerable insight that can influence subsequent waves of modernizations to be more predictable, scalable, and repeatable. The overall productivity and efficiency will also increase in the first few waves before stabilizing at an optimal level. The JMF metrics are also critical for the up-front establishment and consistent measurement throughout the waves of execution.

Some key ingredients are essential to the success of the segmentation and wave planning approach. This planning is advantageous only if subsequent executions also succeed. From that point of view, this planning exercise is narrow in its objectives of identifying, segmenting, and grouping applications into waves. But its influence and impact is broad, because it ignites a large-scale modernization program and all of its supplementary activities.

APM-Driven Segmentation and Wave Planning
As we have previously reviewed, sound APM strategies build a knowledge base and understanding of the applications for an enterprise. To a large extent, segmentation and wave planning rely on this understanding to group

related applications together, taking into account each application's business architecture, infrastructure architecture, and technological characteristics. Comprehensive APM frameworks support objective decision-making at the wave planning stage. Domain and industry best practices must also be incorporated into the application segmentation process. Well-designed waves that rely on low-hanging fruit for the target applications is one way to ensure quick wins and build confidence while rooting out project issues and inherent risks.

Focus on Software Engineering and Process Planning
While the segmentation and wave planning exercise combines business process knowledge, functional domain knowledge, and subject matter expertise associated with the applications, ultimately the automated modernization factory migration approach also relies on excellent software engineering practices. The approach takes into account the complexity of the portfolio and its tight coupling with other applications. Most of the time, unexpected issues in modernization and reengineering efforts are associated with faulty libraries, frameworks, or other functional integrations with other services. The segmentation and wave planning exercise defines and customizes the process governance for factory setup. Similarly, change management protocols must be fundamentally established during this wave. The identification and training of an initial set of resources, preferably from the first wave, is essential to authenticate the collective knowledge and dispel any fear of the unknown.

Modernization Readiness Assessment
The critical self-evaluation during the segmentation and wave planning exercise aims to understand the maturity of an organization and its readiness to undertake the monumental task of large-scale modernization. The workforce that will participate in this modernization program must be assessed and analyzed to determine any functional gaps or inherent risks. It is also important to identify partnerships with outside vendors that can address any disconnect between the enterprise team and the modernization project at hand. Many times, this involves a review of the IT department's ability and available skill sets and a matching of partner resources to cover any functional gaps.

The Pilot Wave

The pilot wave enables an organization to "get its feet wet" as it begins its journey on the modernization, migration, or reengineering path. This initial wave allows for a gentler descent into the large-scale modernization exercise. The primary focus of the pilot wave is a thorough understanding of the entire modernization solution stack, including its customized applications. Even after gaining a fair understanding of the portfolio, instituting APM, and introducing process governance and a customized Java modernization solution stack, several risks and unanswered questions can still exist. The initial pilot wave will help to unearth most of these issues while modernizing a small subset of the applications in the portfolio. The smaller scope helps to refine and customize the solution stack further based on learnings and feedback from this initial foray into the large-scale modernization. The success of the pilot wave strongly indicates that the rest of the modernization program can be accomplished. This well-earned achievement in the initial stages builds momentum for the project while simultaneously demonstrating value to executive management.

Subsequent waves are not necessarily sequenced one after the other. Wave planning can stagger subsequent waves based on the type of modernization factory model employed. During the pilot wave, there is room to shore up or tweak engineering issues, infrastructure and environments, governance policies, and operational processes such as resources, staffing, communication, and program management. The solution stack assets are completely customizable to identify and implement any additional productivity tools or processes necessary for the project.

The end goal of the pilot wave is to showcase modernization successes and resolve key challenges, issues, and risks in execution, operation, and governance of the program. Any identified risks are mitigated and measured against demonstrable metrics for use in subsequent waves. Enterprise teams new to large-scale modernizations may structure the second wave in a similar scope and sequence as the baseline. After a few successful waves, a more staggered approach can be instituted to complete the modernization program effectively and efficiently.

Subsequent Waves of Migration

Once an enterprise understands the dynamics of migrating and modernizing its Java applications through a pilot wave, these learnings are leveraged to tweak engineering processes and factory protocols for future waves.

In subsequent waves of migration, additional resources and alignment of those resources are necessary. This alignment is dependent on the wave design and which applications are grouped together for modernization. It is not necessary to execute subsequent waves in sequence, one after the other. It is not prudent to execute waves in parallel either. The best approach, once sufficient competency has been achieved, is to stagger the waves so that a few projects can be in flight at the same time. This staggered approach brings more efficiency to the factory execution and improves productivity gains.

It is also necessary to implement a release strategy to monitor certain applications that have dependencies or integrations with other applications. Many organizations already have a formal user-acceptance phase to mark the functional sufficiency of successful release cycles. Although subsequent waves of migration will show a noticeable improvement over the initial pilot wave, this metric will eventually level out as the benefits are maximized.

Elastic Sourcing Model

Successful enterprises continually transform their business and technological capabilities to realize returns on IT investments and create their competitive advantage. To do this, an enterprise needs a sustainable process for identifying these new capabilities and enhancing their existing ones.

Even mature enterprises deal with performance issues and resource churn. In any large-scale program, there are phases that require additional resources or resources with a specific skill set. At the same time, enterprises cannot hire and scale up resources only to let them go when a program is completed. Realistic expectations for resources, staffing, and project execution must be established at the outset between the enterprise and a vendor that the enterprise has decided to partner with for this program. Implementing a wave-based approach is the best way to deal with critical resource-related issues in a large-scale modernization program. The ramp-up and ramp-down characteristics of a wave-based approach to modernization can be complex and difficult to anticipate and manage. This continuous process management cannot be resolved overnight. It must be elastic and agile to accommodate these organic operational issues.

One of the key focus areas of the JMF highlights an elastic sourcing approach to modernization. With this method, there is a central pool of resources with specific skill sets to be leveraged across all modernization efforts within an enterprise. Ideally, this group of trained modernization technicians belongs to the factory and not an individual wave. If the enterprise has not yet set up a modernization factory, the next best place to house these skilled resources is within the APM group. When a particular wave is in flight, several core members of that team are involved in the modernization because of their intimate knowledge of the specific applications. The team members embedded with these factory resources benefit from the modernization knowledge and solution stack expertise that they bring. This process ensures that all waves of applications are uniformly approached with similar best practices and methodologies to manage project resources.

As waves of applications move toward modernization closure, resource needs naturally decrease. Factory resources are returned to the modernization factory to await their next assignment in another wave or project requiring modernization expertise. With careful planning, these resources can be leveraged again for another modernization initiative or APM to provide maximum benefit to the enterprise as a whole. If these resources are not able to be used for a specific period of time, one option would be to return the resources to the company's overall IT pool or absorb them into other related groups. Hopefully, this scenario will never arise in an enterprise that continuously manages its portfolio of applications and regularly makes necessary adjustments. Overall, the elasticity provided by this approach enables an enterprise the flexibility to leverage a pool of skilled experts on an as-needed basis without redundancy, additional costs, or untimely delay.

Guaranteeing Successful Java Modernizations

In the modern era of IT, adaptation to complex and unrealistic demands is prevalent. Business models fight to keep up with the torrid pace of technology evolution. Given this high-stakes environment, enterprises are apprehensive about undertaking risky projects. However, by inadequately supporting these initiatives, organizations risk becoming extinct in the ever-changing corporate landscape. This creates a double-edged sword. We have already witnessed the fate of Borders, Mervyn's, and Circuit City, for example. At the time of this writing, Sears, Kmart, and JCPenny face incredible adversity and pressure to close their stores. One thing they all have in common is that their business processes, business models, and IT application portfolios could have benefited from a modernization exercise. Although there is no way to guarantee the success of large modernization initiatives, there are ways to maximize the probability of success. Everything starts with an organization's ability to understand, visualize, and crystallize the business value of modernizing its application portfolio. This goes beyond just modernizing applications to update technology stacks. That should not be the end goal. That, coupled with a convincing business case with a solid return on investment, must be the motivating force.

Several assumptions are made in the creation of a business case. If those assumptions are rooted in a well-entrenched methodology that has evolved over time, then there is a certain confidence in the estimations, interpolations, and extrapolations that result. Following the APM blueprint addressed in earlier chapters of this book will enable an organization to assess its application portfolios and build a useful knowledge base. Projects live and die by their apportioned budgets. The creation of a solid business case and the life cycle management of an application are essential to the total cost of ownership. It is important to ensure that stakeholders are not adversely affected by any large-scale program that fails to manage its program costs. Building support and consensus for a large initiative and mobilizing necessary resources are essential factors to guarantee the success of any modernization initiative.

Modernization does not happen overnight. Similarly, following a pragmatic approach of segmentation and wave planning is not enough. It takes time to execute and migrate these large projects, because ultimately they must co-exist with existing applications in the portfolio. There is a strong need for risk mitigation, detailed planning, and quality control so that business functions are not materially affected. The adoption of a micro-services container approach and modernization to that specific architectural structure will help to minimize any business impacts. This isolation of specific application components will ensure flexibility and agility of the application portfolio in the long run.

Even if a modernization factory is set up, if it is not leveraged properly or socialized within the enterprise to promote its vision and existence, there will be limited traction for its adoption as a core driver in modernization engagements. One of the easiest ways to all but guarantee the success of Java modernizations, especially in large-scale projects, is with a well-executed modernization factory strategy. The key dimensions enabling the success of the factory and the modernization itself are depicted in Figure 14-8.

The dimensions are presented in two layers, with the inner layer focused inward into the organization and the leadership necessary to conceive modernization programs. The outer layer is outward focused to areas that will help enable and execute the modernization programs.

The five dimensions of the inner layer are explained below:

- Strategy and vision need to be set for the factory with clear communication of the strategy, vision, existence, and blueprint.

- The modernization factory must have excellent leadership to drive the vision and strategy forward, and the leadership must be able to engage all key stakeholders across the enterprise.

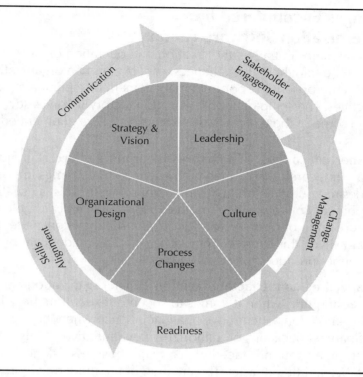

FIGURE 14-8.   *Essential dimensions to ensure success leveraging the modernization factory*

■   The culture of the organization will be affected in various ways by modernization programs. The factory must be able to manage and drive the change that invariably occurs when an enterprise ushers in new processes and technology. This is especially relevant for modernization, which will bring about additional changes.

■   With changes to processes, retooling of enterprise skills, and shifts in the architecture—business, functional, and technical alike— organizational readiness will contribute to the minimization of the risks associated with such shifts. The factory solution stack and its assets should be leveraged to support this readiness.

■   Another key dimension is the impact to the organizational structure with a realignment of skills to ensure that the enterprise is able to take advantage of the modernized portfolios and the newly created business value.

Challenges Encountered by a Modernization Software Factory

As with any major initiative, the creation and operation of a modernization factory can be fraught with challenges, especially in an organization with a lack of an enterprise-wide portfolio management discipline and architectural best practices. The setup of a modernization factory involves several moving parts, and some of the typical issues encountered are enumerated here:

- **Shortcuts or lack of a factory blueprinting effort**   If major activities are not carefully planned with adequate timeframes imposed, the desired outcome of the factory cannot occur. This is usually a major point of concern, since most enterprises hurriedly cobble together a core team of resources and proclaim that they constitute the factory. However, this shortcut approach, without an adequate blueprint, cannot produce successful results.

- **Speeding up the factory creation**   Each organization has its own set of quirks when it comes to speed of execution. Very large organizations often move at a glacial pace when it comes to making financial decisions or authorizing new initiatives. Only when such an organization is faced with a major business risk does it tend to move a little bit faster. The creation of the modernization factory must take into account the velocity of change currently within the organization and must align with the inherent risk in moving faster than the organizational culture allows so that there will be minimal impact to the transition.

- **Not adequately communicating the operational plan**   An enterprise needs to have visibility of the modernization factory from its creation, to its roadmap generation, and finally to its operational characteristics. This ensures that the modernization factory will be aligned with specific initiatives and adequately leveraged by the enterprise.

- **Lack of change management**   Adopting a modernization factory approach and undertaking large modernization initiatives requires a cultural shift within the organization and appropriate change-management processes. Existing resources could be significantly impacted requiring that new skills be brought in to address the gaps. Current execution approaches and software engineering processes may also undergo revisions.

Quantification of Benefits

To capture the benefits of the JMF, organizational teams must first identify and create metrics to measure and quantify the benefits. Each enterprise must decide the specific goals of the factory, useful metrics, and the ultimate measurement of those metrics.

In the context of the modernization factory, there are a set of suggested metrics relevant to the analysis:

- Number of applications migrated, reengineered, and modernized

- Number of applications sunsetted and reduced

- Number of initiatives that factory resources participated in

- Average reduction in time of modernization engagements compared to previous baseline

- Average reduction in cost of modernization engagements compared to previous baseline

- SLA deviations

- Number of business processes impacted

- Number of business units supported

- Number of application owners supported

- Number of resources trained enterprise-wide in APM

- Average number of applications under the factory every year

- Average number of lines of code migrated every year

- Average improvement in productivity computed as saved effort in modernization

- Annual estimated cost savings due to automation

- Reduction in the application maintenance and support cost of each application modernized

- Average reduction in cycle time compared to manual application migration

- End-user satisfaction

This list is basic and should be used as a beginning first step. Several other financial and operational metrics should be periodically measured and used to improve the factory processes. When the factory is initially set up and an enterprise has not yet experienced a large-scale modernization, the derived metrics can substantially deviate between programs and between applications. As such, the pilot wave is a good opportunity to create a baseline to measure subsequent waves and test the validity of those metrics to ensure that the factory is operating as intended.

Ensuring the Success of Java Migrations

At the project execution level, Java migration success depends on processes and people to implement the requisite technology and adopted tools. As we have seen, a tools-based assessment and an automated analysis of the Java source code, compiled class files, and other application assets will enable the development of a deep knowledge base. Cultivating a strong APM practice will ensure that best practices are available to portfolio assessments and Java migration programs. Adoption of a solution stack such as OMSS will bring together the necessary tools and accelerators to complete the implementation successfully. Knowing the depth of the lake is a good idea before wading into it. Similarly, the use of effort and cost estimation approaches can provide a fairly accurate evaluation of the migration effort. Adopting a factory model such as JMF will deliver an end-to-end migration approach to guide the engineering aspects of the migration and standardization for the project. Automation, coupled with strong governance and skilled resources, is the key driver for successfully tackling large-scale migrations.

Although the modernization factory acts as the strategic and tactical entity to maximize the effectiveness of large-scale modernizations, over time the factory becomes more tactical and operational as it becomes entangled in specific programs within the enterprise. It is my view that the strategic and tactical approaches should be separate and independent of each other to drive innovation and embrace the rapid pace of changing Java technologies, libraries, and frameworks that the application portfolio depends upon. Establishing a center of excellence within the factory will prioritize continued research, the adoption of enhanced modernization processes, and the requisite tools to allow for a strategic focus for the factory to flourish as it meets its tactical day-to-day enterprise needs.

Figure 14-9 illustrates the elements of a Java modernization center of excellence and illustrates one way of organizing it by focusing on the activities of the COE to augment the tactical and operational elements of the modernization factory. The COE will strategize, enable, deliver, and measure

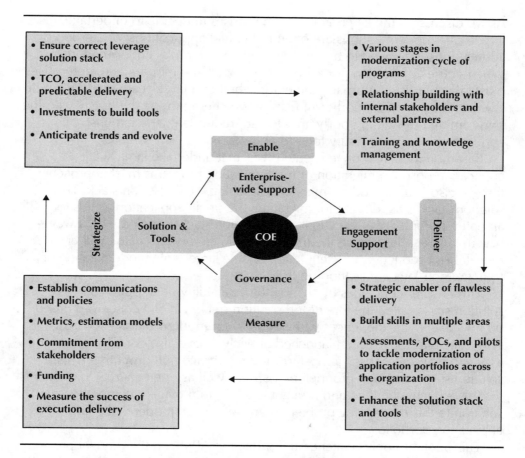

FIGURE 14-9. *Java modernization center of excellence (COE) operated by the modernization factory*

factory operations to advance modernization within the enterprise. The COE will also determine whether the processes, tools, solution stacks, and assets are effective and sufficient for the modernization exercise. This overall coverage of strategic and tactical elements by the COE and the modernization factory will ensure success for the enterprise.

Summary

This chapter addressed how to undertake large-scale Java application portfolio modernizations. Enterprises must have the right solution stack coupled with the right approach to pull off mega-modernization efforts.

As we discussed, the key drivers for enterprises to decide to undertake large-scale modernizations are often individual applications, or a group of applications, that need to be migrated, upgraded, replaced, or modernized. When entire application portfolios are assessed and modernized, enterprises must take a holistic approach to decide whether a large-scale modernization is worth the potential short-term risks or whether ignoring the heady warning signs emitted by aging, poorly architected, redundant, and expensive application portfolios justify long-term impacts to business goals.

Based on identified drivers, enterprises that undertake large-scale application portfolio migration or modernization programs must approach the exercise in a methodical manner, leveraging a full solution stack. This solution stack is as relevant for migrating one single application as it is for an entire portfolio of applications. The solution stack, coupled with a wave-based approach leveraging the modernization factory paradigm, will ensure repeatable, productive, efficient, and scalable large-scale modernization of Java and non-Java application portfolios.

This chapter concludes by sharing the availability of an open-source solution stack called the OpenMod solution stack, which I conceived based on my collective experiences with several prior modernization exercises. This stack has not yet been launched publicly. I have also contributed several assets to help enterprises jumpstart their modernization programs. This solution stack leverages proprietary assets as well as open-source components that have been identified and brought together to provide a comprehensive solution to this burgeoning problem of migrating and modernizing Java application portfolios.

This book has only scratched the surface of APM and the thought process around automation of Java application migration and reengineering. In my next book, I plan to discuss custom rules and migration in great detail and show how to extend the functionality of available tools. I also hope to see a future version of the Java platform provide built-in automated solutions for migrating itself onto new versions and libraries. At the very least, a robust application modernization solution stack should be available as a complement to the Java platform. This solution stack should contain a full set of rules governing the migration of Java source code to the newest release. Until that day arrives, I hope that this book can serve as a reference for providing an approach and solution stack to assist enterprises in starting their own modernization journeys.

Index

T

Beta Test Oracle Software

Get a first look at our newest products—and help perfect them. You must meet the following criteria:

✓ **Licensed Oracle customer or Oracle PartnerNetwork member**

✓ **Oracle software expert**

✓ **Early adopter of Oracle products**

Please apply at: pdpm.oracle.com/BPO/userprofile

If your interests match upcoming activities, we'll contact you. Profiles are kept on file for 12 months.

Copyright © 2014, Oracle and/or its affiliates. All rights reserved. Oracle and Java are registered trademarks of Oracle and/or its affiliates.

Join the Largest Tech Community in the World

 Download the latest software, tools, and developer templates

 Get exclusive access to hands-on trainings and workshops

 Grow your professional network through the Oracle ACE Program

 Publish your technical articles – and get paid to share your expertise

Join the Oracle Technology Network
Membership is free. Visit community.oracle.com

@OracleOTN   facebook.com/OracleTechnologyNetwork

Copyright © 2016, Oracle and/or its affiliates. All rights reserved. Oracle and Java are registered trademarks of Oracle and/or its affiliates.

ORACLE®
CERTIFICATION PROGRAM

BOOST YOUR
PROFESSIONAL
IMAGE

The Value of Oracle Certification

Confidently display your globally recognized skills with an Oracle certification digital badge. Your digital badge can be added to all your on-line profiles and is displayed and validated immediately.

Advance Your Career with Oracle Certification

 Positive impact on professional image **60%**

 Moved to a career in IT **26%**

 Received a salary increase **20%**

 Found a job **19%**

 Got a promotion **14%**

88% of IT professionals said they would recommend certification to a colleague when discussing a career or advancement in IT

Three Oracle Certified Professionals Tell us Their Stories

Saint-Paul, Software Architect and Developer, Oracle Certified Associate, Java SE 8 Programmer
"By becoming certified, I learned about new APIs which helped me update different parts of my programs and improve some of our software performances. It also adds credibility to my knowledge."

Adrienne, Data Administrator, Oracle Database 12c Certified SQL Associate
"Certifications are a way for me to stay current with the breadth and depth of the products."

Giovanni, Oracle Developer, Oracle Certified PL/SQL Associate
"But what the certifications have given me is more confidence and also complimentary attributes to my resume, thus allowing me to increase my salary."

Read more stories at
http://www.oracle.com/certstory

 GET ORACLE CERTIFIED   **http://education.oracle.com/certification/**

ORACLE®

Integrated Cloud Applications & Platform Services
Copyright © 2017, Oracle and/or its affiliates. All rights reserved. Oracle and Java are registered trademarks of Oracle and/or its affiliates. Other names may be trademarks of their respective owners.

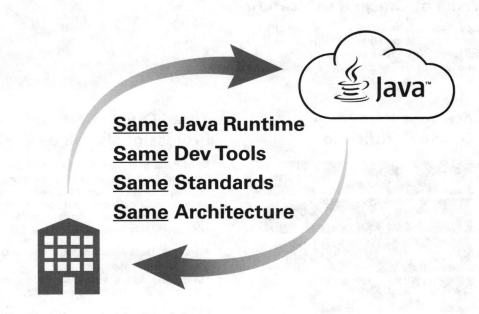

Push a Button
Move Your Java Apps to the Oracle Cloud

Same Java Runtime
Same Dev Tools
Same Standards
Same Architecture

... or Back to Your Data Center

ORACLE®

cloud.oracle.com/java

Copyright © 2016, Oracle and/or its affiliates. All rights reserved. Oracle and Java are registered trademarks of Oracle and/or its affiliates.

Oracle Learning Library

Created by Oracle Experts
FREE for Oracle Users

- ✓ Vast array of learning aids
- ✓ Intuitive & powerful search
- ✓ Share content, events & saved searches
- ✓ Personalize your learning dashboard
- ✓ Find & register for training events

oracle.com/oll

Copyright © 2017, Oracle and/or its affiliates. All rights reserved. Oracle and Java are registered trademarks of Oracle and/or its affiliates.

Reach More than 640,000 Oracle Customers with Oracle Publishing Group

Connect with the Audience that Matters Most to Your Business

Oracle Magazine
The Largest IT Publication in the World
Circulation: 325,000
Audience: IT Managers, DBAs, Programmers, and Developers

Profit
Business Insight for Enterprise-Class Business Leaders to Help Them Build
a Better Business Using Oracle Technology

Circulation: 90,000
Audience: Top Executives and Line of Business Managers

Java Magazine
The Essential Source on Java Technology, the Java Programming Language,
and Java-Based Applications

Circulation: 225,00 and Growing Steady
Audience: Corporate and Independent Java Developers, Programmers,
and Architects

For more information
or to sign up for a FREE
subscription: Scan the
QR code to visit Oracle
Publishing online.

31901060925320

Copyright © 2016, Oracle and/or its affiliates. All rights reserved. Oracle and Java are registered trademarks of Oracle and/or its affiliates. Other names may be trademarks of their respective owners.